Reading History Sideways

POPULATION AND DEVELOPMENT

A SERIES EDITED BY RICHARD A. EASTERLIN

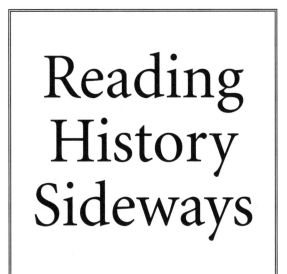

Reading History Sideways

The Fallacy and Enduring Impact
of the Developmental Paradigm
on Family Life

ARLAND THORNTON

The University of Chicago Press
Chicago and London

Arland Thornton is director of the Population Studies Center, research professor at the Survey Research Center, and professor of sociology at the University of Michigan. He is the coauthor of *Social Change and the Family in Taiwan* and the editor of *The Well-Being of Children and Families: Research and Data Needs.*

The University of Chicago Press, Chicago 60637
The University of Chicago Press, Ltd., London
© 2005 by The University of Chicago
All rights reserved. Published 2005
Printed in the United States of America

14 13 12 11 10 09 08 07 06 05   1 2 3 4 5

ISBN: 0-226-79860-7 (cloth)

Library of Congress Cataloging-in-Publication Data

Thornton, Arland.
   Reading history sideways : the fallacy and enduring impact of the developmental
paradigm on family life / Arland Thornton.
      p. cm. — (Population and development)
   Includes bibliographical references and index.
   ISBN 0-226-79860-7 (cloth : alk. paper)
   1. Family—Historiography.   2. Family—Europe, Western—Historiography.
   3. Family—Europe, Northern—Historiography.   4. Family—History.   5. Family—
   Europe, Western—History.   6. Family—Europe, Northern—History.   7. Social
   change.   I. Title.   II. Population and development (Chicago, Ill.)
   HQ503.T48 2005
   306.85′094—dc22

                                                                        2004017204

To Shirley, Richard, Blake, Rebecca, and Amy

Contents

Acknowledgments

I am indebted to many individuals and groups for their many contributions to this book. Particularly crucial in this regard are my colleagues in the Family and Demography Program at the University of Michigan who have participated with me in many discussions about family change, provided insights and sources, and read and commented on numerous drafts. These colleagues include Bill Axinn, Jennifer Barber, Georgina Binstock, Susan Brower, Janet Dunn, Tom Fricke, Dirgha Ghimire, Martha Hill, Julie Josefosky de Jong, Colter Mitchell, Lisa Pearce, Pete Richardson, Elizabeth Rudd, Jeannie Thrall, Yu Xie, Li-Shou Yang, and Linda Young-DeMarco.

Numerous other colleagues, friends, and family members at the University of Michigan and in Ann Arbor have provided useful input of many kinds. These include Julia Adams, Kent Christensen, Ronald Freedman, Bruce Gibb, Muge Gocek, Dena Goodman, Michael Kennedy, Miles Kimball, Howard Kimeldorf, Kim Leavitt, James Lee, Jinyun Liu, Jeffrey Paige, Arlene Saxonhouse, John Schulenberg, Margaret Somers, Amy Thornton Teemant, Leo Teemant, Blake Thornton, Janelle Thornton, Rebecca Thornton, Richard Thornton, Shirley Thornton, Maris Vinovskis, Marty Whyte, and Wang Zheng.

This book has also benefited from numerous discussions at seminars held at the University of Michigan's Family and Demography Program, Department of Sociology, Population Studies Center, and Survey Research Center. Also beneficial have been seminar discussions at Bowling Green State University, Brown University, Cambridge University, the University of Chicago, the University of North Carolina, the University of Pennsylvania, and the University of Wisconsin. A summary of the main themes of the book was presented in my presidential address to the Population Association of America in 2001 (Thornton 2001), the feedback to which also proved useful. In addition, numerous undergraduate and graduate students at the University of Michigan have read and reacted to previous drafts of the manuscript.

My gratitude for assistance in many forms—including the provision of references, ideas, and feedback on drafts—extends to numerous colleagues both in the United States and abroad. Particularly valuable has been input from Jalal Abbasi-Shavazi, John Casterline, Joseph Chamie, Andrew Cherlin, Dilli Dahal, Calvin Goldscheider, Frances Goldscheider, Amy Kaler, Ron Lesthaeghe, Alan Macfarlane, Mansoor Moaddel, Philip Morgan, Phyllis Piotrow, David Popenoe, Steven Ruggles, Roger Schofield, Edward Shorter, Richard Smith, Beth Soldo, Naomi Tadmor, Dirk van de Kaa, Richard Wall, Susan Watkins, Charles Westoff, Tony Wrigley, and Kathryn Yount.

The production of the manuscript has required the efforts of numerous people in the Population Studies Center and the Survey Research Center of the University of Michigan, many of whom are members of the Family and Demography Program. Judy Baughn has provided devoted general oversight and supervision for more than a decade. During the early phases of the production of the book, Kashif Sheikh gave the manuscript the same kind of attention that people usually devote only to their own work, and Julie Josefosky de Jong has done the same for the completion of the manuscript during its later phases. Additional valuable assistance has been provided by Susan Clemmer, Jana Bruce, Pearl Johnson, Yan Fu, Lee Ridley, Nancy Barr, Tera Freeman, Anu Gupta, Stephen McLandrich, Jennifer Richardson, and Linda Young-DeMarco.

The editorial team at the University of Chicago Press has been a pleasure to work with. Both Richard Easterlin and Geoffrey Huck were persistant in their generous support of this project over its very long gestation period. John Tryneski, Rodney Powell, and Christine Schwab have guided the project through the editorial process with considerable helpfulness and efficiency, and the copyeditors hired by the press provided extensive and expert assistance in the copyediting of the manuscript—a service that has substantially improved the readability of the manuscript.

I close this acknowledgment with a quotation from Francis Jennings, whose thoughts about his book match mine in at least one important dimension: "This book ranges widely in subject matter and research disciplines, and it offers more than the ordinary number of opportunities for error; that I have inadvertently taken advantage of some of those opportunities may be the one certainty of the whole process" (1975, x). Although the book has benefited greatly from the input of many individuals and groups, all responsibility for any errors of fact or interpretation remains with the author.

PART ONE

Introduction and Approaches

Introduction and Overview

This book is about developmental ideas, models, and methods and how they have influenced families and the ways in which scholars have studied families. Its overarching thesis is that developmental ideas and frameworks have motivated and guided much of social-science research for centuries, influenced the actions of governments and international bodies, affected world history, and guided the motivations and behaviors of numerous individual actors around the world. In fact, the domination of developmental ideas and approaches has been so overwhelming that knowledge of it is a prerequisite for understanding both the history of family change and the history of scholarly efforts to describe and explain changes in family life. The purpose of this book is to tell two interrelated stories: (1) the influence of developmental thinking on scholarship about families and (2) the influence of developmental thinking on actual family structures, relationships, and processes.

At the core of developmental ideas and methods is the developmental paradigm. As I outline in chapter 2, the developmental paradigm is a model of history that assumes that all societies are on the same pathway or trajectory of change, with each going through the same stages of development. However, the developmental paradigm posits that the speed of movement along this relatively uniform pathway of development varies across societies. Some societies are perceived to have progressed and then become static, others to have progressed rapidly for a time and then fallen back, others to have been static since virtually the beginning of time, and yet others to have been slow starters that later progressed rapidly to new heights of civilization. The result of this differential rate of progress is the existence of various societies at different stages of development at any specific period of history.

The developmental paradigm has had a very long history, as it was known to have existed in ancient Greece and Rome and was influential in the writings of several generations of Christian theologians. Many versions of the developmental paradigm have been promulgated and used in numerous ways by scholars, policymakers, and ordinary people around the world, with its various versions packaged under different labels, including models of progress and civilization, modernization, and social evolution. In its various forms, the developmental paradigm has dominated much of social inquiry and policy in the Western world for centuries.

The key method associated with the developmental paradigm is one that I refer to as *reading history sideways*.[1] As I discuss in chapter 2, reading history sideways is an approach to history that, instead of following a particular society or population across time, compares various societies at the same time. This method takes advantage of the assumption of the developmental paradigm that, at any single point in time, all societies can be pegged at various stages along the same development continuum. It assumes that the previous conditions of life of a more advanced society can be proxied by the life situations of a contemporary society believed to be at an earlier stage of development. That is, the contemporary society perceived as less developed is used as a proxy for circumstances at an earlier historical period of the society that is perceived as more advanced. A belief in this approach makes it possible to portray societal change using information from populations observed at the same time but in different geographic locations.

Scholars have read history sideways for several centuries to construct histories of virtually every dimension of human life. They were especially fascinated with the variety of religious, familial, economic, and political institutions around the world, and they energetically compared these social institutions, crafting the data that they obtained into complex accounts of social change across developmental stages of history. They produced numerous—and often lengthy—treatises on the history of marriage, women, religion, economics, and politics. Although these scholars used similar methods, they created different historical trajectories, resulting in extensive disagreements and debates about the way in which history had unfolded.

Although reading history sideways has been used to construct histories of each of the central institutions of life, my focus in this book is limited to marriage and family life. More specifically, I examine such central dimensions of personal and family life as marriage, relationships between women and men, the bearing and rearing of children, the place of family units in society, intergenerational relations, and living arrangements. Here, the emphasis is on the scholarly use of the developmental paradigm and read-

---

1. *Reading history sideways* is a method whereby cross-sectional data are used to describe history rather than just to make static comparisons.

ing history sideways to describe and explain changes in family life over previous centuries and millennia. I show how this framework and this methodology have dominated the study of changing family life for centuries.

This book tells two main stories. The first is about the way in which scholars from the 1700s through the mid-1900s used the developmental paradigm and reading history sideways to construct versions of, or myths about, the history of family life in the Western world, which were discovered to be myths only in the last half of the 1900s. The overarching myth created by developmental thinking and methods was that, prior to the early 1800s, there had been a great transformation of family life in Northwest European societies.

Prior to the last half of the 1900s, there was a consensus among scholars that, sometime in the past, England and other Northwest European populations had societies that were almost exclusively organized around families, were characterized by extensive family solidarity, and placed little emphasis on the individual. These scholars also held that the Northwest European households of the past were large, with children, parents, grandparents, and married aunts and uncles all living together. Almost everyone in these societies was believed to have married at a young age, with those marriages arranged by parents and with little opportunity for affection to grow prior to marriage. It was also believed that, in these societies, parents had overwhelming authority over children and women were accorded very low status.

Scholars of the 1700s through the mid-1900s also believed that the family structures and processes in England and other Northwest European populations in the past had been transformed at some point into the kind of families observed in this region during the 1700s and 1800s. Among the characteristics of Europe of the 1700s and 1800s that they emphasized was a social system that was less organized around families and placed greater emphasis on the individual as compared to the collective. These scholars perceived Northwest Europe of the 1700s and 1800s to have small households with few grandparents, aunts, and uncles sharing residence with parents and children. They also reported older and less universal marriage, more independence for the young, more affection between couples, and more autonomy accorded to couples in the mate-selection process. Furthermore, although they were aware of continuing gender differentials in authority and status, these scholars believed that the status of women was higher during the 1700s and 1800s than it had been previously.

However, this orthodoxy about the transformation of Northwest European families was seriously challenged by numerous studies conducted during the 1960s and 1970s by family historians, historical demographers, and economic historians using the historical archives. The picture of the family systems of Northwest Europe prior to 1800 that emerged from these studies was very different from that painted by generations of earlier scholars. In fact, many of the distinctive features of Northwest European families in the 1800s that had previously been thought to have been of recent origin—the result of the great transformation—were discovered to have actually existed for many centuries. Some even dated as far back as the 1300s—and possibly even earlier, although lack of data made the latter determination difficult. The evidence of continuity eventually became so pervasive that many came to see the long-believed great transformation of family life as a myth.

Although the family literature contains a few hints about the sources of this myth about family change (see Laslett and Wall 1974/1972; and Macfarlane 1979a/1978, 1987), I know of no systematic discussion of the origins of the myth. This book fills that gap as chapters 3 and 5 are devoted to telling the story of the creation and unmasking of the myth of the transformation of family life in Northwest European societies prior to the 1800s. The main element in the creation of the myth of family change is the application of the developmental paradigm and reading history sideways to extensive quantities of cross-sectional data from numerous populations around the world.

In chapter 3, I discuss the incredible variety of social and family structures and relationships that scholars of the 1700s through the mid-1900s identified in their contemporary observations of the human condition. I also discuss the fact that these scholars found different family types to be concentrated in different regions of the world and that they found Northwest European family systems to be quite different from most others. These scholars utilized the developmental paradigm and the method of reading history sideways to create an account of transformation that relied on the cross-sectional differences in family life that they observed: from the family systems outside Northwest Europe to those of Northwest Europe. This transformation they termed *the great family transition*. Chapter 5 is devoted to a summary of some of the central studies of the late 1900s that discovered that the great transition could not be documented in the historical archives of Northwest Europe.

The paradigms, methods, and narratives of family change that dominated scholarly understandings from the 1700s through the mid-1900s have had substantial influence on family scholarship beyond the creation of myths about changes in family life. As I document in chapter 4, the developmental model and the mythical narratives of family change had great influence on the scholarly understanding and interpretation of the actual historical decline in mortality and fertility that occurred in the 1800s and 1900s throughout Europe and much of the rest of the world. It was very easy for the scholars of the late 1800s and early 1900s to utilize the developmental model and the earlier conclusions about family change to explain the decline in mortality and fertility—a change that they have frequently labeled *the demographic transition.*

In addition, the developmental paradigm and reading history sideways are not just historical curiosities but, in many ways, remain important today. As I document in chapter 6, developmental language and developmental categories remain common in the language and models of scholars and ordinary people. People continue to categorize populations as *traditional* or *developing* in opposition to *modern* or *developed.* In addition, people continue to write about large transitions from traditional to modern. Reading history sideways also continues to be part of the tool kit of social science, although now used with more sophistication and awareness of its potential for error. In addition, the theories formulated by earlier generations of scholars to explain family change remain predominant as explanations today. That is, the theories formulated in earlier times continue to be used as explanations of recent changes in family life around the world even though they were not applicable to the time and place that they were created to explain. Finally, as I speculate in chapter 7, the developmental paradigm, reading history sideways, and mythical conclusions about family change have influenced the very data that some scholars have used to study family change.

The second main story of this book is the use of the developmental paradigm, reading history sideways, and the conclusions of several generations of scholars from the 1700s through the mid-1900s to create a set of propositions about society, family life, and the fundamental rights of human beings that have been an overwhelming force for family change during the last two centuries. This story about actual family change begins with the conclusions about social, economic, and family history that were created by the scholars of the 1700s through the early 1900s. The histories that these scholars created stretched from the beginning of humanity to their own time and provided powerful narratives of the course of human experience, the forces producing societal development, and the direction of the future course of humanity. They also provided new mechanisms for judging human institutions and evaluating the legitimacy and usefulness of the many different ways of organizing human societies. This developmental thinking and these conclusions also provided a model and blueprint for the future. They showed the direction for future change and the mechanisms that human beings could employ to facilitate progress and well-being. In this way, the developmental paradigm, reading history sideways, and the conclusions of generations of scholars became the engine for many social, economic, and familial changes.

More specifically, the developmental paradigm, reading history sideways, and conclusions of generations of scholars grew into a powerful set of propositions that I call *developmental idealism,* propositions that would drive many fundamental changes in family life in recent centuries and decades. I have distilled the propositions of developmental idealism into four basic statements: (1) modern society is good and attainable; (2) the modern family is good and attainable; (3) the modern family is a cause as well as an effect of a modern society; and (4) individuals have the right to be free and equal, with social relationships being based on consent.

The first proposition suggests a preference for a society characterized as modern—that is, a society that is industrialized, urbanized, highly educated, highly knowledgeable, and wealthy in contrast to one that is primarily agricultural, rural, with little formal schooling, and with relatively little economic wealth. The second proposition indicates a preference for a family system characterized as modern—one that emphasizes individualism, the high status of women, mature marriage, marriages arranged by the couple, the autonomy of children, and small households consisting primarily of parents and children. This modern family is in contrast to a traditional family with an emphasis on the family collective, little individualism, large households, parents and children sharing residences with grandparents and married aunts and uncles, marriages arranged by parents, a young age at marriage, and the low status of women. The third proposition of developmental idealism suggests that a modern society and family are causally connected, with modern society being a cause and/or an effect of a modern family system. Finally, the fourth proposition emphasizes freedom, equality, and consent as fundamental human rights.

The propositions of developmental idealism have been disseminated around the world and have become exceptionally powerful forces for changing personal and family lives. Included within this package of developmental idealism is a set of ideas identifying the good life, a framework for evaluating various forms of human organization, an explanatory framework linking the good life as cause and effect of various social patterns, and a statement about the fundamental rights of individual human beings. These propositions provide new models, motivations, and expectations of personal and family life that affect the lives of individuals directly as well as indirectly through their influence on public policy, laws, and the actions of political and administrative leaders.

An essential observation of the book is that, while the centuries prior to the 1800s in Northwest Europe are now noted much more for family continuity than for family change, the 1800s and 1900s in Northwest Europe stand out as a period of dramatic change. In addition, the last two centuries, especially the 1900s, have seen dramatic changes in family life in many other parts of the world. Some of the most important examples of these dramatic changes have been declines in childbearing, increases in age at marriage, the increase in the autonomy of young people, growing egalitarianism between women and men, increases in divorce, independent living among the elderly, increases in sexual activity and cohabitation outside marriage, and the growing emphasis on individual rights as opposed to the norms and regulations of the larger community.

A central thesis of chapter 8 is that these dramatic changes in family life were directly influenced by the developmental idealism that either grew out of or was reinforced by the developmental models and conclusions of earlier periods. In fact, I argue that, during the past two centuries, the package of motivational ideas contained in developmental idealism has become one of the most powerful forces for changing family processes and relationships, both in Northwest Europe and in many other parts of the world. With developmental idealism embedded within a powerful model for understanding the world, it became a force for dealing with and changing that world.

Unfortunately, the power of developmental idealism and the larger developmental paradigm has received too little attention in the study of the historical family changes that have occurred in the 1800s and 1900s. Consequently, the dramatic role that developmental thinking has played in the many family changes that have occurred in the past two centuries is not well understood or appreciated. A major goal of chapters 9–12 is to redress this gap in our understanding by focusing on the ways in which developmental thinking has been influential in changing family structures and processes around the world. Because the mechanisms of the influence of developmental idealism on changes in family life have varied between Northwest European populations and the rest of the world, I focus chapters 9 and 10 on Northwest Europe and the overseas populations from that region. In chapters 11 and 12, I discuss some of the mechanisms by means of which developmental idealism was diffused from Northwest Europe to other parts of the world and influenced family structures and processes there.

As I conclude in the final chapter, there have been a plethora of reasons why the developmental paradigm, reading history sideways, and developmental idealism have been such powerful forces in the descriptions and explanations of scholars and in the lives of ordinary people. For one thing, these explanations begin with the fact that the developmental paradigm and reading history sideways have had the blessings of history in that they have been endorsed for millennia. For another, they account for both cultural diversity and world history. There were no other models of geography and history that could compete with the scope and elegance of developmental approaches in describing and explaining cultural diversity. It is also important to emphasize that, although the power of the paradigm and its conclusions was often sufficient to generate endorsement, in numerous cases skepticism remained. In many of these instances, developmental ideas and conclusions were enforced legally and, when they generated resistance, even militarily. It was, in fact, sometimes the power behind, and not just the power of, developmental idealism that made it so important. That is, developmental idealism spread, not just because it was powerful in itself, but because it was the ideology of powerful people and organizations. This mixture of powerful ideas and powerful proponents permeates the last part of the book and is addressed directly in the final chapter.

Because of this book's strong emphasis on the impact of the developmental paradigm and reading history sideways on the work of scholars, readers may get the impression that I believe that this paradigm and this method have been the only forces influencing scholars. And, because of the book's strong emphasis on the impact of developmental idealism on family change around the world, readers may get the impression that I see it as the only propellant for family change. It is, thus, important for me to disclaim these impressions and assert my commitment to a complex and multivariate view of the forces influencing both scholarship and ordinary people. My goal in this book, however, is not to provide a complete explanation for the behavior and conclusions of scholars and ordinary people, but to explain how the developmental paradigm, reading history sideways, and developmental idealism have played a substantial role in both scholarship and the lives of ordinary people. These forces have not been fully understood and appreciated, and they are the central themes of this book. That said, this book focuses on a single set of causes, without belief that these causes are the only important ones. A full account of family structures, processes, and changes would require a more extensive set of explanatory factors, including social and economic structures, war, religion, and scientific theories and mentalities.

In this book I consider most of the last millennium, although I join with past generations of scholars in lamenting that the quantity and quality of data deteriorate as one moves back in time. The geographic scope of the book is the entire world, although with numerous gaps and with substantially more focus on Europe than other areas. The book considers the writings of social philosophers and scientists for more than 250 years, a period in which an incredible amount of ink was expended to explain social and economic development and family change.

Given the space constraints within which I am working, I must paint with a very broad brush, one that provides only the barest essentials of the big picture. Even in a book-length manuscript, it is impossible to provide anything remotely close to detailed coverage of the entire matrix of family studies and changes in family life defined by the intersection of time, place, and scholarly literature. My account of the scholarship and conclusions of numerous authors must be abstract and general. It must be illustrative rather than comprehensive. And it must also restrict caveats, nuances, detailed empirical data, and appropriate exceptions.

Most of the scholars utilizing the developmental paradigm and reading history sideways were European or of European descent. More specifically, most were French, English, Scottish, Spanish, German, and European American. Although many of the important early scholars were Spanish, most of the important later writers were from Northwest Europe and its overseas migrant communities. Given their geographic location and substantive interests, these later scholars made many contrasts between Northwest European societies and those in other parts of the world, a pattern that I continue. Although the designation *Northwest European* is somewhat fuzzy, I use it to refer both to people living in that region—primarily England and northwest France—and to people whose ancestors migrated from that region to America, Australia, and other places around the world.

The scholars of Northwest Europe used the developmental paradigm and reading history sideways in an ethnocentric way that presumed that Western societies were superior to non-Western societies. Furthermore, the Western authors using this paradigm frequently referred to people of other cultures using language that is today offensive to many, including me. However, although I object to the ethnocentric assumptions and language of the paradigm, it is impossible to demonstrate the conceptual model and the methodology and their power as scholarly tools and motivational forces without following the language of the original literature.[2]

I also emphasize that I am not advocating the developmental paradigm and reading history sideways as a conceptual framework and method for research. As I indicate in chapters 6 and 13, I am very critical of them as research tools and believe that their use has been the source of numerous substantial errors in the description of human history. My purpose in this

2. More discussion of the use of developmental language is provided in the postscript.

book, therefore, is not to endorse them, but to show how they have combined with cross-cultural data to influence both social-science conclusions about the history of family life and actual family change around the globe.

As I noted earlier, developmental idealism includes a set of value and belief statements that have direct relevance to many dimensions of family life, including marriage, childbearing, childrearing, divorce, sex, cohabitation, gender roles, and intergenerational relations. As such, developmental idealism is explicit in stating which forms of family life are good and which types are bad. Not only have these value statements been powerful in changing family life, but they have been controversial as well. In fact, developmental idealism and its value statements about personal and family life are at the center of the culture wars raging in the United States and elsewhere around the world.

It is important to note that I present the propositions of developmental idealism not as factual statements, but as beliefs and values that individuals may accept or reject. I therefore neither endorse nor condemn them. My goal is analysis, not advocacy.

It is also useful to note that, although developmental idealism has historically been linked with developmental thinking, methods, and conclusions, the validity of the propositions of developmental idealism do *not* depend on the validity of developmental concepts, methods, and conclusions. That is, the values and beliefs of developmental idealism can be accepted without a belief in the developmental paradigm, reading history sideways, and the conclusions of generations of developmental scholars.

More explicitly, such values as equality, consent, freedom, independence, and mature marriage can be maintained entirely independently of developmental models and methods. Although these values have received substantial support from developmental thinking and methods, they can be supported on other grounds, including personal preferences and ideals. This means that a rejection of the developmental paradigm, reading history sideways, and the conclusions of developmental scholars does not require a rejection of the principles of freedom, consent, equality, mature marriage, and independent living. It also means that the propositions of developmental idealism can be powerful in the lives of individuals and communities even if the developmental paradigm and reading history sideways are faulty.

I now leave the issue of agendas and values and turn to a more complete discussion of the developmental paradigm and reading history sideways. I begin by explaining the models, methods, and data used by several generations of previous scholars, the topics of the next chapter.

growth, decline, and death to individual societies, he applied it to the overall history of mankind. Mankind as a whole would go through these stages of life only once, and the experiences of individual societies or nations formed the epochs or stages of the larger human experience.

The application of the biological metaphor of growth and development to human societies was transformed again during the 1600s. It was then that "the metaphor of genesis and decay was stripped, as it were, of its centuries-old property of decay, leaving only genesis and growth" (Nisbet 1975/1969, 109)."[8] The crucial new idea was that knowledge and understanding were continuous and that their accumulation over time was natural. This view suggested that the moderns (those living in Europe during the 1600s) had all the knowledge available to the ancients (those living in Greece and Rome centuries earlier) plus all the ideas and information gained in the subsequent centuries. Thus, where the strict application of the biological metaphor suggests eventual decay and death, this transformation of the metaphor eliminated the period of decline and left the growth part of the developmental trajectory intact and operating indefinitely. This idea of continuous accumulation of knowledge and understanding was later applied to many other domains of human life, including government, religion, economics, and the family.

In fact, the idea of continuous growth and improvement was endorsed so enthusiastically by some that they conceptualized mankind as having an innate impulse toward improvement (Hegel 1878/1837). The possibility of indefinite improvement, perfectibility, and eternal progress for all was also posited.[9]

Although the model of continuous and indefinite social growth was to play a very important role in social thought throughout the subsequent centuries, it would be a mistake to believe that it was the only variant of the model to be important during these years. Instead, the old variant of genesis, growth, and decay remained important for many subsequent scholars. In fact, the dynamic tension between the two models of the societal life cycle was to play an important role in debates during the 1700s and 1800s (Mandelbaum 1971; Nisbet 1975/1969, 1980). Some scholars interpreted the social change that they believed they saw as progress; others saw it as decay. The optimistic perception of growth and improvement has, however, overwhelmingly predominated the pessimistic scenario of decline and decay in the last two centuries.

Although there were differences between the two schools of thought on the ultimate prospects for society—with one seeing progress and the other decay—

8. See also Elliott 1972/1970; Hodgen 1964; Meek 1976; Nisbet 1980.

9. See Condorcet, n.d./1795; Godwin 1926/1793; Hegel 1878/1837. See also Elliott 1972/1970; Löwith 1949; Meek 1976.

the two approaches were united in their attachment to the developmental paradigm. Both schools accepted the metaphor comparing human societies to biological organisms, with societies following developmental trajectories through childhood, the young adult years, and maturity. Furthermore, scholars from both viewpoints believed that the developmental experiences of all societies were highly similar. The only disagreement concerned whether developmental changes after maturity represented growth and progress or decay and decline.

Of course, to label uniform and directional change in the developmental model as progress or retrogression is to make a value judgment that depends on the perspective of the viewer rather than on the state of the object (Jennings 1975). That is, like beauty and character, societal progress and retrogression exist in the eye of the beholder and can be interpreted in different ways by different observers. Thus, the labeling of change as progress or retrogression can be removed entirely from the discussion without disturbing the central features of the developmental model itself.[10]

Societal Uniformity and Idiosyncrasy

One of the key elements of the developmental model was that societies at the same state of development had the same fundamental characteristics (see, e.g., Robertson 1780/1777, 1860/1762). That is, the forces associated with a particular developmental stage were believed to be so strong that the various societies in that stage had the same basic customs and lifestyles. However, the extent of the perceived uniformity across societies in the same stage varied across authors. Although the model was sometimes pictured with strict and total uniformity, most scholars were much less rigid in their approach (Carneiro 1973; Sanderson 1990; Sumner and Keller 1929). The developmental paradigm was usually applied to human societies in a way that maintained the unity of the human experience while at the same time recognizing the diversity of culture and social organization. Most scholars recognized that each society was influenced by the special events and circumstances of its environment—especially climate in the 1700s—that resulted in its own idiosyncratic historical trajectory, one that could even include side trips and retrogression.[11] The unfolding of the developmental trajectory of societies was, thus, seen as including both common and unique aspects across the different populations of the world.

10. See Giddens 1984; Goldenweiser 1937; Lenski 1976; Sanderson 1990; Sumner and Keller 1929.

11. See Bock 1956; Carneiro 1973; Harris 1968; Home 1813/1774; Roberson 1780/1777; Sanderson 1990; Sumner and Keller 1929; Tylor 1871.

Scholars recognized that, just as there were differences in the developmental experiences of individual biological organisms, there were differences in the life-cycle experiences of various cultures.

The primary goal of these researchers was the identification and explanation of the essential and common elements of societal development (Bock 1956). They were interested in the laws of change, the true elements of nature, and the dynamics of development inherent in human society. The scholars interested in societal development were, consequently, not interested in the details and idiosyncrasies of the actual histories of particular societies. These were seen by them as trivial, uninteresting, and descriptive rather than the subject of science, which is about the general and the universal. There were, of course, historians who were interested in documenting the details and uniquenesses of the histories of specific societies, but their projects were seen as much less valuable to developmental scholars at the time than was the science of history that focused on the uniformities of development (Bock 1956; Macfarlane 1979a/1978, 2002).

At the same time, some scholars were interested in writing about both the details and idiosyncrasies of historical change and the uniformities of development, sometimes combining them in the same work (Howard 1904; Robertson 1780/1777, 1860/1762). A major problem for the developmental researcher was the separation of the idiosyncratic noise from the substantively interesting ladder of development itself.[12] Conjecture and abstraction were part of this approach because it was necessary to abstract from concrete events and circumstances in individual societies. As a result, social observers generalized from concrete and unique events and conditions to write "natural" or "conjectural" histories that were believed to describe the fairly uniform development of human societies.[13]

Variable Rates of Societal Development

Although most analysts using this societal-developmental perspective thought that the unity of mankind resulted in all societies having similar trajectories of change, most also believed that the velocity and direction of development varied across groups, space, and time.[14] For example, many scholars believed that China and India were the homes of great civilizations for centuries but per-

12. See Bock 1956; Carneiro 1973; Sanderson 1990; Sumner and Keller 1929.

13. See Bock 1956; Harris 1968; Hodgen 1964; Nisbet 1975/1969, 1980.

14. See Condorcet, n.d./1795; Ferguson 1980/1767; George 1938/1880; Hegel 1878/1837; Home 1813/1774; Lieber 1876/1838; Mill 1989a/1859; Millar 1979/1779; Montesquieu 1973/1721, 1997/1748; Robertson 1860/1762; Tylor 1871. See also Carneiro 1973; Nisbet 1975/1969.

ceived those civilizations as having become stagnant. Many analysts also perceived that Northwest Europe itself had been backward for centuries but had then experienced considerable development to bring it to the peak of progress at that time. Many were also poignantly aware of the perceived rise and fall of Greece and Rome. Conditions among certain American Indian groups were also interpreted by some as being the result of retrogression from higher levels. This understanding of the possibility of both retrogression and progression made some people especially concerned about the fragility of development and progress and the very real possibility of big falls backward as well as great leaps forward—realizations that, as we shall see in chapter 9, played a role in subsequent political events.

This view of the different rates of advancement along the trajectory of development is summarized succinctly by John Millar, who in the late 1700s made important contributions to the developmental understanding of changes in family life. Millar said: "There is thus, in human society, a natural progress from ignorance to knowledge, and from rude, to civilized manners, the several stages of which are usually accompanied with peculiar laws and customs. Various accidental causes, indeed, have contributed to accelerate, or to retard this advancement in different countries" (1979/1779, 176–77).

Some contemporary societies had, according to this view, progressed quite far along the development ladder by the 1600s and 1700s, others had only begun the climb, and yet other societies were scattered along the way between the most and the least advanced. This differential development helped account for the enormous cultural diversity that European scholars observed in the world around them.

Of course, abstracting a "natural" history that describes the normal course of societal development, taking into account the experiences of numerous societies and different levels of life-cycle development, was a monumental task. Many of the analysts of the day were poignantly aware of the complexities involved, and the approaches and results varied across observers. Numerous descriptions of the stages of societal development were formulated to summarize the life cycles of social institutions. These schemes often identified the nature of social institutions in the beginning of social life and traced the developmental sequences through the observed social life cycle and, sometimes, into the future.

Although there were many differences in the specific descriptions of the developmental trajectories identified, there was also general agreement about the broad developmental steps. Some scholars maintained great detail in their descriptions of developmental change and had numerous stages in the pathway of development. Many scholars reduced the continuous course of societal development into three or four broad stages. One such scheme that became popular adopted a broad three-step sequence that began with savagery, proceeded through barbarism, and finally culminated in civilization. Many also used simple dichotomies: from rude to polished; from backward to developed; from traditional to modern; and from undeveloped to developed (Kreager 1986; Mandelbaum 1971; Nisbet 1975/1969, 1980).

The Scottish Enlightenment of the 1700s was an especially important locus in the formulation of the idea of development through stages. Several scholars of the Scottish Enlightenment linked the stages of development to economics and the means of subsistence and identified four such stages: hunting; herding; agriculture; and commerce.[15] These scholars were especially influential in suggesting that the changes of society through these stages of development were important for other aspects of social life, including family relationships. This idea of the dominance of the technical-material factors in changing social relationships became especially popular in subsequent decades and has remained tremendously influential over the past two centuries (Lehmann 1979/1960; Meek 1976).

Many of the leading scholars of the era were aware of some of the difficulties of describing the world using the developmental model. There was an understanding among them that the world is hard to describe, that values influence perspectives and labels, that people tend to disparage things that are foreign, that human observation and judgment are fallible, and that barbarism is in the mind of the beholder.[16] Thus, their models and categorization schemes proceeded with at least some awareness of some of the pitfalls.

Empirical Data

Classical Historical Data

Northwest European philosophy and social science had between the 1500s and 1900s considerable data resources available for historical and comparative analysis. Of central importance was the Bible, which provided a theologically approved history. It included accounts of the beginnings of mankind and chronicled significant history for at least one cultural group and its neighbors.

15. See Home 1813/1774; Millar 1979/1779; A. Smith 1976/1759, 1978/1762–63. See also Meek 1976.

16. See Ferguson 1980/1767; Hobbes 1996/1651; Hume 1825/1742; Mill 1989a/1859; Montaigne 1946/1580; Montesquieu 1973/1721; Robertson 1780/1777; Rousseau 1984/1755. See also Bock 1956; Fenton and Moore 1974; Hodgen 1964; Pagden 1982.

Also available to scholars of the era were substantial accounts of life in classical Egypt, Rome, and Greece. These materials provided a great deal of information about life in these societies, including descriptions of historical change. They also described the conquests of Rome and Greece by the peoples from the east and the north.

Northwest European scholars also had some archaeological information from Europe. Extensive knowledge of certain aspects of European history, including political and military events, was also available. European writers were also well aware of economic, scientific, and technological changes in recent European history, including the increase both in the number of schools and in educational attainment.

Cross-Cultural Information

Writers in the ancient Greek and Roman worlds documented life in neighboring societies (Bock 1956; Hodgen 1964; Rives 1999). Perhaps most remarkable in this regard is the account by the Greek writer Herodotus, who left comparative accounts of life in several neighbor countries. Other Greek and Roman writers provided similar accounts, one of the most cited today being that by Tacitus of the Germans (Rives 1999).

Comparative data for various societies continued to accumulate between the demise of Rome and the 1400s, the beginning of the age of sustained European exploration (Biller 2001; Hodgen 1964). Many Europeans had traveled to the Middle East and were familiar with the Islamic societies of that region, with the Crusades playing an important role in the dissemination of cross-cultural knowledge. There was a significant amount of information available in Europe about India. Europeans traveled to East Asia, with the accounts of Marco Polo becoming especially important. The threat that the Mongols posed to Europe resulted in European envoys being sent to that society, with the subsequent circulation of reports of life there. However, despite the slow accumulation of reliable information, much of the European understanding of other cultures in the 1400s consisted of the fantastic, abnormal, and preposterous (Hodgen 1964).

With the dawning of the age of European exploration and conquest, the scope of data from non-European populations available in Northwest Europe expanded dramatically.[17] Whole new populations were discovered in the Americas, Africa, Australia, and elsewhere. European explorers and conquerors

17. See Bock 1956; Chiappelli, Allen, and Benson 1976; Hodgen 1964; Myres 1916; Pagden 1982; Porter 1979; Sheehan 1980.

returned from their travels with accounts of fascinating people, and that information circulated widely within Europe. They also brought back artifacts that became the object of collection and display. In addition, the explorers captured Native Americans, took them to Europe, and exhibited them for the curious. In fact, in his first voyage to America, Columbus captured and transported back to Europe seven Native Americans, and hundreds more followed by the end of the 1400s. Similar displays of artifacts and people appeared in subsequent decades and centuries (Hodgen 1964).

Many of the explorers, travelers, missionaries, and colonists were very curious and eager to share their experiences with others. Published accounts began to accumulate (Hodgen 1964; Sheehan 1980). Hodgen (1964, 183) reports that, between 1480 and 1600 alone, the list of titles on travel and geography in English numbered well over one hundred.

Across the subsequent centuries, the amount of cross-cultural data accumulated rapidly, until scholars had overwhelming quantities of such information.[18] Numerous Western explorers, colonial officials, missionaries, and military personnel lived for extensive periods among other groups and returned to their homes to write accounts of the people they had visited. These non-Western populations also attracted many travelers who sought the cross-cultural experience and subsequently published detailed and extensive summaries of their adventures.

The scholars of the 1600s through the 1800s were incredibly well-read, and they assimilated and used in their work enormous amounts of information— both historical and contemporaneous—from a very large number of places around the world. Even given this extensive use of secondary material, however, many were not content to rely entirely on the data collections of others. Instead, they traveled extensively to make their own observations. The travel of some was extraordinarily prodigious, especially considering the limitations of communication and transportation networks of the 1600s through the 1800s. A few—including Frédéric Le Play, Lewis Henry Morgan, and Edward Westermarck—even collected their own primary data through community studies and ethnographies.[19]

As a result of both the large amounts of secondary data available and the successes of scholars in collecting their own primary data, the research reports

18. See Blaut 1993; Bock 1956; Godelier 1983; Gruber 1973; Harris 1968; Kreager 1986; Lehmann 1979/1960; Myres 1916; Nisbet 1975/1969, 1980; Pagden 1982; Sanderson 1990; Westermarck 1929/1927; Wrigley and Souden 1986.

19. See Baker 1998; Blaut 1993; Le Play 1982c/1855, 1982d/1879; Westermarck 1929/1927.

of scholars during that era are remarkable in the amount of data reported. In fact, social scientists had been overwhelmed by large amounts of comparative data for centuries before the fielding in the late 1900s of such mammoth studies as the World Fertility Survey, the Demographic and Health Surveys, and the World Values Surveys (Blaut 1993; Nisbet 1980).

Prolonged contact with an exceptionally large and diverse group of cultures and societies around the world produced major challenges to European perspectives concerning such fundamental factors as the definition of humanity, the origins of society, the history of Europe and the larger world, and mankind's relationships with deity. The new information and the questions that it raised about fundamental European beliefs and values occupied many of the best minds of Europe during the subsequent centuries. This new scholarship that began in the 1500s was crucially important during the Enlightenment of the 1600s and 1700s, dominated the social sciences of the 1800s and early 1900s, and remains influential in the social sciences today (Jennings 1975; Lehmann 1979/1960; Nisbet 1980).

The new information flowing into Europe was, according to Lehmann, "nothing short of revolutionary in its impact upon men's thinking on problems of human nature, society, politics, the nature and origin and development of social and political institutions, and even on the nature of morals and religion themselves." It greatly expanded the amount of thinking devoted to comparative issues and caused much "reflection and speculation of a historico-sociological nature" (1979/1960, 118–19; see also Comaroff and Comaroff 1997).

One of the profound issues raised by the new cross-cultural data was the nature of creation and the line of separation between humans and the rest of the animal world.[20] At the most fundamental level, some asked if the newly discovered creatures from various non-European parts of the world were human or a different species. This debate was ultimately resolved in favor of defining them as humanity—a conclusion consistent with papal pronouncement. Others asked new questions about the origins and meaning of humanity. Although the Bible contained a theory of human diversity (Cain, Noah, the Tower of Babel), many scholars began to challenge its adequacy as a full account. Some scholars rejected the biblical account of a single creation in their efforts to account for human diversity, suggesting that mankind had descended from multiple creations. Eventually, however, most scholars rejected the poly-

20. See Berkhofer 1978; Bock 1956; Elliott 1972/1970; Hodgen 1964; Huddleston 1967; Lehmann 1979/1960; Meek 1976; Myres 1916; Pagden 1982; Pearce 1967/1953; Porter 1979; Sheehan 1980.

genetic view and accepted the unity of mankind through a single creation. These newly discovered people were, thus, seen as one with the rest of humanity, being on the same development ladder, but, as I note later, viewed as existing at the earliest stages of human development.

The Validity of Cross-Cultural Data

As one would expect, the empirical data from the 1700s and 1800s did not usually meet the standards of today. Censuses and vital statistics were often nonexistent or weak. The wonders of representative sampling and survey research were not yet widely appreciated. The travelers, colonial administrators, explorers, and military personnel who wrote the accounts of people they encountered were generally not trained in data-collection techniques. In addition, those scholars who collected their own data were unaware of many of the data-collection standards that have become commonly accepted today. They also carried with them substantial biases about the superiority of their own customs. Consequently, the empirical information available for analysis in the 1500s and extending through the 1800s often did not meet the standards of anthropology, sociology, or economics in the late 1900s. The data sometimes did not even meet the standards of the scholars themselves (Robertson 1780/1777; see also Pagden 1982).

In some cases, the weaknesses of the available data contributed substantially to the drawing of incorrect conclusions.[21] This was particularly true for populations that were very different from those in Europe. Worldwide, it also seems to be true in political matters and in the areas of family sentiment and the distribution of family labor and authority. For example, there were some inevitable misinterpretations of the cross-cultural data about the meaning of marriage, gender relations, and the role of love and affection in kinship relations.[22] In addition, some of the descriptions of some societies seemed biased and extreme (Jennings 1975; Pagden 1982).

Although there were important deficiencies in some aspects of the conclusions of the scholars of the past, much of their information has been described as being of surprisingly high quality (Blaut 1993; Gruber 1973). As I detail more fully in chapter 3, in a remarkably large number of cases the data were of sufficient quality to portray with general accuracy many of the fundamental and dramatic contrasts in family patterns across cultures (Gruber 1973; Macfarlane

21. See Coontz 1991/1988; Jennings 1975; Lee and Wang 1999; Myres 1916; Pagden 1982; Sheehan 1980.

22. See W. Alexander 1995/1779; Millar 1979/1779. See also Boas 1940; Coontz 1991/1988.

1979a/1978). That is, the differences in family structures between Northwest Europe and many other places were of sufficient magnitude that their general nature could be observed, even if the meaning, details, and nuances of particular patterns were sometimes misunderstood.[23] Thus, such customs in other societies as child marriage, arranged marriage, bride-price, polygamy, foot-binding, and extended households could be described and contrasted with those of Europe with relative accuracy even if they were misunderstood and considered revolting.

Thus, despite data limitations and potential for misinterpretations, many of these cross-cultural conclusions derived by generations of Northwest European scholars were relatively consistent with the reality of family patterns from that same era as understood by scholars today. Numerous recent studies have confirmed many of the most important and fundamental empirical conclusions of research from the earlier generations of scholars about family patterns across regions in that time period.

Scholars of the era recognized the value of all the data sources available to them: the archaeological record; the Bible; the record from Greece and Rome; the European historical record; and the rapidly accumulating comparative materials. All these data sources were used extensively across the centuries from the 1500s into the 1900s. In fact, many scholars used multiple sources simultaneously in an effort to describe societal development.[24]

Making sense of all these data was a time-consuming and complex project. It took time for the new information to filter into public consciousness and into the descriptions and explanations of academics (Elliott 1972/1970; Hodgen 1964).[25] By the early and mid-1500s, books cataloging and describing the customs of numerous people around the world began to appear.[26] Across the subsequent decades and centuries, the discussions became more systematic and exhaustive, although earlier works seemed more interested in agriculture and

---

23. Macfarlane (1979a/1978) found the descriptions and comparisons by international travelers of social and family conditions in the past to be remarkably consistent with his findings from other archival sources.

24. See W. Alexander 1995/1779; Condorcet, n.d./1795; Hegel 1878/1837; Howard 1904; Le Play 1982a/1881, 1982c/1855; Malthus 1986a/1798, 1986b/1803; Millar 1979/1779; Robertson 1860/1762; A. Smith 1978/1762–63. See also Baker 1975; Lehmann 1979/1960; Myres 1916.

25. This process seems to have happened especially quickly in Spain because of that country's early involvement in the Americas (Huddleston 1967; Pagden 1982). Also, the discovery of America by the Europeans played a role in Thomas More's *Utopia*, published in 1516 (More 1997/1516).

26. See Elliott 1972/1970; Huddleston 1967; Pagden 1982; Porter 1979.

commerce than in culture and family systems. In time, scholars became interested in virtually all dimensions of human life and created complex descriptions and explanations of the differences that they saw (Hodgen 1964).

As the scholars of the era began to make sense of their data, they realized that, in many ways, their materials were insufficient for their needs.[27] Both Rousseau (1984/1755) and Hegel (1878/1837) complained about a lack of cross-cultural information that prevented them from covering all types of societies. Other scholars began a lamentation—one that has continued to the present—about the shortage of easily available, reliable information concerning the actual histories of social institutions of particular societies (Malthus 1986a/1798, 1986b/1803; Millar 1979/1779).

Interestingly, however, the same historical records that scholars used in the last half of the 1900s were available to scholars of the 1700s and 1800s. In fact, some historians continued to write detailed histories of actual societies, but the focus of these histories was generally on political, economic, and international matters rather than on mundane domestic things such as marriage and living arrangements.[28] In addition, because these developmental scholars were interested in science and the general rather than the details and particulars of history, they had less interest in the actual historical record of specific societies (Bock 1956). The cross-cultural data were also easily available in large amounts and provided scholars with new challenges and questions requiring answers. Apparently, scholars also became so busy making sense of the abundant cross-cultural data that they did not have the time to undertake the research in the Northwest European libraries that historians would conduct centuries later.

Examples of Scholars Using Cross-Cultural Data

Cross-cultural data from numerous societies permeated the writings of many scholars from the 1600s through the 1800s. In fact, some of the most important treatises of the time were based, at least in part, on international comparative information. I highlight briefly here its use in the work of John Locke, Robert Malthus, Frédéric Le Play, Edward Westermarck, and the scholars of the Scottish Enlightenment. Locke, who had a passion for information about people around the world, provides an important example of the use of inter-

---

27. See Carneiro 1973; Lehmann 1979/1960; Mandelbaum 1971; Sanderson 1990.

28. Several examples of scholars writing histories of social and family institutions from the historical record are provided by Macfarlane (1979a/1978, 2002). Particularly noteworthy here is the work of F. W. Maitland, who wrote a generally reliable and extensive account of England that included information about many social and economic matters in the English past.

national data as early as the late 1600s.[29] When he died in 1704, Locke had a substantial collection of books—approximately 3,600—that scholars have since systematically analyzed to ascertain the sources of his ideas (Ashcraft 1968; Laslett 1965). Of those books, 195 were categorized as travel and voyage volumes and another 85 as geography (Laslett 1965). Apparently, Locke's collection contained more travel and voyage volumes than did other personal libraries of similar size during this period (Ashcraft 1968).

Furthermore, Laslett (1965) indicates that an examination of the various volumes in Locke's library suggests that the books on travel, exploration, and geography may have been the most well used by Locke himself. His preoccupation with cross-cultural customs is further evidenced by the fact that "he was forever noting in his commonplace books the political, economic, and social customs recorded by travellers to non-European countries" (Ashcraft 1969, 53). He was, apparently, generous in sharing his interest in foreign customs with his friends and colleagues, sometimes drawing jibes about his "perpetual references to travellers' tales" (Laslett 1965, 29; see also Laslett 1988/1960). Myres (1916) reported that Locke was so high on the importance of this travel literature that he included a substantial list of such books as recommended reading in his *Thoughts Concerning Reading and Study* (Locke 1996/1693).

Most important, Locke's passion for knowledge of foreign customs was not just a hobby but played a substantial role in his writing.[30] Locke's most important and pathbreaking political work—the *Second Treatise of Government*—is motivated by his interest in human origins and explicitly states that "in the beginning all the World was *America*" (Locke 1988/1690, 301). Locke made numerous references to Native Americans in describing both the origins of society and the development of human institutions. Because of the power and extensiveness of his comparative analysis and its subsequent influence, it has been suggested that he did more than anyone else to establish the field of comparative anthropology (Laslett 1988/1960). He was also especially influential in establishing and popularizing the belief

29. See Ashcraft 1968; Batz 1974; Cranston 1957; Laslett 1965, 1988/1960; Myres 1916. Locke was born in England in 1632 in a family of Puritan background. He was well educated in the classics from a young age and graduated from Oxford in 1658. He received a medical degree and was a teacher of medicine at Oxford. He also served as a diplomat and on the Board of Trade. His extensive philosophical, political, and educational writings were creative and very influential. Despite the fact that he published some of his most important work anonymously, it has been claimed that he died in 1704 as "the most famous and influential philosopher of his age" (Grant and Tarcov 1996, xix; see also Cranston 1957; Laslett 1988/1960).

30. See Ashcraft 1968; Batz 1974; Laslett 1965, 1988/1960; Myres 1916.

that America and similar places represented life in the beginning of human time (Meek 1976; Myres 1916).

By the time of the Scottish Enlightenment in the last half of the 1700s, the use of comparative cross-cultural data was accepted and widespread. Virtually all the major figures of the Scottish Enlightenment—including Adam Smith, David Hume, John Millar, Henry Home, and William Robertson—made extensive use of data from various societies. John Millar was particularly assertive and influential in his use of cross-cultural data concerning family processes and relationships. These Scottish scholars also played important roles in systemizing the use of cross-sectional data to create accounts of social change. By doing so, they made pioneering and substantial contributions to the documentation and explanation of societal family change.

Another important user of international comparative data was Robert Malthus, an English clergyman whose thinking about population dynamics has dominated the field of population studies and policy for the past two centuries.[31] Malthus's *Essay on the Principle of Population* (1986a/1798) is probably the single most influential work ever written concerning population growth and its interrelations with human well-being. His theoretical and policy statements about the growth of population and its role in decreasing economic well-being are well-known today—as are his pleas for the postponement of marriage in order to reduce fertility. Less known today, however, is his empirical work, which led him to important conclusions about how population dynamics and marriage patterns had changed over the course of Western European history.

In 1798 Malthus published a brief essay on his ideas and assumptions concerning population growth. Then, between 1798 and 1803, Malthus gathered an extensive array of empirical evidence both through travel on the European continent and through wide reading in the contemporary comparative literature (Godelier 1983; Wrigley and Souden 1986). The result of this extensive research was the production in 1803 of a very large manuscript that between 1803 and 1826 went through five editions. This four-volume work contained enormous amounts of information about family and population matters from numerous societies around the world.

Nearly a century after Malthus, a young Finnish scholar embarked on an even more ambitious international study, one focused specifically on human

---

31. Robert Malthus was born in England in 1766 and died in 1834. He graduated from Jesus College, Cambridge, with a degree in mathematics in 1788. Also in 1788 he took holy orders and embarked on a career in the ministry. In 1805, after publishing his famous essays on population, he took a position at the East India College, where he served as professor of general history, politics, commerce, and finance (Flew 1986/1970; Wrigley and Souden 1986).

marriage. This was Edward Westermarck, who left his native Finland in 1886 for London, where his principal activity was reading in the British Museum.[32] In addition to his work at the British Museum, Westermarck sent questionnaires to about 125 people living in various parts of the world (Granqvist 1968, 530; Westermarck 1929/1927, 79–80).

The result of Westermarck's work was the collection of an enormous amount of cross-cultural information about numerous aspects of human marriage. The original editions of his *History of Human Marriage* included nearly thirty pages of bibliographic citations, a number that grew to over one hundred pages by the fifth edition. The pages of his book are dense with the documentation of many dimensions of marriage patterns around the world, including age at marriage, the extent of celibacy, courtship patterns, the arrangement of marriage, and patterns of authority and autonomy within families.

The information published by Westermarck was well accepted and widely circulated (Granqvist 1968). His book went into its second edition in 1894, and, by 1921, five editions had been issued, with the fifth edition expanded to three volumes. *The History of Human Marriage* was translated into several languages, including French, German, Swedish, Italian, Japanese, and Spanish (Westermarck 1929/1927, 297).[33]

Frédéric Le Play was one of the giants of social-science history and a prolific collector of social-science data from numerous settings. He began his career in France as a metallurgist and industrial engineer and later became interested in human behavior and family relations.[34] In the mid-1800s, he con-

---

32. Edward Westermarck was born in Helsingfors (Helsinki), Finland, in 1862 and died in 1939. According to Westermarck (1929/1927), in 1889 he finished a draft of his book and used the opening chapters, under the title "The Origin of Human Marriage," as his doctoral dissertation at the University of Helsingfors. He then added more material to the book, polished its contents, and published it as *The History of Human Marriage* in England in 1891.

33. Westermarck was also widely sought after in academic circles. He served as professor of moral philosophy at the University of Helsingfors. He also served as the first head of Abo Academy, where he was also professor of philosophy (Granqvist 1968, 530). After his death, the Westermarck Society was formed to honor his memory.

34. Le Play, who was born in Normandy in 1806 and died in Paris in 1882, began his very successful career in the physical sciences and engineering. As Kellner (1972) wrote: "His life before 1855 would provide enough achievement to fill four life-long careers." Among other things, he conducted and published research on mining, metallurgy, the steel industry, and industrial relations. He was a professor at the Ecole des Mines, sat on three government commissions, and managed a mining and industrial operation in Russia (Brooke 1970).

From the beginning, Le Play displayed a strong interest in the human side of mining and

ducted one of the most monumental and successful studies that social science has ever seen. The data reported in the resulting book—*The Workers of Europe* (Le Play 1982c/1855)—were gathered almost exclusively under his direction from families scattered across the European continent and beyond. Although Le Play did not use sampling techniques, he was aware of the need to choose families carefully in order for them to represent the larger population.

Once the families were selected for study, they were subjected to an intense and multifaceted data-collection effort. Each family participating in the study was observed for between eight days and a month (Higgs 1890). Semistructured interviews with members of the household were also conducted. Finally, information was collected from people in the area who had known the family for an extensive period and who could provide additional information about the family (Le Play 1982b/1862).

A central feature of the Le Play story is that he was not content to study only families living in and around Paris, where he lived, but, instead, launched a truly comparative research effort involving fieldwork in much of Europe and in bordering areas. His research took him to "England seven times, Germany almost as often, Russia and Italy thrice, Spain and the west of Asia twice" (Higgs 1890, 415). Le Play also reported completing detailed studies of three hundred different families from a wide range of European countries, including Austria-Hungary, Bulgaria, England, France, Germany, Norway, Russia, Sweden, and Switzerland (Brooke 1970, 146–53).[35] An important outcome of Le Play's energetic and persistent data collection was his monumental description of the geographic distribution of family types in the mid-1800s in Europe and beyond, which is generally consistent with the best understanding today.

-----

industrial operations (Brooke 1970) and in human welfare more generally (Le Play 1937/1879). He also traveled extensively in his numerous roles as university professor, engineering researcher, government commissioner, and industrial manager, which undoubtedly increased his interest in the issues of social science. According to Le Play himself, his social-science apprenticeship was well advanced by 1843, his metallurgical career dwindled from 1848 to 1855 as he devoted more time to his social-science work, and he devoted himself entirely to social science after the publication of his *Workers of Europe* in 1855 (Le Play 1937/1879).

35. Le Play wrote: "Travel is to the science of societies, what chemical analysis is to mineralogy, what fieldwork is to botany, or, in general terms, what the observation of facts is to all the natural sciences" (Le Play quoted in Fletcher 1969, 53). In all, he was estimated to have traveled approximately 200,000 miles for his research, much of that distance on foot (Farmer 1954). The fact that he spoke five languages facilitated both travel and the collection of information (Higgs 1890).

Reading History Sideways

With appropriate historical data, describing societal change across time is a relatively straightforward matter. For any given society—for example, England—
first arrange the respective periods in chronological order from the beginning
of time to the present. Then describe the changes occurring across this chronological sequence. The scholars interested in societal change understood this
strategy and attempted to follow it when they could. However, the historical
data available to them were limited and difficult to use. They did, however, have
large quantities of cross-sectional data and a method that they believed they
could use to describe societal change.

The scholars of the 1600s through the 1800s used what they called *the comparative method,* that is, an approach that employed cross-sectional data from
multiple places to describe a trajectory of change.[36] I refer to this approach
as *reading history sideways* because it contrasts with a chronological approach
employing a single geographic location.[37] With their belief in the existence
of contemporaneous societies at various levels of development, scholars of
the era believed that they could use information from a less advanced society to proxy for the past conditions of a more advanced society. That is, the
past circumstances of contemporary societies believed to be at higher levels
of development could be ascertained by examining the present conditions of
contemporary societies believed to be at lower levels of development. Making
such comparisons meant interpreting the cross-sectional data as historical
data and variations across space as variations across time.[38] Instead of reading the history of actual societies from the past to the present, scholars
employing the comparative method read history sideways across geographic
and cultural categories.

Apparently, there were classical precedents for this methodology. Several

36. See Comte 1858/1830–42; Sumner and Keller 1929; Westermarck 1922, 1929/1927. See also
Bock 1956; Bryson 1945; Carneiro 1973; Fabian 1983; Mandelbaum 1971; Nisbet 1975/1969;
Sanderson 1990.

37. That is, it is used as a method to describe human history and not to make static comparisons.

38. See Condorcet, n.d./1795; Ferguson 1980/1767; Hegel 1878/1837; Hobbes 1991/1642,
1996/1651; Home 1813/1774; Locke 1988/1690; Mill 1989c/1869; Millar 1979/1779; Robertson
1780/1777, 1860/1762; Rousseau 1984/1755; Senior 1831; A. Smith 1978/1762–63; Sumner and Keller
1929; Teggart 1925; Turgot 1895/1750. See also Berkhofer 1978; Bock 1956; Bolgar 1979; Carneiro
1973; Fabian 1983; Gordon 1994; Harris 1968; Hodgen 1964; Manuel 1962; Myres 1916; Sanderson
1990; Sheehan 1980.

Greek writers, including Thucydides, Herodotus, and Aristotle, were reported to have used it to describe their own origins (Bock 1956; Hodgen 1964; Pembroke 1979). Adam Ferguson, a key advocate of this methodology in the late 1700s, suggested: "Thucydides, notwithstanding the prejudice of his country against the name of *Barbarian,* understood that it was in the customs of barbarous nations he was to study the more ancient manners of Greece" (1980/1767, 80).

The Northwest Europeans also had other precedents for mixing time and place in the construction of history. To the extent that they accepted the Hebrews, Greeks, and Romans as being part of their own pasts, they were mixing time with place. Although the data that they used from the Hebrews, Greeks, and Romans were temporally prior to their own data from Northwest Europe—by more than a millennium—they also came from different cultures and places. This was, of course, a mixing of temporal and geographic variation.

Using the comparative method required a system for converting information from different societies around the world into homogeneous developmental sequences (Nisbet 1980). However, the scholars of the 1500s through the 1900s had few resources with which to accomplish this task. They had no societal age distributions, no geologic clocks, and no layered sediments (Mandelbaum 1971). They had to rely on other means of ordering contemporaneous societies from the origins of mankind to the most developed.

Because of the power of ethnocentrism, we should not be surprised that the people of Northwest Europe would believe that they were at the pinnacle of societal development. This ethnocentrism was undoubtedly reinforced by the traditions and worldview of Christianity, which saw itself as being at the pinnacle of religious progress.[39] God was also perceived in Western tradition as rewarding loyal adherents with more rapid social and economic progress.[40]

Westerners were also aware of their military and political ascendancy since the time of Christopher Columbus and Vasco Da Gama and understood well which countries had the most prestige and power, both military and economic (Blaut 1993; Nisbet 1980; Sheehan 1980). Ferguson, for example, believed that military prowess was related to societal life-cycle development, noting: "Rude nations . . . always yield to the superior arts, and the discipline of more civilized nations" (1980/1767, 95; see also Macaulay 1974/1790).

---

39. See Blaut 1993; Bock 1956; Nisbet 1975/1969, 1980; Pagden 1982.

40. It is worth noting that Northwest Europeans did not have a monopoly on self-perceived superiority. This practice of looking down on others as inferior is widely distributed, as Mennell (1996) reminds us.

Education, scientific knowledge, technology, written language, and urban life were also used by Northwest European scholars as criteria for placing their countries at the pinnacle of the developmental trajectory (Pagden 1982). For example, Edward Tylor, commonly identified as the father of anthropology, wrote in the late 1800s that "the educated world of Europe and America" set the standard for the advanced end of the continuum. According to Tylor: "The principal criteria of classification are the absence or presence, high or low development, of the industrial arts, especially metal-working, manufacture of implements and vessels, agriculture, architecture, &c., the extent of scientific knowledge" (1871, 23).

The scholars of this era in Northwest Europe were also aware of some evidence from the archaeological record and of the technological and economic changes that had occurred in recent European history (Mandelbaum 1971) as well as of the recent expansion in education and knowledge in Europe. This awareness, coupled with ethnocentrism, made it very easy for them to locate the pinnacle of development in their own region of the world.[41] It has also been suggested that the idea of the developmental ascendancy of Northwest Europe may have been strengthened both by the conquest of other groups and by a motivation to legitimize European territorial expansion and the creation and maintenance of the colonial system.[42]

With the advanced end of the continuum of development firmly anchored by Northwest Europe, it was possible to represent as the least developed those societies that were most different from Northwest Europe (Bock 1956; Meek 1976). Following the criteria identified by Ferguson and Tylor, this could be done in terms of military power, industry, education, urbanization, and scientific knowledge.

Having firmly identified Northwest Europe at the pinnacle of development, Tylor (1871, 23–24) could enunciate additional criteria, such as "the definiteness of moral principles, the condition of religious belief and ceremony, the degree of social and political organization, and so forth." Societies most distant from those of Northwest Europe on these criteria could also be placed at the least advanced end of the ladder of development.

Identification of the specific contemporaneous societies considered to be the least developed proved to be challenging for the European scholars.[43] As

41. See Blaut 1993; Bock 1956; Fabian 1983; Jennings 1975; Nisbet 1975/1969, 1980; Sanderson 1990; Stocking 1987.

42. See Berkhofer 1978; Blaut 1993; Jennings 1975; Pagden 1982.

43. See Hodgen 1964; Meek 1976; Myres 1916; Nisbet 1980; Pagden 1982; Pearce 1967/1953.

early as the 1500s, some Europeans believed that some of the populations outside Europe were so different from those in Europe that they could have
advanced only very little, if any, since their creation—or that, if they had
advanced since their creation, they had regressed sufficiently to be back near
their origins. Some even thought it possible that catastrophes—such as the
events occurring at the Tower of Babel, where God dispersed the population
and confused the language—had caused so much retrogression that the state
of these societies had been brought below what it had been at their creation
(Home 1813/1774). Because these societies were believed to be so close to the
origins of humanity, some scholars believed that they could be used as indicators of what life was like all over the world at or near the beginning of time.

The very earliest Europeans to explore the Americas were especially struck
with the exceptionally low levels of development that they perceived among
some indigenous groups.[44] They believed that some Native Americans were so
undeveloped as not to have even the rudiments of social life, such as governments, laws, justice, friendship, social organization, communities, cities, marriage rites, or commerce. This belief was widely accepted among and
disseminated by writers in Western Europe during the 1500s, 1600s, and 1700s.[45]
It was even reflected in some of the important literature of the era, including
the work of Shakespeare and Defoe (Myres 1916).

The extremely low level of development believed to exist in some populations in the Americas—and also in Africa and Australia—led to the idea
that these groups might be even more primitive than the earliest people
described in the Book of Genesis.[46] This idea was supported by several
beliefs, including a belief in multiple creations, a belief in the degeneration
of society after creation, and even rejection of the biblical account of creation altogether. Whatever the perceived cause, this idea became increasingly accepted, and, in the 1600s and 1700s, several scholars openly suggested
that the least developed—or earliest—people were to be found, not in the
Book of Genesis, a position supported by the church and believed for centuries, but among the peoples of the Americas, Africa, and Australia. For

44. See Berkhofer 1978; Huddleston 1967; Myres 1916; Pearce 1967/1953; Porter 1979.

45. See Montaigne 1946/1580; Robertson 1780/1777. See also Axtell 1981; Berkhofer 1978; Elliott
1972/1970; Huddleston 1967; Myres 1916; Pagden 1982; Pearce 1967/1953; Porter 1979; Sheehan
1980.

46. See Beard 1946; Cranston 1983; Hodgen 1964; Meek 1976; Myres 1916; Pagden 1982. The
biblical heritage of Western Europe provided the framework for initially interpreting the origins of the peoples of America. Having interpretations that could be reconciled with the Bible
remained important for centuries (Home 1813/1774; Huddleston 1967).

example, in the mid-1600s, Thomas Hobbes suggested that the beginning of time was to be observed best among the Native Americans (Hobbes 1991/1642, 1996/1651)—a belief that was repeated and popularized by Locke a few decades later (Locke 1988/1690) and by many others subsequently, including Rousseau, Tylor, Robertson, and Lafitau.[47]

The competition of this perspective with the earlier view locating the beginning of time in the Book of Genesis was especially vigorous (Schochet 1975; Soloway 1969). Some of the scholars of the 1600s were so impressed with the contrast between the inhabitants of Northwest Europe and those of the Americas, Australia, and Africa that they began to conceptualize the former as having and the latter as not having society and civilization (Gordon 1994). This contrast played a significant role in defining for the Northwest Europeans, not only what it meant to have society and civilization (Elliott 1972/1970; Gordon 1994; Meek 1976), but also what it meant to live without society and civilization—that is, in a state of nature. It also encouraged Europeans in their beliefs about indefinite improvement and eternal progress, with Europe at the pinnacle of human development (Elliott 1972/1970).

As conceptualized by Hobbes, Locke, Rousseau, and others, a state of nature was one in which all individuals were, by nature, free and equal.[48] Civil society, by contrast, was formed when these free and equal people freely consented to join together by contract to have society, rules, and government. Although there was substantial disagreement about whether life in the state of nature was, as Hobbes put it, "solitary, poor, nasty, brutish, and short" (1996/1651, 84), or the opposite, as Rousseau (1984/1755) suggested, there was little disagreement that it was free and equal and that the establishment of society required free consent.[49] As I document in chapters 8 and 9, this line of reasoning was very influential and had enormous implications for subsequent religious, political, and familial beliefs and behavior—but that is getting ahead of the story (Berkhofer 1978; Hodgen 1964; Myres 1916).

Given the importance of the state of nature—with its freedom, equality, and consent—for subsequent political and feminist theories, it should not be surprising to find that a substantial body of literature emerged in the 1900s

47. See Lafitau 1974/1724; Robertson 1780/1777; Rousseau 1984/1755; Tylor 1871.

48. See Hobbes 1991/1642, 1996/1651; Locke 1988/1690; Macaulay 1974/1790; Montesquieu 1997/1748; Robertson 1780/1777; Rousseau 1984/1755.

49. See also Hegel (1878/1837), who saw the ideal of freedom, not actual freedom, in the state of nature.

concerning the location of the state of nature.[50] This literature placed it either in the imagination of the writers, in a system of morality, or in actual historical experience. However, for Hobbes, Locke, Rousseau, and their contemporaries, the primary location of the state of nature was in geography and culture.[51]

In the context of the developmental paradigm and reading history sideways, it is clear that all these authors located the state of nature and the beginning of time among the native peoples of the Americas, Africa, and Australia. Thus, Locke's (1988/1690, 301) famous statement that "in the beginning all the world was *America*" was referring to those people in the Americas who were perceived as the very least developed. Interestingly, writers referred to all these native peoples as *naturals* (Hodgen 1964). That the colonists of Virginia sometimes referred to Native Americans as *naturals* suggests that the idea of certain peoples existing in a state of nature was current among them (Jennings 1975). Thomas Jefferson also referred to the Native Americans as "living under no law but that of nature" (Jefferson quoted in Nisbet 1980, 198).

Although the state of nature was originally a place, it was transferred to a historical time through the developmental paradigm and reading history sideways. Locke and others merely transferred "America" from a geographic and social location in the 1500s and 1600s to a historical location at the beginning of time. This transference of a geographical place to a historical one was, of course, also an accomplishment of the human mind, which made some later scholars believe that earlier generations were just imagining this state of nature. The state of nature was also eventually located in morality, but that part of the story will have to wait until chapters 8 and 9.[52]

Although the location of earliest humanity living in a state of nature was generally believed to be found somewhere among the peoples of the Americas, Africa, and Australia, there was no agreement on exactly which people repre-

50. See Anglim 1978; Ashcraft 1968, 1987; Batz 1974; Bobbio 1993/1989; Cranston 1983, 1984; Debeer 1969; Dunn 1969; Gaskin 1996; Gourevitch 1988–89; Leder 1968; Macpherson 1962; Meek 1976; Myres 1916; Nicholson 1986; Rendall 1985; Schochet 1975; Tarcov 1984; Tomaselli 1985.

51. See Condorcet, n.d./1795; Ferguson 1980/1767; Hobbes 1991/1642, 1996/1651; Locke 1988/1690; Rousseau 1984/1755. See also Ashcraft 1987; Batz 1974; Berkhofer 1978; Bobbio 1993/1989; Cranston 1983, 1984; Gaskin 1996; Leder 1968; Meek 1976; Myres 1916; Nisbet 1980; Tarcov 1984.

52. It appears that Hobbes (1991/1642, 1996/1651; see also Gourevitch 1988–89) also located the state of nature in relations between sovereign nations and in anarchic relations between individual people. For him, "America" was apparently only one illustration of the state of nature that existed when there was no superior government authority to maintain order.

sented the beginning of humankind (Myres 1916). There were many candidates, varying widely along many dimensions, and one's choice of candidate had enormous effects on how one viewed early mankind and the state of nature. This variance undoubtedly contributed to the substantial disagreements about life in the state of nature (Myres 1916). So, while Northwest Europeans believed that they knew precisely where the pinnacle of civilization was located, they were much more fuzzy on the location of human origins, a fuzziness that has implications for subsequent views of history and political moralizing.

Although the idea of the state of nature was especially important in the 1600s and 1700s, some scholars never accepted it as a useful concept. One objection raised by skeptics was that humans were by nature social beings. Another was that, if there ever was a time when humans were without culture and society, it was too long ago for there to be any information about it available. Yet another was that there were no contemporary peoples without some form of organized society—in fact, no evidence that any group of people had ever been without culture or society.

It was this last objection—no contemporary or historical evidence—that led some scholars to believe that there were no actual data describing such a place as the state of nature.[53] (Interestingly, this view of the ubiquity of society and civilization was consistent with earlier views that there were rules, society, and government in the beginning as described in the Book of Genesis [Schochet 1975; Soloway 1969].) Although this skeptical point of view eventually prevailed, the identification of the native peoples of the Americas, Africa, and Australia as being the closest to the beginning of time nevertheless persisted for centuries (Beard 1946; Hodgen 1964; Myres 1916). And, while the notion remained current, it had important effects on views of history and political and social values, effects that were to remain influential far into the future.

Despite such controversies, most scholars were able to identify—at least to their own satisfaction—a group or groups representing the beginning that they could then contrast with the European peoples at their present pinnacle of development. With the most and least advanced groups identified, Tylor, for example, believed that "ethnographers are able to set up at least a rough scale of civilization" (1871, 24). The rest of the world's population could be arrayed between the least and the most advanced societies. The more a group was like Northwest Europeans, the more civilized, developed, or modern it was judged

---

53. See George 1938/1880; Home 1813/1774; Hume 1825/1742; Lieber 1876/1838. See also Lehmann 1979/1960; Myres 1916.

to be. The less like Northwest Europeans it was, the less civilized, developed, or modern it was judged to be.[54]

Tylor probably assessed the general scholarly opinion of his era quite correctly when he concluded his discussion of the placement of contemporary societies on the development ladder by suggesting that "few would dispute that the following races are arranged rightly in order of culture:—Australian [aborigines], Tahitian, Aztec, Chinese, Italian" (1871, 24). Stocking suggested that, in this statement, Tylor implied "an unstated higher reference point northwest across the English Channel" (1987, 235; see also Carneiro 1973). Thus, with this geographic or cultural ordering, Tylor and numerous others transformed cultural categories into a developmental sequence. By following the directional lines on Tylor's world map, as summarized in figure 2.1, one could use the developmental paradigm to construct scenarios of historical change from geographic diversity.

There were, of course, many variants on Tylor's temporal ordering of contemporary societies, but most retained the same general outline. In addition, there were alternative approaches. Examples of these include Thomas Jefferson starting his development ladder in the western United States with the Native Americans and ending it in the cities of the East Coast (Jefferson cited in Nisbet 1980, 198; also in Pearce 1967/1953; see also Prucha 1984). In the 1500s, several Spaniards, including Acosta and Las Casas, suggested another developmental scheme based entirely in the Americas. This one started with the groups that they conceptualized as least developed and ended with the native kingdoms in Peru and Mexico (Meek 1976; Pagden 1982). This scheme was also used by Locke (1988/1690) in his work (see also Batz 1974; Meek 1976).

The developmental model was sometimes applied internally within Europe. Societies on the periphery of Europe and certain ethnic groups were sometimes viewed as less civilized than others.[55] Thus, such people as the Irish and the Welsh were sometimes described as rude, primitive, and barbaric in contrast to the civilized English, French, and Germans. Similarly, the idea of differential progress was sometimes applied to rural-urban differences within the societies of Europe. According to this scheme, rural and uneducated Europeans were viewed as less advanced than their urban and educated counterparts (Malcolmson 1980; Pagden 1982).

54. See Tylor 1871. See also Bock 1956; Fabian 1983; Meek 1976.

55. See Bartlett 1993; Comaroff and Comaroff 1997; France 1992; Jennings 1975; McClintock 1995; Sheehan 1980.

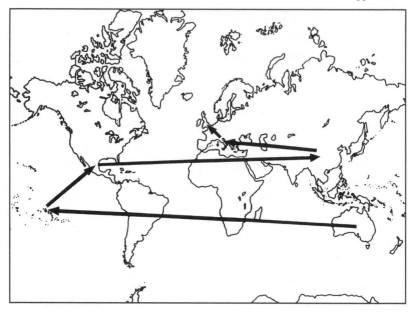

Figure 2.1 Edward Tylor's cross-cultural view of the trajectory of societal development

It is important to understand that users of cross-cultural data to read history sideways believed that their ladders of differentially ranked contemporary societies represented more than a simple cross-sectional ordering. They represented the natural history of civilization and the stages of cultural development. By looking down the ladder, the Western users of the social developmental paradigm and the reading history sideways methodology believed that they could read much of the sweep of human history.[56] They could read the European past from the non-European present. By looking at their next-door neighbors in Southern and Eastern Europe, the Northwest Europeans believed that they could read their relatively recent past. By looking further away—at China and India—they thought that they could distinguish the previous stage of development. By looking at the societies furthest down the ladder, they believed that they could (almost) see their own societal origins. By taking in the entire sweep of the development ladder and the con-

56. See Colden 1973/1727; Comte 1858/1830–42; Home 1813/1774; McLennan 1886/1865; Morgan 1985/1877; Robertson 1780/1777, 1860/1762; Sumner and Keller 1929; Teggart 1925. See also Carneiro 1973; Fabian 1983; Harris 1968; Mandelbaum 1971; Manuel 1962; Nisbet 1975/1969, 1980; Pearce 1967/1953.

temporary societies differentially placed along it, they believed that they could see the entire panorama of their own cultural history.

The examples of the ancient Greeks and the Northwest Europeans of the 1500s and 1600s reading history sideways are fairly simple and without elaborate justification. In fact, in many instances, the methodological approach is implicit and difficult to detect. However, as reading history sideways entered the 1700s, it became more self-conscious, detailed, and elaborate. Scholars also began to map out more complex sequences of the developmental trajectories of interest. For example, scholars such as Turgot, Ferguson, and Millar provided detailed explanations of the method and applied it in relatively complex forms.[57] By the end of the 1700s, the procedure was very widespread in Europe and became even more explicit and well articulated in the 1800s (Harris 1968). Many of the key figures of the 1800s and 1900s explained, justified, and used the method to provide detailed descriptions of societal development from cross-sectional data.[58] In other instances, the method was so well accepted and pervasive that many scholars took it for granted and saw no need to explain or defend it.[59]

Several of the developmental scholars, for example, Tylor and Comte, recognized weaknesses in the comparative approach to studying societal development (Bock 1956). There were also historians in the 1800s who criticized the sideways reading of history and insisted that history should be written from the events happening in precise places and times (Bock 1956; Macfarlane 1979a/1978). Nevertheless, the extensive cross-cultural data and the desire to describe and explicate the scientific, general, and uniform led many developmental scholars to focus primarily on cross-sectional data. For some, the reading of history sideways with comparative data became *the* method of social science (Bock 1956).

Through the use of this powerful conceptual framework and methodology, scholars believed that they could write the natural history of whatever it was that interested them—be it religion, politics, the economy, or marriage and the family. By comparing the patterns of marriage and family life of contemporary societies along the entire developmental spectrum that they had created, these scholars believed that they could trace the stages of marriage and family change stretching out to their own distant past.

---

57. See Ferguson 1980/1767; Millar 1979/1779; Turgot 1895/1750. See also Manuel 1962.

58. See Comte 1858/1830–42; McLennan 1886/1865; Morgan 1985/1877; Senior 1831; Westermarck 1922.

59. See Carneiro 1973; Harris 1968; Hodgen 1964; Pagden 1982; Sanderson 1990.

Using their conceptual framework of societal development, the reading history sideways methodology, and extensive cross-cultural information, scholars of the 1500s through the early 1900s literally wrote history from ethnography and the accounts of international visitors. Although social historians, historical demographers, and family sociologists of today discuss the fine points of the correct way to read history—whether backward from the present to the past or frontward from the past to the present—earlier scholars adopted a much easier solution. They used comparative information to read history sideways across geographic categories.

These earlier scholars believed that, if a world traveler were to schedule his itinerary in the order of the development ladder, he could discover the history of society during a long and interesting trip. If such a traveler were to follow Tylor's view of the development ladder (fig. 2.1 above), he could re-create the history of Western European society by beginning his trip in Australia and then visiting Tahiti, Mexico, China, Italy, and England—in that order. A less expensive procedure would be for a curator to arrange materials from numerous cultures in their "correct" developmental sequence in a museum.[60] Another approach would be for the scholars to arrange information from different societies in the appropriate order in their offices and then write the natural history of the cultural and social traits that emerged from that ordering.[61] Thus, through travel, through a museum visit, or by arranging material in their offices, these scholars believed it was possible to read history sideways and to write their histories from ethnography. In a very real way, these scholars invented, created, or produced a version of history from cross-sectional data rather than documenting it from the historical record.

Many of the major social philosophers and scientists from the 1500s through the beginning of the 1900s utilized at least some elements of comparative data from different societies, reading history sideways, and the developmental paradigm in their scholarly descriptions and explanations. The list of scholars using this approach and contributing to the literature on social development reads like a who's who of social, political, and economic thinkers of the 1500s through the 1800s. For the 1500s and 1600s, it includes such luminaries as Acosta, Montaigne, Hobbes, and Locke. From the 1700s, we have such giants as Smith, Rousseau, Voltaire, Millar, Turgot, Robertson, Homes, Condorcet, Hume, and

---

60. Apparently, museums frequently employed this approach. For a description of a remarkable 1851 display in London that did, see Stocking 1987.

61. Herbert Spencer provides an interesting account of the process he used (Spencer cited in Becker and Barnes 1961).

Malthus. Among the developmental scholars of the 1800s are such notables as Comte, Tyler, Maine, Morgan, Spencer, Marx, Durkheim, Westermarck, and Le Play. In fact, the reading history sideways method was so widespread and well accepted that Harris (1968, 150) wrote: "All theorists of the latter [1800s] . . . proposed to fill the gaps in the available knowledge of universal history largely by . . . the 'comparative method.'" The use of the method also extended well into the 1900s (Carr-Saunders 1922; Kirk 1944; Sumner and Keller 1929).

The Northwest European scholars did not have a monopoly on the use of the developmental paradigm and reading history sideways in the writing of Western history. Apparently, several Russian scholars played a significant role in the writing of English medieval history. Furthermore, Peter Gatrell suggests that they sometimes assumed that "the less developed country shows to the more developed an image of the latter's past" (1982, 24). Given the knowledge of Russian society that the scholars had and the use of the reading history sideways methodology, it would not be surprising if the men and women of medieval England looked more like Russian peasants in the history literature than in reality.[62]

The perceived value of the reading history sideways methodology was, interestingly enough, not limited to reading past history. It was also taken to facilitate predicting the future. By looking at the trajectory followed by Northwest European society, these scholars believed that they could roughly determine the developmental trajectories that would be followed by the societies of Asia and Africa. These developmental trajectories were seen as contingent on these groups actually proceeding along the ladder of development, but, if they did develop, these scholars believed that they knew where that movement would take them. The use of this methodology to predict the future course of development for non-Western societies has very important implications for the lives of ordinary people in those populations, a subject that I take up later, in chapter 8.

It is important to recognize that the scholars of the 1500s through the early 1900s applied the developmental paradigm, reading history sideways, and data from around the world to virtually every activity and organization of humankind. They created new histories of the origins and trends of a wide array of institutions—government, the economy, religion, art, society, culture, and the family. They also evaluated the forces producing the perceived changes in these many dimensions of life.

---

62. I am indebted to Alan Macfarlane for this insight about Russian scholars participating in the writing of English history.

Although it would be possible to describe the influence of the developmental paradigm and reading history sideways on the literature about the origins of and changes in all these topics, I limit my focus in this book primarily to the family arena. Nevertheless, my discussion, of necessity, includes other societal institutions and forces. This is because the family has historically been a central element of the larger social structure and, thus, intricately interconnected with religion, politics, and economics. I devote considerable attention to the issue of political authority, a topic that has been connected explicitly with family authority in the writings of political and social theorists for more than a millennium. Economic and religious forces are also important, both as causes and as effects of family structures and processes.

I turn now to an examination of the actual research findings and conclusions of developmental scholars concerning family history. In the following chapter, I address three specific questions concerning this research. What were the cross-sectional differences in family life that these scholars found in the international data that they assembled and analyzed? How were these cross-cultural family differences transformed into dynamic stories of human family change? And what explanations were formulated to explain the changes in family life that these scholars believed were revealed by their cross-sectional data?

Because so many scholars wrote about societal development and family change, perspectives inevitably varied, and conclusions differed. The story of this scholarship is also complicated by the fact that this research was conducted over many decades, even centuries, with scholarly perspectives and conclusions changing across time. The result, of course, is that the literature prepared by these scholars has numerous voices and variations, which greatly complicates the presentation of it.

PART TWO

Influence on Family Scholars

3

Views of Changes in Family Life from Reading History Sideways

Differences in Family Patterns across Societies

As the scholars of the 1700s through the early 1900s analyzed the data available to them about family structures and processes, they observed important uniformities in social organization across societies as well as remarkable variance. Among the uniformities that they discovered was the importance of family and kinship ties in organizing religious, economic, personal, political, and social relations (Wright 1899; also Sanderson 1990). In all the studied populations, they found that substantial fractions of the activities of individuals took place within family units. Families bore children, socialized them, and reared them to adulthood. Individuals usually lived and worked in family units, received their means of subsistence within the family economy, and experienced a division of labor and authority based on family relationships. This centrality of family relations in the past continues to be a theme in scholarship today.[1]

Because of their importance in human experience, family structure and process have been central to studies of personal and social relationships among scholars for thousands of years and across diverse societies—including Greece, China, and Northwest Europe. The roll call of people contributing to family studies includes some of the most famous names in scholarly history. Such notables from the distant past include Aristotle, Aquinas, and Confucius. In recent centuries, the names of many famous Western European scholars were added to the list, including John Locke, Adam Smith, Montesquieu, Jean-Jacques Rousseau, Georg Hegel, Emile Durkheim, Robert Malthus, Frédéric Le Play, Lewis Henry Morgan, Edward Westermarck, Alexis de Tocqueville, Max Weber, and Karl Marx. Others—

---

1. See Hufton 1995; Laslett 1984/1965; Lee and Wang 1999; Thornton and Fricke 1987; Thornton and Lin 1994; Todd 1985.

even those of once-important players—have largely faded from view: John Millar, William Robertson, Henry Maine, John Lubbock.

The Variety of Family Patterns

Despite—or perhaps because of—its ubiquity, the family is an incredibly flexible institution. It has long been understood that human beings have over the centuries created a great variety of social and family structures and relationships (Herodotus 1942/n.d.; Montaigne 1946/1580; see also Biller 2001). With a worldwide view, the scholars of the 1700s through the early 1900s documented a remarkable variety of these structures and relationships.[2]

As these scholars discovered and more recent research has verified, human beings have created a truly remarkable array of structures and processes to organize family and kinship relations (Broude 1994; Burguière and Lebrun 1996/1986; Goody 1990). Among the many different forms of family and marriage documented by family scholars are monogamy, polygyny, and polyandry; cross-cousin and exogamous marriage; bride-service, bride-price, and dowry; matrilineality, patrilineality, and bilateral descent; arranged marriages and love matches; extended, stem, and nuclear households; child adoption, child fosterage, and servanthood; child and late marriage; patrilocal, matrilocal, and neolocal residence; universal marriage and widespread celibacy; and marriage alliances and couple independence. In fact, family life and marriage have been so varied across the societies of the world that it has been extremely difficult to construct definitions of *family* and *marriage* that are universally applicable (Coontz 1991/1988; Gough 1959; Yanagisako 1979). Although each society has similar concepts, the differences have been substantial enough to prevent easy translation of terms across languages and cultures.

Making sense of this enormous variation posed a significant challenge to the scholars of the 1700s and 1800s—and continues to do so today. Cross-region variation was particularly large, but within-region variation was also significant (Broude 1994; Harrell 1997). Not only were there very important variations in family patterns across the regions of Asia—for example, between East, Southeast, and South Asia—and even within the boundaries of different subregions and countries (Burguière and Lebrun 1996/1986; Harrell 1997), but there was also considerable within-region variation to be found in Europe, even

---

2. See W. Alexander 1995/1779; Home 1813/1774; Hume 1825/1742; Malthus 1986b/1803; Millar 1979/1779; Montaigne 1946/1580; Montesquieu 1973/1721, 1997/1748; Morgan 1985/1877; Roberston 1780/1777; Smith 1976/1759; Sumner and Keller 1929; Westermarck 1894/1891.

within the northwestern area itself (Kertzer and Barbagli 2001; Burguière et al. 1996/1986; Kertzer 1989, 1991).

In the language of statistics, this cross-sectional variation posed a classic analysis-of-variance problem. The scholars of the past approached this variation by dividing the world and its family systems into groups, noting variance in family patterns both across and within groups. Many of these scholars played up the between-group variance and downplayed the within-group variance.

Many scholars of the 1700s through the early 1900s recognized that the differences in family patterns across regions were so great that any categorization scheme adequate to summarize them required large numbers of categories (W. Alexander 1995/1779; Morgan 1985/1877; Westermarck 1894/1891). They therefore used complex categorization schemes in their analyses.

Other scholars were less interested in the full geographic range of variation than in the specific differences between the family systems of Northwest Europe and those of the rest of the world. Especially important to these scholars were the contrasts between Northwest European families and Asian, African, and Native American families. In addition, even though there was relatively little geographic distance between the societies of Northwest Europe and those of Southern and Eastern Europe, there were substantial differences between them in family structures and processes, a contrast made particularly salient by the close geographic proximity.[3]

This approach of highlighting the differences between Northwest Europe and the rest of the world resulted in substantial artificial homogenization of the contrasting categories as there was substantial variation in family organization within Northwest Europe and within other regions of the world. Within Northwest Europe, family behavior and relationships varied by both place and social class.[4] The family patterns of the European elite were especially different from the patterns of the ordinary people. Internal variation in family systems was also great outside Northwest Europe. In addition, the emphasis on the contrast between Northwest Europe and other parts of the world tended to obscure similarities across regions and set up an us/them dichotomy. Furthermore, family systems all over the world were not static but subject to change.

---

3. Remember that, throughout this book, I am using the phrase *Northwest Europeans* to refer, not only to the populations of Northwest Europe itself, but also to overseas Northwest European populations, e.g., those in Australia and North America.

4. See Hufton 1995; Kertzer 1989, 1991; Shorter 1977/1975; Stoertz 2001.

In the following sections of this chapter, I discuss some of the variation in family processes and relationships that scholars of the past found across societies. My description of that variation follows the approach used by many of these scholars and primarily contrasts Northwest Europe with the rest of the world. I also focus on the family patterns of ordinary people rather than on those of the elite. After describing this geographic variation, I show how these scholars transformed it into stories of the history of family change. Finally, I describe these scholars' explanations of the family change that they believed they discovered through reading history sideways.[5]

Family and Nonfamily Organization of Society

When the Northwest European scholars of the 1700s through 1900s looked at their own family systems, they recognized that many social relationships and activities were family based but that there were many nonfamily institutions as well. Among the nonfamily institutions of the period were the state, the church, the military, the market, and the schools. In addition, many young people worked and lived as servants in families that had no kinship relationship to them. The result was numerous opportunities for nonfamily authority and interactions.

In contrast, when these scholars looked outside Northwest Europe, they generally found societies that were more family based and had fewer nonfamily institutions. Although many individuals in these societies did have important relationships and experiences outside the family, the plethora of nonfamily institutions existing within Northwest European societies of the 1700s and 1800s was not generally seen in Eastern Europe, Asia, Africa, and the Americas.[6] Extensive recent research confirms that, historically, the social organization of societies in Northwest Europe contrasted with that in many other parts of the world. Compared with other societies around the world, Northwest European societies of the past continue to be characterized as less organized around the family.[7]

---

5. My decision to emphasize the contrast between Northwest Europe and the rest of the world was prompted by my interest in the ways in which scholars of the past used this variation to describe family change leading to the family systems that they observed in Northwest Europe. The result, of course, is a downplaying of the extensive variation existing both within Northwest Europe and within the rest of the world.

6. See Hegel 1878/1837; Le Play 1982a/1881, 1982c/1855; Maine 1888/1861; Millar 1979/1779; A. Smith 1976/1759, 1978/1762–63; Sumner and Keller 1929; Weber 1958b/1916–17, 1968b/1916.

7. See Cohen 1970, 1976; Coontz 1991/1988; Gallin 1966; Greenhalgh 1982, 1985; Hanawalt 1986, 1993; Herlihy 1985; Kussmaul 1981; Smith 1979, 1992; Thornton and Fricke 1987.

The scholars of the past recognized that solidarity was an important element of family life in Northwest Europe. Families were very important units in organizing and controlling the lives of individuals in Northwest European societies. At the same time, when scholars from Northwest Europe compared their societies with those that they observed elsewhere, they found a contrast in the relative emphasis on the individual compared to family and community relations.[8] Whereas many of the societies of Eastern Europe, Asia, and Africa strongly emphasized family solidarity, in the societies of Northwest Europe, especially that of England, there was relatively more emphasis on the individual. This pattern has also been confirmed by more recent historical research showing that the substantial individualism in the English past contrasts strongly with the emphasis on kinship and community observed in many non-Western societies (Macfarlane 1979a/1978; Shammas 1995; R. M. Smith 1979, 1992).

Household Composition and Structure

According to scholars of the 1700s and 1800s, the nuclear household—one consisting of a married couple and their dependent children—was the most common residential unit in Northwest European societies (Le Play 1982c/1855, 1982e/1872; A. Smith 1976/1759, 1978/1762–63; Sumner and Keller 1929). Less common were stem households—married parents and one married child—although young married couples often maintained residences close to their parents and frequently maintained economic interchanges and social connections with them (see Ben-Amos 2000; Foyster 2001; Seccombe 1992). By contrast, the extended household consisting of parents and two or more married children was, according to these scholars, more common in many other parts of the world—such as Eastern Europe, Asia, and Africa—than in Northwest Europe.

Recent research confirms the nuclear household/extended household contrast between Northwest Europe and other parts of the world.[9] It also suggests, however, that, in the Northwest European societies of the past, stem households were, in fact, relatively uncommon because high mortality and fertility and late marriage and childbearing combined to limit the number of families

8. See Hegel 1878/1837; Le Play 1982c/1855, 1982e/1872; Maine 1888/1861; Smith 1976/1759; Sumner and Keller 1929; Weber 1958b/1916–17, 1968b/1916.

9. See M. Anderson 1986/1980; Czap 1983; Gillis 1985; Hajnal 1982; Halpern 1972; Hufton 1995; Kertzer 1991; Laslett 1978/1977, 1984/1965; Lee and Campbell 1997; Lee, Wang, and Ochiai 2000; Liao 2001; Maynes and Waltner 2001; McCaa 1994a, 2003; Mitterauer and Sieder 1982/1977; Phillips 1988; Ruggles 1987, 1994; Seccombe 1992; Shorter 1977/1975; Thornton and Fricke 1987; Thornton and Lin 1994; Wall 1983, 1995.

that were able to form them (Ruggles 1987, 1994). Nevertheless, there are indications that the age structure of these societies made it possible for large numbers of elderly people to live with their unmarried or married children, and many did so (Kertzer 1991; Ruggles 1987, 1994, 1996, 2001; Wall 1995). However, most married couples living with their children resided only with unmarried children (Ruggles 2001; D. S. Smith 1981). And many of the elderly who lived with married children were themselves widowed (Ruggles 2001; D. S. Smith 1981). Finally, recent research confirms that very few married siblings lived together (Lee, Wang, and Ochiai 2000; Ruggles 1994).

It is also useful to note that many households outside Northwest Europe were neither particularly complex nor large (Liao 2001). This was probably the result of various demographic, economic, and cultural influences on the dynamics of living arrangements and household formation and dissolution processes. However, despite the diversity of living arrangements within various societies, the basic contrasts made by previous generations of scholars between Northwest Europe and many other parts of the world remain valid today.

Marriage and Intergenerational Authority

Earlier generations of scholars contrasted the timing and frequency of marriage in Northwest Europe with marriage patterns in other parts of the world.[10] Because in Northwest Europe marriage generally required the inheritance or establishment of an independent economic unit and household, it was frequently difficult to procure the necessary means for it. Consequently, there was a substantial delay of marriage, and large numbers of people never married, patterns documented by Malthus, Westermarck, and others. In Eastern Europe, on the other hand, marriage was nearly universal and occurred at substantially younger ages. It was nearly universal in many non-European societies as well and often occurred at even younger ages than it did in Eastern Europe. In addition, child marriage was a phenomenon noted by early scholars in some non-European societies (W. Alexander 1995/1779; Montesquieu 1997/1748).

A wealth of research conducted since World War II on Northwest European marriage patterns reconfirms the work of earlier generations.[11] In fact, a clas-

---

10. See Carr-Saunders 1922; Godwin 1964/1820; Hume 1825/1742; Malthus 1986b/1803; Montesquieu 1997/1748; Sumner and Keller 1929; Swindlehurst 1916; Westermarck 1894/1891, 1971/1908.

11. See Flandrin 1980; Hajnal 1965, 1982; Hanawalt 1986; Macfarlane 1986; McDonald 1985; Seccombe 1992; Smith 1979, 1992.

sic 1965 paper by John Hajnal divided Europe around 1900 into eastern and western regions—with a dividing line extending roughly from Trieste to Leningrad that was remarkably similar to that indicated by earlier scholars, including Westermarck. Hajnal wrote: "So far as we can tell . . . [the Western European pattern is] unique or almost unique in the world. There is no known example of a population of non-European civilization which has had a similar pattern" (1965, 101). He also paralleled Westermarck in concluding that the prevalence of marriage was even higher in Africa and Asia than in Eastern Europe.

Additional research has provided only modest clarification of the geographic distribution of marriage timing and prevalence as outlined by both Westermarck and Hajnal.[12] It should be noted, however, that neither Westermarck nor Hajnal was interested in exploring in detail the differentials in marriage within the broad range of countries outside Europe, and subsequent research has demonstrated rather considerable variations in non-European marital patterns.[13] It has also recently been shown that in at least some non-European places—China, for example—marriage was significantly less universal for men than for women (Lee and Campbell 1997; Lee and Wang 1999).

Another central difference between Northwest Europe and elsewhere concerns the independence of children and the authority of parents. Northwest European children undoubtedly received substantial guidance and supervision from parents and other adults both during childhood and during the transition to adulthood. Yet, when compared with young people elsewhere, they were observed to enjoy a remarkable degree of autonomy.[14]

---

12. See Coale, Anderson, and Härm 1979; Coale and Treadway 1986; Dixon 1978; Jones 1981; Maynes and Waltner 2001; McDonald 1985; Sklar 1974; D. P. Smith 1980; Watkins 1986b.

13. See Durch 1980; McCaa 1994a, 1994b, 2003; D. P. Smith 1980; P. C. Smith 1980.

14. See Engels 1971/1884; Hegel 1878/1837; Kent 1873; Le Play 1982c/1855, 1982e/1872; Maine 1888/1861; Millar 1979/1779; Montesquieu 1973/1721; A. Smith 1976/1759, 1978/1762–63; Sumner and Keller 1929; Westermarck 1894/1891, 1922, 1971/1908. Westermarck created a more nuanced model. He saw young people as having the most autonomy in the least and the most advanced societies and the least autonomy in the moderately advanced societies (Westermarck 1894/1891, 1922, 1971/1908; see also Sumner and Keller 1929). (According to Westermarck, gender equity also followed the same pattern.) Also, because couples in Northwest Europe often established their own households and economic units early in marriage, they enjoyed more independence from parents throughout most of their lives than did those living in households with parents. In addition, in some non-Western societies, the veneration of ancestors meant that children's obligations to their parents extended beyond their parents' lifetimes (Hegel 1878/1837; Montesquieu 1997/1748; see also Thornton and Lin 1994). This was easily interpreted as a sym-

The freedom of young people in Northwest Europe was especially marked in decisions about marriage.[15] In many other societies, parents had the responsibility and the authority to determine when and whom their children married, and young people had little or no say in the matter. The control of parents over marriage was undoubtedly related to the young age at marriage—either because a young age at marriage allowed parental control or because marriage occurred at young ages as a result of parents arranging it. Contact between marrying couples before marriage was often extremely limited, and the couple would often not be introduced to each other until just prior to or at the time of the marriage ceremony.

Among the common folk of Northwest Europe, however, the consent of the couple was an essential element of marriage (W. Alexander 1995/1779). Most young people in Northwest Europe had remarkable autonomy when it came to courtship and mate selection.[16] Although parents could influence the marriage process in many ways, in contrast to the marriage systems so common elsewhere, the Northwest European marriage system could be described as being largely directed and managed by the young people themselves.

Affection, love, and companionship were essential elements of the courtship system in Northwest Europe during the 1700s and 1800s. Although economic prospects, religion, and family connections undoubtedly played a role in mate selection, love may have been the most important element in the choice of whom to marry. By contrast, in the arranged marriage systems so common elsewhere, affection and companionship could not play an important part in the choice of marriage partners as mate selection was handled almost entirely by the older generation.[17]

A substantial amount of recent historical research confirms conclusions of earlier generations of scholars about the importance of the autonomy of young people, the consent of the couple, and affection, love, and companionship in the mate-selection process in the Northwest European past.[18]

---

bol of the extensive and indefinite control of parents over children, a pattern that contrasted sharply with that found in Northwest Europe.

15. See W. Alexander 1995/1779; Engels 1971/1884; Home 1813/1774; Kent 1873; Millar 1979/1779; A. Smith 1976/1759, 1978/1762–63; Swindlehurst 1916; Westermarck 1894/1891, 1922, 1971/1908.

16. Among elite families, however, parents often maintained more control.

17. See W. Alexander 1995/1779; Engels 1971/1884; Home 1813/1774; Lubbock 1889/1870; Malthus 1986b/1803; Millar 1979/1779; Morgan 1985/1877; Robertson 1780/1777; Smith 1976/1759; Sumner and Keller 1929; Swindlehurst 1916; Westermarck 1894/1891.

18. See Brundage 1987; Gillis 1985; Hanawalt 1986; Macfarlane 1970, 1986, 1987; Olsen 2001; Pierre 2001; Rothman 1984; Wrightson 1982.

Recent research also suggests that this youth-run mate-selection system contrasts dramatically with the arranged-marriage systems in numerous other areas of the world (see, e.g., Broude 1994; Lee and Wang 1999; Thornton and Lin 1994).

The contrast in the mate-selection process was so dramatic that some Northwest Europeans overstated the difference by saying that people elsewhere did not even care who they married. Some also suggested that there was no love and affection in marriage at all—either before or after marriage.[19] This notion probably grew out of misinterpretations of the meaning of family relationships in some other societies. Others, however, more properly noted that, while love and support were often not precursors to non-Western marriage, they often existed in abundance after marriage (Westermarck 1894/1891). A recent review of the cross-cultural evidence supports the conclusions of Westermarck that love between husbands and wives exists in nearly every culture (Broude 1994). It should not be surprising that such cross-cultural misunderstandings occurred in the past as it is easy for them to occur today, even with greater awareness of the problem.

The Rights and Autonomy of Women

The writers of the 1700s and 1800s observed important differences in the treatment of women between Northwest Europe and other areas of the world. And, in describing those differences, they deemed women outside Northwest Europe to be accorded fewer rights, to have less autonomy, and in general to live in worse conditions than women in Northwest Europe. In fact, some drew such emphatic contrasts between the conditions of women in Northwest Europe and elsewhere that it seems likely that ethnocentrism and cultural ignorance substantially affected their evaluations. One contemporary observer—Adam Ferguson—suggested as much when he wrote: "We are apt to exaggerate the misery of barbarous times, by an imagination of what we ourselves should suffer in a situation to which we are not accustomed" (Ferguson 1980/1767, 105; see also Robertson 1780/1777).

Interestingly, Ferguson judged the contrasts less sharply than did others, but he seems to have been in a very small minority. Observers from other cultures or later times may also have drawn similar conclusions to Ferguson's when comparing the status of women in Northwest Europe and in other parts of the world in the 1700s and 1800s. Be that as it may, the rel-

---

19. See W. Alexander 1995/1779; Lubbock 1889/1870; Millar 1979/1779; Montesquieu 1973/1721, 1997/1748; Morgan 1985/1877; Robertson 1780/1777; Smith 1976/1759. See also Goody 1990.

evant evaluations were made by Northwest Europeans, and I report their observations and judgments.[20]

There was a substantial number of customs in the non-Western world with which the scholars of Northwest Europe were unfamiliar and that they deemed to be degrading to women (Comaroff and Comaroff 1997; Coontz 1991/1988; Cott 2000). Polygyny (a man having more than one wife), for example, drew widespread attention and was judged by one observer to be so terrible that no woman would enter it voluntarily.[21] Other observers reacted very negatively to the elaborate exchanges of labor and money that accompanied marriage in many non-Western societies, practices frequently interpreted as reflecting the buying and selling of women.[22] Also noted was the ease with which men could divorce their wives, an arrangement suggesting that women could be discarded at will.[23] Hume (1825/1742) noted the practice of foot-binding female children and its crippling effects on personal mobility. Other authors commented on women's confinement more generally along with their perceived isolation through the wearing of veils (W. Alexander 1995/1779; Hume 1825/1742; Montesquieu 1973/1721, 1997/1748). The condemnation of widowed women to death, child marriage, female infanticide, and the superior authority of men were also noted with great disapproval (W. Alexander 1995/1779; Home 1813/1774; Millar 1979/1779).

One of the common themes in the literature of the period was the heavy labor performed by women in many non-Western societies, with men sometimes seen as lazy and unproductive—an interpretation frequently applied to Native Americans and Africans.[24] William Alexander (1995/1779) contrasted this situation with that in the countries of Northwest Europe, where there was

20. It is also worth noting that relations between women and men everywhere are complex and multifaceted. Consequently, the construction of overall indicators of women's status is very difficult. Comparisons across societies are even more problematic.

21. See W. Alexander 1995/1779. See also Hegel 1878/1837; Home 1813/1774; Hume 1825/1742; Millar 1979/1779; Montaigne 1946/1580; Montesquieu 1973/1721, 1997/1748; Paley 1793; A. Smith 1978/1762–63 as well as Coontz 1991/1988; Porter 1979.

22. See W. Alexander 1995/1779; Grimké 1988/1838; Hegel 1878/1837; Home 1813/1774; Lubbock 1889/1870; Mill 1989c/1869; Millar 1979/1779; Robertson 1780/1777; Sumner and Keller 1929; Wright 1899. See also Coontz 1991/1988; Goody 1990.

23. See W. Alexander 1995/1779; Home 1813/1774; Millar 1979/1779. See also Axtell 1981; Berkhofer 1978; Coontz 1991/1988.

24. See W. Alexander 1995/1779; Ferguson 1980/1767; Home 1813/1774; Millar 1979/1779; Robertson 1780/1777. See also Axtell 1981; Boserup 1971/1970; Shammas 1995; Sheehan 1980; Vaughan 1995/1965.

a fairly strict gender division of labor, women being responsible for activities in and around the home, men for farmwork and product distribution. (Alexander did note that this arrangement did not hold for lower-class women.) This distinction between societies where women as opposed to men performed most of the agricultural labor has been reported by more recent research (Boserup 1971/1970; Harrell 1997).

The contrast between the status of women and that of men in Northwest Europe and the Americas was probably exaggerated by the inability of the Europeans to understand Native American circumstances.[25] Among many Native American groups, women were generally responsible for agricultural work and performed many other manual tasks, while men took care of hunting and fishing. Many Europeans considered hunting and fishing to be leisure activities and, therefore, perceived Native American men to be lazy. At the same time, they saw farm labor as men's work and believed the heavy involvement of women in it to reflect their low position in society. Scholars today suggest that, in Native American societies, both the labor contributions of men and the equality of the sexual division of labor were greater than originally believed.

All the differences in the treatment of women in Northwest Europe and elsewhere suggested to many Northwest Europeans a profound degradation of the rights and standing of women in many other parts of the world.[26] Many characterized women's relation to men in non-European societies as servitude or slavery.[27] It was suggested that some women in these societies were so depressed by their conditions that they killed their female children rather than have them suffer under the circumstances (Home 1813/1774). Europe, in contrast, was characterized as a region where women were treated significantly better. Interestingly, one observer suggested that "England is the heaven of women" and that things were even better for women in France and Spain (W. Alexander 1995/1779, 1:317).

Northwest European families were, nevertheless, seen as characterized by considerable male dominance and privilege. In fact, some writers, especially those trying to bring more egalitarianism to male-female relationships, equated

25. See Axtell 1981; Coontz 1991/1988; Shammas 1995; Vaughan 1995/1965.

26. See Home 1813/1774; Lubbock 1889/1870; Millar 1979/1779; Morgan 1985/1877; Robertson 1780/1777; Sumner and Keller 1929; Westermarck 1894/1891, 1922, 1971/1908.

27. See W. Alexander 1995/1779; Condorcet, n.d./1795; Home 1813/1774; Hume 1825/1742; Lubbock 1889/1870; Macaulay 1974/1790; Millar 1979/1779; Montesquieu 1973/1721, 1997/1748. See also Cott 2000; Tomaselli 1985.

marriage in Northwest Europe with slavery, a theme that I take up again in chapter 9.[28] Even these writers, however, recognized that consent was an essential element of marriage in Northwest European practice, a crucial feature separating marriage there from marriage in many other settings (Grimké 1988/1838; see also Cott 2000).

The Northwest European perspective on gender relations in different societies also failed to take into account the fact that the gender division of labor in some non-Western societies may have actually given women more autonomy and authority than they enjoyed in Northwest Europe. In Northwest Europe, there was, as we have seen, a fairly strict division of labor between wives and husbands. This gender division became even more marked with industrialization and the increased specialization of women as housewives and men as breadwinners. The result was women's even more limited involvement in and control over economic production and distribution.

This situation in Northwest Europe contrasted with that in many other settings. Their substantial involvement in farming and trading in some societies would have given women many opportunities to know about and influence decisions about economic production and exchange. As a result, they were likely to have had more economic autonomy and authority in these settings than in Northwest Europe. Thus, to the extent that high status is marked by autonomy and authority, the status of women may have been lower in Northwest Europe than in other societies.

Of course, while such perspectives on the relative status of women and men are common today, they were little understood and appreciated in Northwest Europe during the 1700s and 1800s. For Northwest Europeans of the 1700s and 1800s, it was clear that the status of women was generally higher in Northwest Europe than elsewhere. And this conclusion permeated the scholarly literature of the period.

Le Play's Map of European Families

The Workers of Europe—Frédéric Le Play's monumental work documenting family patterns—provides a useful summary of the way in which scholars of the 1800s understood the distribution of family types across Europe and beyond. Having first engaged in an intensive data-collection effort (see chapter 2), Le Play proceeded to formulate a tripartite typology of family patterns.

---

28. See W. Alexander 1995/1779; Grimké 1998/1838; Macaulay 1974/1790; Mill 1989c/1869; Thompson and Wheeler 1994/1825; Wollstonecraft 1975/1792. See also Brace 2000; Cott 2000; Offen 2000; Rendall 1985.

The three categories of his typology formed a continuum, with the end points defined as the patriarchal family and the unstable family and the midpoint as the stem family.

Le Play stated that, in patriarchal family systems, married sons generally lived with or near their parents, often in large extended households. He also said that, when households became too large, they would divide, but, even then, second-generation family members would often continue to live together after the first-generation head of the family had died (Le Play 1982c/1855). These patriarchal family groups lived under the authority of the parents. The property of the family remained undivided, and the father directed the labor of the family and oversaw the distribution of the family's production. Le Play observed that any desire of the younger generation for independence was neutralized by economic considerations (Le Play 1937/1879, 1982e/1872).

What Le Play referred to as *the unstable family* is what is today referred to as the nuclear family.[29] This family type starts, according to Le Play, with the marriage of the husband and wife. The family expands as children are born but then contracts as these children leave home. Finally, the family is dissolved when the parents die. Thus, this family is always nuclear in that it never contains multiple married couples. It is usually, but not always, small. Le Play emphasized that considerable independence and a lack of integration between the generations characterized the unstable family system (Le Play 1982e/1872). He also reported that individuals in unstable families were not responsible for the well-being of their relatives. In addition, the authority of parents was significantly weaker in these types of families than in others (Le Play 1982e/1872).

The third kind of family in Le Play's typology was the stem family. It occupied a middle position between the patriarchal and the unstable family and was seen by Le Play as more desirable than the two other types. In this kind of family system, one of the children married and stayed with the parents while the other children moved away. Unlike the unstable family, the stem family offered its members a permanent source of security and protection. It was also seen as striking a balance between the great freedom that children had in the unstable family and the great authority that parents had in the patriarchal family (Le Play 1982e/1872).

Besides developing his typology, Le Play also prepared a detailed map showing the geographic distribution of family types (see fig. 3.1). A review of that map reveals a remarkably regular distribution of family types across the coun-

---

29. The labeling of households consisting of a wife, a husband, and their dependent children as *unstable* reflects Le Play's negative judgment of them.

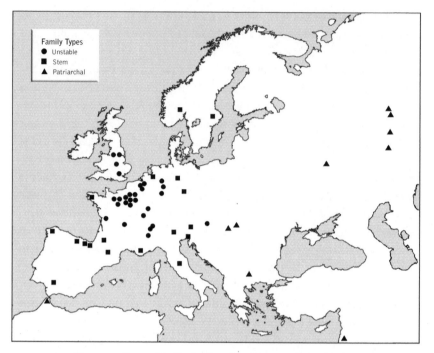

Figure 3.1 Geographic distribution of families according to Le Play
(adapted from Le Play 1879, 646–47)

tries of Europe. As Le Play observed, patriarchal families were very common among "Eastern nomads, Russian peasants, and the Slavs of Central Europe" (Le Play 1982e/1872, 259). In fact, all the Russian, Moroccan, and Syrian families, and none of the families located outside Eastern Europe, the Middle East, and North Africa, were patriarchal. As Malthus, Westermarck, and others documented, these patriarchal families were characterized by young and universal marriage, frequently with extensive parental control of the marriage process.

Moving to the other end of his typological continuum, Le Play observed: "The unstable family prevails today among the working-class populations subject to the new manufacturing system of Western Europe" (Le Play 1982e/1872, 260). More specifically, as can be seen from the map, he classified as unstable all the families of England, Belgium, and northern France. Also categorized among the unstable families were some German families and one family in Vienna. These areas were also characterized by Malthus, Westermarck, and others as having late marriage, widespread celibacy, and courtship systems involving extensive involvement of the young.

Finally, Le Play characterized southern France, Spain, and Italy as being dominated by stem families. He also found stem families in Germany, the Netherlands, Norway, and Sweden.

Le Play's map of European family patterns is remarkable, not only for the amount of data that it summarized, but also for the way in which it has stood up in the face of an enormous amount of research done in the subsequent century and a half. As Emmanuel Todd (1985) has written, Le Play's description of cross-sectional patterns has gone virtually unchallenged. Similarly, Richard Wall was generally impressed with the close parallels between Le Play's report and views today about the geographic distribution of family types in the European past. Wall concluded: "It is suggestive that Le Play found multiple-family households in southern, but not northern, France, in North Africa, Russia, and in parts of Italy, that is in just those areas where more extensive research at the level of the community has confirmed their presence or where the existence of the multiple-family household seems likely" (1983, 20–21). Substantial additional research also reports a geographic distribution of family types that is remarkably consistent with the one provided by Le Play.[30] The current understanding of the historical distribution of family types in Europe may now be more complex and detailed than Le Play's, but Le Play's geographic picture of the distribution of European families in the middle 1800s is remarkably compatible with that provided by the scholarship of the late 1900s.[31]

Developmental-Trajectory Interpretations

The conceptual apparatus of the developmental paradigm and the reading history sideways methodology provided a ready framework for the scholars of the 1700s through the early 1900s to interpret developmentally the differences that they observed across societies. With this framework they trans-

---

30. See M. Anderson 1986/1980; Czap 1983; Hajnal 1982; Halpern 1972; Kertzer 1991; Laslett 1978/1977; Mitterauer and Sieder 1982/1977.

31. Interestingly, Le Play's map has several commonalities with one published by William Smith in the early 1800s of the geological formations of England. (Smith's map made an important contribution to furthering the understanding of geology, the location of geographic strata, and the history of the physical world [Winchester 2001].) Both maps represent a colossal amount of work; the descriptions of the locations of the phenomena in question have generally been accepted as accurate; and both maps were interpreted in temporal terms. However, whereas the historical interpretation of geologic strata in England continues to be accepted today, the developmental interpretation of LePlay's family map has fallen from favor.

formed the geographic differences that they observed into a series of developmental sequences of changes in family patterns.[32]

Although the specific family dimensions were actually studied separately or in various clusters according to the interests and perspectives of individual scholars, they could also be grouped into a package of family changes. Kingsley Davis (1948) would later endorse virtually this entire package of family changes as *the great family transition*. Taken as a whole, the family scholarship of the 1700s through the early 1900s concluded that, in the past, Northwest European families had been characterized by features that were now found among Eastern European, Asian, Native American, and African families. It further concluded that those past features had been transformed by the developmental process into the features characteristic of families at the pinnacle of the developmental ladder.

Specifically, this scholarship suggested that, in the Northwest European past, societies were overwhelmingly organized around family and kinship relations, that they were familistic rather than individualistic, that they were relatively undifferentiated (i.e., contained few nonfamily institutions), and that they were characterized by a household structure that was extended rather than nuclear. It also indicated that parental authority was overwhelming, marriages were arranged, marriage occurred early and was universal, love and affection were absent in the marital-arrangement process, and the status of women was exceptionally low.

Furthermore, the scholarship of the era indicated that, over the course of Northwest European history, the developmental process resulted in much more differentiated societies (i.e., societies containing many more nonfamily institutions), increased individualism, decreased parental authority, more nuclear households, an improved status for women, more marriages that were love matches, later marriages, and more people never marrying. Many of these themes survived intact into the mid-1900s as several influential scholars of the period came to very similar conclusions.[33]

---

32. See W. Alexander 1995/1779; Condorcet, n.d./1795; Durkheim 1978/1892; Engels 1971/1884; Home 1813/1774; Le Play 1982c/1855, 1982e/1872; Maine 1888/1861; Malthus 1986b/1803; Millar 1979/1779; Morgan 1985/1877; A. Smith 1976/1759, 1978/1762–63; Sumner and Keller 1929; Thwing and Thwing 1887; Westermarck 1894/1891. See also Gordon 1995; Weisbrod and Sheingorn 1978. As in earlier chapters, my purpose here is to describe interpretations, not to endorse them.

33. See Bosanquet 1915/1906; Burgess and Locke 1953/1945; Calhoun 1960a/1917; Davis 1948; Ellwood 1910; Lynd and Lynd 1929; Sumner 1934/1880; Sumner and Keller 1927; Thomas and Znaniecki 1974/1918; Weber 1968a/1922.

Many scholars of the era also offered a developmental interpretation of the data available on political institutions.[34] These scholars believed that, after the initial formation of society (either after or without a state of nature), government forms generally lacked political liberty, which was acquired gradually and only with development.[35] Ancient Greece and Rome sometimes served as examples of the association of political liberty with development, but with the warning that serious retrogression was not only possible but had actually occurred in history. Northwest European societies—most notably those of England and Germany—were pictured as being at the pinnacle of development in terms of political freedom. Thus, the increase in family freedom with development was perceived to have been accompanied by an increase in political freedom.

With a model that placed all humanity on the same development ladder, it was easy for the community of scholars from the 1700s through the 1800s to use these results to predict the futures of Eastern Europe, Africa, and Asia. Assuming that the societies therein developed further, these scholars predicted that they would take the same developmental trajectory experienced by Northwest Europe and eventually come to exhibit Northwest European family and political patterns. That is, with development, these societies too would eventually be characterized by political liberty, many nonfamily institutions, an individualistic orientation, nuclear families, later marriage, many people never marrying, marriages that were love matches, and higher status for women.

The transformation of international cross-sectional data into narratives of family change through the reading of history sideways occurred in different ways. Westermarck, for example, explicitly employed this methodology, which enabled him to utilize a range of cross-sectional data and produce *The History of Human Marriage* even though he did not have enough data to write a history of marriage in either Finland, his native country, or England, where he lived for many years. However, other scholars—Malthus, for example—employed the reading history sideways approach only implicitly.

Malthus was, nevertheless, profoundly affected by the developmental paradigm and interpreted the large amounts of empirical data that he accumulated through consistently and pervasively using the reading history side-

---

34. See Condorcet, n.d./1795; Hegel 1878/1837; Hobbes 1991/1642; Hume 1825/1742; Locke 1988/1690; Mill 1989c/1869; Millar 1979/1779; A. Smith 1978/1762–63.

35. Rousseau (1984/1755) was an important exception, as he believed in a steady deterioration of freedom across time.

ways method for studying social change.[36] In book 1 of his *Essay on the Principle of Population* (entitled "Of the Checks to Population in the Less Civilized Parts of the World and in Past Times"), he lumped together as examples of societies at an earlier stage of development the ancient inhabitants of Northern Europe, Greece, and Rome and such contemporary societies as those of the American Indians, the South Sea islanders, the Chinese, and the Japanese. He also included in this category the peoples of Turkey, Persia, India, Siberia, and Africa. Then, in book 2 ("Of the Checks to Population in the Different States of Modern Europe"), he presented contemporary information about Norway, Sweden, the Baltic areas of Russia, Central Europe, Switzerland, France, England, Scotland, and Ireland, whose societies he grouped together because, for him at least, they represented a more advanced or developed stage of societal growth. On comparing these two groups of societies (the less and the more advanced), he interpreted the differences in marriage patterns that he found as the natural product of societal development (Malthus 1986b/1803).

Frédéric Le Play's implicit use of the reading history sideways approach illustrates the power of the developmental paradigm and its use in the social sciences of the 1800s. This metallurgist-turned-sociologist had a strong commitment to an inductive approach that relied on empirical observations and eschewed preconceived theoretical orientations. He wrote that physical scientists understand that science is based on observation but that many social scientists are less empirically grounded, being still guided by preconceived ideas and tending to disdain the facts. "Social science thus remains," he suggested, "in a situation comparable to that of the physical sciences when they were based on the conceptions of astrology and alchemy; social science will not be established until it is founded on observation" (Le Play 1982b/1862, 179).

Interestingly, this inductive, empirically grounded scholar who was repulsed by preconceived conceptual frameworks noted a strong correlation between geography and family patterns, with a gradient of family and household structures running from east to west. And, despite his self-conscious caution, Le Play concluded that the different household structures were the result of differential social and economic development. The subtle, but powerful, influence of the developmental paradigm and reading history sideways thus determined the conclusions that Le Play drew from his cross-sectional data.

36. See Béjin 1983; Coleman 1988/1986; Eversley 1959; Godelier 1983; Kreager 1986; Nisbet 1975/1969; Wrigley and Souden 1986.

Historical Data

Although the conclusions of the scholars from the 1700s and 1800s about family change in Northwest Europe were largely based on reading history sideways
with cross-sectional data, they were also based on some historical data (Le Play
1982c/1855; Malthus 1986b/1803; Westermarck 1970/1936). Malthus, for example, made efforts to use the European historical record to evaluate the history
of demographic processes within actual European populations. Unfortunately,
both the quantity and the quality of the historical data available to Malthus
were deficient, a circumstance that would continue to plague generations of
future demographers (Macfarlane 1986; R. M. Smith 1979, 1981, 1992; Wrigley
and Schofield 1981). Despite his awareness of the enormous data deficiencies,
Malthus made some strong assumptions about the data and connections
between mortality and marriage and concluded that marriage had declined in
the past. Thus, his conclusions from historical data converged with his conclusions from comparative data, giving him added confidence that he was correct (Malthus 1986b/1803). As I note in chapter 5, more technically sophisticated
research on England nearly two centuries later refutes his conclusions (Smith
1999; Wrigley and Schofield 1981).

The scholars of the 1700s and 1800s also had extensive historical evidence
showing that Northwest European societies had become more differentiated
and less family organized across time. That is, numerous nonfamily institutions such as schools, factories, businesses, and government agencies had been
introduced or expanded.[37] The historical record thus gave these scholars
increased confidence in the developmental story of changing social organization that they had derived from reading history sideways. With the increasing
specialization and proliferation of nonfamily institutions confirmed by both
the historical and the comparative record, this idea became a central element
of most discussions of social change both in Northwest Europe and elsewhere.
More discussion of this and other actual family trends in the history of
Northwest Europe is provided in chapter 5.

Two other sources of reading family change sideways may have reinforced
these scholarly conclusions. The locus of one lies in the Middle Eastern origins
of the Judaic and Christian heritages of most people in the West. The sacred
texts of Judaism and Christianity pictured Hebrews in the past as having
extended and patriarchal families. By comparing these family images from the

---

37. See Condorcet, n.d./1795; Engels 1971/1884; LePlay 1982/1855; Marx and Engels 1965/1848;
Millar 1979/1779; A. Smith 1978/1762–63.

Middle East with those of the West, it would be very easy for a Jew or a Christian to conclude that families had become less extended and less patriarchal over time, a conclusion that ignores the problems of history being confounded with differences in both geography and culture.

The immigrant experience of many people in the United States provides another opportunity for reading history sideways. Many immigrants came to the United States from countries with extended families. As these people settled in the United States, they tended to assimilate, and their family structures began to resemble those of the host population. Comparing the lives of these immigrants with those of their ancestors without taking account of the cultural and geographic differences involved, one might conclude that the shift from extended to nuclear households represented a historical trend, thus reinforcing the conclusions of family scholars.[38]

Declining Family Functions

One particularly important use of the observation that nonfamily institutions had proliferated was its incorporation into the structural-functionalist perspective by Emile Durkheim and others (Durkheim 1984/1893; Weber 1968a/1922). In the functionalist framework we encounter another comparison of societies with biological organisms. Just as organs can be seen as structures that perform functions for biological organisms, social institutions are seen as performing functions for society. Durkheim compared early human societies to simple organisms that were internally homogeneous with few specialized organs and suggested that, at the dawn of human civilization, most functions of human life were performed in just one undifferentiated institution—the family. Just as biological organisms were believed to have evolved numerous specialized organs, Durkheim believed that human societies had developed many specialized institutions such as churches, schools, factories, and government agencies. The result was a transfer of functions from the family to nonfamily institutions, and, in the process, the family became just one of many specialized institutions. In short, the functions of the family were seen as declining, an idea that would have exceptional longevity in family scholarship.

Durkheim believed that the expansion of social organizations outside the family circle and the declining functions of the family were part of a long-term developmental process that extended indefinitely into both the past and the

38. I am indebted to Calvin Goldscheider for the first of these reinforcing ideas and to Martin Whyte for the second.

future. These considerations led him to posit a "law of contraction" with specialized groups increasingly absorbing the "whole of family life" (Durkheim 1978/1892, 232). Durkheim believed that the law of contraction had, in fact, reduced the functions of the family to such a great extent that the occupational group and state were replacing the family. In fact, he believed that the corporation would eventually take the place of the family (Durkheim 1978/1892). The law of contraction was also apparent to Durkheim in other aspects of family life, including the contraction from extended families to nuclear families and from family solidarity to individualism and personal autonomy (Durkheim 1984/1893). Similar views about the withering away of the family and its functions being assumed by the larger society were expressed by Marx and Engels (see Geiger 1968).

The Timing of the Perceived Changes in Family Life

Although the scholars of the 1700s and 1800s believed that there had been substantial changes in family life sometime in the past, it was difficult for them to date these trends in historical time. The problem was that the reading history sideways methodology provided no mechanism for assigning dates to transitions (Bock 1956). This is true because the comparison points came from cultural groups rather than from historical time periods and thus there were no dates to be attached to the changes they believed they had observed from reading history sideways. Dating therefore became a matter of conjecture. The result, of course, was widespread disagreement about the timing of specific transitions even if there was consensus as to the nature of the general trends (see Macfarlane 1979a/1978; Wallerstein 1991).

We can with confidence, however, place one boundary on the timing of these perceived changes in family patterns in that they had to have occurred prior to the time they were first reported. With one possible exception, all the family transitions reviewed in this chapter had been reported at least by 1803 in the work of such scholars as Millar, Smith, Alexander, Robertson, and Malthus, which implies that they had to have occurred prior to that time.

Although there is conclusive evidence that most elements of the great family transition were documented through reading history sideways by 1803, the documentation of the transition from extended to nuclear households was not definitive until 1855, with the work of Le Play. There are, however, at least three reasons to think that the transition from extended to nuclear households was, in fact, documented by 1803.

First, it is very likely that Adam Smith believed that there had been a transition from extended to nuclear households in Northwest Europe as early as the late 1750s (A. Smith 1976/1759, 1978/1762–63; see also D. S. Smith 1993). In a brief comment in *Lectures on Jurisprudence* (A. Smith 1978/1762–63), for example, he suggested that, in the past, married children lived with their parents while, at the present time, they lived alone. Although Smith was not explicit on his methodology, it appears that this conclusion came from reading history sideways. Similarly, in *The Theory of Moral Sentiments* (1976/1759), he discussed the tendency seen in pastoral societies for even distant relatives to live together in the same neighborhood. Smith suggested that this arrangement had existed among the Scottish Highlanders "not many years ago," "among the Tartars, the Arabs, the Turkomans, and . . . among all other nations who are nearly in the same state of society in which the Scots Highlanders were about the beginning of the present century" (1976/1759, 223). By contrast, he indicated that, in commercial societies, relatives tend to disperse geographically, become unimportant to each other, and, after a few generations, even forget about their common ancestral heritage. According to Smith, regard for remote ancestors decreased the longer a society had been in a commercial state.

Smith (1976/1759) also spent considerable time discussing affection in families—presumably in Northwest Europe—and its relation to living arrangements. He suggested that affection arises from living together in the same household and occurs most dramatically between siblings and between parents and children. He went on to indicate that adult siblings usually establish separate households, with the result that their children seldom live in the same household. Consequently, he argued, the emotional ties between cousins are much weaker than those between siblings. Smith went on to suggest that only in fiction did strong family ties exist without actual personal connections—and even then only between "those who are naturally bred up in the same house; between parents and children, between brothers and sisters. To imagine any such mysterious affection between cousins, or even between aunts or uncles, and nephews or nieces, would be too ridiculous" (1976/1759, 222). This suggestion—that married siblings and cousins seldom lived together—was, clearly, consistent with the implication that the transition to nuclear families had occurred by the 1700s.

Second, the Northwest European marriage system documented by Malthus (1986b/1803) is intricately linked with a nuclear- or (at most) a stem-family household system. This suggests that Malthus understood that, at the time of his writing, Northwest Europe had a nuclear (or stem) household system. If there had been a change from an extended-family household system, that change would have had to occur before Malthus conducted his research.

Finally, there were authors prior to 1800 who wrote normatively rather than descriptively about family patterns. Some of these writers based their comments on the understanding that nuclear-family households were at least acceptable and probably common. This is true of Montaigne's (1946/1580) discussion of parent-child relations where he suggests the advisability of parents living apart from children. Also, Locke's (1988/1690; see also Smith 1993) discussion of parent-child relations indicates an assumption that many children will grow up and live independently of their parents. Although both Montaigne and Locke were giving advice rather than describing family behavior, it would be difficult to understand that advice if it assumed that fathers always lived with children and married children always lived with parents, that is, an extended-family system. This suggests that if the great transition in household structure did occur, it occurred before Montaigne wrote in 1580 or before Locke wrote in 1690.

Even if all these arguments are not found to be totally compelling, it is nevertheless clear that the perceived transition from extended to stem to nuclear households had been documented by Le Play (1982c/1855) by the mid-1850s. This means that the family transitions discussed above must have occurred by the mid-1850s at the latest, and probably by the very early 1800s, and, perhaps, decades or even centuries before that.

Theoretical Explanations

The researchers of the 1700s and 1800s were not content to describe what they believed to be the trajectory of family change. They also formulated an array of explanations for that change, explanations that, as is to be expected, grew more sophisticated as scholarly understanding of the relevant social and economic factors involved was refined. Because most of these explanations remained powerful through the 1900s and will, therefore, be familiar to most readers, I discuss them only briefly in the paragraphs that follow.

The first, and perhaps foremost, explanation of family change centered on the changing modes of economic production (Lehmann 1979/1960; Meek 1976). Numerous scholars emphasized the importance of the shift in modes of subsistence from hunting, to herding, to agriculture, and, finally, to manufacturing for the transformation of other elements of society. Particularly important for the immediate creation of the Northwest European family was the process of industrialization, which transferred many aspects of economic production from family enterprises to bureaucratic organizations and relied mostly on wage labor. This meant that fathers no longer controlled the means of production and that people no longer relied on family enterprises for their livelihoods. Fathers, thus, often had less control over the activities and well-being of wives and children.[39]

Related to industrialization was the urbanization of society. Several aspects of urbanization were mentioned by these scholars, including differences between rural and urban life, the transformation of life associated with rural-urban migration, and the urbanization of rural life. These were seen as modifying family structures, processes, and relationships.[40]

There was also an awareness of the important expansion of education that had occurred over the course of Northwest European history and widespread support for the idea that education was an important element of social progress (Macaulay 1974/1790; see also Ekirch 1951). Many saw increased education levels as powerful influences on family change.[41] These increased education levels, along with subsequent delayed entrance into industrial employment, were believed to modify gender relations, decrease the authority of elders, and postpone marriage, among other things.

Related to this awareness of advances in education was an awareness of an increase in knowledge and information. And many scholars believed that this increase was associated with a growth in prudence and foresight, with implications for family change (e.g., Malthus 1986b/1803; Millar 1979/1779). For example, increased prudence and foresight were believed to increase awareness of the requirements and demands associated with marriage and childbearing, and this increased awareness was, in turn, believed to motivate young people to delay marriage and childbearing until their living standards were higher.

Many scholars believed that the growth of industry, education, and income was associated with rapidly expanding aspirations for consumption and social mobility. These changes were, in turn, believed to lead to deferred gratification,

39. See Burgess and Locke 1953/1945; Calhoun 1960c/1919; Davis 1997/1937; Durkheim 1978/1892, 1984/1893; Ellwood 1910; Engels 1971/1884; Groves and Ogburn 1928; Le Play 1982c/1855; Marx and Engels 1965/1848; Millar 1979/1779; Morgan 1985/1877; Thomas and Znaniecki 1974/1918; Westermarck 1922.

40. See Billings 1893; Burgess and Locke 1953/1945; Condorcet, n.d./1795; Durkheim 1984/1893; Groves and Ogburn 1928; Le Play 1982a/1881, 1982c/1855; Millar 1979/1779; Thomas and Znaniecki 1974/1918; Westermarck 1922.

41. See Brentano 1992/1910; Calhoun 1960b/1918, 1960c/1919; Condorcet, n.d./1795; Durkheim 1984/1893; Groves and Ogburn 1928; Le Play 1982a/1881, 1982c/1855; Millar 1979/1779; Westermarck 1922; "Why Is Single Life Becoming More General?" 1868.

a postponement of marriage and childbearing, and a decline in family size, among other things.[42]

Also considered important was religious change. The rise and expansion of Christianity generally was believed to be an important force in social, political, and family change.[43] The Protestant Reformation in particular was seen as expanding religious pluralism and liberty and shifting the focus of religious devotion from the community and the church to individual relationships with God (Condorcet n.d./1795; see also Phillips 1988). Its role in the legitimization of divorce may have been especially important (Phillips 1988). Another important religious shift cited was secularization, the decline of religion as a force in the lives of individuals (Thwing and Thwing 1887).

Political change—particularly the rise of democracy—was considered important. Also mentioned was the growing power of the state: besides providing increased security, this was also seen as decreasing the authority of families over their children.[44]

Finally, many scholars suggested that changes in some dimensions of family life itself propelled changes in others. For example, the movement from a family to a nonfamily mode of organization was seen as changing living arrangements, marriage, and parent-child relationships.[45] The movement from familism to individualism was seen as affecting parental authority (Maine 1888/1861; Thwing and Thwing 1887). The emancipation of women was sometimes believed to increase age at marriage and modify intergenerational relations.[46] And the decline of parental authority was viewed as increasing love and affection within families (Le Play 1982c/1855; Tocqueville 1955/1835).

As we consider these theoretical explanations for family change, it is useful to note that, for the most part, the theories of the scholars of the 1700s and 1800s were formulated to explain the products of the developmental paradigm and reading history sideways. By this I mean that the methodology of reading

42. See Alison 1840; Billings 1893; Brentano 1992/1910; Davis 1997/1937; Ferguson 1980/1767; Franklin 1961/1751; Jones 1859; Malthus 1986a/1798, 1986b/1803, 1986c/1830; Millar 1979/1779; "The New England Family" 1882; Ross 1907; Senior 1831; Sumner and Keller 1927; Westermarck 1922; "Why Is Single Life Becoming More General?" 1868.

43. See Condorcet, n.d./1795; Hegel 1878/1837; Home 1813/1774; Lieber 1876/1838. See also Cott 2000; Ekirch 1951; Löwith 1949.

44. See Calhoun 1960b/1918, 1960c/1919; Millar 1979/1779; Morgan 1985/1877; Smith 1976/1759; Thomas and Znaniecki 1974/1918; Thwing and Thwing 1887; Tocqueville 1955/1835. See also Nisbet 1980.

45. See Le Play 1982c/1855; Millar 1979/1779; Morgan 1985/1877; Thwing and Thwing 1887.

46. See Billings 1893; Brentano 1992/1910; Ungern-Sternberg 1931; Westermarck 1922.

history sideways had created a fascinating new body of perceptions concerning social change that called out for explanation. The scholars of the 1700s and 1800s met this challenge with great vigor and formulated many interesting explanations for the changes that they perceived in their international cross-sectional data. In fact, the data generated from reading social change sideways were influential in the formulation of the important and general theories of the 1700s and 1800s.[47]

I noted earlier that most of the changes in family life that these scholars set out to explain were observed from reading history sideways. However, many of the changes in the factors believed to produce the perceived changes in family life were observed by reading history from the past to the present.[48] That is, these scholars knew from the historical record that there had been several dimensions of Western European societies that had changed significantly in previous decades and centuries, including religion, education, modes of production, communication, transportation, and location of residences in rural or urban areas. It was, therefore, easy for them to use these historical changes to explain the trends in family structure and relationships that they observed from reading history sideways.

Although my discussion in this section has pictured family change as a dependent variable—the product of changing social, economic, and religious structures and ideas—it is possible to reverse the direction of causation and posit family change as a force influencing social, economic, and religious change. In fact, some scholars of the period were sensitive to the possibility that family patterns and relationships could be causes as well as effects (Ferguson 1980/1767). In addition, numerous scholars suggested that family, religious, and political changes were, indeed, important forces for changing many other dimensions of society (e.g., Weber 1958a/1904–5, 1968b/1916). This, however, is a topic that must be postponed to chapter 8.

47. Again, my purpose here is description, not endorsement, of these theories.
48. For example, Le Play 1982a/1881, 1982c/1855; also Condorcet, n.d./1795; Millar 1979/1779; A. Smith 1978/1762–63.

4

The Fertility Decline in Northwest Europe

In this chapter, I turn my attention to childbearing among married couples—including fertility-control practices and the number and spacing of children. Childbearing is a dimension of family life that is particularly important to population studies because it is the process that renews the population by replacing those who die. Fertility, along with mortality and the geographic movement of individuals, also determines population size, population growth, and age structure. Thus, this family dimension has captivated the interest of demographers and other social scientists in the last half of the 1900s, with great intellectual and financial resources devoted to describing and explaining trends in the reproductive behavior of men and women throughout the world.

At the same time that childbearing is a central element of population size, structure, and dynamics, it is a crucial dimension of family life, along with marriage, living arrangements, intergenerational relations, family authority, and gender roles and status. Given the central importance of childbearing behavior for families, it might seem a little odd that the previous chapter—about a range of family behaviors—was largely silent on this issue. This silence was not, however, due to any decision to treat fertility separately from the other family dimensions. Instead, it largely parallels scholarly treatments of family behavior and change during the 1700s and most of the 1800s, in which it was treated as of little interest.

Scholars of the earlier era, including Malthus, wrote extensively about overall levels of fertility, but their interest centered primarily on marriage, rather than on childbearing within marriage, as the central influence on birthrates and population renewal. As we have seen, the timing and prevalence of marriage varied widely across populations, with well-recognized ramifications for childbearing. In fact, in his policy recommendations concerning the control of fertility to limit population growth, Malthus argued for restricting marriage rather than for controlling childbearing within marriage. In fact, Malthus believed that contraception was a vice that should not be practiced.

Differentials in marital fertility between Northwest Europe and elsewhere were either moderate or not well documented before the late 1800s. Thus, marital fertility was not included as part of the great family transition in scholarly treatises before the late 1800s. In addition, the decline in marital fertility that occurred in Northwest Europe in the late 1800s and early 1900s had either not yet occurred or not yet been documented in the historical record. For these reasons, there was little for scholars interested in grand developmental trajectories to discuss about marital fertility before the closing decades of the 1800s.

Documenting Declines in Fertility and Mortality

All this changed at the end of the 1800s, when, using time-series census and vital-statistics data, scholars began to document a dramatic and substantial decline in fertility in many of the countries of Northwest Europe as well as in the overseas populations from this region.[1] Fertility had fallen so low by the early 1900s that scholars and politicians began to worry about the ability of some populations to reproduce themselves and the implications of this supposed inability for population composition and the differential power of competing groups and countries (Teitelbaum and Winter 1985).

Scholars of the late 1800s and early 1900s hypothesized that a decline in marriage had led to this decline in fertility. However, as they examined their time-series data for the societies experiencing fertility decline, they found little empirical evidence of a general decline in marriage associated with the fertility decline. Apparently, the large fertility decline of the late 1800s and early 1900s was the result, not of changes in marriage, but of declines in childbearing among married couples.[2]

Some scholars looked to changes in physiological capacity to explain the declines in marital fertility.[3] They believed that, as societal development

---

1. See Billings 1893; Carr-Saunders 1936; Engelmann 1903; "The New England Family" 1882; Ross 1907, 1927; Thompson 1929, 1930a, 1930b; Ungern-Sternberg 1931; Wright 1899. See also Hicks 1978; Hodgson 1983; Piotrow 1973; Reed 1978; United Nations 1953.

2. See Carr-Saunders 1936; Engelmann 1903; Ross 1907; Thompson 1930a, 1930b; Ungern-Sternberg 1931; United Nations 1953.

3. See Brentano 1992/1910; Reed 1978; Spengler 1991/1932; United Nations 1953.

emphasized education and the use of the mental faculties, it had led to the deterioration of physiological capabilities to reproduce. However, it eventually became clear that physiological deterioration was not the cause of the decline in fertility.[4] Indicated instead was the use of various methods of contraception and abortion to limit the number of children born.[5]

As scholars documented changes in childbearing and the control of fertility, it became clear that the earliest changes had occurred primarily in the populations of Northwest Europe. Furthermore, the geographic lines demarcating the changes in Northwest European fertility were remarkably similar to those demarcating the distribution of various family patterns noted by generations of earlier scholars. Consequently, by the early 1900s, scholars were describing the same types of geographic differences in marital fertility that had been documented earlier for other dimensions of family behavior and structure.[6]

The scholars of the late 1800s and early 1900s also documented from the historical record a marked decline in mortality and an associated increase in life expectancy (Thompson 1929, 1930b; Ungern-Sternberg 1931). The geographic distribution of this mortality decline was similar to that of the fertility decline (Thompson 1929). Although the mortality decline of the last two centuries would eventually occur in virtually all populations of the world, it was first documented among the peoples of Northwest Europe (Thompson 1929, 1930b; Ungern-Sternberg 1931).

A Framework for Interpreting Declines in Fertility

It is important to emphasize that these trends in mortality, childbearing, and fertility control were documented, not with cross-sectional data and by reading history sideways, but with data from multiple censuses and vital statistics across time and by reading history from the past to the present. Nevertheless, the strong geographic correspondence between previously identified family

4. See Billings 1893; Englemann 1903; "The New England Family" 1882; Reed 1978; Ross 1907, 1927; Spengler 1991/1932; Sumner and Keller 1927; Thompson 1930a, 1930b; Ungern-Sternberg 1931; United Nations 1953.

5. See Billings 1893; Carr-Saunders 1922, 1936; Notestein 1945, 1983/1964; Ross 1907, 1927; Rubinow 1907; Spengler 1991/1932; Thompson 1929, 1930a, 1930b; Ungern-Sternberg 1931; United Nations 1953; Willcox 1907.

6. See Brentano 1992/1910; Kirk 1944; Notestein 1945; Thompson 1929, 1930a, 1930b; Ungern-Sternberg 1931. See also Chesnais 1992; Hauser 1964; Hodgson 1983; McDonald 1993; Stolnitz 1964; Szreter 1993; United Nations 1953.

patterns and the fertility and mortality declines undoubtedly influenced the way in which this generation of scholars interpreted the fertility trends documented with historical data from multiple time points in the same population.

In the late 1800s and early 1900s, the developmental paradigm, substantive conclusions, and theoretical apparatus formulated by earlier generations of scholars to explain changes in family patterns documented by reading history sideways provided a ready framework with which to interpret the decline in martial fertility in Northwest Europe.[7] And scholars capitalized on this framework—a process undoubtedly made easy by the geographic correspondence between fertility trends and other family patterns—incorporating marital fertility into their already-formulated model positing the powerful effect on family change of social and economic change. It was obvious to these scholars that the great family transition documented by earlier generations of scholars by reading history sideways had preceded the fertility decline. Following the principle of the time ordering of causes and effects, they simply incorporated fertility change as the ultimate dependent variable in the model (see Hodgson 1983, 1988; Szreter 1993). The fertility decline was conceptualized as an ultimate product of the changing social and economic environment. Socioeconomic change was seen as operating both directly and indirectly on fertility change, through its influence on family structures and relationships. Changes in the family were seen as crucial intervening determinants of changes in marital fertility (Davis 1997/1937; Notestein 1983/1964; United Nations 1953). In this way, the intellectual products of reading history sideways were used to explain the actual historical record of fertility decline.

Specific Explanations of Fertility Decline

Of central importance here is the declining centrality of the family as a mode of social organization, with the activities of humans increasingly organized and conducted outside the family.[8] A related issue is the perceived shift from familism to individualism (Carr-Saunders 1936; Notestein 1945). These changes were

---

7. See Brentano 1992/1910; Davis 1948; Kirk 1944; Notestein 1945; Sumner and Keller 1927; Thompson 1930b; United Nations 1953; Vance 1952a; Wright 1899. See also Chesnais 1992; Cleland and Wilson 1987; Goldscheider 1971; Greenhalgh 1993, 1996; Hodgson 1983; Szreter 1993, 1996; van de Kaa 1996; Watkins 1986a.

8. See Carr-Saunders 1936; Davis 1948, 1997/1937; Notestein 1945, 1983/1964; Thompson 1930a, 1930b; Ungern-Sternberg 1931; United Nations 1953. See also Cleland 1985; Coleman 1990; Freedman 1964; Goldscheider 1971; Teitelbaum and Winter 1985.

believed to modify family relations and decrease the value of children to parents and the larger community and, thus, to motivate couples to limit the number of children born.

Increased school attendance and the decline of child labor were seen as having particularly important implications for fertility. They were perceived as modifying relations between parents and children. They were also perceived as increasing the cost of—and, therefore, reducing the desire for—children.[9]

The growing independence, employment, and status of women were also seen as important factors in the decline of marital fertility. As women entered the paid workforce, the amount of time that they could devote to bearing and rearing children decreased. In addition, their increased financial resources and higher status gave them more opportunities for independence apart from their families.[10]

Descriptions of the influence of changing social and family organization on the decline in fertility were sometimes couched in the terms of the structural-functional model of changing family functions (see chapter 3). That is, scholars suggested that declining fertility was part of—and influenced by—the decline in family functions (Davis 1997/1937; Notestein 1945). For example, in a line of argument paralleling Durkheim's (1978/1892) earlier discussion of the law of family contraction, Kingsley Davis (1997/1937) suggested that the loss of family functions—and the resulting decline in fertility—was inevitable and would continue indefinitely. Unlike Durkheim, however, Davis argued that the state, not the corporation, should take over the functions that the family could no longer handle.

Moving one step back in the causal chain, note that the early theorists of the fertility decline incorporated into their models virtually all the social and economic factors used by previous generations of scholars to explain family change. They posited the importance of industrialization and economic expansion—with the associated shift from an agricultural, rural society to an urban, bureaucratized economy based on wage labor—as an influence on marital fertility.[11] They also posited the importance of increases in informa-

9. See Bailey 1907; Brentano 1992/1910; Carr-Saunders 1922, 1936; Notestein 1945, 1983/1964; Ross 1907, 1927; Spengler 1991/1932; Sumner and Keller 1927, 1929; Thompson 1930a, 1930b; Ungern-Sternberg 1931; United Nations 1953. See also Cleland 1985; Teitelbaum and Winter 1985.

10. See Billings 1893; Brentano 1992/1910; Carr-Saunders 1936; Ross 1907, 1927; Spengler 1991/1932; Thompson 1930a, 1930b; Ungern-Sternberg 1931; United Nations 1953.

11. See Kirk 1944; Notestein 1945, 1950, 1983/1964; Spengler 1991/1932; Thompson 1929, 1930a, 1930b; Ungern-Sternberg 1931; United Nations 1953. See also Hodgson 1983.

tion, knowledge, and education.[12] However, some formulated extremely sophisticated arguments suggesting that the correlation between education and fertility was not the result of education influencing childbearing, but the result of exogenous factors influencing both (Emerick 1909; Engelmann 1903; Nearing 1914).

The old arguments about prudence and foresight increasing with development and leading to the postponement of marriage were also applied to the expansion of fertility control and the decline in the number of children born. Increased prudence and foresight were seen as leading, not only to a postponement of marriage, but also to decreased childbearing within marriage.[13] And, just as rising aspirations for consumption and social mobility were cited as reasons for the earlier perceived decline in marriage, they were cited as motivations for the decline in marital fertility.[14]

Yet another factor that this generation of scholars used to explain the fertility decline was religious change, including the Protestant Reformation and increased religious pluralism, liberty, and secularization.[15] Political change, particularly the rise of democracy and the growing power of the state, was also seen as a causal force (Ross 1907). Increased religious and political freedom was considered an important influence on the fertility decline because it loosened the control of communal institutions over family-size preferences and permitted the adoption of contraception.

The theorists of the late 1800s and early 1900s also incorporated mortality decline into their explanations of the adoption of birth control and the decline in fertility. The socioeconomic changes outlined earlier were viewed as important determinants of improvements in health and, therefore, the decline in mortality, which, in turn, was seen as leading to reductions in childbearing.[16] This was because the decline in mortality was most dramatic during infancy and early childhood. Consequently, had fertility remained

12. See Ross 1907; Spengler 1991/1932; Ungern-Sternberg 1931; United Nations 1953.

13. See Notestein 1983/1964; Ross 1907; Spengler 1991/1932; Sumner and Keller 1927; United Nations 1953.

14. See Bailey 1907; Billings 1893; Brentano 1992/1910; Carr-Saunders 1922, 1936; Engelmann 1903; Knibbs 1928; "The New England Family" 1882; Notestein 1945, 1983/1964; Ross 1907, 1927; Rubinow 1907; Spengler 1991/1932; Sumner and Keller 1927; Ungern-Sternberg 1931; United Nations 1953. See also Hodgson 1983.

15. See Carr-Saunders 1936; Notestein 1983/1964; Ross 1927; Thompson 1930b; Ungern-Sternberg 1931; United Nations 1953.

16. See Brentano 1992/1910; Thompson 1930b, 1952; United Nations 1953. See also Knodel 1978; Matthiessen and McCann 1978; Preston 1978; Sandberg 2002.

constant, the decline in child mortality would have increased the number of children reared within a family. This increase in family size would have disrupted social, economic, and familial relations and would have led to desires to reduce the number of children born in order to bring family size and child-rearing responsibilities back into their previous balance. That is, a fertility decline would be required to counterbalance the mortality decline and keep the number of children in the family constant.

The Demographic Transition

Although some of the authors of the early 1900s took a relatively nondevelopmental or contingent approach to studying the fertility decline,[17] many of the writings of this period had a developmental tone to them as they included such features of the developmental paradigm as uniformity and naturalness in their discussions of the fertility and mortality declines.[18] The tendency of demographers toward developmental interpretations of fertility and mortality declines was probably encouraged by the more general emphasis at the time on developmental approaches in the social sciences under the general rubric *modernization theory* (Hodgson 1983; Sanderson 1990; Szreter 1996). In fact, this controlled and low fertility was labeled *modern fertility* by some authors, consistent with its incorporation into the developmental model.

In fact, the declines in fertility and mortality were soon incorporated into a general developmental model of demographic change known as *the demographic transition*. The demographic transition became one of the central narratives of demography, and an understanding of it is required of virtually all certified demographers. This model begins with all societies having high and fluctuating fertility and mortality and little population growth. Mortality then declines, leading to a period of population growth, that growth being particularly dramatic when the mortality decline is sharp. At some point subsequent to the mortality decline, fertility declines as well. Later, both mortality and fertility become moderately stable at relatively low levels. All these changes were, as we have seen, driven by the social, economic, and family changes that had been perceived through a reading of both the comparative and the historical record. At first, this model of the demographic transition was applied to Northwest Europe, but it would also come to be

17. See Davis 1951; Notestein 1945; Thompson 1929, 1952; United Nations 1953; Vance 1952a.
18. See Davis 1948; Kirk 1944; Notestein 1983/1964; United Nations 1953.

applied to non-European populations as they experienced social, economic, fertility, and mortality changes.

The picture that I have sketched here in very broad terms indicates the general status of social science's understanding of the fertility decline as the world entered the last half of the 1900s.[19] This model of the demographic transition would continue to be applied to both Northwest Europe and other regions of the world for several additional decades.

19. See, e.g., Coale and Hoover 1969; Freedman 1964; Goldscheider 1971; Hauser 1964; Hodgson 1983; Szreter 1993; United Nations 1953; Vance 1952b.

5

Changes in Family Life in the Northwest European Historical Record

New Family Research

In the years following World War II, family and childbearing patterns and trends continued to be central topics of social-science studies. Like their intellectual ancestors, scholars of this era were interested in both the diversity of family patterns and historical changes in family structures and relationships. Their studies of family change departed from earlier generations of family research by making considerably more use of historical data, specifically, the Northwest European historical record. Making intensive use of such documents as census records, vital statistics, parish records, and diaries, this new research extended the database available to scholars back in time until it reached the 1300s. It thereby permitted a substantial reading of history from the past to the present rather than sideways.

Although this new historically oriented research was conducted in many places, the work done in England, especially at Cambridge University, was particularly important. Scholars such as Peter Laslett, John Hajnal, Alan Macfarlane, Roger Schofield, Richard Smith, Richard Wall, and Edward Wrigley investigated historical trends in living arrangements, family interactions, marriage, and childbearing. The concentration of this new historical research in England was to give it and its findings a particularly English emphasis. Another important center was Princeton University, where a team of demographers led by Ansley Coale utilized census and vital-statistics data from across Europe to document both geographic variations and historical trends in marriage and childbearing.

The Continuing Search for Origins

Although the new historical studies of the mid-1900s departed substantially from earlier generations of research in emphasizing more extensively the historical record, the two did share one interesting commonality. As we have seen, one of the key features of earlier scholarship was a fascination with the origins of human institutions, including the family. Many scholars were interested both in finding the ultimate beginnings of specific social institutions and in tracing the development of these institutions throughout history to their Northwest European apex. Other scholars had more limited goals and searched more specifically for the origins of their own Northwest European institutions in the not-so-distant past.[1]

The writers of the new history appear to have been motivated by some of the same questions. Many of these scholars were searching for the origins of Northwest European society.[2] Hajnal was interested in the English marriage system, specifically its emphasis on later marriage and widespread celibacy (Hajnal 1965). Macfarlane focused on English individualism and the English marriage system, specifically its emphasis on affection, autonomy, and later marriage (Macfarlane 1979a/1978, 1986, 1987).[3] And Laslett researched the nuclear family (Laslett 1984/1965; Laslett and Wall 1974/1972).

It is impossible to understand fully the assumptions and expectations of these scholars when they designed and began their research. However, their writings hint that they expected to find in the historical data many of the central elements of the great family transition as described by Millar, Malthus, Le Play, Durkheim, Westermarck, and other earlier scholars. That is, they apparently believed that, at some point in the past, the Northwest European family system prevailing in the 1800s had emerged from a dramatically different family system.

Alan Macfarlane (1979a/1978, 1987) explicitly acknowledges his acceptance of the old models of change when he began his historical research, his expectation of finding in the English past a social and economic system similar to the one described by generations of previous scholars. Peter Laslett also acknowledged that, when he began his pathbreaking research on historical living arrangements, he too supposed "that our ancestors lived in large familial units": "Family groups, it seems to be almost universally agreed, ordinarily con-

---

1. As I wrote this section of the book, I was amused by a personal reflection. The research for this book was originally motivated by a desire to find the roots of the myths about Western family life. It continues a long tradition of searching for origins.

2. Gillis, e.g., indicated: "When I began this study I too was searching for the origins of the conjugal ..." (1985, 4).

3. Macfarlane even titled one of his books *The Origins of English Individualism* (1979a/1978) and a chapter in another "The Malthusian Marriage System and Its Origins" (Macfarlane 1986).

sisted in the preindustrial past of grandparents, children, married as well as unmarried, grandchildren and often relatives, all sleeping in the same house, eating together and working together" (Laslett 1984/1965, 90). Given the discussion of previous chapters, it should not be surprising that the households that Laslett expected to find sound very much like the extended households observed in many places outside Northwest Europe and attributed to preindustrial Northwest Europe by earlier generations of scholars.

What many of these scholars appear to have been searching for were the circumstances and timing of the great family transition. When and under what circumstances did it occur? Hajnal, for example, noted: "If the [Western] European marriage pattern is unique, it is natural to ask, 'when did it arise?'""Curiously enough," he continued, "this question seems scarcely to have been asked, let alone adequately answered" (1965, 106). Similarly, after describing the distinctive features of Western family life, Laslett asked "how old the pattern was": "Can it yet be said when 'the West' began to diverge from the rest of Europe and the rest of the world in its familial outlook and behaviour?" (1978/1977, 46). In a similar vein, Stone noted: "Family history is inextricably involved in the great issue of the change from traditional to modern society, . . . [and] no other question is more important to historians of the West than the causes, nature, timing, and consequences of this transition" (1982, 82). Thus, it appears that determining the timing of the great family transition was a major motivation for much of the new historical research—an issue that does not seem to have occupied much of the energy of the earlier generation of scholars.

In fact, Hajnal, Macfarlane, Laslett, Stone, and their contemporaries can in some ways be seen as setting out to complete the work of previous generations of scholars. The earlier researchers believed that they had discovered many great family changes by reading history sideways, but, as we saw in chapter 3, their methods uncovered no evidence of the timing of those changes. Their research indicated only that the changes had occurred at some unspecified time before the 1800s. In attempting to date those changes more precisely, this new generation of scholars combed the historical archives. And what they found there was surprising.

Surprise in the Historical Record

The results of this new stream of historical research were shocking, revolutionary, and paradigm shifting. Study after study of the Northwest European past found family and household patterns very different from those described by previous generations of scholars. These new historical investigations—many extending back in time hundreds of years—found little evidence of the family structures and relationships that had previously been imputed to the Northwest European past. Instead, they found the same general outlines of family structures and relationships that characterized England and other areas of Northwest Europe in the 1700s and 1800s. I turn now to the specifics of this research.

Living Arrangements

The new historical research found that, in Northwest Europe, households had been predominantly nuclear (or a weak stem form) for hundreds of years.[4] Laslett, for example, reported that expectations of large and complex extended households "have been demonstrated to be false ... for traditional England. ... It is not true that most of our ancestors lived in extended families. ... It is not true that the elderly and the widowed ordinarily had their married children living with them, or that uncles, aunts, nephews and nieces were often to be found as resident relatives" (1984/1965, 91; see also Laslett and Wall 1974/1972). In short, Laslett found that there was no evidence that family arrangements seven hundred years ago were markedly different from those of "early modern times." "The further we go back," he wrote, "the more elusive the origins of the interrelated characteristics of the Western family. As of the present state of our knowledge we cannot say when 'the West' diverged from the other parts of Europe" (Laslett 1978/1977, 48).

Steven Ruggles subsequently called the idea of extended households in the past *the extended family myth,* noting: "There are now few adherents to the myth that extended families predominated in the world we have lost" (Ruggles 1987, 4). Examples of other scholars maintaining this view include M. Anderson (1986/1980), Goode (1982/1964), Hareven (1977), Levine (2001), Mitterauer and Sieder (1982/1977), Mount (1982), Segalen (1986), Seward (1978), Smith (1979, 1992), and Stone (1982). There was, thus, apparently no evidence for the purported substantial decline in extended households in Northwest Europe during the centuries preceding the 1700s and 1800s.

In fact, one of the remarkable findings to emerge from this new wave of research was that extended family living probably increased in England and the United States in the 1800s (Ruggles 1987; Wall 1995). This increase was

---

4. See M. Anderson 1986/1980; Goode 1970/1963, 1982/1964; Hareven 1977; Laslett 1984/1965; Laslett and Wall 1974/1972; Mitterauer and Sieder 1982/1977; Mount 1982; Ruggles 1987; Seccombe 1992; Segalen 1986; Seward 1978; Stone 1982; Wall 1995.

likely related to the fact that the existing household system was structured so that significant percentages of the elderly lived with a married child but that married children almost never lived together. With this system, the prevailing demographic conditions of high mortality and fertility and late marriage and childbearing meant that in relatively few instances were the appropriate family members available to form stem households. As mortality and fertility declined in the 1800s, the potential for living in stem households expanded, and the fraction of extended households increased.

Individualism and Autonomy

The emphasis on individualism rather than familism or communalism was also discovered to extend far back in English/Northwest European history (Macfarlane 1979a/1978, 1986; R. M. Smith 1979, 1981). The archives also revealed that young people had considerably more independence than would have been suggested by the circumstances of young people in many other parts of the world (Macfarlane 1979a/1978; Pollock 1985/1983; R. M. Smith 1979, 1981).

According to Alan Macfarlane, for example, individualism, freedom, and equality were much more important in the English past than had been previously recognized. In his research, Macfarlane searched back eight hundred years in the historical archives for the origins of English individualism. What he found was not individuals and their nuclear families dominated by kinship and community influences but a tradition of individualism so old that "it is not possible to find a time when an Englishman did not stand alone." He concluded: "[It] now seems clear . . . that England back to the thirteenth century was not based on either 'Community' or 'communities'" (1979a/1978, 196, 163). In short, the levels of individualism and autonomy documented in the historical archives were very different from those derived from reading history sideways (see also Macfarlane 2002). Nevertheless, recent research indicates that there was still considerable interaction and exchange between individuals and their relatives, their neighbors, and the larger community (Ben-Amos 2000; Wrightson 1982).

Richard Smith (1979, 1981, 1992) investigated English social and family relationships back into the 1300s. Although Smith placed greater emphasis on the existence of community and family relationships and less on individual autonomy than had Macfarlane, his conclusions about the continuity of family systems and structures were very similar. For example, he found that many elements of later English society (social fluidity, autonomy among young people, geographic mobility, the rotation of young people as servants among households, wage labor, and individualism, etc.) could be found as far back as the 1300s. In fact, according to Smith, as far as the historical record would allow any reasonable understanding, life in England in the 1300s was very different from life in places like Russia or Tuscany—Eastern and Southern European societies that had been used by some of the previous generations of scholars as proxies for the English past.

In an important recent study, Linda Pollock (1985/1983) examined the historical evidence about parent-child relationships in the past and asserted simply and strongly that "the history of childhood is an area dominated by myths." Continuing this theme, she wrote: "The thesis of a dramatic transformation in the capacity for experiencing emotion is a myth. There is no such transformation" (1985/1983, viii, 140; see also 270).

Using data from the United States and Britain, Pollock concluded that, in the American and British pasts, "parents took a great deal of interest in their children and experienced much pride with regard to their behaviour and achievements" (1985/1983, 102). She revealed a great variance in disciplinary styles and argued that, in the past, there were both strict and indulgent parents. She also reported that, while parents strove to exert authority over their children, young people actually enjoyed considerable autonomy. Although Pollock did document some changes across time in parent-child relationships, she clearly saw the big story of the period 1500–1900 as being one of continuity. Her views concerning the emotional relationship between parents and children in the Northwest European past have been echoed by many other researchers.[5]

The Timing of Marriage

A similarly extensive search for the origins of the Northwest European marriage system failed to find a period when marriage was early and universal. The pattern of late marriage and widespread celibacy was an ancient one, extending back in time for at least half a millennium.[6] Hajnal's primary conclusion was impressively straightforward: "The distinctively [Western] European pattern can be traced back with fair confidence as far as the seventeenth century in the general population" (Hajnal 1965, 134). Later research by Smith and Macfarlane suggested that there was no substantial evidence of a trend in mar-

---

5. See Gies and Gies 1987; MacDonald 1981; Morgan 1966/1944; Mount 1982; Smith 1977; Wrightson 1982.

6. See M. Anderson 1986/1980; Goode 1970/1963, 40–42; Hajnal 1965, 1982; Hanawalt 1986; Herlihy 1985; Hufton 1995; Levine 2001; Macfarlane 1986; Mount 1982; O'Hara 2000; Seccombe 1992; Seward 1978.

riage patterns between the 1300s and 1650 (R. M. Smith 1979, 1981, 1992; Macfarlane 1979a/1978, 1986), and Levine (2001) has suggested that these same marriage patterns existed as far back as 1000. Lawrence Stone reported: "This late marriage pattern, which is unique to the West, . . . is the most startling and significant finding of the past two decades of demographic history as it affects the family" (Stone 1982, 58).

The monumental work of Wrigley and Schofield (1981; see also Smith 1999) indicates that Malthus's conclusion of a decline in marriage in England during the 1700s was also wrong. These scholars found that, in England during the 1700s, marriage rates were generally increasing rather than decreasing (as Malthus had concluded) and that both age at marriage and the proportion of the population never marrying decreased rather than increased (again, as Malthus had concluded). In fact, they concluded that increasing marriage rates during this period led to increases in fertility, which in turn fueled a growth in the English population.

Marital Arrangements

Historical research in Northwest Europe also revealed, not a system of arranged marriages among the common folk, but, instead, a marriage system that involved active courtship and emphasized love and affection between prospective spouses. Also, marriage required the active consent of prospective spouses. Although the marriage system involved family, community, and economic considerations, the ultimate responsibility for choosing a spouse and contracting a marriage rested with the couple, who married for both love and money. And the essentials of this system had been in place in Northwest Europe for many centuries.[7]

One important example of such research was Macfarlane's examination of love and marriage in England between 1300 and 1840 (1986, 1987). Macfarlane believed that the English marriage system as described by Malthus was distinctive—not only because, under it, people generally married late and many did not marry at all, but also because, in it, sentiment and autonomy played such an important role. He therefore wanted to find its origins.

7. See Brundage 1987; Chaytor 1980; Davies 1981; d'Avray 1985; d'Avray and Tausche 1981; Donahue 1976, 1983; Gillis 1985; Glendon 1977; Gottlieb 1980; Hanawalt 1986; Herlihy 1985; Hufton 1995; Ingram 1981, 1985; Leclercq 1982; Macfarlane 1970, 1986, 1987; Morgan 1966/1944; Mount 1982; Noonan 1967, 1973; O'Hara 1991; Olsen 2001; Outhwaite 1995; Ozment 1983; Pierre 2001; Riley 1991; Rothman 1984; Sarsby 1983; Seccombe 1992; Shahar 1983; Sheehan 1971, 1978; Wrightson 1982.

As did his efforts to find the beginnings of English individualism, Macfarlane's efforts to find the origins of the English marriage system ended in failure. Even as far back as 1300 Macfarlane found no evidence of a parentally controlled system of mate choice, with parents making marriage decisions for their children. What he found instead was a pattern of young adults making their own choices, admittedly often in consultation with parents and friends (see also R. M. Smith 1979; Wrightson 1982).

An interesting recent study of English marriage patterns in the 1500s suggests that Macfarlane may have underestimated the amount of family and community involvement. O'Hara (2000) suggests that marriages were influenced by collective values, by friends and relatives, and by economic circumstances more than Macfarlane allowed (see also Foyster 2001; Outhwaite 1995). However, she does emphasize the importance of love, freedom, consent, and the active involvement of the prospective partners in the mate-selection process. And she explicitly notes that Macfarlane was comparing England with China and India and that the extent of community and family involvement was of a different order in England than in these other countries. O'Hara also found no evidence of changes in marriage patterns during the 1500s, the period she examined.

Macfarlane further concluded that, in the past, "marriage was both a psychological and an economic enterprise." He reported that companionship between husbands and wives was an important element of marriage. And he argued that "love was the essential prerequisite of marriage": "As far back as we can easily go, there is evidence of the same insistence [on the importance of love]. If we leap back to the early thirteenth century we find . . . a similar emphasis on love, 'fellowship,' affection, consideration" (1986, 165, 175, 183; see also Macfarlane 1987). In fact, Rothman (1984) found that, in colonial America and the early republic of the 1700s, love may have been more important in the choice of a mate than economic prospects, religious affiliation, or family connection. It was in courtship that young people found and developed love and affection, and it was in marriage that they promised to love, cherish, and honor each other throughout life (Book of Common Prayer 1888/1552).

Thus, Macfarlane, O'Hara, Rothman, and others found no evidence that affection and autonomy in the marriage process were the products of a relatively recent societal transformation in England or the United States.[8]

---

8. See Olsen 2001; Ozment 2001; Smith 1979; Wrightson 1982.

Indeed, analyses of an extensive body of American love letters from the early 1800s reveal that romance, affection, and emotional commitment in both courtship and marriage were widespread, at least among the literate population. These elements were seen as essential to the marriage process as well as the goals and duties of marriage (Lystra 1989). The practice of exchanging love letters was common in Europe well before the 1800s, so common, in fact, that, in the 1600s, the love letter was an established theme in Dutch art. Furthermore, images of romance, courting, and affection abound in the scenes of ordinary life portrayed in Dutch and Flemish paintings and literature of the 1500s and 1600s, attesting to the fact that all the elements of romantic love had long since been established.[9]

Ironically, there is considerable evidence showing that, from about 1500 to the mid-1900s, individual couples may have lost rather than gained control over some aspects of the marriage process. Through the 1400s, the power to form a marital union ultimately rested with the couple so inclined,[10] marriage involving only an exchange of vows between the partners themselves and the sexual consummation of the union. This autonomous and decentralized marriage system sometimes led to disagreement over whether a marriage had, in fact, occurred—a problem that kept the ecclesiastical courts of the era clogged. Consequently, beginning in the 1500s, attempts were made to eliminate potential confusion by inserting the authority of the church and/or the state in the process and requiring such things as announcements, licenses, certificates, and ceremonies presided over by clergymen with witnesses in attendance.[11]

This process of instituting tighter community control over the initiation of marriage itself has been successful enough over the last several hundred years that the common understanding today is that the church and/or the state, not the prospective partners, has the ultimate authority to effect a marriage. Of course, with the rise in the last few decades of the 1900s of cohabitation among the unmarried, the process of union formation has become

9. See de Jongh 1997/1971; Nevitt 2001; Roberts-Jones and Roberts-Jones 1997; Sluijter 2000; Vergara 2001.

10. See Brundage 1987, 1993; Donahue 1976, 1983; Gillis 1985; Koegel 1922; Murray 1998; Rheinstein 1972; Sheehan 1971, 1991a, 1991b; Smith 1986.

11. See Biller 2001; Bowman 1996; Brundage 1987; Burguière 1987; Donahue 1983; Flandrin 1980; Gillis 1985; Howard 1904; Hufton 1995; Jeaffreson 1872; Kelly 1973; Koegel 1922; Macfarlane 1986; Outhwaite 1995; Pollock and Maitland 1968; Witte 1997. The apparent outcome of one restrictive law in England in the mid-1700s was an increase in marriage within rather than outside the local community (Snell 2002).

much more unstructured and individually controlled—another trend to which I return in chapter 9.

The Rights and Autonomy of Women

In the past several decades, extensive research has been conducted on the rights and autonomy of women in the Northwest European past. This new research has shown that marriage and family life were deeply gendered religiously, socially, and legally—a characteristic that would form the basis for substantial controversy and battle from the 1800s on.[12] The merger of a man and a woman into a family unit through marriage was accomplished primarily by the incorporation of the wife's interests and identity into the husband's.[13] The husband was considered the head of the family, with the authority to represent his wife and children in the larger community. At marriage, women lost the legal ability to control property, to make contracts, and to sue and be sued. That women were subordinate was even made clear in many marriage ceremonies, with wives promising to obey their husbands.[14] Although typically both husband and wife were involved in a wide range of productive activities, the husband was generally seen as having financial responsibility for family affairs, and the wife as having responsibility for the care of the home and the children.[15]

Research also, however, demonstrates considerable autonomy and rights for women in the Northwest European societies of the past.[16] This is especially apparent when those societies are compared with non-Western societies of the 1700s and 1800s rather than with an abstract egalitarian ideal or with Northwest European societies of the late 1900s. As noted earlier, consent in the choice of a spouse and love and respect in marriage had been ideals for centuries. Thus, for centuries, the marriage vows included the promise of the husband to love and cherish as well as the promise of the wife to obey (Book of Common Prayer 1888/1552). In addition, despite her generally subordinate role in the family, the wife was a junior partner who

12. See Ammons 1999; Cott 2000; Flexner 1975; Hanawalt 1986; Koehler 1980; Nock 1998; Norton 1980; Pollock and Maitland 1968; Ulrich 1982; Weitzman 1981.

13. See Ammons 1999; Cott 2000; Flexner 1975; Norton 1980; O'Donnell and Jones 1982; Weitzman 1981.

14. See *Book of Common Prayer* 1888/1552; Cott 2000; Koehler 1980; Pollock and Maitland 1968; Whitelock 1952.

15. See Cott 2000; Hanawalt 1986; Norton 1980; Pinchbeck 1969; Weitzman 1981.

16. See Cott 2000; Hanawalt 1986; Macfarlane 1979a/1978; Morgan 1966/1944; Norton 1980; Ozment 1983, 2001; Sarsby 1983; Ulrich 1982; Wrightson 1982.

had considerable authority as she directed child care and managed household activities.[17]

Thus, the conclusions of earlier generations of scholars once again fared poorly. The practices of foot-binding, polygamy, and child marriage that had been deduced through reading history sideways as characteristic of the Northwest European past were not found in the historical record. In addition, the notion that, over the course of the Middle Ages, women had emerged from drudgery and slavery to the heights of enlightenment may have been turned on its head, evidence having been uncovered that, in some respects at least, the status of women may in fact have declined over the centuries leading to the 1700s.[18]

It is also likely that some Western observers were led to exaggerate the low status of women in non-Western societies by the sheer novelty of the family patterns observed there. Although the gender inequalities in non-Western societies were frequently substantial, they were probably not as extreme as suggested by much of the rhetoric of the Western literature of the 1700s and 1800s, including the designation of marriage in these settings as slavery. This exaggeration of the low status of women outside of Northwest Europe is important to note because these societies were used as proxies for the Northwest European societies of the past. Consequently, this exaggeration would have led to a perception of the status of women in the Northwest European past as having been lower than it actually was, thereby providing an exaggerated contrast with the Europe of the 1700s and 1800s.

The Place of Families in the Organization of Society

The research of earlier generations of scholars suggested, and recent research has confirmed, that, in the Northwest European past, there was a fundamental reliance on the family to structure society.[19] For the most part, individuals lived in family households, and activities such as production, distribution, consumption, and socialization were organized around the family. The family was also central in structuring, and, to a large extent, controlling access to, information and ideas.

There is also general agreement that, in the societies of Western Europe and the United States, nonfamily institutions have become increasingly pow-

17. See Bailey 2002; Hanawalt 1986; Morgan 1966/1944; Norton 1980; Sarsby 1983; Ulrich 1982; Wrightson 1982.

18. See Beard 1946; Berg 1978; Levy, Applewhite, and Johnson 1979; Sarsby 1983.

19. See Coleman 1990; Demos 1970; Gies and Gies 1987; Hanawalt 1986; Laslett 1984/1965; Lesthaeghe 1980; Thornton and Fricke 1987; Tilly and Scott 1978.

erful in people's lives.[20] Prior to 1800, churches, guilds, and governments increasingly became the focus of activity. This trend continued with the Industrial Revolution as bureaucratic economic institutions such as factories increasingly organized production outside the family and schools took on a bigger role in the education and socialization of children. As a result of these trends, the family vied for influence with a wide variety of nonfamily institutions. Thus, on this particular dimension of family life, previous generations of scholars were correct; there has been a general movement in society away from family and toward nonfamily modes of organization.[21]

There is, however, reason to believe that these scholars overstated the magnitude of this change. First, as has recently become clear, they underestimated the influence in the past of nonfamily institutions on individuals' lives (Macfarlane 1979a/1978, 1987, 2002; R. M. Smith 1979, 1981; Wrightson 1982). For example, England has for centuries had a significant number of day laborers who worked for wages in the economic enterprises of nonrelatives. Also, there have long been in many Northwest European countries significant numbers of young people working as servants in the homes of nonrelatives (although it should be noted that the lives of servants, whether in the homes of relatives or nonrelatives, were organized around the basic family system). In addition, the power of both religious institutions and the state in Europe has long been significant (although it should be noted that the state itself was in the past more familially organized). And, in at least one European country, England, there has long been a government system to help provide for the economic needs of the poor.[22]

Second, because earlier scholars used contemporary non-Western societies to proxy for past Western societies, they exaggerated the importance of the family in the Western past. This occurred because many non-Western societies have historically been more familially organized than those in the West. For example, in China, the activities of many people were organized almost exclusively around family units.[23] Many Chinese villages were com-

20. See Demos 1970; Gies and Gies 1987; Hall 1977; Hareven 1977, 1987; Harrell 1997; Hufton 1995; Laslett 1984/1965; Lesthaeghe 1980; Thornton and Fricke 1987; Tilly and Scott 1978.

21. There is also substantial evidence suggesting that a similar movement can be found in non-Western societies. See Cain 1977, 1978; Caldwell 1982; Cohen 1970, 1976; Fricke 1986; Gallin 1966; Goode 1970/1963; Greenhalgh 1982, 1985; Shah 1974; Shanin 1972; Thornton and Fricke 1987; Thornton and Lin 1994.

22. See Hajnal 1982; Kussmaul 1981; Laslett 1984/1965; Macfarlane 1979a/1978; Wilson and Dyson 1992.

23. See Cohen 1970, 1976; Gallin 1966; Greenhalgh 1982, 1985; Thornton and Fricke 1987; Thornton and Lin 1994.

posed entirely of people of the same clan, meaning that everyone in the village was kin. This arrangement helped ensure that village life was organized
around family relationships. Furthermore, there was little in the way of formal religious organization in China, and family members (including ancestors) played a significant role in defining the sacred. Thus, although Western
societies were substantially more family based in the 1700s than in the 1900s,
they were still less family based in the 1700s than many non-Western societies had been and continued to be.

Family Functions

Many scholars of the mid-1900s, like those of previous generations, employed
functionalist language to express the shift to nonfamily modes of social organization. That is, they suggested that, over time, the functions of the family were
declining and were being transferred to other social institutions.[24] However,
several recent scholars have seriously challenged this idea (Caplow et al. 1982;
Fletcher 1973/1962; Goode 1970/1963). In fact, according to Ronald Fletcher, just
the opposite has happened. Family functions have actually increased rather
than decreased. He argued that "both in the sense of being concerned with a
more detailed and refined satisfaction of the needs of its members, and in the
sense of being more intricately and responsibly bound up with the wider institutions of society, the functions of the family have been increased in detail and
in importance. As the provisions of wider agencies have been increased, the
functions of the family have not been diminished, but have themselves been
correspondingly extended. These wider provisions are *additional* to the conditions of the family in pre-industrial Britain" (1973/1962, 222–23).

Although reading history sideways played a significant role in the over-
statement of the amount of change in the centrality of family units in
Northwest European societies, it cannot account for the extensive controversy
over whether family functions have declined or increased in vitality and number. Instead, the problem here lies in the reification of the metaphor comparing societies to biological organisms. As discussed in chapter 3, when Durkheim
conducted his insightful analysis of social change, he explicitly discussed the
structure of biological organisms and the functions that were carried out within
them, comparing the social sphere to this biological world. He also explicitly
based his model of change on the notion of increasing specialization and

24. See Demos 1970; Gies and Gies 1987; Hareven 1987; Mitterauer and Sieder 1982/1977;
Popenoe 1988.

division of labor within individual organisms, applying this notion in his analysis of social change.

Unfortunately, we cannot literally observe family functions directly, which means that we cannot measure whether they are, as functionalist analysis would have it, "increasing" or "decreasing," "strengthening" or "weakening," "expanding" or "contracting," or whatever. Without the ability to measure the metaphor in concrete social life, it is difficult to make statements about whether the family is fulfilling more or fewer functions. I would suggest, moreover, that the conclusions that we reach regarding family functions depend on whether we focus primarily on family institutions or nonfamily institutions.

On the one hand, scholars who focus on nonfamily institutions are likely to emphasize the growing number of activities being conducted within them. As Fletcher (1973/1962) pointed out, there is a tendency to conclude incorrectly that, as the social milieu outside the family expanded, the family itself contracted. (This is exactly what Durkheim did.) This fallacy can explain the mistaken conclusion that the family no longer has an economic function when such a great deal of productive activity (cooking, sewing, washing) takes place within the home and when bureaucratic economic enterprises employ people who are members of families. This fallacy can also explain the mistaken conclusion that the family no longer has an educational function when young children are primarily socialized within families, when school-age children continue to receive extensive teaching and training from parents, when school systems involve parents in the formal education process, and when parents pay many of their children's college expenses.

On the other hand, scholars who focus on families are invariably impressed with how many activities continue to be conducted within them. As Fletcher (1973/1962) noted, the expansion of such nonfamily institutions as health-care facilities may actually increase the amount of time and resources that a family allocates to taking care of its members' health. This observation led Fletcher (1973/1962) to conclude that the family's health function was increasing rather than decreasing. The underlying assumption here, of course, is that a function (in this case, a "health function" or a "protective function") is operationalized by time or resources being devoted to it.

In many respects, the functionalist metaphor and the recognition by scholars and laypeople alike that, today, many activities are carried out within specialized institutions results in activities being labeled according to the sphere within which they are conducted. This clearly happens when only economic activities conducted outside the home in bureaucratic institutions, and not comparable activities conducted within the household, are labeled *work*. This also happens when only socialization and learning that occur in formal school settings, and not comparable activities conducted within the household, are labeled *education*.

This differential labeling of course distorts our view of the kinds of activities taking place within different contexts and leads to our differential valuation of them. For example, work in factories and education in schools are often valued more highly than work and education in the home. This differential valuation is made clear by the fact that many home activities are not included in national income accounts and the gross national product while similar nonhome activities are. Ultimately, to devalue home relative to nonhome activities in this way is also to devalue the contributions of those who perform the home activities, usually women, relative to the contributions of those who perform the nonhome activities, usually men, and, thus, implicitly to devalue women relative to men, with serious implications for the well-being and priorities of both.

For all these reasons, it must be concluded that the functionalist approach has not been a helpful one. That is, it has not provided a useful elaboration of the fundamental changes that have occurred in the organization of society.

The Emergence of the Theme of Family Myths

As we have seen, the historical investigations of the late 1900s confirmed the results of earlier studies in documenting the growth of nonfamily organizations and activities, but they also showed that these changes were not as great as had previously been believed. More important, however, is that these new investigations revealed that most of the family patterns identified by previous generations of scholars as distinctive of Northwest European society in the 1700s and 1800s were not the result of recent change but had, in fact, existed for a very long time. As early as the 1300s, Northwest European society had a nuclear or a weak stem household system, an emphasis on individualism, substantial autonomy of young people, late marriage, widespread celibacy, and a courtship system in which the young were actively involved. This is not, of course, to say that there was no change whatsoever. However, changes of the magnitude postulated by earlier scholars were nowhere to be found in the historical record between the 1300s and the 1700s (Macfarlane 1979a/1978; R. M. Smith 1979, 1981).

Eventually, the evidence against a great family transition before 1800 in Northwest Europe became so overwhelming that a new theme emerged in family scholarship—that of the historical family myth. Several scholars have written about the myth of the extended household, the myth of early and universal marriage, the myth of arranged marriages, the myth of affection-less families, and the myth of declining family functions.[25] In fact, it is probably not an exaggeration to suggest that the theme of the family myth has dominated recent discussions of Northwest European family history.

It is important to note that I am not saying that there have been *no* changes at all in family structures and relationships in Northwest Europe. In fact there were some changes before 1800, but nothing remotely resembling the large changes described by earlier generations of scholars through the sideways reading of history.[26] Substantial changes have also been documented for the centuries after 1800. However, the central point that I wish to make here is that most substantial family changes in Northwest Europe occurred *after*, not *before*, 1800—and, thus, *after* most of these earlier scholars were writing—and that those few changes that did occur before 1800 were misidentified—either in magnitude or in direction—by earlier scholars.[27] The post-1800 changes are, of course, highly relevant to the arguments of this book, and I return to them in chapters 8–10.

A Dissenting Voice

My argument that the myth of the great family transition in Northwest Europe sometime before 1800 was constructed by scholars in the 1700s and 1800s contradicts a recent argument of Daniel Scott Smith (1993) that the myth originated in the first half of the 1900s. Smith agrees that in the 1950s there was a belief that an important change had occurred in the past from extended to nuclear households but that this idea of change emerged during the first half of the 1900s and not before. Smith came to this conclusion on the basis of a review of the work of such writers as Adam Smith, John Locke, and Alfred Marshall. Smith argued that it was well known to these scholars of the 1600s, 1700s, and 1800s that, in Northwest Europe, parents and their married children tended to maintain separate residences and lead relatively independent lives.

25. See Caplow et al. 1982; Goode 1970/1963, 1982/1964; Hareven 1991; Laslett 1984/1965; Laslett and Wall 1974/1972; Macfarlane 1979a/1978, 1986; Mount 1982; Ozment 2001; Pollock 1985/1983; Ruggles 1987; Seccombe 1992. See also Kertzer 1991.

26. For example, Tadmor (2001) has identified changes in family and kinship terminology.

27. For example, the change in social structure from more to less family organized was, as we have seen, not as great as had previously been believed. Also, the control of church and state over marriage has increased, not decreased, as had been suggested (Brundage 1987; Glendon 1977; Ingram 1981, 1985).

For this reason, Smith suggests that these scholars could not have believed in a great transition from extended to nuclear families.

My interpretation of the views of scholars from the 1700s and 1800s about family life in their own societies is entirely consistent with Smith's. As I noted in chapter 3, Northwest European scholars of the 1700s and 1800s were well aware that the classic extended household was *not* a common characteristic of their societies.[28] Scholars of this era mentioned nuclear and stem households in their societies but no large extended households.[29] Recent research also reveals that such an understanding of households consisting primarily of married couples and their children dates back to the 1500s and 1600s (see Freedman 2002).

Unfortunately, Smith shows no awareness that, using the developmental paradigm and the reading history sideways method, scholars of the 1700s through the early 1900s based their descriptions of Northwest Europe in a yet earlier period on the non–Northwest European present. He does note that they sometimes contrasted the family systems of Northwest Europe with those elsewhere, but only to establish that they were well aware of the contrast and, therefore, of the actual circumstances in Northwest Europe. He misses the fact that these scholars were not just making cross-cultural comparisons, but were using non-Western societies as proxies for the Northwest European past. By doing so, they came to believe that households in Northwest Europe had been transformed from extended ones to the nuclear ones they knew in their own time. Thus, this myth was created in the 1700s and 1800s, not in the 1900s.

This conclusion brings us to a final point. I have heard in talks by and informal conversations with colleagues in family studies the idea that the various family myths were constructed out of people's fantasies about the past, that is, out of an uncritical acceptance of a nostalgic notion of family life being different in the past. However, as we have seen, those myths had a basis in reality—or, rather, a reality of sorts. Clearly, they were constructed from cross-sectional data obtained from societies outside Northwest Europe using the dominant social-science tools of the 1700s and 1800s, the developmental paradigm and reading history sideways.

---

28. As I also indicated in chapter 3, these scholars were also aware of what are now properly understood to be the marriage, authority, and gender patterns characteristic of their time.

29. Alfred Marshall recognized, according to Smith, that the Northwest European family system of recently married couples usually establishing their own households could be found throughout Europe during the Middle Ages.

The Decline in Fertility

In the second half of the 1900s, social scientists intensified their efforts to understand the history of childbearing in Europe. Numerous studies were designed and implemented to document historical patterns and trends in fertility. One particularly important and comprehensive project was the Princeton European Fertility Project, which gathered extensive historical data concerning mortality, marriage, and fertility for virtually all the countries of Europe. In addition, in the late 1900s, social scientists undertook massive contemporary data collections in many non-European populations to document and explain fertility patterns and trends worldwide. Among these large-scale studies were the World Fertility Survey and the Demographic and Health Surveys.

The new historical European fertility studies confirmed the findings of earlier fertility studies (Coale and Treadway 1986). The historical record showed that, during the last part of the 1800s and the early 1900s, Northwest Europe had experienced a dramatic decline in the number of children born to married couples (Coale and Treadway 1986). This decline apparently began first in France in the early 1800s, with the United States following by mid-century. By the last decade of the 1800s, most of the countries of Northwest Europe were experiencing declines in marital fertility. Although there were pockets of Central and Eastern Europe, such as parts of Hungary and Baltic Russia, that experienced declines in marital fertility in the late 1800s, fertility generally remained high in that region throughout the 1800s (Coale and Treadway 1986). However, by the early 1900s, it had begun to fall throughout most of Eastern and Southern Europe (Coale and Treadway 1986).

Then, in the second half of the 1900s, fertility began to fall in many countries outside Europe, with most populations of Asia and Latin America experiencing significant declines.[30] In many parts of East and Southeast Asia, these declines were rapid and substantial. There are also now beginning to be declines in marital fertility in parts of Africa. So, rather than the decline in fertility in Northwest Europe being a myth, it was a very substantial and important reality that has now been experienced in many other places as well. In fact, it may be one of the crucial changes in human populations in the past century.

However, even while confirming the fertility decline, the new historical studies have challenged earlier explanations of it. The research documented

---

30. See Bongaarts and Watkins 1996; Casterline 1994, 1999; Casterline and Bulatao 2001; Chesnais 1992; Guzmán et al. 1996; Harwood-Lejeune 2001; Jones et al. 1997.

earlier in this chapter showing that most elements of the so-called great family transition in Northwest Europe were myths had enormous ramifications for explanations of fertility decline. If, as we have seen, the great family transition was in large measure a figment of the scholarly imagination, it cannot be used to explain the fertility decline. Simply put, the relative constancy in the various dimensions of family life makes it difficult to maintain that any or even all of them could explain a substantial change in childbearing patterns (Cleland and Wilson 1987).

Of course, as discussed earlier, the social organization of Northwest European societies has changed in important ways over the past two centuries. For example, nonfamily organizations have grown in power and importance with the dramatic expansion of schools, government agencies, and production outside the household. Such changes can, as earlier generations of scholars suggested, change the value of children to parents in terms of economic production and old-age security. They can also change the costs of rearing children to adulthood and shift the desire from child quantity to child quality. They may still, therefore, be relevant as explanations for fertility change. In fact, some recent research suggests that they are (Lesthaeghe 1980; Lesthaeghe and Wilson 1986).

However, recent research has also shown that there is no simple or precise connection between the fertility decline and social and economic change in Europe. Fertility fell in some places in Europe that experienced only limited social and economic change and remained high in others that experienced significant change.

The classic comparison here is between France and England. Although industrialization came to England earlier and more extensively than it did to France, the fertility decline was under way in France by the early 1800s, about three-quarters of a century earlier than the decline in England, which did not begin until the 1880s or 1890s (Coale and Treadway 1986). In addition, fertility began to decline in England at about the same time as or later than it did in parts of Hungary, a country characterized by substantially less industrialization and urbanization (Coale and Treadway 1986; Demeny 1968). Interestingly, a major theme of the Princeton European Fertility Project was that the fertility decline often followed cultural and linguistic lines rather than social and economic change (B. A. Anderson 1986; Watkins 1986a).

Research conducted outside Europe has also questioned the link between fertility decline and social and economic change. Just as in Europe, those countries outside Europe experiencing a fertility decline exhibit various levels of social and economic circumstances. A total transformation of family life is certainly not a prerequisite for fertility decline in these settings (Freedman 1979). Many populations have experienced substantial fertility declines while maintaining many historic family patterns. Many contemporary scholars have, therefore, concluded that no clear, precise connections can be made between fertility decline and social and economic change.[31]

As discussed in chapter 4, the fertility decline has for decades been linked with mortality decline in a widely accepted developmental model known as *the demographic transition.* That model suggests a long period of fluctuating but high mortality and fertility, a pattern transformed by a mortality decline, which in turn led to a fertility decline. Many recent discussions have challenged the link between fertility and mortality, maintaining that it is not supported by the historical record.[32]

Thus, the new empirical research about the causes of fertility decline has seriously challenged—even discredited—the previous ideas of the demographic transition as a substantive or theoretical model of fertility decline. A simple developmental version of mortality and fertility decline linked together causally and interconnected with familial, social, and economic change is not tenable in the face of our current understanding of the facts. It has become clear that no single theory can explain fertility decline worldwide.[33]

However, several recent discussions suggest that the total rejection of the demographic-transition model may be premature, that only narrow and rigid versions of the model should be rejected, not more general or approximate ones (Burch 1996; Chesnais 1992; Mason 1997a). For example, Chesnais (1992) defends the connection between fertility decline and social and economic change by suggesting that early fertility-transition theorists had suggested only a general, not a detailed, correspondence and that later critics have tested a version of the model that is too rigid and corresponds hardly at all to the one actually advocated by earlier scholars. In fact, he suggests that the general correspondence is strong and persuasive.[34] Chesnais also suggests that

31. See Cleland 1985; Cleland and Hobcraft 1985; Cleland and Wilson 1987; Demeny 1968; Freedman 1979; Goldscheider 1971; Greenhalgh 1993; Tilly 1986; Woods 1987.

32. See Cleland and Wilson 1987; Goldscheider 1971; Knodel and van de Walle 1979; Mason 1997a; McDonald 1993; Tilly 1986; van de Kaa 1996; van de Walle 1986; Watkins 1986a.

33. See Chesnais 1992; Greenhalgh 1990, 1993; Hirschman 1994; Hirschman and Guest 1990; Mason 1997a; McDonald 1993; Szreter 1993, 1996; Teitelbaum and Winter 1985; Tilly 1978, 1986; van de Kaa 1996; Watkins 1986a; Woods 1987.

34. See also Bongaarts and Watkins 1996; Knodel and van de Walle 1979; Mason 1997a; Watkins 1986a.

the empirical evidence refuting the influence of mortality decline on fertility decline either is more apparent than real or has been overemphasized. The crucial importance of mortality decline for fertility decline, especially in non-European populations, has also been argued by others (Cleland 2001; Freedman 2001; Sandberg 2002).

Summary and Conclusions

As documented in previous chapters, European social philosophers and scientists from the 1500s through the early 1900s used the developmental paradigm, reading history sideways, and vast amounts of data from various societies to create descriptions of the origins of humanity and the history of human experience. Of particular interest here, they interpreted the significant differences between family patterns in Northwest Europe and those in many other parts of the world as representing the results of a great family transition that had occurred in Northwest Europe. They also formulated an extensive and impressive array of theories explaining the dramatic changes that supposedly characterized that transition. During the late 1800s and early 1900s, these explanations were applied to the dramatic fertility declines then being documented in many Northwest European populations. And these conclusions and theories remained virtually unchallenged until the mid-1900s.

Then, in the last half of the 1900s, instead of looking for the Western past in such places as the East European and Asian present, scholars turned to the Northwest European historical record, where they found evidence that contradicted the research of several previous generations of scholars. Instead of finding a great family transition in the Northwest European past, they found that family systems had remained remarkably continuous in the centuries before 1800. They thus came to view the notion of the great family transition as a myth. And they also challenged the prevailing theories of fertility decline.

The historical data do not, of course, prove that the notion of the great family transition is erroneous, just that, if it did occur, it occurred before the 1300s. Nevertheless, continuing to believe in the transition before the 1300s is very much a step of faith, at least on the basis of currently available evidence (see Levine 2001; Smith 1979). And demonstrating that it did occur prior to the 1300s will be an arduous, if not impossible, task.[35]

---

35. Although documenting and explaining family change in Europe prior to the 1300s is extremely difficult, this has not totally deterred efforts to do so. For one such effort, see Goody 1983.

It is important to emphasize that the errors of previous generations of scholars were the result primarily of faulty models and methods, not faulty data. To be sure, as indicated previously, these scholars made some empirical errors, but their reading of the comparative data was in many ways remarkably accurate. Numerous studies have confirmed their most important and fundamental empirical conclusion, that, when family life in Northwest European societies in the past is compared with that in numerous other societies around the world, it proves to be quite distinct in many of the ways identified by earlier scholars. Thus, the crucial problem was methodological, using the developmental paradigm and reading history sideways to transform the differences across societies into narratives of family change.

6

The Scholarly Legacy

The previous chapters have centered on how several generations of scholars used the developmental paradigm, reading history sideways, and cross-sectional data to draw conclusions about changes in family life and, concomitantly, on how in the last half of the 1900s it was discovered that the conclusions drawn from reading history sideways were largely inconsistent with the actual Northwest European historical record. In this chapter and the next I ask whether the developmental paradigm and reading history sideways are simply historical curiosities, of interest only to those fascinated by intellectual history, or whether they have implications for scholarship today. Has the developmental paradigm disappeared from scholarly thought, has reading history sideways been abandoned as a scholarly method, and have cross-sectional data lost their fascination for those interested in social change? Have the models, methods, conclusions, and theories of previous generations of scholars been discarded and forgotten, or is their influence ongoing?

My answer to these questions is that the developmental paradigm, reading history sideways, and the conclusions and theories of earlier scholarship do, indeed, have real and direct significance for scholarship today. The developmental paradigm continues to influence thinking about social change and the way in which populations are classified. Scholars continue to use cross-sectional data to reach conclusions about social change. The theories that generations of scholars formulated to explain the great family transition that never happened are very much alive and well today—in fact, they remain the dominant explanations of family change around the world. Although scholars are now more theoretically and methodologically sophisticated than were their predecessors, earlier models, methods, conclusions, and theories remain highly relevant. The current chapter focuses on the continuing influence of earlier models, methods, and theories, while the next considers the ways in which the conclusions of several generations of social scientists concerning changes in family life may have influenced the data used today by some scholars interested in family change.

The Developmental Paradigm

As we have seen, the developmental paradigm was a key feature of the scholarly apparatus of the 1700s and 1800s. Then in the 1900s it became the subject of withering attacks from critics, lost considerable credibility in the academic community, and has been largely abandoned as an explicit conceptual framework.[1] Teleology and the assumptions of uniform, necessary, and directional change now seldom figure explicitly in analyses. Nevertheless, the developmental paradigm is not an inert relic of the past, but continues to influence scholarship in subtle but powerful ways.

The continuing influence of the developmental paradigm can be seen in the fact that one of the most popular procedures for categorizing world populations—ranking societies according to their degree of development—is based squarely and explicitly on it. This categorization scheme is often employed by governments and international organizations, and developmental language continues to be used in scholarly frameworks (Blaut 1993; Greenhalgh 1993, 1996). The categories *modern, developed, traditional,* and *developing* can be found in discussions of familial, social, and economic conditions. *Modernization* and *development* are sometimes invoked as processes that transform traditional societies and family systems into modern ones. Frequently, however, no clear definitions of these terms are provided.[2] It is important to recognize that central to the language of modernization and development today are the same concepts that scholars employed through the 1800s to frame their analyses of the development of family structures and relationships across the societal life cycle.

Use of the Developmental Model
The developmental model of uniform change figured importantly, albeit in different ways, in the work of several family scholars prominent in the last part

---

1. See Baker 1998; Boas 1940; Bock 1956; Giddens 1984; Gillis 1985; Goldenweiser 1937; Goldscheider 1971; Greenhalgh 1993, 1996; Hodgen 1964; Jennings 1975; Kreager 1986; Mandelbaum 1971; Nisbet 1975/1969, 1980; Szreter 1993; Tilly 1978, 1984.

2. I have used the framework in this implicit way myself (see Thornton 1984), and numerous other examples could be cited (see, e.g., Chesnais 1992; Easterlin and Crimmins 1985; Goode 1970/1963; Hirschman and Minh 2002).

of the 1900s. These scholars seem to have believed, for example, that there was a high degree of uniformity in the nature of the family transitions that they described and significant variation only in the pace of those transitions. They also used the language of developmental transitions.

Edward Shorter (1977/1975, 21) talked explicitly about the "Great Transformation" in family life occurring everywhere and how this transformation occurred at different times and at different rates in different places. Similar evidence of the influence of the developmental paradigm can be found in the work of Mitterauer and Sieder (1982/1977).

A more recent example is provided by David Popenoe, who adopted what he called a *neoevolutionary* perspective and discussed the worldwide movement of family changes through historical stages. Popenoe (1988, 45) argued that these changes represented an "evolutionary trend of social differentiation and the family's loss of functions." While he recognized that these "depictions of the trend can have a nineteenth-century 'evolutionism' aspect," he believed that his interpretations of this evolutionary trend "differ considerably from those of the past century" in two ways. First, he argued that social evolutionists of the 1800s believed that social change represented improvement in the human condition but that his neoevolutionary perspective was much less optimistic. Second, he suggested that "the nineteenth-century evolutionists considered the trend to be a relatively consistent, unilinear development over time." In contrast to this linear view, Popenoe claimed that the trend had been uneven and circuitous, had waxed and waned, and had even gone back on itself.

I would argue, however, that there is not a clear and meaningful distinction between Popenoe's neoevolutionary approach and the developmental approach of the scholars of the 1800s. On the issue of progress, earlier scholars were divided over the question of whether the changes that they believed were occurring represented improvement or deterioration in the human condition (see chapter 2). On the issue of unilineal development, they were more sophisticated than is suggested by Popenoe's description. Although they perceived a highly uniform trajectory of social change (again, see chapter 2), they also recognized that within that trajectory could be found dimensions of reversal, unevenness, and circuitousness.

Use of Grand Developmental Epochs

Scholars today continue to employ the notion of the grand developmental epoch to describe individuals and societies as moving through developmental stages. This is particularly true in demography, where the demographic transition concept is frequently used. As we have seen in chapter 4, what has generally come to be called the *demographic transition*—the dramatic and substantial decline in both fertility and mortality—was first identified in many countries of Northwest Europe during the late 1800s and the early 1900s. More recently, substantial declines in marriage rates and substantial increases in divorce rates, out-of-wedlock childbearing, and cohabitation outside marriage during the last few decades of the 1900s have prompted the identification of a *second demographic transition* (see Lesthaeghe and Neels 2002; Lesthaeghe and Surkyn 2002; van de Kaa 1987, 1994, 2001). The identification of these changes in marriage and divorce as the second demographic transition has led to a relabeling of the decline in fertility and mortality as the first demographic transition.[3]

Especially problematic for those describing social change as epochal *transitions* is the fact that the dichotomy *traditional/modern* is useful for understanding only the movement from traditional to modern. To understand any other type of change, a different language is required. The category *postmodern* has, therefore, been suggested as a useful analytic tool when faced with changes in societies that have already been labeled as modern.[4] This has led to the suggestion that the postmodern demographic transition is a useful analytical tool (van de Kaa 2001).

The use of the term *demographic transition* itself has recently been questioned by Dirk van de Kaa, who was instrumental in identifying the recent changes in marriage, divorce, sexuality, and cohabitation as the second demographic transition. Van de Kaa noted that Adolphe Landry, an eminent French demographer of the early and mid-1900s, had written about the great decline in mortality and fertility in Europe as a *revolution,* not as a *transition.* According to van de Kaa, that the language of *transition* prevailed over that of *revolution*

> may have been a serious mistake. This simply for the reason that as far as the outcome of a regime change is concerned the term demographic revolution is more

---

3. Interestingly, some scholars (see Caldwell 1982; Chesnais 1992; Coale 1973; Freedman 1979) identified the supposed decline in marriage in Northwest Europe before 1800 as the first demographic transition because it supposedly predated the decline in fertility and mortality. Because this supposed decline in marriage was subsequently called into question, it has been dropped as a demographic transition and the decline in fertility and mortality is generally referred to as the first demographic transition.

4. See Crook, Pakulski, and Waters 1992; Giddens 1991; Kloeze and Hoog 1999; D. S. Smith 1994; van de Kaa 2001. The categories *high modernity* and *late modernity* have also been used (see Giddens 1991).

neutral than the term demographic transition. The term demographic revolution implies nothing more than the replacement of one demographic regime by another. Implied in the use of the term demographic transition, however, was the idea that over time, a long-term equilibrium seeking demographic regime would be replaced by the next. More specifically, a regime characterized by quasi stability resulting from the combination of a high level of mortality with a high level of fertility to match that, would be replaced by a new balance in the components of natural growth at low levels of both mortality and fertility. (van de Kaa, in press)[5]

I agree with van de Kaa that the use of the language of transitions in demography has been a mistake, as it has perpetuated the view of a developmental model with stages having long-term equilibrium. I believe that what demographers have called the first and second demographic transitions would be better discussed in neutral terms such as "mortality reduction," "fertility decline," "the increase in divorce," and "changes in marriage," with such nondevelopmental modifiers as *substantial* or *tremendous* added as the observer thought appropriate to indicate the significant magnitude of observed changes. This approach would not only remove the developmental implications of the demographic transition concept, but also, by identifying mortality, fertility, divorce, marriage, and other central aspects of family and demographic behavior as distinct phenomena, facilitate the examination of the linkages between them.

Developmental Assumptions

Social science today has received from its intellectual ancestors a heritage of teleological thinking—an approach inherent in the developmental model of necessary, uniform, and directional change. Teleological thinking is, according to Sewell (1996), the practice of explaining changes in terms of abstract processes that necessarily lead to a future condition rather than in terms of specific historical events whose outcomes depend on the circumstances prevailing at the time. Sewell argues that the long tradition of developmental thinking in the social sciences makes it easy for scholars today to continue to think in teleological terms despite having explicitly rejected the teleological approach.

Social science has also inherited from the tradition of developmental thinking the heritage of interpreting history as unfolding unidirectionally. For example, it is easy to assume that recent trends represent the continuation of long-term trends. It is also easy to assume that current trends will continue indefinitely.

---

5. It should be noted that van de Kaa applies this argument to the second demographic transition as well as to the first.

As a result of this developmental heritage, social, economic, and demographic change is sometimes pictured as a necessary outcome rather than a contingent process that depends directly on both initial conditions and specific causal forces. Change thus conceptualized as inevitable either is automatically explained or does not require explanation, thus limiting the scope for interpretation. In a similar way, the language of *transition* lends an element of irreversibility to descriptions of change.

The Search for the Origins of the Northwest European Past

As indicated in chapter 2, scholars of the 1700s and 1800s had an interest in tracing the origins of the Northwest European family system, origins that they found in Eastern Europe, Asia, and elsewhere. As indicated in chapter 5, scholars of the late 1900s inherited from their intellectual ancestors this interest, but they conducted their search for origins in the historical record (see also Macfarlane 2000, 2002). It also appears that they may have inherited the faith that, sometime in the past, Northwest Europe had a family system dramatically different from that which prevailed between 1300 and 1800 and that, when that family system was eventually documented, it would have much in common with the family systems of Eastern Europe and Asia (Macfarlane 1979a/1978, 1987; Laslett 1978/1977). In some cases, they appear to have been genuinely disappointed when they did not find what they were looking for (Macfarlane 1979a/1978).

My impression is that the failure to document the great family transition in Northwest Europe did not necessarily destroy faith in that transition. My own experience with both the general public and a generation of undergraduate students is that the idea of the great family transition is alive and well in the minds of many Americans today. To my great interest—and sometimes dismay—I have found that this notion is so strongly embedded in American culture that a semester course is not always sufficient to dislodge it. Although it is possible that this may be the result more of my limited teaching effectiveness than of the power of belief, I have found that my colleagues report having a similar difficulty convincing students of the mythical nature of many beliefs concerning family change.

If such ideas as the great family transition do indeed enjoy as wide a currency as I suspect, they may bias scholars investigating them. The dim pictures generated by the archives—the result of the poor-quality data available—are likely easily overwhelmed by the more compelling images generated by strong faith. That is, reports that archival evidence has been found of family systems in the Northwest European past that are similar to non-Western family systems may reflect more a long heritage of faith than actual evidence.

Of course, my assertion that the developmental paradigm and the idea of the great family transition continue to have influence could very well be unfounded. But if it is, why are few scholars today asking such interesting questions as the following: Can the basic elements of family systems observed in Northwest Europe in the 1700s be traced back indefinitely? Are Northwest European family systems as old as those in Eastern Europe, China, India, and elsewhere? What are the origins of the family systems observed outside of Northwest Europe? Could non-Western family patterns have evolved from systems similar to Western patterns?

Why are such questions not being asked? In theory, questions about the origins of non-Western families are just as legitimate and interesting as questions more narrowly focused on the origins of Western family patterns. They may even be more compelling given that the origins of Western family patterns are now being pushed back to the 1300s and beyond. Certainly, we should not assume that non-Western family systems have remained unchanged for millennia.

That such questions are not being frequently asked implies that Western family systems are perceived by scholars as inherently more interesting than non-Western ones. But why would that be? One obvious reason is that many of the scholars pursuing family history today are from Western societies and may, therefore, be more interested in their own societal origins than in those of others. Another is the observed uniqueness of Western family patterns, a uniqueness that would call out for explanation.

Yet another reason—and one that I think must be taken seriously—is that scholars today continue to be influenced by the developmental paradigm and the idea of the great family transition in the West. This heritage suggests a dynamic and developing West in contrast to a non-Western world that has been static for long periods.

The preconception that societal development produces change from non-Western family systems to those of Northwest Europe may still bias interpretation of non-Western trends. It could very well obscure the detection of two different and contradictory patterns in non-Western settings: change that moves away from and not toward the West; and strong persistence and stability in family patterns. It could thus lead to the interpretation of changes as moving toward Western patterns when that directionality exists only in the eye of the beholder, not in the data under consideration.

Possible Effects of Developmental Idealism

In the next few chapters I argue that developmental idealism—a product of the developmental paradigm—influences social scientists as well as ordinary people.[6] Although most social scientists try to separate their scholarship from their values and beliefs, few, if any, are completely successful. Consequently, scholars' approaches and conclusions will be affected to the extent that they are influenced by their values and beliefs, in this case developmental idealism.

For all of these reasons, the developmental paradigm is not simply a conceptual framework that dominated social thought for centuries, was then abandoned, and now has no power to influence conclusions about families and family change. Instead, it continues to have considerable potential to influence the approaches and conclusions of social science research today. We must, therefore, be explicitly aware of the heritage of developmental thinking that we have inherited from our intellectual ancestors if we are to escape its influence.

Reading History Sideways

Reading history sideways with comparative data was a crucial element in the creation of the myths about changes in family life in Northwest Europe by scholars of the 1700s and 1800s. As noted in chapter 2, the weaknesses of the method were recognized by both developmental scholars and historians in the 1800s (Bock 1956; Macfarlane 1979a/1978). And strong critiques of it were written in the 1900s.[7] As a result, scholars today are enormously more methodologically sophisticated than were their predecessors. The hazards of drawing dynamic inferences from cross-sectional data are now well-known, as are the dangers of making causal inferences from static data. In addition, scholars today are blessed with considerably more longitudinal data than were previously easily available.

However, scholars today must still deal with many of the same problems faced by their predecessors. The necessary longitudinal data are frequently lacking, which means either remaining silent on an issue or relying on cross-

---

6. Developmental idealism will be discussed at length in chapter 8. For the moment it will suffice to know that the four propositions of developmental idealism are as follows: modern society is good and attainable; the modern family is good and attainable; the modern family is a cause as well as an effect of a modern society; and individuals have the right to be free and equal, with social relationships being based on consent.

7. See Boas 1940; Bock 1956; Goldenweiser 1937; Mandelbaum 1971; Nisbet 1975/1969.

sectional data. For this reason, scholars from many disciplines—including history, the social sciences, and biology—continue to employ the method of reading history sideways.[8] In the following sections, I provide some examples of how reading history sideways has been used in the last part of the 1900s by both historians and social scientists.

Use of Cross-Sectional Data by Historians

Macfarlane suggests (1979a/1978, 1979b, 1987) that using information from one society to proxy for information from another society has been widespread among historians. I provide examples of this from three particularly influential historians of the last half of the 1900s—Lawrence Stone, Philippe Ariés, and Edward Shorter. I suggest that reading history sideways was particularly important in the work of Stone and Ariés and played a more subtle, but nontrivial, role in that of Shorter.[9]

Turning first to Ariés and Stone, we should note that, although these researchers relied more heavily on the actual record of the Western past than did their predecessors, they also utilized information from non-Western societies on which to base their discussions of the nature of family relationships in Western history. This approach contributed to these two scholars reaching conclusions about family sentiments and relationships in the Northwest European past that were similar in several respects to those of earlier scholars.

Two examples will illustrate how Ariés explicitly used the method of reading history sideways by imputing the Western past from information from the present in other societies. First, Ariés concluded that, in the past, Western parents were extremely open about sexual matters in the presence of children. He also suggested that, in the past, Western parents felt comfortable handling their children's genitals and that the practice was commonplace. After citing a few anecdotes from the French past in support of this conclusion, he turned to Muslim experience, reporting: "The practice of playing with children's privy parts formed part of a widespread tradition, which is still operative in Moslem circles. These have remained aloof not only from scientific progress but also from the great moral reformation, at first Christian, later secular, which disciplined eighteenth-century and particularly nineteenth-century society in England and France. Thus in Moslem

---

8. See Bulatao 1980; Caldwell 1982; Harris 1968; Harvey and Pagel 1991; Ho 1988: Howell 1986; Kluge, n.d.; McDonald 1985; Nisbet 1975/1969; Sanderson 1990; Smith 1973; Stocking 1987.

9. Another example of the use of reading history sideways is provided by Mitterauer and Sieder (1982/1977).

society we find features which strike us as peculiar but which the worthy Heroard [Henri IV's physician] would not have found so surprising" (1962/1960, 103). Ariés went on to cite a passage from a novel written by a Tunisian Jew in which a Muslim boy in Tunis has his genitals manipulated by an adult. After describing the incident, Ariés concluded: "This twentieth-century scene surely enables us to understand better the seventeenth century before the moral reformation" (105).[10]

Second, Ariés asserted that, in the past, Western family life was not kept private, secluded behind the walls of the family home, but extended into the street. He wrote: "As in modern Arab towns, the street was the setting for commercial and professional activity, as also for gossiping, conversation, entertainments and games.... This medieval street, like the Arab street today, was not opposed to the intimacy of private life; it was an extension of that private life, the familiar setting of work and social relations" (1962/1960, 341).

Stone's extensive use of comparative data has been thoroughly documented and analyzed by Macfarlane (1979b). I therefore summarize Macfarlane's conclusions only briefly here, referring the reader to his essay for a more extended discussion.

According to Macfarlane, Stone used a technique that "may be termed the argument by analogy and involves the wholesale importation of foreign evidence. The book is entitled The Family, Sex and Marriage in *England*..., but if one counted up the footnote references, a large proportion of them come from outside England" (1979b, 16). Much of the non-English data that Stone used came from continental Europe, particularly France:

> When we pursue Stone's argument and proof on many topics, we find again and again that the evidence is from France. His basic premise, that we can deduce from French evidence the nature of English experience unless there is strong proof to the contrary, is stated openly on a number of occasions.... What is most insidious about this approach is that nearly always the evidence is used to close a gap which Stone believes will one day be filled by material from England. He does not consider that the absence may have occurred because England was different from France.... It really is not satisfactory to project nineteenth-century French peasant social structure back onto the English in the sixteenth century. If we threw

---

10. Although my purpose in describing this example is to illustrate the use by Ariés of the comparative method of describing history, serious questions could be raised about how useful this story is in summarizing even the ordinary experience of Tunisian Muslims. Does a novel written by a person of one religious persuasion about the behavior of people from another religious group provide reliable information about "widespread tradition" in Muslim Tunisia?

away all of Stone's French evidence, there can be little doubt that many of his hypotheses would collapse since their weak evidential basis would crumble into almost nothing. (119–20)

Macfarlane also points out that Stone relied on contemporary anthropological data from societies outside Europe for evidence of the English past. For example, in describing interpersonal relations in the 1500s and early 1600s, Stone wrote: "Children were neglected, brutally treated, and even killed; adults treated each other with suspicion and hostility; affect was low, and hard to find. To an anthropologist, there would be nothing very surprising about such a society, which closely resembles the Mundugumor in New Guinea in the twentieth century, as described by Margaret Mead" (1977, 99). In describing the status of women, he wrote: "The lot of a working wife was probably like that of many women today in underdeveloped countries" (200). And he found confirmation of his views of past English marriage in "anthropological studies of the many societies where love has not been regarded as a sound basis for marriage, and where one girl is as good as another, provided that she is a good housekeeper, a breeder, and a willing sexual playmate" (181).

While my purpose here has been to illustrate how extensively Stone used non-European anthropological data in describing the English past—how he read the English past, at least in part, from the non-English present—Macfarlane also argued that Stone's characterization of the bulk of the anthropological data was inaccurate and misleading. For example, according to Macfarlane, anthropologists would, contrary to Stone's assertion, be surprised to find a society characterized by neglect, brutality, and murder. In fact, Macfarlane indicates that they were surprised to find such a society in New Guinea. Macfarlane also took exception to Stone's assertion that "one girl was as good as another," suggesting that "there is a vast literature which shows that one girl is not as good as another since there are usually elaborate rules concerning proscribed and prescribed marriage" (Macfarlane 1979b, 112).

In the next chapter, I discuss in detail Edward Shorter's (1977/1975) extensive study of family change. Although Shorter primarily relied on historical data, cross-sectional data from France, Britain, and the United States played a significant, although subtle, role in his analysis. Shorter recognized considerable geographic and cultural differences in family forms despite espousing a developmental model of societal change that posited the transformation of a fairly uniform traditional family into a quite homogeneous modern family. He was particularly impressed with the unique nature of the family in Britain and the United States, a uniqueness that has been observed by others

(Macfarlane 1979a/1978; Stone 1977). After noting several ways in which England was an outlier (Shorter 1977/1975, 21, 30, 42, 47, 125, 225), he offered an explanation of the important difference between France and England:

> What we may be picking up . . . is the early modernization of domestic relationships in England that we have observed at other points. As egalitarian relationships between husband and wife diffused, the community began to perceive as intolerable such vestiges of earlier patriarchal authority as the right to slam one's wife about; and so it moved to rebuke the wife-beaters. In French domestic relations, such egalitarianism arrived so late in time that the charivari [a form of community control] was already dead as an active custom—having expired for entirely unrelated reasons—before it could be turned against the violent husband. (225)

Thus, like several generations of scholars before him, Shorter interpreted the cross-sectional differences between two societies as reflecting differential progress along a uniform societal life cycle. However, while this time-honored practice of explaining variation in terms of differential development was sufficient to explain the French-English data to his satisfaction, apparently it was insufficient to explain the even greater differences that Shorter perceived to exist in the United States. In order to account for the distinctiveness of the American experience, Shorter proposed a new twist to the societal-life-cycle paradigm: that societies could skip the traditional stage and be born modern.

Shorter suggested that the family patterns in Colonial America during the 1600s were so modern that America must have been born modern—skipping the traditional stage that characterized Europe of the period. Particularly important to Shorter were the conclusions of Edmund Morgan (1966/1944) and John Demos (1970) that romance was an integral part of the lives of the Puritans of Massachusetts in the 1600s and 1700s—a pattern that Shorter saw as remarkably modern and discrepant from the pattern of little romance that he believed to exist in traditional European society. Shorter reported: "References to romantic love as an active force in the life of the couple began with the Puritans and never ceased thereafter. John Demos believes it impossible to say anything conclusive about companionate marriage in Plymouth Colony, but talks anyway—and convincingly—about the 'instinct of love.' Edmund Morgan is forced time and again to use the word 'love' in describing the Massachusetts Bay settlement" (Shorter 1977/1975, 65). Shorter also provided evidence that similar sentiment existed in Virginia. Furthermore, he was "impressed by the Puritans' casual acceptance of sexual needs for both men and women." The data seemed to suggest to Shorter that there was "a certain changelessness in American patterns over two hundred years of time [from about 1760 to 1960]" (250).

Shorter explained the distinctiveness of America as follows: "The American family was probably 'born modern' because the colonial settlers seem to have seized privacy and intimacy for themselves as soon as they stepped off the boat" (Shorter 1977/1975, 242). He also opined that "the easy availability of land" may have allowed the settlers to set aside the psychology of the Old World. Unfortunately, Shorter provided no further details about how a group of traditionalists from Europe could be so fundamentally transformed into a modern society by a trip across the Atlantic and settlement in North America. Nevertheless, the notion that a society could be born modern instead of traditional seemed to explain the American case to his satisfaction. Those less enamored of the societal-life-cycle paradigm will likely be less convinced of the transformational nature of the migration experience.

The Use of Cross-Sectional Data by Social Scientists

Shifting the discussion to the use of the comparative method by social scientists, I begin with David Popenoe's (1988) important substantive analysis of social trends. Focusing on family change, Popenoe wrote: "The trend is most clearly visible (and most analyzed) today in comparing less- and more-developed countries and in studying Third World development over time; contemporary economic and social development in the Third World to some extent mirrors the historical development in the West. The less-developed countries today are much more kinship oriented than are the advanced industrial societies, which are the most nuclear, and over the long-term nuclear familism grows with economic and social development" (48). He continued:

> If one looks not just at currently modernizing societies but at the full range of world societies, from tribal to highly developed, a slightly different picture of family change emerges. Taking this range of societies as a rough indication of long-term evolutionary development, there is evidence that some dimensions of the historical evolution of family-kinship systems have been curvilinear and that the recent trend of the family toward the nuclear form has in a sense brought the world full circle. . . .
>
> Nuclear households predominate in the "simpler societies," such as those based on hunting and gathering. . . . Only when local economies become more sophisticated, for example, when they are based on settled agriculture (the stage at which most Third World industrializing societies are today), can the large, complex household be supported. Then, at a still later stage of development, the nuclear-family household again becomes predominant as societies move into the industrialized age. (49)

Apparently, Popenoe drew his conclusions about changes in family structure at least partially by reading history sideways. He used a range of contemporaneous societies to inform him of "long-term evolutionary
development." He read changes in family life sideways from today's hunting-
and-gathering societies to, first, industrializing and, then, industrialized societies. The fact that all these societies were contemporaneous did not appear
to be an issue for Popenoe, just as it was not for previous generations of social
scientists using comparative data to describe social change.

The ambitious and sophisticated study by Stevan Harrell (1997) also used
cross-sectional data to describe family change. Harrell identified four stages
of societal evolution from nomadic bands to modern industrial societies,
with great transformations marking the movement from one societal stage
to the next. Although Harrell used recent over-time data to describe family
trends accompanying his last great transformation, that to a modern industrial society, his descriptions of family forms at earlier stages of development
were based on contemporaneous information from societies judged to be at
those stages of development. Harrell also explicitly recognized the importance of culture and how it could influence trajectories of change and differences among societies he categorized at the same stage of development.

Another social-science example of reading history sideways comes from
a very sophisticated recent analysis by Ronald Inglehart and Wayne Baker
(2000; see also Inglehart, Norris, and Welzel 2003). Within a modernization
perspective, the authors utilized cross-sectional data collected in the 1990s
from sixty-five countries to compare those countries on a wide range of cultural values summarized in the two indices of traditional versus secular-
rational and survival versus self-expression. At the national level, these
summary indices are, according to Inglehart and Baker, closely related to several measures of individual and family behaviors and relationships. Most
important for our purposes is the strong correlation between these two summary indices and measures of gross national product and industrial structure. Wealthy industrialized countries score much higher in terms of
secular-rational and self-expression values than do poor countries that are
not industrialized. The authors interpret these cross-sectional differences in
developmental terms, suggesting that they represent the results of economic
development and cultural modernization.

Inglehart and Baker do not stop with reading history sideways but go on to
provide considerable further evidence to buttress their developmental interpretation of the international cross-sectional data. They analyzed longitudinal
data over brief periods of the 1990s for a subset of thirty-eight of the original

sixty-five countries. Using these data, they show that economic fortunes in the 1990s were generally positively correlated with increases in secular-rational and self-expression values, outcomes consistent with their developmental inter-pretations of the cross-sectional data. They also examine differences in indi-vidual values by birth cohort. They find that, in wealthy countries, younger individuals have more secular-rational and self-expression values, cohort/age differences that they interpret as indicating historical trends rather than the effects of aging per se. Contrasted with these substantial cohort differences in wealthy countries are the small or nonexistent cohort differences found in poor countries, a contrast suggesting a lack of change in the latter.

Inglehart and Baker also provide a sophisticated discussion of the path dependence of cultural change, the extent to which modernization is prob-abilistic rather than deterministic, and the persistence of cultural patterns accumulated over centuries. In short, their work represents a very impres-sive example of the combination of many kinds of data, including both cross-sectional and longitudinal information. Yet their sweeping conclusions about the effects of economic development and cultural modernization as societies move from agrarian to industrial and then to postindustrial rely primarily on national cross-sectional evidence.

Yet another example of the use of the comparative method is provided by Bulatao (1979). Rodolfo Bulatao utilized cross-sectional data and an explicitly developmental model to compare the value of children across sev-eral countries with different levels of development. What he observed were substantial cross-sectional differences that he interpreted as the result of development processes. Interestingly, he also provided a clear discussion of the problems involved in inferring development processes from cross-sectional data. Nevertheless, his conclusions about developmental processes were offered with a substantial degree of confidence.

Two additional examples merit attention. The first is Bongaarts's sophis-ticated examination (2001) of trends in living arrangements that uses both cross-sectional and temporal data. Like Inglehart and Baker, Bongaarts com-bined the two types of data with a full awareness and appreciation of the lim-itations of employing comparative data in a temporal analysis. The second is an investigation by Smits, Ultee, and Lammers (1998) that uses interna-tional cross-sectional data to examine whether development results in hus-bands and wives having more nearly comparable education levels. The authors' methodology was challenged by Raymo and Xie (2000) in a study that obtained somewhat different results using longitudinal data for a small number of countries. This challenge prompted Smits, Ultee, and Lammers

(2000) to conduct a reanalysis of the original data, but with a temporal component introduced, that modified and extended the earlier results.

Reading History Sideways Using Individual-Level Data

Although the central interest of this book centers on the analysis of change and dynamic processes observed at the societal level, it may be useful to note that the reading history sideways method is sometimes used at the individual level as well. Instead of following an actual birth cohort of people across time to determine how people age, scholars sometimes create synthetic cohorts of individuals from cross-sectional data to serve as proxies for real cohorts. This procedure involves identifying a series of contemporaneous age-based groups and using the successive age groups as proxies for the temporal life-course trajectory of a single cohort. It is comparable to reading history sideways at the societal level because it is presumed that an actual cohort will experience life in the same way as suggested by the synthetic cohort consisting of contemporaneous age groups. However, today it is generally recognized that the "experience" of such synthetic cohorts is hypothetical and does not necessarily reflect any actual life-course trajectory. Of course, because such an approach relies on an actual time metric for ordering people into age groups, its employment is less problematic than is the employment of the comparative method at the societal level, which has no such metric for ordering countries into stages of development.

Another common way for researchers to read history sideways at the individual level is to use cross-sectional data to make comparisons between people in terms of their experiences. This procedure involves estimating the influence of a particular factor (say education level) on a particular trait (say church attendance) by focusing on the cross-sectional correlation between the factor (education) and the trait (religiosity). However, it is today generally recognized that, unless the individuals are studied longitudinally (e.g., measuring church attendance through the high school and college years and beyond), it is impossible to determine with any degree of confidence whether any observed correlation is due to the effect of the factor on the trait (in this case, education level affecting church attendance), the effect of the trait on the factor (church attendance affecting education), or some unidentified other factor (say ethnicity) affecting both.[11]

---

11. Although the use of panel data helps to ameliorate this problem, it does not totally solve it, as panel data can also be plagued by such problems as selectivity bias, unmeasured variables, unobserved heterogeneity, and misspecification bias, problems that have been extensively addressed elsewhere and are beyond the scope of this book.

The Persistence and Appropriateness of the Old Theories

As we have seen, employing the methodology of reading history sideways, the scholars of the 1700s and 1800s created a fascinating new set of propositions—perceived as facts—about the ways in which family life changed as societies developed, propositions that called out for explanation. The challenge of explanation was met with great vigor, and many insightful and powerful theories were created. It was proposed that family change was the natural product of the unfolding of the developmental potential of human societies. In addition, specific social and economic forces influencing family change were identified, including industrialization and growth in wage labor; urbanization; increases in knowledge, information, and education; growing consumption aspirations; growth in prudence and foresight; the rise of democracy; and the Protestant Reformation and increased religious pluralism and secularism. By the early 1900s, several of these causal factors were well accepted as determinants of family change.

These old theories have persisted to the present, and their influence is not limited to understanding changes in family life identified by earlier scholars employing the method of reading history sideways. Indeed, because they have provided a ready framework, they have often been used by scholars to explain trends in family life, documented not through comparative data, but by chronological data. For example, as we have seen in chapter 4, modified versions of these theories were used in the early 1900s to explain the fertility decline that began in Northwest Europe in the 1800s. Many elements of these theories have also been used throughout the 1900s to explain other historical trends in Northwest Europe, such as divorce and the division of authority within the family.[12]

Given that these theories were originally designed to explain the transformation of families from non-Western to Western forms, it should not be surprising that they have also been used—sometimes modified, sometimes not—to explain a broad range of family trends identified in non-Western settings.[13] Indeed, as with studies of change in Western family forms, these theories now dominate studies of family change in non-Western societies. Ultimately, they have come to constitute the great bulk of theories currently available in the social sciences to explain family change.

12. See Dike 1885; Ellwood 1910; Thwing and Thwing 1887; Willcox 1891.
13. See Chesnais 1992; Cleland and Wilson 1987; Goode 1970/1963, 1982/1964; Mason 1997a; Thornton and Lin 1994.

It is profoundly ironic that, as we have seen, recent research has shown there to be no basis in fact for the trends that these theories were created to explain. And the evaluation of theories designed to explain nonexistent changes presents us with an interesting dilemma. Under normal circumstances, false predictions of this sort would be seen as disconfirmation of a theory and grounds for its rejection. It could be argued, however, that these theories were not invalidated by the experiences of Northwest Europe prior to 1800 but inappropriately applied there. The rationale for this argument is that the theories were created to apply to societies having family systems that never existed in Northwest Europe. The theories were also designed to explain the influence of certain causal factors on the rise of family characteristics that, it turns out, antedate those causal factors by centuries.

Although these theories may not have been applicable to Northwest European family life prior to 1800, they may be applicable in other places or other times. They may, for example, be applicable in explaining family change in non-Western societies, because many of these societies had precisely the kinds of family systems that the causal forces in the theories were meant to apply to. It could also be argued that, while the old theories are inappropriately applied to the pre-1800 Western world when family change was relatively limited, they may be appropriately applied to the post-1800 Western world when family change was substantial. Thus, these theoretical forces may not have produced the family changes posited by earlier generations of scholars for Northwest Europe, but may be relevant for later periods in Northwest Europe and for other parts of the world.

It would, of course, be an incredible coincidence for a set of explanations with no relevance to the time and place for which they were created to have great relevance to other times and places. This would imply that theories invented to explain a nonexistent past would be powerful explanations of an actual future. Although this conjunction of events is possible, some skepticism about it seems in order.

Since most of the theories currently available in the social sciences to explain family change were formulated in response to trends identified by reading history sideways, they are not a random sample of all theories that might be generated to explain family change. They are, ultimately, theories specifically designed to explain how family systems characteristic of non-Western societies could change into family systems characteristic of Western societies. The result is that most theories of family change today reflect the results of the developmental paradigm and reading history sideways.

The consequence of this conclusion for research projects designed today to study non-Western family systems is that it is difficult to avoid theories with the results of the developmental paradigm and reading history sideways built into them. This makes it hard to reach conclusions and explanations different from those of the scholars of the 1700s and 1800s. As a result, social change can seem less contingent and diverse and more necessary and regular than it is.

All of these considerations suggest the need for a reorientation of our theoretical frameworks for understanding changes in family patterns. One useful element here would be a decreased predisposition toward acceptance of these old theories. A second useful element would be an expansion of alternative theories for explanations of changes in family life. These alternative theories would have a different starting point from the transition of non-Western family forms into Western ones.

Specifying Comparison Points

One of the essential questions motivating scholars of the 1700s and 1800s—What is the nature of Northwest European family life in the past?—continues to fascinate many people today. An important element in answering this question at the present time concerns the appropriate comparison point. This is important because the choice of comparison points for evaluating Northwest Europe in the 1700s could be as different as China in the 1700s and Northwest Europe in the late 1900s, with the choice having substantial implications for the ways in which Northwest Europe of the 1700s is described. Such widely divergent comparison points are possible—even likely—in family research today and can greatly complicate communication and cumulation of knowledge.

Of course, the scholars of the 1700s and 1800s could not compare Northwest Europe of their day with Northwest Europe of the late 1900s. Their comparisons could only be with societies outside of Northwest Europe—often with Eastern Europe, the Middle East, and South and East Asia. As we have seen, with these comparisons it was easy for these scholars to describe Northwest European society as individualistic, households as nuclear, marriages as occurring at older ages, the marriage system as youth-run, and parental authority as weak.

Similar comparison points guided many scholars of the late 1900s, including Laslett, Macfarlane, and Hajnal, as they sought to describe past Northwest

European family life. Thus, it was easy for them to emphasize the same aspects of Northwest European family life in the past that had been described by previous generations of scholars. Unlike their predecessors, however, these latter scholars reported that these family patterns had existed for many centuries longer than had been imagined by earlier generations of scholars.

Of course, scholars today can use Northwest Europe in the late 1900s as the comparison point for describing Northwest European families of the past, with dramatic implications for the conclusions reached. Because of the enormous changes that have occurred in Northwest Europe during the past two centuries toward individualism, nuclear households, and freedom of young people, it is now very easy to describe Northwest European society before the 1800s as familistic, having extended families and involvement of parents in marital choices. This comparison point may have affected the emphases of some scholars in recent years, for example, Ruggles (1987, 1994) and O'Hara (2000). These observations highlight the necessity of being explicit about comparison points in describing the past.

7

The Legacy of Data

In this chapter, I shift the focus from models, methods, and theories and speculate about the effects of the theories and conclusions of scholars of the 1700s and 1800s about family change on the secondary data available in the historical archives, effects that are, I suggest, substantial. I also provide some limited data in support of this hypothesis.

I hypothesize that the conclusions of scholars in the 1700s and 1800s about family change were widely disseminated and believed among the educated elite members of Northwest European societies. Many of these educated people observed and described the family behavior and relationships of the ordinary people in their own societies. It is likely that as the beliefs of scholars about family change spread among the elite of Northwest Europe, the views of these educated observers about ordinary people would change. More specifically, the new ideas would motivate these educated European observers to compare people from Eastern Europe, Asia, or Africa with Northwest Europeans. But because scholars had transplanted Eastern Europeans, Asians, and Africans into the Northwest European past, it was easy for these observers to view their comparisons in terms of social change rather than cross-cultural differences—just as the developmental scholars had done.

If this hypothesis is correct, the emergence of the new conclusions about changes in family patterns in the 1700s and 1800s would have led to a change in the ways educated observers reported past and present family life. That is, it would have led to an upswing in comments about modern family behaviors in Northwest Europe in the accounts of educated observers, with the supposedly new circumstances contrasted with the old traditional ways. Consequently, any time series of reports of educated observers about family life and family change in Northwest Europe would have been biased by the influence of the flowering in the 1600s and 1700s of erroneous information about family change. This possibility is important because significant amounts of the historical research of the 1900s relied on data that came, not from primary sources, but from secondary accounts written by educated observers of the 1700s and 1800s (Pollock 1985/1983).

In what follows, I discuss this possibility in the area of family sentiment and romance, focusing largely on Edward Shorter's *The Making of the Modern Family* (1977/1975), a particularly germane example because Shorter was very much aware of the dangers involved in using secondary data in historical research. I conclude the chapter with a brief discussion of similar influences on work conducted in non-Western settings.

Edward Shorter and Secondary Data in France

Like generations of historically minded scholars before him, Edward Shorter lamented the shortage of primary historical data about ordinary people. Shorter therefore assembled a time series of accounts of families and family change written by three kinds of observers (all educated and well informed): antiquarian scholars, medical doctors, and minor bureaucrats. He was aware, however, that these accounts of ordinary family life were likely to be biased because the lifestyles of ordinary people were often seen as reflecting a lack of culture rather than as indicating a different culture. Thus, Shorter said that these accounts could not be reliable descriptions of peasant life, but he made the reasonable assumption—one made by numerous other students of social change—that the biases in the reports were constant across time. He was also explicit in noting that if this assumption was not met, his analysis would reveal only how views of family life have changed, not how family life itself changed.

Reports of Changes in Family Life

The picture that Shorter painted of family life in the West before the last half of the 1700s is in many ways one of an emotional and affectional desert. For example, he concluded that "marriage in former centuries was usually affectionless" and that "on the farm, man and wife got along in quiet hostility and withdrawal" (1977/1975, 55–57). According to Shorter, farmers of the past placed more value on their livestock than on their wives, and men were "selfish, brutal, and unsentimental" (78). Although he was willing to admit that "some sort of affection binds the young couple together before marriage," he also insisted that "neither in intensity nor form was it what the modern world was to call 'romance'" (142).

The picture that Shorter painted of modern family life in the late 1800s is, by contrast, very different. One of the most important changes that he identified is what he called a "surge of sentiment": "Romantic love unseated material considerations in bringing the couple together" (1977/1975, 5). Young people, according to Shorter, shifted their allegiance from the lineage and the community to personal happiness and self-development, and, as a result, mating and dating became "privatized," and sentiment and romance blossomed.

The timing of the explosion in reports about sentiment on which Shorter based this conclusion is particularly interesting. Shorter indicated that numerous reports of affectionate marriage relationships in urban areas in France began to appear in the late 1700s. He said that he had not encountered these kinds of reports before 1775 and that the clustering of such remarks "in the last quarter of the eighteenth century and first quarter of the nineteenth points quantitatively to an important evolution" (Shorter 1977/1975, 229)—the surge of sentiment. However, Shorter offered no explanation for why this surge of sentiment occurred where and when it did.

What Shorter missed is that this explosion in reports of sentiment overlaps to a great extent the dramatic flowering of the research about changes in family life based on cross-cultural data and the sideways reading of history, which can be dated to the mid-to-late 1700s. As we have seen, the scholars of this period—for example, John Millar, William Robertson, Henry Home, William Alexander, and Thomas Malthus—came to important conclusions about the lack of marital sentiment in the past and the enormous increase in such sentiment with modernization. We also know that the ideas of the Enlightenment, including those about family change, were widely disseminated in Europe (Goodman 1994; Meek 1976). The overlap of this new wave of scholarship about changes in family sentiment read from sideways history with the burst of reports about family sentiment documented by Shorter is truly remarkable—and, I speculate, not coincidental.

Although historical change in family sentiments was a theme in the writings of several widely read scholars, the work of John Millar may have had a particularly important influence.[1] *The Origin of the Distinction of Ranks*, Millar's best-known and most influential work, is one of the first major social-science treatments of marriage, gender, and family relationships, with

---

1. John Millar was born in Scotland in 1735, the son of a minister of the Church of Scotland. He attended the University of Glasgow, where he received an education in the classics. He also became first a student, then later a colleague and friend, of Adam Smith's. Millar was elected to the chair of Civil Law at the University of Glasgow in 1761, and he served in this position until his death in 1801 (Lehmann 1979/1960).

approximately half the book devoted to such topics. William Lehmann (1979/1960) has documented the significant influence that the book had on scholars from the late 1700s well into the 1800s (see also Moaddel 2005).[2] And the fact that many of its ideas have persisted in the literature makes it one of the most important works in the history of family studies. Particularly prominent in the *Origin* is the thesis that a great deal more sentiment characterized the husband-wife relationship of Millar's day than was typical of the husband-wife relationship before his time.

The *Origin* was first published in England in 1771 as *Observations concerning the Distinction of Ranks in Society,* then reissued in a revised and expanded edition in 1779 as *The Origin of the Distinction of Ranks.* According to Lehmann (1979/1960, 59), the book was even from its first appearance "well received by the public" and met with great acclaim during Miller's lifetime, going through what Lehmann calls a "goodly number" of English-language editions, including, apparently, pirated editions in Dublin and Basel. The *Origins* was translated into German in 1772 and French in 1773, and both English- and foreign-language editions were widely distributed. At least one copy of the first edition reached the United States as early as 1772, when it was acquired by the Harvard University Library. The Library of Congress holds a copy of the third edition that bears the autograph of the fourth president of the United States, James Madison.

The fact that the *Origin* was translated into French in the early 1770s suggests that it circulated to some extent in the urban areas of France in the late 1700s and, therefore, that it had some currency among the scholars, doctors, and bureaucrats who were Shorter's sources. The ideas of other scholars such as Alexander, Malthus, Homes, and Robertson were also current among the elite of France in the late 1700s and early 1800s—as acknowledged by Comte (Lehmann 1979/1960). Thus, Shorter's sources most likely had considerable knowledge of the emerging ideas and theories of family change. That discussions of family relationships and structures were also part of the philosophy instruction at many European academic institutions in the 1500s and 1600s (see Freedman 2002)—an emphasis that likely continued into the 1700s and 1800s—further supports this contention since Shorter's sources were

2. John McLennan, who played a pivotal role in the family-history debates of the mid-1800s, acknowledged his discovery of Millar's work a century after it was first written, referring to the *Origin* as an "admirable review" that "every student of history should be acquainted with" (McLennan 1886/1865, 324–25). McLennan also noted that Millar largely anticipated the work of at least one important later scholar.

likely educated at major centers of learning or by teachers who themselves had been educated at those centers.[3]

All of these considerations suggest the possibility that it was a change in the perspectives of the educated doctors and bureaucrats—and not changes in the relationships and behaviors of ordinary people—that led to the upsurge in accounts of family sentiment reported by Shorter. The reasonable assumption that Shorter had made about constant biases of reporting was likely violated, making his study, as he indicated, more about changing views of family life than about actual changes.

Evidence of Possible Effects of Developmental Scholarship

The language of the accounts of family observers in the 1700s and 1800s cited by Shorter is consistent with the idea that their authors were influenced by the new family scholarship. Many authors of the period emphasized the high degree of affection and support in urban French families beginning in the late 1700s. They indicated that "unity reigns in the families"; that there is "fatherly tenderness, filial respect and domestic intimacy"; that "paternal affection" is common; that "spouses are united and appear to be mutually affectionate"; that "wives . . . see the perfection of their happiness in caring for their children and cherishing their husbands"; and that "for the most part wedlock is not a yoke but rather a soft exchange of consideration, of kind attentions." Especially to the point is the following: "Husbands have come closer to their wives, mothers to their children. All have felt the need for mutual support, to create for themselves consolations and resources, to give themselves to domestic concerns which formerly they had disdained" (1977/1975, 228–29).

Although Shorter interpreted these statements about family affection as a surge of positive sentiment among family members, he also recognized a problem with this thesis. He suggested, "We obviously cannot believe all this. The romanticism of these doctors and administrators leaps from the context, and the values they so blithely attribute to the entire bourgeoisie were doubtless to have been found, first of all, in their own households" (Shorter 1977/1975, 229).

These statements present a problem to Shorter's central thesis because these writers of the late 1700s and early 1800s were describing a very high degree of love, emotion, and commitment to the nuclear family. If French

---

3. For example, one of those sources, who wrote his observations in 1808, was described by Shorter (1977/1975, 191) as a "retired natural history teacher" and "an aging nostalgic."

families through the mid-1700s had in fact been emotional deserts, as Shorter characterized them, the burst of sentiment required to bring them to the level of love and emotion that his sources described would have been so rapid and overwhelming as to be unbelievable. Shorter may have thought that this surge of sentiment had taken place and that his sources were simply exaggerating its extent. But if so, he offered no explanation of what would motivate such exaggeration.

Although the statements of these French observers are not particularly believable when interpreted as reflecting shifts in French family behavior, they make more sense when interpreted as the product of a burst of new scholarly conclusions about family change. The flowering of new ideas concerning the origins and history of family relationships could have caused observers in the late 1700s and early 1800s to emphasize in entirely new ways the romantic and sentimental natures of their own family lives. With Millar and other scholars describing the family experiences of earlier societal life cycle stages as being almost totally lacking in affection, romance, and autonomy—even describing marriage as slavery—it would not be surprising for later observers to begin to emphasize the enormously contrasting nature of family life that they could observe in their own neighborhoods and families, even though there had been no change in actual family relationships. The romanticism of their reports about family life in their own time, which Shorter found unbelievable, becomes understandable when placed in the context of the important new and apparently authoritative information about unloving and uncaring families in the past.

The observers of family life in the 1700s and 1800s also made explicit use of the developmental language of the period. Shorter wrote that "these writers believe themselves living witnesses to a historical change, for they often explicitly compare the Bad Old Days to 'our glorious times'" (Shorter 1977/1975, 229). Since several generations of developmental scholars had compared the lives of so-called barbarians and savages with the perceived glories of civilized Europe, it is easy to suspect that the writers cited by Shorter were greatly influenced by the methods and conclusions of Millar and similar scholars. Given the prevailing developmental paradigm and the practice of reading history sideways, it is even likely that the "bad old days" of these observers did not exist in the European historical record at all but in perceptions of family conditions outside of Europe.

Shorter provided one particularly striking account of an observer who contrasted the present with the past as follows: "In former times there was a great distance between husband and wife, between father and children, from family to society. Talk came less easily, human ties were less intimate, relationships more distant" (1977/1975, 230).[4] Like the work of the family scholars of the 1700s and 1800s, this account provides no specific time frame for the comparison made, indicating only that the writer is speaking of "former times." Also, like the work of those early scholars, this report sounds more like a generalization about family relationships than a report of specific features of family life. One quick sentence covers husband-wife, parent-child, and family-society relationships. Could this writer, like those early scholars, have been relying not on the actual European past but on European perceptions about non-Western families?

The Need for Additional Research in Northwest Europe

All of the considerations of the previous sections lead me to the plausible hypothesis that the conclusions of developmental scholars during the 1700s and 1800s had an important effect on secondary observations concerning ordinary life. These conclusions, in effect, led to a change in the point of view of the observers that affected the kinds of reports they wrote. In turn, Shorter attributed these changes in reports quite reasonably to changes in family relationships.

It is important to emphasize, however, that I consider my interpretation of Shorter's data as a plausible hypothesis rather than a demonstrated fact. Further research is needed to document the extent to which the developmental paradigm, reading history sideways, and specific conclusions about the history of family relationships and sentiment permeated and affected the views and writings of doctors, bureaucrats, antiquarian scholars, and other educated and elite observers in the past. However, if, after further research, it is confirmed that I am correct to conclude that the work of the early developmental scholars led to a change in the point of view of secondary observers, it must then be concluded that a substantial amount of the available secondary data used to study social change is badly biased. The extent of the bias will, however, be difficult to determine and, therefore, control for, because it is highly unlikely that the influence of the developmental paradigm was at all times and in all places uniform.

---

4. This account was from the 1820s, but Shorter also cited similar accounts from the 1880s.

Possible Effects of Developmental Scholarship
outside of Northwest Europe

Although the main focus of this speculation about the influences of developmental thinking and research on secondary reports of family life and trends has centered on the West, there is no reason to believe that these influences would be limited to Western settings. In fact, it is likely that as the ideas and conclusions about development spread around the world, they affected observers outside the West as well. Thus, both the interpretations and misinterpretations of Western scholars would be reflected in indigenous reports of family life in other parts of the world.

Evidence for such influence in the non-Western world has, in fact, been reported by Shakry (1998) and Abu-Lughod (1998b), both of whom comment on the remarkable similarity between the language used in European and Egyptian descriptions of family life in Egypt in the 1800s. Abu-Lughod, for example, notes that, in the highly influential *Liberation of Women* (1992/1899), Qasim Amin included references to Western developmental writers, held Western family forms in high regard, and described Egyptian family life in very negative terms, even suggesting that Egyptian family members despised and hated each other. An experienced observer and student of family life in Egypt, Abu-Lughod wondered about the origins of such a "strange and negative depiction of marital life . . . in Egypt," noting the "striking" similarities between Amin's "descriptions and those of the missionaries and colonial officials," who also "described the Muslim family as loveless" (Abu-Lughod 1998b, 258).

Although this example of the influence of Northwest European developmental scholarship and travelers on indigenous accounts of Egyptian family life comes only from one country, it would be surprising if this influence was felt only in Egypt. Instead, it is likely that this kind of influence was widespread in other countries as well. However, this is only speculation and further research is needed to establish the extent to which those connections actually existed.

I turn next to an examination of developmental idealism and its influence on the actual family behavior and relationships of ordinary people around the world.

PART THREE

Influence on Individual and Community Actors

8

Developmental Idealism

To this point, I have argued that the developmental paradigm and reading history sideways have had a profound influence on the thinking and conclusions of several generations of social scientists. In this chapter, I suggest that the conceptual paradigm, research methodology, and substantive conclusions that dominated social science for hundreds of years have had enormous power beyond the walls of the academy. This occurred as concepts, theories, and conclusions were translated into a set of paradigms or models that showed individual and government actors how to deal with the world and motivated them to change their behaviors and relationships.[1] That is, the ideas of development and the specific conclusions about its content and direction became much more than an academic lesson in world history—and much more than a framework for understanding the history of social, economic, and familial relations.

Specifically, the developmental paradigm, reading history sideways, and the conclusions of generations of social scientists have offered meaningful and powerful narratives of human origins and history. And these developmental histories themselves provided new criteria for evaluating the legitimacy and value of the many existing ways of organizing human society. The pinnacle of history in these narratives—Northwest Europe—became for many the standard by which to judge the value of human institutions and the mechanisms for attaining the good life. Developmental thinking and conclusions also provided a blueprint for the future, showing the direction of change and the mechanisms that could be employed to facilitate progress and well-being. And they made the defining elements of Northwest Europe part of the inexorable march of history.

---

1. See Kulick 1992. See also Fricke 1997a, 1997b; Geertz 1973; Meyer et al. 1997.

The motivational power of the developmental paradigm has been felt worldwide.[2] Developmental ideals and influences have been known by many names: *the march of civilization, progress, economic and social development,* and *modernization.* These forces are also sometimes referred to as Westernization because the concepts of modernity and development were defined by the characteristics of the West. These forces of modernization and development have affected almost every dimension of life, including the political, psychological, economic, familial, cultural, and social. However, since in this book I am concerned with changes in family ideas, behavior, and values, I focus here not on the broad set of developmental ideals and influences, but only on those that have direct implications for family change.

Included among the relevant ideals and influences is a package of powerful propositions and aspirations that I call *developmental idealism.* Within this package is a set of ideas identifying goals to be achieved, means with which to evaluate forms of social organization, an explanatory framework linking social and economic achievement as both cause and effect of specific family patterns, and statements about the fundamental rights of individual human beings. I argue that developmental idealism has affected the family ideas and behavior of billions of individual women and men around the world.

Developmental idealism has been disseminated around the world through many mechanisms. Among the most important mechanisms have been schools, the mass media, travel and immigration, European conquest and colonization, and the spread of Christianity. Also important have been the United Nations, international aid programs, Marxism, family planning programs, and women's organizations. And all this was facilitated by industrialization and urbanization, which both brought people closer together and enhanced communication channels.

In many ways, the spread of developmental idealism was fueled by the positive power of its message, a compelling story of human progress. Developmental idealism, which had been legitimized by the empirical evidence of the wealth and health of the West, provided goals to be achieved and mechanisms to attain them. For many, therefore, it became a motivational force, even

2. See Amin 1989; Blaut 1993; Comaroff and Comaroff 1997; Dahl and Rabo 1992; Dussel 1995/1992; Escobar 1988; Kahn 2001; Kulick 1992; Lee 1994; Lerner 1958; LiPuma 2000; Myrdal 1968; Nisbet 1980; Pigg 1992; Robertson 1992; Samoff 1999; Sanderson 1990; Wallerstein 1997/1979, 1991; Welch 1999.

a secular religion with the power to define morality and motivate behavior and relationships (J. C. Alexander 1995).

For many others, however, developmental idealism was not compelling, and it was resisted, sometimes energetically. This resistance was successful in many instances, but at other times it was met with effective military and police enforcement. Developmental models and programs were also sometimes imposed through legal mechanisms and financial incentives and disincentives. In addition, developmentalism was at times embraced in order to obtain the resources and knowledge to resist Western domination.

In addition to being a framework for social change, the developmental model and ideology were sometimes used as ideational tools to justify Western dominance over other people. This occurred because being at the top of the developmental ladder provided justification for colonization and subjugation. It gave some Europeans a rationalization—even a mission—for civilizing those in other parts of the world.

My goal in this chapter is to describe developmental idealism, explain some of the mechanisms of its transmission around the world, and describe how it has influenced the lives of billions of people. I will show how it has been disseminated through both the attractiveness of its message and the force of those propounding it. I will also describe how it has been accepted, rejected, and modified in various places.

It is important to note that I am not attempting to provide a comprehensive theory of family change, but to indicate the potential power of developmental idealism in changing family life. My emphasis on developmental idealism as a force in family change, therefore, should not be viewed as an effort to emphasize the ideational to the exclusion of the structural and economic. Ultimately, developmental idealism is only one—albeit crucial—factor influencing family change; attention to all relevant forces is necessary to understand family change fully. Among these other relevant forces are the social, economic, political, psychological, and technological. Developmental idealism is also not the only cultural or ideational force influencing family change, as religious changes, new theories of the world, and other changing ideas can influence family beliefs and behavior. In addition, because all of the causal forces influencing changes in family patterns are interrelated, it is very difficult to isolate precisely the influence of developmental idealism. Thus, my purpose here is to explain why developmental idealism is an essential, but underappreciated, component of a comprehensive model of changes in family life.

The Components of Developmental Idealism

Although the concept of developmental idealism shares many features with the general concepts of modernity and development, the latter two have over the years acquired a variety of different meanings that inhibit precise definition and operationalization. For this reason, I introduce the term *developmental idealism* to allow me to define precisely what is included in the definition.[3] Another advantage is that the term clearly indicates that I am referring to the ideational components of development and not the structural components, although, as I make clear, developmental idealism does contain ideas about social structure.

There are four fundamental propositions that constitute the notion of developmental idealism: (1) modern society is good and attainable; (2) the modern family is good and attainable; (3) the modern family is a cause as well as an effect of a modern society; and (4) individuals have the right to be free and equal, with social relationships being based on consent. Although these four propositions are interconnected in that they are all deeply embedded in developmental thinking and conclusions, each is, in fact, independent and conceptually distinct. As I suggest below, these four basic propositions are also buttressed by related propositions about the value of modern political institutions and the power of the forces of history.

My argument is that the four basic propositions of developmental idealism constitute a system of beliefs that can motivate and guide a wide range of behaviors and relationships. If the ideas of developmental idealism are widely believed, they can become powerful forces for changing a wide range of family patterns, including marriage, childbearing, parent-child relations, living arrangements, and gender relationships. The power of developmental idealism would, of course, be greatest if all four propositions were widely and deeply believed. However, even if only one or two of the propositions were widely embraced, developmental idealism would still have considerable power.

Three things should be noted here: First, I am introducing these propositions not as factual statements, but simply as ideas. The issue is not whether they are true or false, but whether people believe them, are motivated by them,

3. After I formulated and labeled the propositions of developmental idealism, I discovered their similarity to Yang's (1959) notion of family idealism. As I explain in chapter 11, the closeness of the two concepts should not be surprising given that both Yang and I distilled our ideas directly from the developmental thinking and conclusions of generations of earlier scholars. I use the term *developmental idealism* rather than *family idealism* to emphasize the linkage of this package of ideas to the developmental paradigm that was so important in generating it.

and change their lives because of them. Second, I am neither endorsing nor criticizing these propositions as good or bad, but simply discussing them as propositions that might motivate individuals and change culture and behavior. Although the question of whether the effects of these propositions are positive or negative is an important one, its answer lies beyond the scope of this project. Third, these propositions are not the direct formulations of any particular scholar or group of scholars, but represent my own distillation from the vast and often complex literature on development produced over the last several centuries. Another effort to distill the basic motivational ideas from developmental approaches and conclusions could take a different form and produce a different, although related, set of propositions.

The reactions of individuals and groups to these propositions are likely to be not simple, but complex and multifaceted. Any, all, or none of the propositions might be believed, and belief can be complete or partial. And complicating matters further is the fact—explained below—that each proposition is composed of several subpropositions.

Modern Society Is Good and Attainable

As we have seen in chapter 2, for centuries the developmental trajectory was seen as consisting of long periods of growth followed by periods of decline, decay, and, eventually, death. That is, the most advanced periods were seen as negative and certainly not as goals to drive human imagination and energy toward greater development. However, in recent centuries, the overwhelmingly predominant view of development has eliminated the decay part, thereby leaving the full trajectory of development as eternal progress.[4] Each stage of the developmental trajectory is seen as bringing additional wealth, health, power, and happiness to individuals and populations. This positive image of development can make it a powerful motivator for many people.

Societies considered to be traditional have for centuries been associated with agricultural production, rural life, low levels of school attendance, and limited transportation and communication facilities, whereas societies considered to be modern have been associated with industrial production, urban life, high levels of education, and rapid transportation and communication systems. These latter dimensions of social and economic life have been seen as representing the height of development and are associated with wealth, health, prestige, happiness, power, and resources.

4. See Condorcet, n.d./1795; Godwin 1926/1793; Hegel 1878/1837. See also J. C. Alexander 1995; Ekirch 1951; Nisbet 1980.

Traditional and modern societies as they are defined under the first proposition of developmental idealism—modern society is good and attainable—are characterized by these same socioeconomic factors. Note that these various factors are conceptually distinct and that, for the purposes of this discussion, there is no reason to assume causal connections among them. I group them together simply because they have historically been grouped in the traditional/modern continuum rather than because they measure the same thing or are causally connected in some way.

The motivational power of this first proposition is evident in the fact that socioeconomic development—industrialization, urbanization, and the expansion of education and economic productivity—has become one of the highest priorities, if not the highest priority, of national governments and international organizations (Donaldson 1990a; Johnson 1987; Mauldin et al. 1974). In the last hundred years, and especially the last fifty, most countries have made socioeconomic development one of their primary goals. Such change is now increasingly seen as both good and possible, and the route to prosperity, health, and power.[5] The universality of socioeconomic development as a worthy goal is exemplified by the fact that it transcends the boundaries of culture, geography, and political ideology, becoming, according to Meyer et al. (1997), one of the central elements of world culture. In addition, aspirations for economic progress may extend past such currently available things as factories, schools, and rapid communication and transportation to include the hope that no matter how advanced people might consider themselves to be, the future will bring yet more technological and economic progress, with an increase in knowledge, wealth, health, power, and happiness.

This first proposition of developmental idealism would, if generally accepted, have great power for family change. It would provide an ideational force for leading governments and individuals along the pathway to social and economic change that could, in turn, influence family behavior and ideas. It could also lead to increased consumption aspirations, a heightened demand for education, and increased costs of rearing children. In addition, aspirations for socioeconomic development could run ahead of actual attainments, with important implications for family behavior. Furthermore, these social and economic changes could provide conduits for dissemination of many ideas, including developmental idealism.

---

5. See Banister 1987; Kulick 1992; Lapham and Simmons 1987; Mauldin et al. 1974; Notestein 1983/1964; Szreter 1993; Wallerstein 1991; Watkins and Hodgson 1998; White 1994.

The Modern Family Is Good and Attainable

The second proposition of developmental idealism is that the modern family is good and attainable. In formulating this proposition I employ the same traditional/modern family dichotomy used by generations of previous scholars (see chapter 3). As defined by these scholars, the traditional end of the dichotomy was defined to include the following dimensions: a familistic society, family solidarity, extended households, young and universal marriage, extensive parental authority, lack of affection before marriage, and low regard for women's rights and autonomy. Other dimensions of family life that were used by previous generations to define traditionality are polygamy, concubinage, child marriage, foot-binding, and the wearing of veils.

The modern end of the continuum is characterized by the same features of family life discussed in chapter 3 that generations of earlier scholars identified as modern. Among these characteristics are a social system with many nonfamilial elements, extensive individualism, many nuclear households, older and less universal marriage, extensive youthful autonomy, marriage largely arranged by the couple, affection in mate selection, and high regard for women's autonomy and rights. Although low and controlled marital fertility was not included in the original conceptualization of modern families in the 1700s and early 1800s, the decline of fertility in the late 1800s and early 1900s in Northwest Europe brought it into the modern family package. I therefore include family planning and low fertility as modern family patterns in developmental idealism.

Although developmental idealism rates all of these dimensions of family life along the same continuum from traditional to modern, the various dimensions are conceptually distinct, and I make no assertions about any causal connections among them. They are considered together not because they measure the same thing or are causally connected, but because they have historically been included as part of the traditional/modern continuum of family life.

This proposition of developmental idealism provides a framework for evaluating the different components of any family system, with traditional patterns defined as inferior and modern patterns defined as superior. Developmental idealism legitimizes and empowers the ideas and behaviors of modern families by associating them with some of the most powerful words in the English language: progress, enlightenment, development, and civilization. Thus, these modern dimensions of family life are defined as good and, perhaps equally importantly, at the pinnacle of progress and enlightenment (J. C. Alexander 1995; Spencer 1851). As such, they provide powerful motivations for desiring these family patterns. And even if one does not personally approve of these modern family patterns, opposition to them might be moderated because they are associated with enlightenment and progress.

In developmental idealism traditional family elements are discredited and disempowered by association with the powerful label of underdevelopment, with some traditional family features—for example, concubinage, polygamy, child marriage, and foot-binding—being associated with even more odious and powerful words such as backwardness or barbarity. Thus, traditional dimensions of family life are pictured in developmental idealism as inferior, part of the past, and in opposition to progress. With these associations, even advocates of cultural and family systems inherited from the past might decrease their efforts to defend and maintain family dimensions that have been defined as traditional, while opponents of them might become particularly energetic in their opposition. Also note that it is not necessary for all elements of the modern family to be endorsed for developmental idealism to be powerful. Even if only one or two aspects of the modern family are endorsed, the effect could be substantial.

As we have seen in earlier chapters, Northwest European societies of the 1700s and 1800s essentially defined what it means to be modern. But social life changed over the course of the 1900s, with the changing nature of family life in Western societies modifying what was meant by a modern family. Particularly important was the creation of the breadwinner/housewife family model as industrialization separated home and work, thereby increasing the specialization of men in activities outside the home and women in domestic activities. This breadwinner/housewife model increasingly became seen as modern. More recently, however, with the entrance of women into paid employment outside the home, modernity is increasingly associated with the dual career family.

The last several decades in Western societies have also witnessed dramatic increases in premarital sex, divorce, out-of-wedlock childbearing, single parenthood, and openness about sexuality. As these new dimensions of social life have arisen, they have become associated by some people with the idea of modernity, while others have identified these emergent aspects of social life as Western rather than modern. By interpreting these new social phenomena as negative and Western, people could embrace the modern family fully while at the same time opposing certain family dimensions they defined as Western. My definition of the modern family of developmental idealism excludes these new forms of Western life, although recognizing that this exclusion is relatively arbitrary. This means that my definition of the modern family in the developmental idealism framework refers to family patterns of Northwest Europe experienced in the 1700s, 1800s, and early 1900s.

Social thought in many societies of the world, including Northwest Europe, has linked together authority structures in families and government.[6] Therefore, I also identify a proposition of political idealism that is closely related to this second proposition of developmental idealism: modern political systems are good and attainable. I define *modern political systems* in this framework as those that emphasize freedom, liberty, and the consent of the governed. Because of the strong linkage of ideologies about political and familial authority, acceptance of this political proposition could spill over into ideas about family structures and processes.

The Modern Family Is a Cause as Well as an Effect of a Modern Society

The third proposition of developmental idealism is that a modern family is a cause as well as an effect of modern society. This proposition rests on the same observations that social scientists have made for the last several hundred years: that social and economic structures and productivity are strongly correlated with family structures and relationships, a correlation that was interpreted as reflecting an inevitable causal connection between socioeconomic development and modern family life. This correlation could be interpreted causally as a modern family causing a modern society, a modern family being an effect of a modern society, or both, with any of these causal interpretations encouraging acceptance, even embracement, of Western family forms. As I discussed in chapter 3, several generations of scholarly literature have asserted that a modern society produces modern family forms. As for the position that modern family forms produce modern society, some scholars have emphasized political and familial freedom as the driving force,[7] some equality,[8] and some women's rights and autonomy.[9]

6. See Condorcet, n.d./1795; Filmer 1949/1680; Hegel 1878/1837; Montesquieu 1997/1748; Spencer 1851; Wollstonecraft 1975/1792. See also Beard 1946; Butler 1978; Cott 2000; Hunt 1994; Nicholson 1986; Schochet 1975; Shanley 1979; Tarcov 1984; Traer 1980.

7. See Condorcet, n.d./1795; George 1938/1880; Godwin 1926/1793; Hegel 1878/1837; Hume 1825/1742; Mill 1989a/1859, 1989/1869; Paine 1984/1791–92; Robertson 1860/1762; Smith 1937/1776; Turgot 1895/1750; Weber 1968b/1916. See also Baker 1975; Collini 1989; Ekirch 1951; Nisbet 1980.

8. See Condorcet, n.d./1795; George 1938/1880; Mill 1989c/1869; Robertson 1860/1762. See also Tomaselli 1985.

9. See W. Alexander 1995/1779; Condorcet, n.d./1795; Lieber 1876/1838; Mill 1989c/1869. See also Tomaselli 1985.

Two events in the last half century have given added impetus to the idea that the modern family has produced modern society. The first is the discovery (discussed in chapter 5) that most elements of the modern family system could not have been *caused* by modern society because they *predate* it.[10] This led to an emphasis on the idea that a modern family system is a cause and not a consequence of a modern society. The second is the widespread acceptance of the Malthusian notion that well-being can be increased through fertility and population control.

For hundreds of years population growth was viewed as good and associated with social and economic well-being and national power and prestige.[11] However, a tradition extending back to David Hume (1825/1742) and Robert Malthus (1986a/1798, 1986b/1803) held that rapid population growth would lead to war, catastrophe, and misery. This negative view found other adherents over the centuries, but it remained a minority position well into the 1900s.[12] Then, in the mid-1900s, it became apparent that, in non-Western settings, improvements in public health and medicine were beginning to reduce mortality levels significantly at the same time as fertility levels were remaining relatively stable, leading to substantial rates of population growth.[13]

Many in the academic and policy communities came to the essentially Malthusian conclusion that the countries of Africa, Asia, and Latin America would not be able to absorb their rapidly growing populations into their social and economic systems. Although there were some worries that the rapid rates of population growth might lead to absolute declines in living standards and health, the more widespread fear was that rapid population growth would impede social and economic development.

Although the prevailing view at that time was that extensive social, economic, and family changes were required before fertility would decline, there had also been a long tradition extending back to Malthus that humans could

10. See Berger and Berger 1984; Goode 1970/1963; Kertzer 1991; Maynes and Waltner 2001; Todd 1985.

11. See Ferrero 1994/1922; Finkle 2001; Finkle and McIntosh 1994; Godwin 1964/1820; Mundigo 1996; Piotrow 1973; Reed 1978; Teitelbaum and Winter 1985; United Nations 1953; van de Walle 1978.

12. See Carr-Saunders 1936; Ross 1927; Swindlehurst 1916; Thompson 1930a.

13. See Barrett and Frank 1999; Carr-Saunders 1936; Caldwell and Caldwell 1986; Coale and Hoover 1958; Critchlow 1999; Finkle 2001; Hodgson 1983, 1988; Kirk 1944; Notestein 1950, 1982; Piotrow 1973; Reed 1978; Rockefeller 1977/1952; Ross 1927; Spengler 1972; Symonds and Carder 1973; Szreter 1993; Thompson 1930a, 1952; United Nations 1953; van de Walle 1978; Vance 1952a; Warwick 1982; Wilmoth and Ball 1992.

increase their well-being through the control of fertility and population. This view became increasingly influential in the second half of the 1900s as many academics and policymakers became convinced that well-planned and energetic family planning programs could be effective in lowering the birthrate, thereby enhancing prospects for economic development as well as improving health, maintaining political stability, and preventing poverty.[14] Although there were many reasons for instituting family planning programs, Barrett and Frank (1999) argue convincingly that it was the link between fertility and population growth on the one hand, and economic and social development, on the other, that gave the family planning movement its power.

Many academics, foundations, and governments lent their support—financial and otherwise—to this cause.[15] Achieving socioeconomic development through population control even became the stated program of the United Nations and several of its agencies.[16] Population control and family planning came to have such high priority that some observers have suggested that only the prevention of nuclear war took precedence (e.g., Donaldson 1990a). There was only limited opposition to these policies from Western religious bodies such as the Vatican.[17]

It is, of course, not necessary to have an explicit causal interpretation of the association between family patterns and economic prosperity for the empirical association to have motivational power. Individuals aware of the association but unaware of any imputed cause for it could easily conclude that, by adopting the family patterns prevailing in the wealthy parts of the world, they will enhance their prospects for socioeconomic advancement. Such mimicry has, in fact, been documented. Srinivas (1956), for example, found that lower-

14. See Barrett and Frank 1999; Critchlow 1999; Donaldson 1990a; Finkle 2001; Greenhalgh 1996; Harkavy 1995; Hodgson 1983, 1988; Hodgson and Watkins 1997; Johnson 1987, 1994; Kasun 1988; Lapham and Simmons 1987; Notestein 1983/1964; Piotrow 1973; Reed 1978; Sharpless 1996; Szreter 1993; Warwick 1982; Watkins and Hodgson 1998.

15. See Bogue 1993; Cabrera 1994; Caldwell and Caldwell 1986; Chamie 1994; Critchlow 1999; Demeny 1988; Donaldson 1990a, 1990b; Finkle 2001; Finkle and McIntosh 1994; Finkle and Crane 1985; Freedman 1984, 1987; Greenhalgh 1996; Harkavy 1995; Hodgson 1983, 1988; Hodgson and Watkins 1997; Johnson 1987, 1994; Kasun 1988; Knodel, Chamratrithirong, and Debavalya 1987; Krannich and Krannich 1980; Notestein 1968, 1982; Piotrow 1973; Reed 1978; Sharpless 1996; Sretzer 1993; Thomas and Grindle 1994; Warwick 1982, 1994; Watkins 1993, 2000; Watkins and Hodgson 1998.

16. See Donaldson 1990a; Finkle and McIntosh 1994; Hodgson and Watkins 1997; Johnson 1987, 1994; Piotrow 1973; United Nations Economic Commission for Africa 1984; Warwick 1994.

17. See Critchlow 1999; Donaldson 1990a; Keely 1994; Piotrow 1973.

caste Indians attempt to climb the caste ladder by adopting the social patterns of the higher castes. And Henrich and Boyd (1998) argue that the imitation of the more successful by the less successful is an important element in biological and cultural evolution.

Although the developmental paradigm and developmental idealism are not necessary for social imitation, they facilitate it by bringing to the process a worldview that identifies Western family forms as both good and attainable. The developmental paradigm also places all societies on the same developmental trajectory, thereby providing confidence that societies and individuals with fewer resources can make the necessary adjustments and become more like those at the pinnacle of the developmental hierarchy. In addition, developmental idealism provides a set of theories linking family forms to the achievement of the social and economic goals of health, wealth, and power.

Individuals Have the Right to Be Free and Equal, with Social Relationships Being Based on Consent

The fourth proposition of developmental idealism is that individuals have the right to be free and equal, with social relationships being based on consent. Although the ideas of freedom, equality, and consent existed long before the 1600s and 1700s,[18] in the 1600s and 1700s they became the subject of renewed interest as social thought focused on the origins of humanity. As I discuss in more detail in chapter 9, several influential writers—including Hobbes (1996/1651), Locke (1988/1690), Montesquieu (1973/1721), Rousseau (1984/1755, 1997/1762), and Robertson (1780/1777)—believed that, at the beginning of time, people lived in a state of nature, without society, laws, or government.[19] These writers argued that, in this state of nature, individuals were both free and equal and that, when they left the state of nature to form societies with laws and governments, they did so freely and consensually.

Many scholars of the era also extracted normative principles—what ought to be—from the conditions they believed existed in this state of nature at the beginning of time.[20] Most important here is the idea that because people were created with freedom, equality, and the right to consent/dissent in social relationships, these are natural rights that are retained forever. These inalienable rights could be abrogated by no form of social organization, be it government

---

18. Freedom and democracy were, of course, important elements of ancient Greek society.

19. See also Ashcraft 1987; Baker 1990; Cranston 1983, 1984; Gordon 1994; Gourevitch 1997; Myres 1916; Schochet 1975; Tarcov 1984.

20. See Berkhofer 1978; Butler 1978; Schochet 1975; Tarcov 1984.

or family, because government existed by the consent of the governed, and family life involved free and equal individuals whose relationships were consensual after the age of maturity.

The notion of inalienable rights was particularly powerful in a world where kings and fathers ruled by divine right.[21] It was most directly applicable to the political arena, becoming a driving force in the creation of democratic political principles worldwide, and playing a prominent role in the French and American Revolutions.[22] But, given the historical link between government authority and family authority, it was also applied to family relationships. For example, Locke (1988/1690) suggested that people had the right to freedom and equality within the family as well as within the polity.[23] According to Locke, men and women should come to marriage as equals, form the marital union on the basis of consent, and even have the right to dissolve that union if they so desired. Similarly, Locke believed that parents and children were, in principle, created equal and free, but he also recognized that children were born in an immature state and, therefore, dependent on the goodwill and subject to the authority of their parents. However, on reaching adulthood, children achieved full equality and independence.

It should not be surprising that Locke's description of the natural rights of individuals within the family—men and women, parents and children—is much closer to the actual circumstances in his native England than to those in, say, China and India (see also Smith 1993; Laslett 1988/1960). However, in Northwest Europe at the time, gender relationships were characterized by considerable inequality and male control in marriage. Locke's ideas played a substantial role in the drive for equality and freedom for women in the family.[24]

---

21. Writing about human origins, religious unorthodoxy, freedom, liberty, and the divine rights of individuals was both revolutionary and dangerous in Europe during much of the 1600s through the 1800s. Government censorship in this era was rampant, books were burned, and people writing about these issues were frequently under the threat of exile, imprisonment, and execution—with the threats sometimes being carried out. The threat of government reprisal led Locke to publish several of his books, including the *Two Treatises of Government*, anonymously. It also led, it has been suggested, to Locke, Rousseau, and others engaging in both self-censorship and purposive obfuscation (see Macpherson 1962; Meek 1976).

22. On democratic political principles generally, see Ashcraft 1968, 1987; Leder 1968; Myres 1916; Schochet 1975; Tarcov 1984. On the French and American Revolutions in particular, see Ashcraft 1968; Baker 1990; Cott 2000; Tarcov 1984.

23. See also Butler 1978; Fliegelman 1982; Fuller 1941/1845; Schochet 1975; Shanley 1979; Spencer 1851; Tarcov 1984.

24. See Abray 1975; Butler 1978; Laslett 1988/1960; Okin 1982; Shanley 1979.

In addition, in Northwest Europe marriage was, with only very limited exceptions, indissoluble (Phillips 1988). This meant that while women and men had the right to consent in the formation of marriage, they had no legal ability to consent/dissent once the union was formed. For these reasons, application of the Lockean principles of freedom and consent to the termination of marriage, as well as to its initiation, was an important legitimization for the right to divorce and would have dramatic implications for Northwest European patterns of marriage and divorce.

Locke's ideas of intergenerational freedom, equality, and the necessity of consent when children reach adulthood could also have substantial implications for parent-child relations in Northwest European populations because they emphasized the independence of children rather than the authority of parents.[25] Furthermore, the impact of these Lockean principles on gender and intergenerational relations in other places in the world—where there was less historical commitment to them—could be especially dramatic.

The fourth proposition of developmental idealism therefore represents a powerful force for family change. By designating freedom, equality, and consent as basic human rights, it challenges in fundamental ways social relationships based on coercion and inequality.

Note that the fourth proposition of developmental idealism, emphasizing freedom, equality, and consent, is closely related to several aspects of the second proposition, which states that the modern family is good and attainable. This is true because several specific elements defining the traditional family can themselves be opposed because they are seen to deny freedom, consent, or equality. For example, one reason for opposing child marriage is a belief that immature young people are unable to make informed choices and to give their consent to marriage. In addition, marriages arranged by parents and matchmakers can be opposed because they violate the necessity of personal consent. Similarly, the lack of autonomy for women can be opposed on the grounds that it denies equal treatment.

Thus, in some ways freedom, consent, and equality lie at the core of developmental idealism. They provide an integrating philosophical and value framework that can shape other values. In fact, in many ways these principles can be—and have been—accepted as unchallenged, taken-for-granted principles that guide crucial social and individual decisions. As such, they can be powerful forces for family and social change.

25. See Ashcraft 1987; Fliegelman 1982; Schochet 1975; Shanley 1979; Tarcov 1984.

The Diffusion of Developmental Idealism

In order for the ideas of developmental idealism to influence the lives of ordinary people in Northwest Europe, they had to be disseminated from the halls of academia. Because developmental idealism originated in Europe, its dissemination outside Europe would require an even more extensive process to transcend the strong barriers of physical distance, language differences, and the strength of local cultural patterns.

The spread of developmental idealism to community leaders and ordinary people in Northwest Europe was facilitated by the fact that these people were immersed in the same cultural heritage and understandings as the scholars of the region. The ideas of development and the ascendancy of Northwest Europe had permeated the culture of the region and had given scholars and ordinary people similar models for understanding the world around them, thereby facilitating the widespread acceptance of developmental idealism.

One of the reasons for similar cultural models among scholars and ordinary people was that many aspects of developmental thinking and methods are ancient, extending back to Greece, Rome, and a long line of Christian theologians. Also old is the Western European belief that Western society represents the pinnacle of development and progress, with Western culture, society, and family patterns seen as superior to those of other societies. In fact, these propositions of developmental idealism, undoubtedly, were available to affect family life during the period of extensive European exploration and expansion. Just as these ideas could influence travelers and scholars, they could influence government leaders and ordinary people in the same time period.

Many factors have facilitated the dissemination of developmental idealism both in Northwest Europe and throughout the world. To begin with, there was an active international community of scholars in the 1700s and 1800s in Europe, and scholarly writings circulated widely between countries. In addition, there was an overlap between the scholarly and the political elites, with the result that community leaders had easy access to scholarly ideas and manuscripts. Further, many of the most important works of the period were translated into non-European languages and circulated outside Europe, where they became particularly influential in many elite circles.

Schools are likewise an important avenue for the dissemination of ideas, particularly so in the last 250 years, which have witnessed the introduction and expansion of mass education throughout the world. In the countries of Northwest Europe, elementary education became widespread in the 1800s, secondary education in the early 1900s, and postsecondary education in the last few decades of the 1900s. A similar, but in some ways more rapid, expansion of education has occurred elsewhere. And many young people from non-Western countries have been educated in Europe, returning home to influential academic and government positions.

The mass media represent another excellent conduit for information and new ideas. They are particularly relevant here because the last two hundred years have witnessed a great increase in circulation of newspapers, magazines, and other printed material, while the years since the early 1900s have seen the invention of new and even more powerful forms of communication, including radio, television, and, more recently, the Internet. The result has been an almost complete media saturation in many countries.

From the 1500s through the 1900s, European exploration, conquest, and colonization helped the dissemination of developmental idealism. In recent decades, the creation of more rapid and more efficient modes of international transportation networks has facilitated international travel by both Westerners and those living outside the West, thereby facilitating the spread of developmental idealism. The spread of developmental idealism has also been facilitated by industrialization and urbanization, with the movement from agricultural to industrial and especially bureaucratic employment producing new networks of people and, thus, new channels for information flow. The movement from farms to cities also produced greater population density and more effective communication networks.

The ideas of development and developmental idealism have not only found their ways inertly through the information channels of schools, the mass media, bureaucratic organizations, and urban networks, but have been propagated vigorously and widely by numerous advocacy organizations.[26] Some of the earliest and most powerful advocates—particularly in the non-Western world—were the Christian churches. Since the 1400s Christianity has spread widely throughout the world by the power of the word, the sword, and the pocketbook, a process that is continuing in many parts of the world today (Barrett 1982). Not only are the populations of Europe primarily Christian, but so are the populations of the Americas. In addition, more than half of the people in many countries of sub-Saharan Africa are at least nominally Christian. There are also considerable numbers of Christians in Asia, although the percentages are much smaller than in the rest of the world. And with the spread of Christianity has come the idea that Western ways of doing things—including

26. I mention only a few of these movements here in order to illustrate their scope. They are discussed at greater length in chapters 9 and 11.

family forms and relationships—have the approval of deity, are morally and socially superior, and are to be emulated by others.[27]

Political and economic movements have also played an active role in the spread of developmental idealism. Advocates of liberal democracy, for example, have espoused the freedom of individuals and equal access to government. Marxism was built explicitly on the developmental framework and has advocated actively for economic development and equality among social groups, including between women and men. Developmental idealism even became embedded in American foreign policy during the last part of the 1900s through such programs as the Alliance for Progress and the Peace Corps. The United States portrayed itself as the model of development to be emulated by the people of Africa, Asia, and Latin America (Latham 2000).

Also influential have been the United Nations and other international organizations. These organizations have been important players in the creation of a world culture, and among the ideas that have been disseminated through them are those of individual and social development, freedom, and equality (Meyer et al. 1997). In fact, these central elements of developmental idealism are written into foundational UN documents (United Nations 1948, 1962, 1979). In addition, many international aid organizations have spread the ideas of progress and development as they have advocated and financed industrialization, education, and international information and commodity exchange. In many ways, these development programs have helped to change the face of much of the non-Western world.[28]

Other strong proponents of developmental idealism have been the civil rights movement, the women's movement, and numerous family-planning organizations. The abolitionist movement of the 1800s and the civil rights movement of the 1900s were particularly powerful in advocating racial freedom and equality. Organized feminists were effective in the late 1800s, early 1900s, and late 1900s in advocating and spreading the core developmental idealism principles of equality and freedom. Also, as noted earlier, the international family planning movement has been especially powerful in the last half of the 1900s in mobilizing national and international groups and governmental agencies to spread the developmental idealism beliefs concerning family planning and small families. A movement related to both the family planning

27. See Bernard and Gruzinski 1996/1986; Caldwell 1982; Dozon 1996/1986; Lardinois 1996/1986; Locoh 1988; Mayhew 1941; O'Malley 1941; Pillai 1976b; Ross 1927; Watkins 2000.

28. See Amin 1989; Blaut 1993; Dahl and Rabo 1992; Kulick 1992; Latham 2000; Lerner 1958; Myrdal 1968; Pigg 1992.

and feminist movements has been the drive to allow a woman the right to terminate an unwanted pregnancy.

Through these various mechanisms the ideas of developmental idealism have been widely disseminated both in Northwest Europe and in many other parts of the world, where they have for centuries been powerful forces for changing family ideologies and behaviors.[29] I move in the next section to a discussion of the changes that have been introduced through the spread of these ideas.

The Influence of Developmental Idealism

Although developmental idealism has been disseminated widely around the world, it is likely that its diffusion and mechanisms of influence have varied greatly across geographical and social locations. Developmental idealism, of course, originated in Northwest Europe and was embedded in the culture and social structure of this region, whereas it was, at least initially, foreign in other cultures and required dissemination across geographical, cultural, and linguistic boundaries. There were also great power and resource differentials between Northwest Europe and the rest of the world that substantially affected the way developmental idealism influenced family change. For these reasons, I discuss the Western and non-Western worlds separately. I turn first to the Western world.

Northwest Europe

One might at first glance conclude—incorrectly, as it turns out—that developmental idealism would have no effect on most Northwest European populations because these populations have defined what it means to be modern. The question then arises how developmental idealism could have provided models or motivations for change in these societies already defined as modern.

The answer is that all societies—including those of Northwest Europe—have both traditional and modern traits as defined here, with the mix varying among both individuals and groups within any society (Gasster 1968). As long as there is no system with which to evaluate these traits as inferior or superior, they remain simply traits, with no value ranking. But developmental idealism

29. See Amin 1989; Blaut 1993; Comaroff and Comaroff 1997; Dahl and Rabo 1992; Inkeles and Smith 1974; Kulick 1992; Myrdal 1968; Pigg 1992; Welch 1999.

provided a traditional/modern continuum that designated some traits as both traditional and inferior and others as both modern and superior. In this way the developmental paradigm became not just a scientific model but an ideology defining and ordering the various dimensions of life (J. C. Alexander 1995; Comaroff and Comaroff 1997; Latham 2000).

The placement of the modern traits of developmental idealism within the broad developmental model also causes them to be seen as part of the processes leading to Northwest European progress, both in the past and in the future. As a result, those elements of family life denoted as modern in developmental idealism take on an aura of inevitability that they would not have without the developmental paradigm and its conclusions.[30] Those aligned with developmental idealism, thus, have the comfort and legitimacy of knowing that the power of history is on their side while their opponents are left mentally swimming against the currents of history.

For all these reasons, developmental idealism tips the ideational and normative balance in favor of the familial traits it locates at the modern end of the continuum. In a powerful and subtle way, it provides to advocates of family patterns labeled modern an enormous ideational tool in their struggles with advocates of positions labeled traditional.

Two of the most important general themes of developmental idealism—freedom and equality—have been especially influential in the last 250 years. Numerous scholars have credited them with effecting important economic and political change.[31] They played pivotal roles in the French and American Revolutions, the abolitionist movement of the 1800s, and the civil rights movement of the 1900s. In fact, according to Tarrow (1998), they have become today the central forces framing and organizing social movements. More to the point for our purposes, the notions of freedom and equality were linked early and powerfully with change in family relationships. It should, therefore, not be surprising that many changes in family life that have occurred over the past 250 years can be attributed, at least in part, to

---

30. See Condorcet, n.d./1795; Hegel 1878/1837; Mill 1989a/1859, 1989c/1869; Spencer 1851. See also Baker 1990; Collini 1989; Degler 1980; Gordon 1994; Kraditor 1965; Löwith 1949; Nisbet 1980; Offen 2000; Rendall 1985, 1994.

31. See Ashcraft 1968, 1987; Bailyn 1967; Baker 1990; Bartlett 1988; Cott 2000; Cranston 1984; Ekirch 1951; Fliegelman 1982; Fox-Genovese 1987; Goodman 1994; Gordon 1994; Laslett 1988/1960; Leder 1968; Levy, Applewhite, and Johnson 1979; Macfarlane 2002; May 1976; Newman 1992; Offen 2000; Rendall 1985, 1994; Rotenstreich 1971; Tarcov 1984; Traer 1980; Wills 1978; Witte 1997; Wood 1969.

the influence of developmental idealism in general and the notions of freedom and equality in particular.[32] Among these are changes in women's roles and status, the shifting legal and normative acceptance of divorce, the increasing divorce rate, increases in independent living, and the increased acceptance and incidence of premarital sex, unmarried cohabitation, and childbearing outside of marriage.[33]

Of course, the political, familial, and economic systems of the Western world in the 1600s were deeply entrenched and had powerful forces supporting the status quo. Consequently, the family and political changes that have occurred during recent centuries have usually come as a result of extensive— sometimes violent—conflict and coercion.[34] The French and American Revolutions are part of this story of conflict, as is the struggle for racial equality and minority rights and the movement for equal rights for women. In addition, there continues today what some call a culture war over the family and the rights of individuals to decide for themselves issues about marriage, divorce, living arrangements, sex, childbearing, and gender roles (Hunter 1991).

Populations outside of Northwest Europe

As one would expect, developmental idealism has had a tremendous effect on family life in most non-Western populations where it has been spread and accepted. One reason for this is that these are the populations that have defined what it means to be traditional, with a substantial gap between them and the modern family and society defined by developmental idealism. Furthermore, developmental idealism specifies that the route to progress for non-Western peoples requires abandonment of at least some historical ways and adoption of at least some Western patterns.[35]

32. See Bartlett 1988; Cott 2000; Fox-Genovese 1987; Levy, Applewhite, and Johnson 1979; Offen 2000; Phillips 1988; Rendall 1985, 1994; Scott 1998; Shanley 1979; Smith 1990; Tarcov 1984; Thornton 1989; Thornton and Young-DeMarco 2001; Traer 1980; Veroff, Douvan, and Kulka 1981; Wilson 2002.

33. Not only has Smith (1990) identified the endorsement of individual choice and equal rights for all as the most important among post–World War II attitude changes, but, as we have seen in chapter 6, such changes overall have been so great as to prompt the identification of a *second demographic transition.*

34. See Abray 1975; Anthony 1897; Baker 1990; Degler 1980; Ekirch 1951; Foner 1970; Glendon 1977; Grossberg 1985; Hunter 1991; Kraditor 1965; Offen 2000; Phillips 1988; Rendall 1985; Schochet 1975; Traer 1980; Witte 1997.

35. See Ahearn 2001; Amin 1989; Blaut 1993; Kahn 2001; Knauft 2002b; Lee 1994; LiPuma 2000; Pigg 1992; Spitulnik 2002.

As developmental idealism has spread, non-Western populations have been given a choice between two conflicting models of family life: the indigenous family systems received from the ancestors and the modern family as defined by developmental idealism. The acceptance of developmental idealism among non-Western populations undermines indigenous family systems in that these systems are stigmatized as traditional, are associated with poor health and low living standards, and are seen as impediments to socioeconomic development. At the same time, the modern family of developmental idealism is associated with wealth, health, and the route to progress.[36] I turn now to the general conflict as it has been played out in various parts of the non-Western world.

The general conceptual conflict is illustrated well by the struggle on the African continent over the last hundred years or so concerning the nature of African culture and consciousness in the face of the cultural incursions of the West (Brock-Utne 2000; Comaroff and Comaroff 1991). Part of that struggle involves the issue of competing family forms: the indigenous African model, characterized particularly by large families, and the Western model, foreign to African culture because of its emphasis on such factors as not only small families, but also "personal choice of partner, primacy of the conjugal unit over the extended family, privileged care for immediate offspring, the sharing of property by the couple, and the ideal of monogamy" (Locoh 1988, 61; also see Comaroff and Comaroff 1997).[37] The distance between the two models is great, as has been resistance to the Western model (Comaroff and Comaroff 1991; Hetherington 2001).

One response to this conflict has been the creation of various intermediate models. Watkins (2000), for example, has identified a model that arose during the colonial period in Kenya, in which Kenyans accepted the ideology of the small family but rejected contraception as the means by which to attain it. Watkins has argued that in the most recent period the Western small-family model has become domesticated as a legitimate and powerful model within Kenya, but with Kenyans still using the English words to refer to the imported model of family planning. There has also been in recent years some movement in African urban and educated sectors toward having small families.[38]

36. See Abu-Lughod 1998a, 1998b; Ahearn 2001; Ahmed 2002; Hoodfar 2002; Inkeles and Smith 1974; Knauft 2002c; LiPuma 2000; Najmabadi 1998; Zafiri 2002.

37. On African familiy forms, see Bledsoe 1994; Caldwell 1982; Comaroff and Comaroff 1991; Dozon 1996/1986; Fuglesang 1992; Hetherington 2001; Locoh 1988; Ndeti and Ndeti 1980; Watkins 2000.

38. See Comaroff and Comaroff 1991; Dozon 1996/1986; Fuglesang 1992; Harwood-Lejeune 2001; Hetherington 2001; Watkins 2000.

Contrasts and competition between indigenous family systems and those of Northwest Europe have also been reported for Egypt, Iran, and Turkey.[39] Middle Eastern scholars in the 1800s and early 1900s wrote about the perceived backwardness of Middle Eastern family forms such as gender segregation, veils, arranged marriage, and extended households in contrast to the modern forms of developmental idealism in Europe. Furthermore, these writers noted the correlation between family forms and economic well-being, arguing that family reforms would be necessary for economic progress. Some of these arguments were translated into changes in family laws in order to bring social and economic development.

In many ways this competition between indigenous and Western family forms in the Middle East continues to the present. Western family patterns often motivate the familial and personal decisions of young people (Amin and Al-Bassusi 2002). At the same time, many people believe that the penetration of Western ideas and lifestyles is a problem. In fact, recent surveys (2000–2001) in Egypt, Jordan, and Iran reveal that between 55 and 85 percent of the people "considered cultural invasion by the West among very important problems facing their country" (Moaddel and Azadarmaki 2003, 73).

Competing family forms have also been described in India—an indigenous model and an English model. Beginning with British rule, and continuing to the present day, the indigenous model has been described in India as backward and a deterrent to social and economic development (Madan 2000). Under English influence, millions of Indian parents have over the years come to send their children to school to attain the advantages of a Western—in this case, a British—lifestyle, advantages popularized by the mass media (see Caldwell, Reddy, and Caldwell 1988). Changes—sometimes interpreted by Indians as "the advance of civilization"—introduced in the indigenous model as a result of Western influence include a perceived decline in the benefits of children relative to their costs, a partial transfer of authority from the older generation to the younger and from men to women, and the freedom to choose one's own spouse (Mody 2002).

Nepal, a neighbor to India, provides another example of the competition between two kinds of family systems. Many aspects of the world, including family and personal relationships, are now divided by Nepalis between those they perceive as backward or traditional and those they perceive as developed or modern, with this distinction being understood even in very remote parts

---

39. See Abu-Lughod 1998a, 1998b; Cuno 2003a; Fahmy 1998; Kandiyoti 1998; Moaddel 1992, 2005; Najmabadi 1998; Shakry 1998; Starr 1989.

of the country (Ahearn 2001; Pigg 1992). Many Nepalis define as traditional such family traits as arranged and capture marriage, coerced choice of spouse, extended households, and working in family enterprises, while the developed model is characterized by love marriage, free choice of spouse, nuclear households, and working in factories and other nonfamily enterprises (Ahearn 2001).

Crucially important in Nepal is that many people now believe that there is a causal linkage between economic success and the modern family (Ahearn 2001). This belief has likely contributed to increases in the choice of one's own spouse, companionate marriage, and love letters in Nepal.[40]

Ahearn (2001) has suggested that even the labeling of family practices in Nepal as uncivilized is a powerful force for change. She described a long-standing practice of daily feet washing of the husband by the wife that has declined sharply in a Nepali village because it now fits less well with daily practices, because of growing embarrassment among women in doing it, and because husbands tell their wives that it is uncivilized and not to perform it.

Similar examples of the power of language in the competition between various models of family life can be found in other places. For example, an Israeli woman, the daughter of Indian immigrants, summed up a competition among Indian, Moroccan, and Egyptian immigrants to be the most modern by saying: "No one wanted to be primitive" (cited in Goldscheider 2002, 130). Similarly, female circumcision has been attacked in Nigeria as "a cultural/traditional heritage that should be discarded, as it is barbaric" (Aziz 2002, 595). In addition, a Kenyan Christian speaking at a funeral noted: "Now although I am a polygamist, I am a civilized polygamist," apparently wanting to reduce the stigma of polygamy and to legitimize himself as a modern person.[41]

Abundant evidence suggests that the effects of developmental idealism extend well beyond a conceptual conflict between family models to changes in family life itself. We know that in many parts of the non-Western world there have been dramatic changes in family processes and structures.[42] Many, but

---

40. See esp. Ahearn 2001; but also Fricke 1997b; Fricke et al. 1991; Fricke, Thornton, and Dahal 1998; Ghimire et al. 2002.

41. From field notes taken by Rebecca Thornton in the Busia District, Kenya, June 2002. An interesting parallel to these three examples is a mother who, in the 1830s in the United States, "described any action she might take to thwart her daughter's choice [in marriage] as 'barberous,' [*sic*] literally uncivilized" (Lystra 1989, 159).

42. See Abbasi-Shavazi 2000b; Abbasi-Shavazi et al. 2002; Ahearn 2001; Amin and Al-Bassusi 2002; Audinarayana and Krishnamoorthy 2000; Banister 1987; Beillevaire 1996/1986; Bernard and Gruzinski 1996/1986; Bledsoe and Cohen 1993; Caldwell 1993; Caldwell, Reddy, and Caldwell

not all (Amin and Cain 1997; Caldwell, Reddy, and Caldwell 1988), of these changes have been along the lines predicted by the international spread of developmental idealism. These changes include moving from extended to nuclear households, from familism to individualism; from early to late marriage, from universal marriage to the potential for extensive celibacy, from parental control to youthful independence, from arranged marriages to love matches, and from natural fertility to controlled fertility.

Although most changes in family patterns outside the West have clearly been along the lines predicted by developmental idealism, interpretation of changes in the status of women is less clear. One reason for this is that the concept of women's status is relatively ambiguous and subject to different interpretations. In the Northwest European world of the 1700s, high female status meant a fairly strict family division of labor with women primarily responsible for activities in and around the home and men primarily responsible for agricultural and other economic activities away from the house. With industrialization, this distinction between male and female roles became even more marked.

In parts of the non-Western world, by contrast, women were historically more involved with such nonhome economic activities as farming and trading, and men were more involved with other activities such as hunting and fishing (see chapter 3). Europeans of the 1700s and 1800s viewed such arrangements with disdain and felt that reform was needed, since to them the non-Western pattern indicated low status of women and slothfulness on the part of men. Efforts to push non-Western gender relationships in the direction of Western ones met with some success (Boserup 1971/1970; Comaroff and Comaroff 1991, 1997; Coontz 1991/1988).

However, it is not clear whether these changes increased or depressed the status of women. If the gender division of labor along the lines prevailing in the West in the 1700s and 1800s is employed as the standard of high female status, then such changes as did occur in the non-Western world were in the direction of improved status for women. However, if individual autonomy and

---

1988; Cartier 1996/1986; Casterline 1994; Chackiel and Schkolnik 1996; Chesnais 1992; Cohen 1993; Comaroff and Comaroff 1991, 1997; Freeze 2002; Friedl 2003; Ghimire et al. 2002; Goode 1970/1963; Guengant 1996; Guzmán 1996; Harwood-Lejeune 2001; Hetherington 2001; Hull and Hull 1997; Jones 1997; Kaufman 1983; Lardinois 1996/1986; LiPuma 2000; McCaa 1994a, 1994b, 2003; McDonald 1985; Mehryar et al. 2000; Raymo 1998; Rele and Alam 1993; Thornton and Lin 1994; van de Walle 1993.

control of economic resources constitute the standard for high status for women, then those changes may have worsened women's status because they reduced female nonhome economic activity, which, in turn, deprived women of the autonomy and economic control they had previously enjoyed. Boserup (1971/1970, 1990) suggests that this is exactly what happened in many parts of the world, including large parts of Africa. Ahmad (2002) suggests a similar result in the Philippines under Spanish rule.

Of course, developmental idealism, like any commodity or idea, cannot be exported willy-nilly, but must also be imported, ignored, resisted, modified, accommodated, or hybridized according to the circumstances and conditions existing in a specific non-Western setting.[43] Although virtually all non-Western people have come into contact with developmental idealism, they have had to respond from their own perspectives and understandings. Although there have been examples of quick and simple acceptance, sophisticated evaluation, resistance, and adaptation have been more frequent responses. The adaptation process occurs as the component ideas of developmental idealism are incorporated into an existing set of cultural values and economic and social relationships (Taylor 1999), requiring an adjustment and integration of both the existing culture and the newly introduced culture.

The reactions of non-Western people to developmental idealism have, of course, been contingent upon the characteristics of the non-Western population and the nature of its interactions with Western societies. Relevant elements of a non-Western society include its religious and cultural heritage, its social and economic organization, its historical experience, and its political, economic, and military power. Given the differences among cultures worldwide, the process of adjustment to and integration with developmental idealism will inevitably differ among cultures, resulting in a variety of hybrid forms (Kahn 2001; Lee 1994; Taylor 1999).

Among the important external factors relevant to reactions to developmental idealism in non-Western countries are historical and contemporary relationships with Western governments. Of particular importance are communication and interaction networks, the cultural traditions of the Westerners involved, and the economic and power differentials among the

---

43. See Abu-Lughod 1998a, 1998b; Ahearn 2001; Benefo 1999; Cammack, Young, and Heaton 1996; Comaroff and Comaroff 1991; Dussel 1995/1992; Hannerz 1987; Hetherington 2001; Lee 1994; Lerner 1958; LiPuma 2000; Mody 2002; Stromquist 1999; Sullivan 1998; Taylor 1999; Warwick 1982.

actors. Also relevant is the extent to which Western powers actively try to change indigenous patterns through incentives and military force.[44]

There are, of course, many reasons for non-Westerners to resist Western forms of family life, not the least of which is that, as a foreign import, developmental idealism does not fit well with indigenous social forms and cultural values, often running counter to them. Sometimes resistance to family change was sufficiently strong that it could not be put down without the use of physical force (Comaroff and Comaroff 1991; Hetherington 2001), and, in some cases, opposition to Western forms became the rallying point for mobilization of a more general revolt (Hetherington 2001).

All of these considerations suggest that the spread and influence of developmental idealism are both contingent and path dependent. Although global and local environments and forces may constrain choices, there is considerable contingency in the pathways taken.[45]

Developmental Idealism and Theories of Change

My argument that developmental idealism is an important motivational force behind family change is consistent with many critiques of previous research and calls for new directions in theorizing. Although many of these critiques have noted a general or rough correspondence between family change and changes in such structural factors as economic organization, rural-urban population distribution, and educational attainment, the correspondence has not been precise or direct. This has led many to argue that cultural or ideational components are important and must be included in theories of family change.[46]

My emphasis on the ideational forces of developmental idealism is also consistent with the conclusions of Ronald Freedman (1979, 1987), John Caldwell (1982), and Dirk van de Kaa (1996) about the importance of the spread of

44. Although I am mainly interested in the flow of influence from the West to other places, Western societies also are often altered as they come into contact with other cultural and social systems.

45. For a broader discussion of contingency and path dependence, see Axtell 1981; Casterline 1999; Quadagno and Knapp 1992; Sewell 1996; Warwick 1982.

46. See Bongaarts and Watkins 1996; Caldwell 1982, 1999, 2001; Caldwell and Caldwell 1997; Chesnais 1992; Cleland and Wilson 1987; Freedman 1979, 1987; Knodel and van de Walle 1979; Lesthaeghe 1983; Lesthaeghe and Wilson 1986; Mason 1997a; Pritchett 1994; Szreter 1993; Woods 1987.

Western ideas for family change. My framework, however, adds something that is missing from the arguments of Caldwell, Freedman, and van de Kaa—a reason why the non-Western world would even begin to care about, let alone be powerfully influenced by, Western ideas of family and reproductive behavior. It is the desire for social and economic improvement and the intellectual connection of the good life with Western family forms that motivates non-Westerners to adopt Western family patterns. Without these aspirations and the intellectual connections between Western family ways and the good life, it is easy to believe that many outside the West would be repulsed by the Western family system rather than motivated to adopt its ways. That is, Western family ways are not inherently appealing to all, but have their attraction primarily through their connection with health, wealth, power, and progress.

This emphasis on ideational explanations is consistent with Goode's classic study (1970/1963) of family change around the world. Although Goode's explanation of family change can properly be thought of as structural, emphasizing as it does the reconfiguration of social relations generally by industrialization, urbanization, new forms of economic specialization, and geographical and social mobility, he also recognizes the importance in this process of such ideas as economic progress, the conjugal family versus the extended family, technological change, and egalitarianism. These ideas, according to Goode, often enter a society before structural changes, affect changes independently of structural forces, and accelerate change beyond the impetus provided by structural forces alone.

Goode argued that as of several hundred years ago there was a diversity of family systems that subsequently became more like the family forms in the West of the middle 1900s. Although Goode emphasized such things as industrialization and urbanization as the main motors of this convergence, it is not obvious why the social and economic organization associated with industrial society would produce such uniformity when agricultural society did not. It seems likely that ideational influences and the fact that many people have consciously modeled the West—or have been coerced in that direction—have had a substantial role in any such convergence.

Note that the theorized role of developmental idealism in family change is at least partially consistent with a number of other approaches. These include Greenhalgh's political economy approach (1990, 1993), which takes account of international actors and interests, differential power relations, and political, economic, and military influence over time, and the proposal by Watkins and her colleagues that communication networks and interactions between global and local actors must be considered (Bongaarts and Watkins 1996; Watkins

2000; Watkins and Hodgson 1998). The suggested importance of developmental idealism in family change is also consistent with the theories of the diffusion literature involving social transmission, learning, and influence.[47]

I do not claim that only ideational explanations matter when dealing with family change. Any comprehensive explanation of family change must consider structural explanations, including explication of the ways in which ideational and structural forces intersect to influence family change. My goal here has not been to provide a comprehensive theory of family change but simply to show how developmental idealism is a central component of any such comprehensive theory.

It is ironic that developmental idealism may provide a directionality to history that was not previously present. To the extent that people believe that the propositions of developmental idealism are valid, they have a goal or model to guide their behavior in a specific direction. That is, developmental idealism may very well have become a self-fulfilling prophecy with particular goals and endpoints.

It should be noted, however, that the directionality of change produced by developmental idealism is not teleological, as the developmental model was in the scholarly analyses of the 1700s and 1800s. This directionality is, rather, the result of contingent human choices based on real aspirations, knowledge, beliefs, resources, and constraints.

I turn in the next several chapters to a detailed discussion of the ways in which developmental idealism has influenced changes in family life around the world. The next two chapters deal with the Western world, later chapters with the non-Western world.

47. See Casterline 2001; Montgomery and Casterline 1993; Rogers 1973; Rosero-Bixby and Casterline 1993.

9

Freedom, Equality, and Consent in Northwest European Family Relationships

In this chapter and the next, I trace in detail some of the ways in which developmental idealism has influenced changes in Western family forms. I begin with a discussion of the role that political idealism—the new drive for freedom, equality, and consent—played in revolution and regime change. Then I move to the influence of developmental idealism on family forms per se, dealing first with gender relations, next with marriage and divorce, and finally with parent-child relationships. In the next chapter, I discuss some ways that developmental idealism has been used as an ideological tool to attack nonmainstream family forms in the United States.

Political Idealism and Regime Change

For centuries, most Northwest Europeans had believed that descriptions of life at the origins of humanity could be found in the Bible, where family and political relationships were characterized by considerable inequality and authoritarian parents and sovereigns. Most also accepted that such relationships represented God's will and that the way things were in the beginning of time was the way they should continue to be.[1]

As we saw in chapter 2, in the 1500s and 1600s, John Locke and like-minded people relocated the origin of humanity from that described in the Bible to a state of nature predating society and government, with revolutionary results for families and governments.[2] Mankind in this state of

---

1. See Condorcet, n.d./1795; Filmer 1949/1680; Montesquieu 1997/1748; Wollstonecraft 1975/1792. See also Beard 1946; Butler 1978; Cott 2000; Hunt 1994; Nicholson 1986; Schochet 1975; Shanley 1979; Tarcov 1984; Traer 1980.

2. See Hobbes 1996/1651; Locke 1988/1690; Rousseau 1984/1755, 1997/1762. See also Beard 1946; Berkhofer 1978; Lehmann 1979/1960; Nisbet 1980.

nature was believed to be free and equal, and society was believed to have been formed through the free consent of individual human agents as they contracted to live in a community of people with government and laws. Given the belief that the way things were originally was the way they should continue to be, it was only a small leap for these writers to conclude that, in forming societies and governments, mankind retained from the state of nature the natural rights of freedom, consent, and equality.[3]

Of course, the ideas of freedom, consent, and equality date to much earlier than the 1500s and 1600s. However, the political implications of this new emphasis on these principles were revolutionary because most governments fell well short of according their citizens freedom, consent, and equality. Because of the revolutionary nature of these ideas, some authors experienced severe political persecutions.[4] Consequently, many of them were careful both about what they said and about how openly they associated their names with their works. Nevertheless, despite the caution and persecution, the ideas of freedom, consent, and equality spread rapidly (Ashcraft 1987; Baker 1990).

Rousseau provided a particularly vivid and powerful—although exaggerated—description of the disconnect between theory and reality when he opened his *Social Contract* with the ringing challenge: "Man is born free, and everywhere he is in chains" (1997/1762, 41). Rousseau suggested that in order for mankind to regain the freedom that it originally possessed, it would have to transform and renew the social order (Rousseau 1984/1755, 1997/1762; see also Cranston 1983, 1984, 1991; Gourevitch 1997). Over the last half of the 1700s, the ideas of freedom, equality, and the right of active rebellion were echoed by numerous writers and became part of public consciousness.[5]

The ideological influence of these forces on the American and French Revolutions is easily distinguished in the classic documents of those revolutions, including the American Declaration of Independence and the French Declaration of the Rights of Man and of the Citizen. These documents literally boomed the message of the inalienable rights of human beings to liberty, equality, and the right to dissent (Wills 1978). In addition,

3. See Ashcraft 1987; Baker 1990; Myres 1916; Schochet 1975; Tarcov 1984. It is also useful to note that Locke also argued against the ideas of hierarchy, dictatorial government, and family power using the Bible itself. Thus, the Bible was open to multiple interpretations and could itself be used to defend the ideas of freedom and equality.

4. On the persecution of writers holding revolutionary ideas, see Ashcraft 1987, 1968; Betts 1973; Cranston 1983, 1991; Laslett 1988/1960; Macpherson 1962; Meek 1976.

5. See, e.g., Paine 1984/1791–92. See also Ashcraft 1968; Bailyn 1967; Baker 1990; Cott 2000; Cranston 1984; Fuller 1941/1845; Leder 1968; Nisbet 1980; Schochet 1975; Traer 1980; Wills 1978.

the long list of charges against the English monarch in the Declaration of Independence included the accusation of "cruelty and perfidy scarcely paralleled in the most barbarous ages, and totally unworthy the head of a civilized nation" (quoted in Wills 1978, 377). The ideas of development influenced the American Revolution in other ways as well. One particularly important line of thinking was built on the Northwest European family life course, where children were seen as dependent on their parents' resources and subject to their authority only until they reached adulthood, at which point they established their own households and exercised their own authority. By analogy England was held to be the mother and colonial America the child ready to make the transition from adolescence to independent adulthood (Cott 2000; Fliegelman 1982). A related line of thinking was the perceived domestic tyranny of England the parent, a tyranny so bad that it justified America the child in declaring its independence. The relationship between England and America was also sometimes compared to a marriage that had gone sour (Cott 2000; Fliegelman 1982).

Many of the American colonists applied the developmental metaphor of growth and decline to England. Although they believed that England and America were already very advanced societies, they were also optimistic that even greater progress could be attained (Hume 1825/1742; Millar 1979/1779; see also Ekirch 1951). At the same time, many of the colonists believed that societies could regress as well as advance. Some perceived in England signs of corruption and worried that, like Rome, it had begun to decline and would eventually fall (Bailyn 1967; Ekirch 1951; May 1976; Wood 1969). Some colonists mixed this worry about England with optimism about America, suggesting that the leading edge of progress was shifting across the Atlantic from Europe to America, where, if nourished properly, it would carry America to even greater heights (Paine 1879/1776, 1984/1791–92; see also Nisbet 1980; Wood 1969).

These developmental ideas also motivated the French Revolution. Society was to be renewed, and the forces of history would carry France to new heights of liberty and equality, setting an example for the rest of the world (Condorcet, n.d./1795; see also Baker 1990). In subsequent centuries, freedom and equality have been advocated in many places as forces that would bring social and economic progress, and these principles have been enshrined in numerous constitutions as basic human rights.[6]

---

6. See Condorcet, n.d./1795; Hume 1825/1742; Mill 1989b/1859–69; Paine 1984/1791–92; Stimson 1886–92. See also Baker 1990.

Developmental Idealism and Gender Relations

As was noted in chapter 3, Northwest Europe had a long history of giving priority of decision making and control to men rather than to women. But this gender division of authority and opportunity was strongly challenged by the ideas of developmental idealism. The roots of the women's movement can be traced directly to the Enlightenment, and developmental arguments permeated and energized the movement through the 1800s and persisted through the 1900s. In this section, I highlight some of the ways in which developmental thinking and conclusions influenced the course of events.

The Principles of Freedom, Equality, and Consent

I begin with John Locke because his work has been considered an important source of ideas for the women's movement,[7] particularly his conclusions about freedom, equality, and consent as they apply to marriage. According to Locke (1988/1690), men and women come to marriage as equals, and this equality persists throughout the marriage relationship, applying to all circumstances except the practical problem of a disagreement between husband and wife, in which case the husband's superior strength gives him the deciding vote. Despite this substantial limitation, Locke's position was revolutionarily feminist, especially when judged by the standards of the day. In addition, Locke extended the long-standing practice of husband and wife consenting to form a marriage to permit them to decide both the nature of gender roles in their marriage and how long their marriage would last. This explicitly challenged the idea that marriage was indissoluble—or dissoluble only in certain limited circumstances.

Of course, Locke's statements were prescriptive, not descriptive. In actual fact, the terms of marriage in Northwest Europe at the time made the union nearly indissoluble and privileged husbands over wives. Nevertheless, Locke provided a set of principles that would become increasingly powerful and persuasive and would drive the women's movement for centuries. For example, the call for gender freedom and equality is evident in many major and influential pronouncements and programs during the past several centuries, including the 1791 French Declaration of the Rights of Women (Levy,

---

7. See Abray 1975; Butler 1978; Fliegelman 1982; Kraditor 1965; Laslett 1988/1960; Okin 1982; Shanley 1979; Zagarri 1998. I do not, however, mean to suggest that Locke was the first feminist writer. He was not (Hufton 1995), but he was an especially important figure in the feminist movement, his arguments having shaped feminism for centuries.

Applewhite, and Johnson 1979), the 1848 Seneca Falls Declaration of Sentiments (Hole and Levine 1984), and the American Equal Rights Amendment (Boles 1979; see also Abray 1975).

The contradictions between Locke's prescriptions about marriage and women's actual position in the marriage relationship soon led to significant protest. Early in the 1700s, Mary Astell (1970/1730, 107) explicitly challenged the legitimacy of gender inequality and the existing authority structure, asking the simple, tough, and penetrating question: "If *all Men are born Free,* how is it that all Women are born Slaves?" This challenge to male privilege and dominance has been the central theme of feminist arguments ever since. Even the rhetoric of "female slavery"—referring to the restriction of women's self-governance in any relationship—would figure importantly into the late 1900s.[8]

Civilization and the Advancement of Women's Rights and Autonomy

The feminist literature of the 1700s and 1800s also relied on ideas and conclusions about history drawn from the developmental paradigm and reading history sideways.[9] Arguments were built directly on the understanding that there had been long-term improvements in the status and autonomy of women. The fact that future progress was not guaranteed justified mobilization of efforts to ensure additional improvements in women's status.

Many writers of the era applied the charge of barbarism—a particularly powerful accusation—to the conditions of women in Northwest Europe, although at the same time believing that conditions there were better than elsewhere and had improved over time.[10] They believed that it was the duty

8. See W. Alexander 1995/1779; Fuller 1941/1845; Grimké 1988/1838; Macaulay 1974/1790; Mill 1989c/1869; Millar 1979/1779; Montesquieu 1997/1748; Price 1776; Thompson and Wheeler 1994/1825; Wollstonecraft 1975/1792. See also Bartlett 1988; Berger and Berger 1984; Brace 2000; Collini 1989; Conklin 1974; Cott 2000; Degler 1980; Levy, Applewhite, and Johnson 1979; Offen 2000; Rendall 1985.

The rhetoric of slavery was used to condemn any relationship where agency was restricted, including limitations on political freedom and the choice of a spouse by parents (Grimké 1988/1838; Hume 1825/1742; Montesquieu 1997/1748; Price 1776; also see Conklin 1974; Cott 2000; Fox-Genovese 1987). In addition, many of the leaders of the women's movement were active as well in the abolitionist movement (Fuller 1941/1845; Grimké 1988/1838; Hole and Levine 1971, 1984; Kraditor 1965; Offen 2000).

9. See Fox-Genovese 1987; Kraditor 1965; Offen 2000; Rendall 1985, 1994; Tomaselli 1985; Traer 1980.

10. See W. Alexander 1995/1779; Fuller 1941/1845; Grimké 1988/1838; Mill 1989c/1869; Paine 1984/1791–92; Spencer 1851; Thompson and Wheeler 1994/1825; Wollstonecraft 1975/1792. See also Cott 2000; Levy, Applewhite, and Johnson 1979; Phillips 1988; Rendall 1985, 1994; Tomaselli 1985.

of people in this enlightened era in Northwest Europe to shake off the last remnants of barbarism and treat women with the respect and status they deserved in a civilized society.

Some feminist writers linked women's status and overall societal progress so tightly that they argued that the status of women was not only an outcome of development but an indicator of a society's progress.[11] Alexander (1995/1779, 1:151), for example, claimed:

> On this account, we shall almost constantly find women among savages condemned to every species of servile, or rather, of slavish drudgery; and shall as constantly find them emerging from this state, in the same proportion as we find the men emerging from ignorance and brutality; the rank, therefore, and condition, in which we find women in any country, mark out to us with the greatest precision, the exact point in the scale of civil society, to which the people of such country have arrived; and were their history entirely silent on every other subject, and only mentioned the manner in which they treated their women, we would, from thence, be enabled to form a tolerable judgment of the barbarity, or culture of their manners.

John Stuart Mill (1989c/1869, 138) repeated this position nearly a century later: "Experience does say, that every step in improvement has been so invariably accompanied by a step made in raising the social position of women, that historians and philosophers have been led to adopt their elevation or debasement as on the whole the surest test and most correct measure of the civilisation of a people or an age."

Improvement in the status of women was also considered a cause of development and progress generally.[12] It was believed, for example, that improved status would allow women to have a more positive influence on their children and to play a greater role in the larger society. This notion was expressed especially eloquently by Mill (1989c/1869, 195), who was of the opinion that if women were not tyrannized by men, "society must already have reached a paradisiacal state."[13]

11. See Fox-Genovese 1987; Goodman 1994; Offen 2000; Rendall 1985; Tomaselli 1985.

12. See W. Alexander 1995/1779; Anthony 1897; Condorcet, n.d./1795; Grimké 1988/1838; Lieber 1876/1838; Mill 1989c/1869; Stanton 1900. See also Baker 1975; Beard 1946; Goodman 1994; Offen 2000; Rendall 1985.

13. Mill's work is considered particularly influential in the expansion and success of the women's movement in the late 1800s and early 1900s (see Beard 1946; Offen 2000; Rendall 1985, 1994). And his *Subjection of Women* remains powerful to this day.

The literature about the rights of women and their place in the progress of humankind was widely disseminated in the 1800s (Zagarri 1998). The ideas in this literature powered a women's movement that affected all of the Northwest European world (Cott 1994; DuBois 1994; Offen 2000). This movement was especially active in the late 1800s and early 1900s—and then again in the late 1900s. The various phases of the movement have mobilized substantial energy and activity, as well as considerable opposition. As a minimum, the movement has greatly publicized issues of female freedom and equality and has probably been successful in modifying the course of history (Anthony 1897; Degler 1980; Hole and Levine 1984).

Changes in Women's Status and Rights

Although it is hard to identify the causes of long-term trends precisely, it is clear that the last three hundred years have seen dramatic changes in the status and rights of women in Northwest Europe (Anthony 1897; Degler 1980). For example, women can now vote and own property. Wives have a legal and community identity separate from that of their husbands. The number of women participating in the paid labor force has increased dramatically in recent years,[14] and women increasingly hold important and well-paying jobs. Differential treatment based on gender is generally met with disapproval, although earnings differentials between men and women do still exist (Goldin 1990). Women are also much more involved in politics and government, holding offices at all levels in some countries. Their education attainment is now very similar to that of men, with women attending college and graduate and professional schools in substantial numbers (Bianchi and Spain 1986). And attitudes about women's roles in society generally have become increasingly egalitarian, especially in the last half century, and probably prior to that, although data deficiencies make it hard to document earlier trends (Thornton 1989; Thornton and Young-DeMarco 2001).

Developmental Idealism and Divorce

An important extension in Northwest Europe of the Lockean ideas of freedom and consent to family relationships was the right of individuals to terminate a marriage. The indissolubility of marriage had long been a principle in Northwest Europe, but Locke challenged that principle as an inappropriate

---

14. See Bianchi and Spain 1986; Davis 1984; Goldin 1990; Goldscheider and Waite 1991; Spain and Bianchi 1996.

constraint on the principles of freedom and consent (W. Alexander 1995/1779; Hume 1825/1742; Mill 1989c/1869).

Consent in the Initiation and Termination of Marriage

The notion of consent was generally consistent with the way in which marriages had been initiated in Northwest Europe for centuries. Young couples were themselves largely responsible for introductions, courtship, engagement, and entrance into marriage.[15] Marriage was, moreover, a sacrament in the Catholic Church that the couple administered to themselves.[16] As one would expect, parents, friends, and the larger community were often actively involved, for example, setting the overall terms of the marriage, monitoring the marriage process, and arranging the home and economic unit.[17] Nevertheless, the couple's consent was fundamental.[18]

The point at which the notion of consent found itself in conflict with the marriage system of Northwest Europe was when it came to the dissolution of marriage. That marriage was indissoluble had been a central tenant of the Catholic Church from about 1200 on.[19] With the Protestant Reformation came the acceptance of divorce, but only in very limited sets of circumstances (Phillips 1988; Witte 1997). Marriage continued to be viewed legally, socially, and religiously as a lifetime commitment.[20] Clearly, Lockean principles were fundamentally at odds with the notion of indissoluble marriage.

The contradictions between the notion of indissoluble marriage and those of freedom and consent remain to this day the subject of considerable discussion, the terms of which have been remarkably consistent across more than three centuries. Numerous writers suggested that indissoluble marriage violated the principles of freedom, consent, and equality.[21] Some said that,

15. See Brundage 1987, 1993; Donahue 1976, 1983; Gillis 1985; Hanawalt 1986; Macfarlane 1986; Murray 1998; Pollock and Maitland 1968; Rothman 1984; Sheehan 1971, 1991a, 1991b.

16. See Burguière 1987; Murray 1998; Rheinstein 1972; Sheehan 1971; Witte 1997.

17. See Brundage 1987; Chaytor 1980; Donahue 1976; Gillis 1985; Gottlieb 1980; Hanawalt 1986, 1993; Haskell 1973; McSheffrey 1998; Nicholas 1985; O'Hara 1991, 2000; Rothman 1984; D. S. Smith 1978.

18. See Brundage 1987; Chaytor 1980; Donahue 1976, 1983; Gottlieb 1980; McSheffrey 1998; O'Hara 1991; Pollock and Maitland 1968; Sheehan 1971.

19. See Hanawalt 1986; Howard 1904; Phillips 1988; Pollock and Maitland 1968; Rheinstein 1972; Whitelock 1952.

20. See Howard 1904; Phillips 1988; Weitzman 1981; Witte 1997.

21. See W. Alexander 1995/1779; Hume 1825/1742; Mill 1989c/1869; Montesquieu 1973/1721; Rousseau 1984/1755; Thompson and Wheeler 1994/1825. See also Phillips 1988; Rendall 1985; Traer 1980.

in doing so, it restricted love, happiness, and dignity (e.g., A. Smith 1978/1762–63; see also Traer 1980). However, the movement toward the liberalization of divorce laws was slow as many people continued to believe that divorce would have negative consequences, not just for adults, but also, and more importantly, for children. Even some of those who recognized the value of allowing couples to dissolve a marriage, such as Hume (1825/1742) and A. Smith (1978/1762–63), opposed divorce because of these perceived negative consequences for children.

Although the availability of divorce was sometimes viewed as a necessary mechanism to give women equality and protection from abusive relationships, divorce did not, at first, receive the full support of everyone in the women's movement. In fact, the tensions between divorce as a solution to women's problems and as a cause of personal and family difficulties split the women's movement in the 1900s (Phillips 1988). This issue also remains at the center of many family debates in the 2000s.

The existence of gender inequality in marriage and the difficulty in terminating an unsatisfactory marriage also led to a critique of marriage itself (Grimké 1988/1838; Mill 1989c/1869; see also Hole and Levine 1971). The basic argument was that any institution that violated the principles of equality and freedom was problematic—thereby calling into question the value of marriage. This association of marriage with inequality and subservience has persisted for more than a century, undermining faith in the institution. This theme became particularly salient in the 1960s and 1970s, when some portrayed marriage as not only being in need of reform, but as a fundamentally negative institution that hurt many people, especially women.[22] This perspective has received widespread attention in the United States, and only recently has it been seriously challenged.[23]

22. See Berger and Berger 1984; Bernard 1982/1972; England 2000; Hart 1972; Hole and Levine 1971.

23. A substantial body of empirical research in recent years has seriously questioned the proposition that marriage is bad for people. Numerous studies have now found that married people—both women and men—experience better physical and mental health, greater financial success, more satisfying sex lives, less violence, and greater satisfaction with life than do single people. Although the causal mechanisms producing such marital status differences have not been settled, there is growing evidence that marriage is a causal force increasing social, economic, and emotional well-being. For recent discussions of these issues, see England 2000; Glenn 1997; Stanton 1997; Trost 1981; Waite 1995; Waite and Gallagher 2000; Waite et al. 2000.

Changes in Law, Attitudes, and Behavior regarding Divorce

Although the reform of divorce laws was generally a slow and laborious process, the French Revolution of 1789 provides a remarkable example of the power of the message of freedom, consent, and equality when the social institutions protecting historical patterns are in disarray. The primary ideological themes of the French Revolution, freedom and equality, were applied to both the public and the family spheres, and, in a few short years after the Revolution, these principles were being enacted into French family law. For example, where marriage had previously been legally indissoluble, in 1792 a permissive no-fault divorce law was passed that had virtually no restrictions on divorce. In addition, the revolutionaries passed laws restricting the influence of parents and the church over marriage and providing for the equal treatment of children within families, in terms of both legitimacy and inheritance (Traer 1980). The Revolution also emphasized the equality of men and women but apparently passed no substantial legislation in this regard (Hufton 1995; Traer 1980). French history took an uneven course following the Revolution. By the early 1830s the changes in family law had been largely undone, with a return in 1816 to indissoluble marriage (Phillips 1988; Traer 1980).

It is difficult to evaluate the causes of the dramatic changes in family law following the French Revolution, but both Traer and Phillips did so using the language of developmental idealism. They suggested that the changes were the result of the revolutionaries believing that modern families are not only good and attainable but should be achieved immediately. Traer (1980, 16), for example, found that "'modern' marriage and family developed out of the literature and criticism of the French Enlightenment": "Freedom of choice and affection were to be the basic elements of the modern marriage. Husband and wife were to be equals, and children more nearly equal to parents." Similarly, Phillips (1988, 190) indicated: "It might be unhistorical to refer to an innovation as having been in advance of its time, but in the context of the history of divorce in Western society, the French divorce law of 1792 certainly was that. We cannot but be struck by the modernity of that law. Its liberal terms ... are only now, two centuries later, being matched by national divorce policies and legislation in the Western world."

The experience of France suggests that, when opposition to developmental idealism is in disarray—as it was during the Revolution—the principles of freedom, consent, and equality have the power to rapidly overturn historical family patterns in existence for centuries. That experience also suggests, however, that old patterns can be quickly reinstated once the opposing forces mobilize and gain the upper hand. In addition, in more normal, settled times, the legal implementation of the ideas of developmental idealism takes substantially longer. As Phillips (1988) points out, it took two hundred years to achieve again the changes in family law that the Revolution had wrought in a mere two or three.

The Revolution and its dramatic family law changes had contradictory effects on the subsequent history of family changes in France. They likely prompted a conservative backlash (see Phillips 1988; Offen 2000), but, at the same time, they made the larger public aware of the applicability of the ideas of freedom, consent, and equality to family life, thus setting the stage for sub-sequent, more long-lasting change.[24]

The argument for developmental idealism affecting family law in revolutionary times is bolstered by the reform of divorce laws in the United States following the American Revolution. Cott (2000), for example, suggested that the revolutionary ideals of freedom and consent prompted a string of divorce law reforms in the new United States that made it easier to end a marriage (see also Coontz 1991/1988; Phillips 1988; Shammas 1995). The American divorce law reforms were less dramatic but more permanent than those fol-lowing the French Revolution.

There has been a general movement toward the liberalization of divorce laws throughout Northwest Europe since the 1600s—part of a long-term movement away from state and community regulation of intimate behavior (see Schneider 1985)—culminating in the truly remarkable changes of the 1800s and, especially, the 1900s.[25] By the late 1900s, divorce had become very easy to obtain in many jurisdictions. For example, no-fault divorce laws— first introduced in the United States in 1969—had by the late 1970s been adopted by almost every state in the Union (Freed and Foster 1980; Glendon 1976), and similar trends were observed in Europe (Phillips 1988).

Associated with these legal changes have been changes in attitudes toward divorce. Although data deficiencies prevent direct documentation of divorce attitudes prior to the mid-1900s, it is likely that those attitudes were becom-ing more liberal. And in the last half of the 1900s the liberalization of atti-tudes toward divorce has been remarkable.[26] The centuries-old tension

24. See Hufton 1995; Levy, Applewhite, and Johnson 1979; Traer 1980; Varenne 1996/1986.

25. Of course, changes in divorce law depended on location and were not always in the direc-tion of liberalization. Still, Phillips (1988) notes a general trend toward an acceptance of the dis-solubility of marriage. See also Chester 1977; Rheinstein 1972; Riley 1991.

26. See Thornton 1989; Thornton and Young-DeMarco 2001; van de Kaa 1987; Varenne 1996/1986.

between the rights of adults and the well-being of children seems to have been resolved by many in favor of the former—or perhaps divorce is increasingly seen as promoting the well-being of both adults and children when there are marital difficulties. The long-term increases in tolerance toward divorce have been accompanied by substantial increases in the prevalence of divorce in Northwest European societies from the middle 1800s through the latter decades of the 1900s.[27] By the beginning of the 1980s divorce rates were high enough to suggest that approximately one in two marriages would end in divorce in the United States.

All these changes in divorce attitudes, laws, and behavior are consistent with the hypothesis that developmental idealism has had a powerful influence in the Western world in the past several centuries. Of course, these trends have undoubtedly been influenced by other forces as well.

Developmental Idealism and Marriage, Sex, Cohabitation, and Childbearing

As we saw in chapter 3, Northwest European society was in the 1600s and 1700s structured around the family unit, which was, in turn, structured around the institution of marriage.[28] Sex and childbearing were proscribed outside marriage,[29] and full membership in society required marriage.[30] Even economic self-sufficiency depended on marriage, as households were usually coterminous with an economic production and consumption unit, with the husband and wife directing and organizing household activities (Gillis 1985; Macfarlane 1986). Clearly, the developmental idealism principles of freedom, consent, and equality were severely restricted.

Interestingly, there is little evidence that the scholars of the period who challenged so many of society's constraints on freedom and equality also challenged the limitations of sex, childbearing, and household headship to marriage. However, the situation changed dramatically in the 1900s, especially the last half of the century, when the power of society to regulate

---

27. See Ahlburg and DeVita 1992; Jacobson 1959; Phillips 1988; Preston and McDonald 1979; Prinz 1995; van de Kaa 1987. While there have, of course, been fluctuations—associated with, e.g., war and economic depression—the overall trend is toward rising divorce rates.

28. See Gillis 1985; Hanawalt 1986; Hufton 1995; Phillips 1988.

29. See Davis 1985; Macfarlane 1986; Nock 1998; Rothman 1984. Prohibitions against sex outside marriage were often written into legal codes (Weyrauch 1965).

30. See Chambers-Schiller 1984; Hanawalt 1986; Nock 1998; Perkin 1989; Rothman 1984.

through marriage such activities as sex, childbearing, and living arrangements declined significantly. The rights and opportunities accorded the married and the unmarried have been significantly equalized. And this growing freedom, especially of the unmarried (see Axinn and Thornton 2000; Nock 2000), is consistent with the hypotheses of developmental idealism.

The decline in the importance of marriage as a legitimizer of certain activities is reflected in the fact that prohibitions on sex, cohabitation, and childbearing among the unmarried have weakened dramatically, with the incidence of these activities among the unmarried increasing substantially.[31] It is also reflected in the fact that the courts now enforce a "right of privacy" that prohibits government regulation of sexual behavior among consenting adults, married or unmarried (Ihara and Warner 1978), negating laws prohibiting nonmarital sex, even though such laws remain on the books in many places (Weyrauch 1965). For many Americans, love and consent—and often only consent—have replaced marriage as the conditions permitting sex, cohabitation, and childbearing.[32]

Similarly, there is little pressure on couples today to have children. As we saw in chapter 4, the social imperative to reproduce began to weaken in the late 1800s, as increasing numbers of couples used sterilization, contraception, and abortion to limit their childbearing. In addition, whereas through the 1950s it was still more or less mandatory for couples to have children, today it is much more voluntary, although most couples do have at least one child.[33] The societal pressure to marry has also declined dramatically in recent decades (Thornton and Freedman 1982; Thornton and Young-DeMarco 2001; Veroff, Douvan, and Kulka 1981).

Although in this section I have focused on Northwest Europe, I should also note that, in recent years, changes in the dimensions of family life under discussion here have been recorded in other areas of Europe as well. Although the tempo and degree of change have varied from region to region, the direction, at least in the 1990s, has been relatively uniform (Lesthaeghe and Surkyn 2002).

31. See Abma et al. 1997; Axinn and Thornton 2000; Bumpass and Lu 2000; Bumpass and Sweet 1989; Laumann et al. 1994; Lesthaeghe and Surkyn 2002; Morgan 1996; Nock 2000; Pagnini and Rindfuss 1993; Shorter 1977/1975; Thornton 1989; Thornton and Young-DeMarco 2001; Ventura et al. 1995.

32. See Klassen, Williams, and Levitt 1989; Michael et al. 1994; Modell 1989; Reiss 1967; Rothman 1984.

33. See Nock 2000; Thornton 1989; Thornton and Young-DeMarco 2001; van de Kaa 1987.

Developmental Idealism and Parental Authority

The work of John Locke offers a good base from which to understand the association between developmental idealism and changing intergenerational relationships.[34] In his *Second Treatise of Government*, Locke included children in his definition of those who were naturally free and equal. According to Locke, God, not parents, created children, who were then entrusted to parents for care and upbringing. In return, children were enjoined to obedience until they reached the age of maturity and left their parents' home. Parents, according to Locke, could demand obedience from their adult children in exchange for the children's receiving an inheritance, but that obedience was reckoned to be part of an economic transaction, not part of the natural parent-child relationship. Children were to honor their parents always, but honor did not necessarily mean obedience. Once children reached the age of maturity, they could enjoy the equality and freedom of which their immaturity had deprived them. This emphasis on the autonomy of children was also included in Locke's *Some Thoughts concerning Education* (1996/1693), described as the most influential text on childbearing practices in the Anglo-American Enlightenment (Fliegelman 1982). These ideas continued to have advocates well into the 1800s, being picked up by Herbert Spencer (1851) and others.

Laslett (1988/1960), it is useful to note, suggests that Locke derived his notion of the rights of children from observation. These observations were probably made in Locke's native England because the parent-child relationship that Locke outlines in theory is very similar to that which existed in England at the time. Because Locke's prescriptions about correct parent-child relations are very similar to what actually existed in England, those prescriptions would not be expected to have an immediate revolutionary effect on intergenerational relationships there (see Schochet 1975).

The ideas of Locke could, however, have a gradual influence on parent-child relations in England and elsewhere in Northwest Europe because there was variation in these relationships, ranging from the relatively permissive to the relatively tyrannical. By opposing parental authoritarianism and tyranny, Locke and others would have given encouragement to the more permissive end of the childrearing spectrum. Over long periods of time, this emphasis on children's independence could gradually, but persistently, lead to more autonomy in parent-child relations.

34. See Locke 1988/1690, 1996/1693. See also Fliegelman 1982; Schochet 1975; Tarcov 1984.

Although there is little direct evidence about trends in childrearing practices before the 1900s, data from the 1900s in the United States indicate that there have been dramatic changes from the 1920s into the 1980s in the relative emphasis placed on obedience and autonomy (Alwin 1984, 1986, 1987, 1988). For example, Americans placed considerably more emphasis on loyalty to church, conformity, and obedience as values to be instilled in their children in the 1920s than they did in subsequent decades, and the reverse holds for the values of tolerance, autonomy, and independent thinking. Similar changes have occurred in Germany and Japan (Alwin 1988b). Such shifts are clearly consistent with both the decline of the strength of central family norms and the increased power of developmental idealism during the same period.

Developmental Idealism and Living Arrangements

Developmental idealism, particularly its endorsement of intergenerational independence, has probably played a significant role in the dramatic changes in the living arrangements of unmarried young people in Northwest European societies over the past two centuries.[35] Independent living among single people was exceptionally rare prior to the 1800s, but numerous young people did work and live apart from their parents in the homes of other families—that is, entering service—a practice that virtually disappeared as the workplace shifted from the home to the factory or the office and from rural agricultural to urban industrial areas. Boarding and lodging in factory-owned dormitories or in private rooming houses then became common as young people migrated to cities in pursuit of work. As college attendance increased in the late 1800s and the 1900s, it resulted in more and more young people living in college dormitories—but overseen by a resident adult and segregated by gender. The phenomenon of boarding/lodging has now largely disappeared, as has that of the "dorm parent" and the gender-segregated dormitory. Most single young people now live independently in their own houses or apartments, either with non-relative housemates or by themselves.

Trends toward independent living have also been marked among the elderly in the Western world. Substantial numbers of the elderly lived with their children—frequently with unmarried rather than married children—in the

35. For a discussion of trends in living arrangements, see Kobrin 1976; Modell and Hareven 1972; Thornton and Freedman 1983.

1700s and 1800s (Ruggles 1987, 1994, 1996, 2001; D. S. Smith 1981). From the mid-1800s on, however, the fraction doing so declined dramatically, with the result that, by the last few decades of the 1900s, the phenomenon was quite uncommon (Ruggles 1994, 1996, 2001; Thornton and Freedman 1983; D. S. Smith 1981).

There are many potential explanations for these dramatic increases in independent living across the life span. Some focus on structural changes in economic and social conditions. For example, the disappearance of servanthood is clearly related to the economic shift from an agricultural to an industrial economy. Ruggles (2001) makes a very plausible case that the same economic shift can account for much of the decline in intergenerational living from the late 1800s through the early 1900s. The growth of income across the 1900s probably also played a role in this process, as did the institution and expansion of social security (Ruggles 1994, 2001; Thornton and Freedman 1983).

Structural changes cannot, however, fully explain increases in independent living. For example, they offer little insight into why the phenomenon of boarding/lodging would disappear and that of living alone or with roommates would emerge to take its place or why the phenomena of the dorm parent and the gender-segregated dormitory would largely disappear and that of male and female college students living together unchaperoned would emerge to take their place. It seems highly likely that these changes were strongly associated with ideational shifts: an increased desire for privacy and independence among young people and the acceptance of the new arrangements by the older generation. The importance of ideational shifts is also suggested by the fact that, between the 1950s and the 1970s, most of the elderly indicated that they preferred to maintain their independence—while still desiring to live in the same area as their children (Ruggles 2001; Thornton and Freedman 1983).

The reports by Ruggles (1994, 2001) of aggregate analyses showing that education at the county and state level is strongly associated with the living arrangements of the elderly—particularly that increased levels of education can account for the trend of independent living among the elderly in the late 1900s—lend further support to the idea that ideational shifts have been important influences on trends in living arrangements. Ruggles (1994) himself interpreted the strong correlation between education and living arrangements as representing the influence of ideational factors, suggesting that there have been changes in preferences for living arrangements that are tied to more general changes in attitudes toward single parenthood, cohabitation, divorce, and premarital sex.[36] This conclusion is consistent with the postulated influence of developmental idealism.

Conclusion

In this chapter, I have focused on developmental idealism and its power to change family laws, values, and behavior in the Western world. I have emphasized freedom, equality, and consent, three fundamental principles associated with developmental idealism, and shown how these ideas created new definitions of the good life and how it should be achieved. Because these ideas grew out of the developmental paradigm, reading history sideways, and the conclusions of social science, they had the force of history behind them. They were seen both as part of past history and as part of the force for future progress. As such, they played a dramatic role in the personal and family lives of individual men and, perhaps more important, women.[37]

Endorsement of these developmental idealism principles of freedom, equality, and consent has increased dramatically over time, and they are now taken for granted by many people in Northwest European populations. For example, acceptance of the principle of freedom and the right of privacy has meant the erosion of the importance of the government and society as regulators of behavior (Schneider 1985; Shammas 1995). Acceptance of the principle of equality has meant that distinctions based on race, ethnicity, religion, age, gender, marital status, and sexual orientation have become increasingly suspect—and even illegal. In many places, equal protection under the law is now virtually an article of faith.[38] Acceptance of the principle of consent has meant that, as a social value, obedience to parents has been downplayed while emphasis on independent thinking has increased (Alwin 1984, 1986, 1987, 1988). Generally, the normative prescriptions and proscriptions of the past have been replaced by a belief in the toleration of difference (Caplow, Bahr, and Chadwick 1983; Roof and McKinney 1987).

Of crucial importance is the linkage of the principles of freedom, equality, and consent to the substantial trends in family life that have occurred in

36. In a more recent article, Ruggles (2001) again suggested that the preferences of both the young and the old for independent living have grown stronger in the late 1900s. However, in this article, unlike the earlier one, he does not discuss possible links between these changes and more widespread cultural or ideational shifts.

37. See Berger and Berger 1984; Cott 2000; Glendon 1976, 1977; Witte 1997; Varenne 1996/1986.

38. See Berger and Berger 1984; Cott 2000; Glendon 1976, 1977; Witte 1997; Wallerstein 1997/1979, 1991.

the past half century—including changes in gender roles and increases in divorce, unmarried cohabitation, sex and childbearing outside marriage, and independent living. Recent family change has been especially dramatic, suggesting that these principles may have had their greatest influence in the past few decades. In fact, these recent changes have been so enormous and interconnected that, as we have seen in earlier chapters, some scholars have felt compelled to label them *the second demographic transition*.[39] Thus, even though the drive toward freedom, consent, and equality has roots that are very old, it remains very relevant today.

Of course, the principles of developmental idealism have yet to be fully realized. Men and women are still treated differently in many ways. So are the young and the old. So are the married and the unmarried. And these differences are substantial enough to generate considerable controversy. Still, the change from the world of the 1600s is so great as to render things largely unrecognizable to a Locke or a Filmer were they able to see things as they are today.

It is important to note, however, that such change did not come easily.[40] When the principles of developmental idealism were introduced in the 1600s and 1700s, they ran counter to many beliefs then prevailing, and they therefore met with considerable opposition. The controversy and conflict thus generated were central elements of the French and American Revolutions and the American Civil War. Controversy and conflict also dogged the women's movement—which met with especially strong opposition and achieved its successes only after years of struggle.[41] The fight to liberalize divorce laws also extended over centuries (Cott 2000; Phillips 1988; Traer 1980).

Among the forces resisting adoption of new family forms, the Christian churches have been especially powerful. The churches have vigorously defended the prescriptions and proscriptions of personal and family life as they were taught hundreds of years ago. However, among many denominations in recent decades, the strength of opposition to these trends has waned and the norm of tolerance has been emphasized.

---

39. See Lesthaeghe and Neels 2002; Lesthaeghe and Surkyn 2002; van de Kaa 1987, 1994, 2001.

40. See Cott 2000; Ekirch 1951; Fuller 1941/1845; Offen 2000.

41. See Abray 1975; Kraditor 1965; Offen 2000; Rendall 1985. The power of developmental idealism can be further illustrated by the fact that even the opponents of the women's movement employed its arguments. For example, one opponent of female suffrage argued that it would return Western civilization to savagery and barbarism (see Coontz 1991/1988).

There is considerable irony in the opposition of the Christian churches in the past two centuries to the ideas and propositions of developmental idealism. In the 1600s and 1700s developmental models specified Christianity as part of modernity, with the Western Christian family defining what was meant by the modern family. In addition, Christianity was identified as one of the forces of progress producing the modern society of Northwest Europe. In the 1800s and 1900s, however, developmental idealism and other forces greatly modified family life and changed what was meant by the modern family. Thus, by continuing to support the family system that was considered modern in the 1600s and 1700s, the churches have become associated with traditionalism and backwardness.

The fact that the dramatic family changes of the past two centuries occurred despite the strong and general opposition indicates that the forces for change had to have been extremely powerful. Although it is beyond the scope of this book to formulate a comprehensive theory of family change in the Western world over two centuries, I note here that such a theory would need to take into account many structural changes in society, including industrialization, urbanization, income growth, increased levels of education, and the growth of science and technology. In addition, such a comprehensive theory would have to include the ideas of developmental idealism, because they have played a powerful role in transforming the Western world, powering the passions and energies of generations of reformers, and affecting the lives of ordinary people. Of course, this is not to say that developmental idealism was the only force operating. But it was certainly important—and probably crucial. I turn in the next chapter to some different kinds of examples of the power of developmental idealism in Northwest European family life.

10

Fighting Barbarism in the United States

The previous chapter may have given readers the impression that the developmental paradigm and developmental idealism were used exclusively to further freedom and equality—that the advocates of developmental thinking were consistently opposed to hierarchy and control and passionately supportive of freedom of conscience and choice. But that impression would be incorrect because some family forms, such as polygamy and arranged marriage, were viewed as violations of the norms of developmental thinking and were, in fact, strongly opposed and even suppressed. How could such suppression coexist with the principles of freedom and equality, so central to developmental idealism? Because the notion of progress was accorded an even higher priority and sanctioned action taken against practices considered to be backward.

Opposition to perceived backwardness was also facilitated by the belief that progress was not inevitable as society could stagnate or even retrogress. Many believed that ancient Rome and Greece provided examples of such retrogression. Some theories about Native Americans suggested that their perceived low level of development also resulted from a significant retrogression. This motivated many to fight perceived backwardness, or barbarism, wherever it was found in the Western world. In fact, in many respects the fight against barbarism took precedence over the drive to promote the principles of freedom, equality, and consent.

The fight against perceived barbarism has figured particularly prominently in American history. For that reason, I focus in this chapter on the United States and, specifically, on the campaigns to eliminate barbarism that targeted Native Americans, non–Northwest European immigrants, Mormons, and the Oneida Community. Practices identified as barbaric in the 1800s and 1900s included (very) early marriage, arranged marriage, polygamy, and group or complex marriage. Each of these practices was linked with the traditional, or backward, end of the development continuum, and this provided a strong justification for suppression of them.

It is important to note that my purpose here is not to provide a full account of each group's historical family patterns and trends. This limitation of chapter goals is required because the groups under discussion are very different from one another and also exhibit substantial internal variation. In addition, each of the groups has experienced different historical trends, with a range of causal forces influencing each group. Complete documentation of these groups and the forces affecting them would, therefore, be a substantial undertaking, one that is clearly beyond the scope of this chapter. Instead, I focus on the mainstream American reaction to these groups and how that was influenced by the ideas of developmental idealism—and the notion of progress in particular. I begin with Native Americans.

Native Americans

The English colonists brought with them to North America the understanding that the indigenous inhabitants were living in or near the state of nature, that is, with little or no society or government.[1] They perceived that the natives were primitive enough to be savages (either not having progressed to the level of barbarism, let alone civilization, or having previously advanced but then fallen back into savagism). Some colonists believed that the natives were so depraved spiritually that their religions were the work of the devil (Pearce 1967/1953; Prucha 1984; Sheehan 1980).

The colonists also brought with them a clear mandate from the English government to bring to the native population the intertwined attributes of civil society, stable government, and the Christian religion.[2] Their effort to civilize the natives extended to virtually every dimension of indigenous society.[3] It meant changing economies from hunting and gathering to agricultural, religions from indigenous to Christian, and family systems from native

---

1. See Colden 1973/1727. See also Axtell 1981; Berkhofer 1978; Hodgen 1964; Jennings 1975; Meek 1976; Pagden 1982; Pearce 1967/1953; Porter 1979; Prucha 1984; Vaughan 1995/1965; Washburn 1971.

2. See Axtell 1981; Berkhofer 1978; Jennings 1975; Pearce 1967/1953; Prucha 1973, 1984; Sheehan 1980; Vaughan 1995/1965.

3. See Axtell 1981; Berkhofer 1978; Cott 2000; Pearce 1967/1953; Prucha 1973, 1984; Vaughan 1995/1965.

to Northwest European. It also meant convincing the natives to give up self-government and accept English political authority and to adopt the English language and Western forms of education. The effort was continued by the American government after Independence.

The civilizing effort of the colonists was complicated by the fact that the family patterns among the various Native American groups were both very diverse and in many ways greatly different from those in Europe.[4] Some native groups practiced polygamy, some made it easy for men to divorce their wives, some placed little emphasis on the nuclear family relationship, some formed alliances between families through marriage, some practiced abortion and infanticide, and some wore very little clothing. All these practices received considerable attention in the writings of European travelers and colonists.

Especially noteworthy to Europeans were Native American gender relationships. Some groups were matrilineal in that descent was traced through the maternal line. Native societies often accorded women great autonomy as well as great influence in the decision-making process. The division of labor often made women responsible for agricultural tasks and other burdensome activities and men responsible for hunting and fishing. As a result of this division of labor, Europeans often considered native women to be in a servile position and native men to be indolent.[5]

The civilizing process took many forms, including missionary work, education, legislation, and coercion (McLoughlin 1986; Pearce 1967/1953; Prucha 1973, 1984). Of particular importance was missionary work, which was frequently intense and sometimes achieved significant results.[6] In places like New England, where colonists expended considerable effort on missionary work, significant numbers of Native Americans converted to Christianity and made efforts to adopt European ways. Some Native Americans even left their native villages and lived in towns modeled after those of the colonists. After Independence, the U.S. government sometimes cooperated closely with the churches to Christianize and civilize the Native Americans, but only with

4. See Axtell 1981; Berkhofer 1978; Coontz 1991/1988; Cott 2000; McLoughlin 1986; Plane 2000; Prucha 1973; Shammas 1995; Vaughan 1995/1965.

5. In Europe, hunting was often seen as a leisure activity, which led Europeans to the conclusion that Native American men who devoted considerable time to this activity were slothful. Europeans also frequently criticized the gender division of labor in Africa. As they did in North America, European colonists in Africa tried to bring native women into conformity with the Western model of the housewife (Comaroff and Comaroff 1991, 1997).

6. See Axtell 1981; Berkhofer 1978; Jennings 1975; McLoughlin 1986; Pearce 1967/1953; Prucha 1973, 1984; Vaughan 1995/1965.

mixed success. Closely related to missionary work was the effort to educate native populations in Western ways. Western-style schools—in whose curricula the English language and the Christian religion figured prominently—became so widespread that, by the late 1800s, nearly half of all Native American children were reported to be enrolled in school and, by 1970, the average years of schooling completed among Native Americans had risen to ten years.[7]

When proselytizing and education failed, Western ways could be coerced through legislation and the power of the police and the military (Jennings 1975; McLoughlin 1986; Porter 1979). Of course, the level of coercion varied. In colonial New England, for example, the rights of Native Americans were largely respected and the choice of whether to adopt Western ways tended to remain with the natives (McNickle 1973; Vaughan 1995/1965). In other times and places Native Americans were left with little choice but to adopt Western ways[8] and sometimes faced genocide if they resisted.[9] The program of strict enforcement was frequently pursued by both the British colonial and the American national governments, and among its advocates were some of the strongest spokesmen for the principles of freedom and equality, including Thomas Jefferson.

The spread of Western-style civilization was facilitated by several factors. Of great importance was the decimation of native populations by previously unknown diseases brought to America by the Europeans. These new diseases caused epidemics that reduced the ability of the natives to resist European influence.[10] One significant outcome of the devastating epidemics—which left the Europeans virtually untouched—was the loss of faith in the indigenous gods and enhanced receptivity to Christianity (Axtell 1981; Plane 2000; Vaughan 1995/1965). Also enhancing the prestige and desirability of the European way of life were the greater wealth, technological capabilities, and military power of the settlers (Sheehan 1980; Vaughan 1995/1965).

Relations between Native Americans and the settlers were, of course, complex and evolved over time. From the very beginning, however, these relations were guided by the notion that the Europeans had a right to any land

---

7. Berkhofer 1978; Sorkin 1978. See also Dippie 1982; McLoughlin 1986; Pearce 1967/1953; Prucha 1973, 1984; Vaughan 1995/1965; Washburn 1971.

8. See Axtell 1981; Berkhofer 1978; Dippie 1982; Jennings 1975; McLoughlin 1986; Vaughan 1995/1965.

9. See Berkhofer 1978; Cott 2000; Dippie 1982; Pearce 1967/1953; Prucha 1973, 1984.

10. See Axtell 1981; Coontz 1991/1988; Jennings 1975; McLoughlin 1986; Vaughan 1995/1965.

occupied by non-Christians even if the occupants had been in possession for centuries (Washburn 1971).[11] This notion was justified ideologically by the belief that the rights accorded civilized people (i.e., the Christian Europeans) did not apply to savage or barbarian peoples and that discovery, conquest, and settlement were sufficient to establish control. The right to land so obtained was, in the United States at least, affirmed by an 1823 Supreme Court decision that left native populations only the right of use.[12] That decision, authored by Chief Justice John Marshall, assembled an impressive list of precedents. It also suggested that certain attributes (including the "character and religion") of the original inhabitants—for example, that they were heathens, barbarous, savages, that they were preoccupied with war, that they drew their means of subsistence primarily from the forest, that they let the country remain a wilderness—justified the ascendancy of European Americans. This decision became the basis for subsequent determinations of Native American rights. And, as we will see later, the same underlying logic was applied subsequently to other groups perceived to be outside the bounds of civilization.

Over the centuries many Native Americans energetically and resourcefully resisted colonial authority, customs, and encroachments on their lands.[13] But they were ultimately unsuccessful as native populations were decimated and the survivors largely removed to reservations (McLoughlin 1986).

There were, of course, efforts by Native Americans to adopt Euro-American civilization (McNickle 1973; Sorkin 1978), among which the effort of the Cherokee of the southeastern United States is a particularly pertinent example (McLoughlin 1986). By the early 1800s, the Cherokee had begun the process of establishing farms, building schools, accepting missionaries, creating a written language, and adopting a Western-type system of government. The Cherokee proclaimed English as their official language, even though relatively few were conversant with it. And a conscious effort was

11. This belief can be clearly seen to underlie English charters and land grants. In the early years of colonization, however, the English had only a weak military presence in North America and thus were forced to negotiate treaties and purchase land. The result was that, in some instances, Native Americans were accorded many of the same rights as the settlers possessed (McNickle 1973; Vaughn 1995/1965; Washburn 1971). Most often, however, the perceived status of Native Americans as heathen and barbarous led to violations of their human rights (see Jennings 1975; McLoughlin 1986; Porter 1979; Washburn 1971).

12. See *Johnson and Graham's Lessee v. William McIntosh* 1823. See also Jennings 1975; McNickle 1973; Washburn 1971.

13. See Axtell 1981; McLoughlin 1986; Pearce 1967/1953; Prucha 1984; Vaughan 1995/1965.

made to adopt European family patterns. The clan system emphasizing large kinship groups declined in importance. Gender relationships were modified as the matrilineal lineage system was de-emphasized, the daily activities of women and men changed, and the locus of authority shifted from women to men. Polygamy, abortion, and infanticide were outlawed and Western notions of female chastity adopted. All these changes were introduced rapidly, so rapidly, in fact, that some Cherokee openly rebelled against these tribally initiated changes. Despite the extensive efforts of the Cherokee to adopt Euro-American lifestyles, they were forcefully removed from their native lands and made to live elsewhere.

Coontz (1991/1988) suggests that, over time, many of these changes occurred among Native Americans generally. She reports that there has been less emphasis on broad kinship and community relationships and more on the nuclear family and individual ownership of property. She also indicates that the gender division of labor drew closer to the Euro-American pattern and that women had less and less of a role in the decision-making process as a more patriarchal division of authority was adopted.

It should be noted that while some Native Americans have largely been assimilated into mainstream American society, many others have held to many of their core culture beliefs, kinship structures, and language. Thus, despite centuries of contact with European Americans, many elements of indigenous culture continue (McNickle 1973; Sorkin 1978).

One interesting and little-known dimension of the early experience of Europeans in America was the concern that the encounter with the Native Americans would result in the colonists regressing into barbarism and savagery (Axtell 1981; Plane 2000). This concern was, apparently, well founded as significant numbers of colonists did adopt Native American ways, some even becoming members of native societies. (Ironically, observers like Benjamin Franklin suggested that the Native Americans were more successful in assimilating Europeans than the Europeans were in civilizing the Native Americans [Axtell 1981; Sheehan 1980].) The concern—and the reality—led to legislation sanctioning Europeans who assimilated to native cultures (Axtell 1981). The reality also, undoubtedly, reinforced fears of retrogression and energized efforts to ensure the victory of civilization over barbarism.

Immigrants from outside Northwest Europe

Except for the Native Americans—who did not become citizens until the early 1900s—the United States has always been a nation of immigrants. At first, most of those immigrants were from Northwest Europe, with a modest number from Asia and, of course, a great many Africans who had been brought across the Atlantic as slaves. However, the mid-1800s saw the beginnings of an enormous influx of immigrants from other regions of the world, first Southern and Eastern Europe, then, more recently, Latin America, Asia, and the Middle East. Obviously, this influx introduced different social and cultural systems into the American mix.

Migration of necessity involves adjustment and assimilation, and the problems presented by this process can be more difficult and complex the greater the social, cultural, and geographic distance traversed. Although immigrants commonly maintain many elements of their native cultures in their new surroundings—often for several generations—there is inevitably pressure toward acculturation, especially on those generations born in the new country. I argue that, through at least the mid-1900s, developmental thinking and conclusions have played significant roles in the acculturation of immigrants to America, providing both incentives and constraints motivating the abandonment of old customs and the adoption of new ones. In this section, I present this argument briefly—in the context of immigration to the United States—a full discussion being clearly beyond the scope of this book.

The dominant culture in the United States through at least the mid-1900s originated in Northwest Europe, with the perspective that America and its society were at the pinnacle of development and non–Northwest European migrants were not as developed. The same forces propelling the drive to civilize native populations therefore propelled a new civilizing project, this one directed at recent immigrants. Of course, this civilizing project differed in many ways from the old one. A crucial difference was that the newcomers were just that—newcomers who had left their previous homes and had no prior, established communities in America. In addition, the cultural gap was, in most cases, nowhere near as great as that between the colonists and the Native Americans, especially when it came to immigrants from Southern and Eastern Europe. Therefore, as compared to Native Americans, it was often easier to assimilate the new immigrants into the dominant belief and value systems of the United States.

The ideas of developmental idealism influenced all aspects of the civilizing project, including decisions about which immigrants would be allowed to enter the country. Of particular importance for our purposes is the exclusion of people whose family forms were considered barbaric, most noteworthy among whom were practicing polygamists, who were banned from the 1800s on.[14] In the early 1900s, the ban on practicing polygamists was expanded to include anyone who supported the practice of polygamy, a provision that was sometimes interpreted as meaning anyone associated with a religion or cultural group allowing or encouraging polygamy (Cott 2000). And, despite the growth of an increasingly tolerant society in recent years, the ban on polygamists and those advocating polygamy remains in effect today.[15]

For some, the decision to migrate to America was motivated by developmental idealism and the common perception of America as an economic and political paradise with great personal and social freedom (Glenn 1990). Younger immigrants also saw America as a place where they could love and marry with less parental interference (Glenn 1990).

What immigrants found when they arrived in America was a society anxious to assimilate them, to have them adopt American customs and practices. And the reeducation awaiting them was in the hierarchies of developmental idealism, promoting American progress over Old World customs, civilization over backwardness, and modernity over traditionality.[16] In many ways, settlement workers, reformers, educators, and government officials were crusaders for modernity and the abandonment of the old ways of life. They were agents of developmental idealism, linking the ideals of individualism and freedom with social mobility and progress.

The crusade for modernity was particularly vigorous regarding marriage, emphasizing freedom and affection in mate selection. It painted parental control of marriage outside the bounds of American culture and legal practice, with arranged marriage sometimes pictured as slavery and savagery.[17] In fact, marital consent and romance, along with freedom and individualism, became important symbols of the contrast between the old and new—backward and progressive—worlds of the migrants (Cott 2000; Haag 1999; Khater 2003).

As one would expect, immigrant parents who were socialized in a world of strong family solidarity and parental authority did not automatically accept the call for freedom and individualism in their new society (Ewen

14. Polygamy had been singled out as particularly barbaric by generations of writers (Cott 2000). Also excluded were anarchists, paupers, felons, and the insane (Cott 2000).

15. Information on current U.S. immigration law was obtained from the Immigration and Naturalization Service Web site, which can be accessed at www.ins.gov.

16. See Cott 2000; Ewen 1985; Glenn 1990; Haag 1999; Khater 2003.

17. See Cott 2000; Ewen 1985; Glenn 1990; Haag 1999; Khater 2003.

1985; Glenn 1990). Instead, immigrant parents relied heavily on the social and familial customs of the old country—although in adapted form (Ewen 1985; Glenn 1990). This adherence to the old customs was undoubtedly reinforced by living in ethnically segregated neighborhoods, retaining religious institutions, and maintaining native languages (Goldscheider and Goldscheider 1993).

At the same time, immigrant parents understood that they were now in a new world, with their children being socialized into a different culture (Ewen 1985). The children usually became fluent in English, received more education than their parents, and had more access to new ideas and customs. In addition, children sometimes became the interpreters of the new culture for their parents.

As one would expect, this situation created powerful tensions across generations—with parents being the defenders of Old World customs while children were advocates of progress and modernity (Ewen 1985). Consequently, immigrant parents were frequently criticized for being unreasonably old-fashioned and lacking in appreciation for the new progressive ways. This generational-cultural-developmental gap was recognized by both parents and children, with children sometimes speaking of their efforts to civilize their parents (Ewen 1985). The children, of course, had the ideology of progress and modernity on their side while parents were associated with backwardness. Consequently, the children of immigrants often adopted many American customs, with each generation becoming more assimilated than the last. The result was frequently composite or hybridized societies, as people incorporated into their lives various aspects of old and new cultures. In many places, ethnic differentials still exist and are more pronounced when individuals reside in ethnic communities and use the languages of their ancestors.[18]

American Modifications

Foreign cultures were not the only challenges to American family patterns. Similar challenges came from within, experiments with family patterns that had long been branded as barbaric. These experiments were vigorously opposed by the proponents of civilization. In this section I discuss two such

18. For example, there is less personal autonomy and more respect of family authority among Asian and Hispanic families than among people of European and African origins (Goldscheider and Goldscheider 1993).

experiments: polygamy among the Mormons and complex marriage within the Oneida Community of New York.

Mormon Polygamy

Polygamy, or plural marriage—the practice of a man having more than one wife—is recorded approvingly in the Bible but had, by the 1700s, become a key symbol of barbarism for Northwest Europeans.[19] Generations of scholars interpreted polygamy within the context of the developmental paradigm and the story of the growth of civilization. Polygamy was identified as a roadblock to progress and was clearly associated with societies outside the Northwest European cultural sphere, political despotism, and non-Christian religions. It was argued that polygamy was, in itself, an evil and that it undermined family life (especially the institution of marriage and the rearing of children), degraded women (making of them little more than slaves), and, ultimately, threatened the very foundations of Western civilization.

With this widespread prejudice against polygamy, many Americans and the U.S. government itself reacted with condemnation and repression when the Mormon Church adopted the practice in the early 1800s. The Mormon religion was founded in upstate New York in 1830 by Joseph Smith and his followers, who soon moved west to Ohio, Missouri, and Illinois. Plural marriage was an early innovation by Smith, who justified the practice, at least partially, on the grounds that some of the Old Testament patriarchs had multiple wives (Linford 1964; Poll 1957; Van Wagoner 1986). Because of the strong antipathies toward polygamy held by most Americans, including many Mormons, Smith initially limited the knowledge and practice of plural marriage to himself and a few close associates.[20]

By the early 1840s, polygamy had become an open secret in the Mormon community in Illinois, and strong opposition to it emerged within the Mormon leadership itself (Quinn 1985; G. D. Smith 1994). In 1844 a small group of Mormon leaders founded a newspaper to expose several policies of the Church, especially the practice of plural marriage. After the publication of one issue, Smith and his associates destroyed the press, thereby shutting the paper down. This action soon led to his arrest and subsequent murder by non-Mormons who were incensed by the destruction of the press and a number of Mormon practices, including polygamy.

---

19. See W. Alexander 1995/1779; Hume 1825/1742; Lieber 1855; Mill 1989a/1859; Montesquieu 1973/1721, 1997/1748; Paley 1793; A. Smith 1978/1762–63; Wollstonecraft 1975/1792.

20. See Linford 1964; Poll 1957; Quinn 1985; G. D. Smith 1994; Van Wagoner 1986.

With Smith's murder, leadership of the Mormon Church passed to Brigham Young, one of Smith's polygamist associates. Recognizing that Mormonism, with its practice of plural marriage, could not survive in Illinois, Young and his followers left Illinois in 1847 for the West, where they settled in the Great Basin, parts of which became the Territory of Utah with Young as the first territorial governor. Feeling sufficiently safe in Utah, the Church hierarchy in 1852 publicly announced that plural marriage was part of their religion (Linford 1964).

The reaction of the American public to the 1852 announcement of polygamy came swiftly and vigorously.[21] Polygamy was denounced from pulpits and podiums across the country. By the 1856 election, the newly founded Republican Party had pledged in its national platform to eliminate polygamy among the Mormons as one of the "twin relics of barbarism"—the other being the enslavement of African Americans.[22] In 1857, the victorious Democratic president, James Buchanan, sent the army to Utah to ensure Mormon obedience to federal authority and to replace Brigham Young with a new territorial governor. The Mormons initially resisted militarily but soon capitulated to the army and accepted the new governor. However, they refused to budge on the principle of polygamy (Gordon 1995; Larson 1971).

The first federal legislation outlawing polygamy was not passed until 1862, the attention of Congress having been deflected from the issue, first by the national debate over slavery and then by the Civil War. This initial legislation was ineffective, but it was followed over the next three decades by a series of laws and enforcement efforts that were increasingly potent—and increasingly punitive.[23] As of the late 1880s, the federal government had succeeded in disincorporating the Mormon Church, was taking action to seize its property, and had disenfranchised Mormons (including the majority who were not polygamists) by barring them from voting and holding public office. As a result of this crusade—which the Mormons called *the Raid*—over a thousand people were convicted of polygamy, numerous women who refused to

---

21. See Cott 2000; Firmage and Mangrum 1988; Grossberg 1985; Larson 1971; Linford 1964. The reaction was probably heightened by the theocratic tendencies of the Mormon church, which resulted in its high level of involvement in Utah's economic and political life, a level of involvement that ran counter to the general American preference for the separation of church and state. However, the main issue that legitimated the reaction of the American public remained polygamy.

22. See Cott 2000; Linford 1964; Gordon 1995; Poll 1957.

23. See Cott 2000; Firmage and Mangrum 1988; Gordon 1995; Larson 1971; Linford 1964.

testify against their husbands were jailed, large numbers of families were broken up, and many more fled the country or went into hiding.

This overwhelming governmental power achieved partial success in 1890 with the public announcement by the Church that it was abandoning plural marriage (Hardy 1992; Quinn 1985). The practice, however, continued in private into the early 1900s, but persistent governmental pressure and change within the Mormon leadership led to its complete abandonment by the Church in the first two decades of the 1900s (Hardy 1992; Quinn 1985). Today, the Church actively disassociates itself from polygamy, and virtually all mainstream Mormons espouse monogamy. However, the government—now allied with the official Mormon Church—has not been able to eliminate polygamy completely. Practicing polygamists with a Mormon heritage, but without Church sanction, are now estimated to exceed twenty thousand (Quinn 1998; see also Bradley 1993).

Why such a confrontation? What motivated the irresistible force and the immovable object? Although full discussion of Mormon motivations lies beyond the scope of this book, the Mormon position can be summarized as follows. Church spokesmen argued that plural marriage was a fundamental tenet of the Mormon religion and that its abandonment could be sanctioned only by the word of God. They also argued that the practice of plural marriage was protected by the freedom-of-religion clause of the U.S. Constitution and that plural marriages were being entered into by consenting individuals (Firmage and Mangrum 1988; Gordon 1995). Therefore, the Mormons argued that the government should immediately recognize their right to practice polygamy.

What about the arguments of the opponents of polygamy? The opponents accepted the claim that plural marriage was a fundamental tenet of the Mormon religion, but, because Mormonism embraced plural marriage, they saw the religion itself as illegitimate (Gordon 1995). They also recognized that the Constitution provided for religious freedom, but religious freedom, they argued, was not the same as religious license. As for the assertion that plural marriages were being entered into by freely consenting parties, they argued that the government had the right to restrict religious practices that went beyond the boundaries of morality and decency. This allowed them to exclude polygamy from the religious freedom clause. Their conclusion was, therefore, to come down firmly against the practice of plural marriage, even for religious reasons, a position sanctioned by Supreme Court decisions (e.g., *The Late Corporation of the Church of Jesus Christ of Latter-Day Saints v. United States* 1890; *Reynolds v. United States* 1878; see also Lieber 1855).

No effort was made, however, to demonstrate the harmful effects of polygamy empirically (Firmage and Mangrum 1988; Gordon 1995; Linford 1964). Nor did the public support of polygamy by vast numbers of women in Utah matter, except as evidence of just how degraded those women had become (Gordon 1995). Instead, to make their case, the opponents of polygamy relied on the principles of developmental idealism, in the process elevating developmental thought to the highest of legislative and judicial levels.[24] In short, they associated polygamy with savagery and barbarism and, thus, with despotic government, slavery, and the degradation of women. At the same time, they associated monogamy with civilized society and, thus, with democratic government, freedom, and the just treatment of women. Furthermore, because family structure and gender relationships were viewed as causal forces in the development of modern society, polygamy was considered a threat, not only to further progress in America, but also to current levels of development. There was, in fact, virtually unanimous agreement that this threat was sufficiently serious to justify the withholding of basic, constitutionally guaranteed rights.

The influence of developmental idealism can perhaps best be illustrated by a series of Supreme Court decisions.[25] In 1878, the Court ruled: "Polygamy has always been odious among the northern and western nations of Europe, and, until the establishment of the Mormon Church, was almost exclusively a feature of the life of Asiatic and of African people." Appealing to the work of Francis Lieber, a leading developmental scholar of the day, the Court went on to declare: "Polygamy leads to the patriarchal principle, and which, when applied to large communities, fetters the people in stationary despotism, while that principle cannot long exist in connection with monogamy" (*Reynolds v. United States* 1878, 164, 166). The Court was even more explicit and dramatic when it ruled in *The Late Corporation of the Church of Jesus Christ of Latter-Day Saints v. United States* (1890) that polygamy was "a crime against the laws, and abhorrent to the sentiments and feelings of the civilized world . . . [a] barbarous practice . . . a blot on our civilization," going on to declare: "The organization of a community for the spread and practice of polygamy is, in a measure, a return to barbarism. It is contrary to the spirit of Christianity and of the civilization which Christianity has produced in the

24. See Cott 2000; Firmage and Mangrum 1988; Gordon 1995; Grossberg 1985; Linford 1964; Weisbrod and Sheingorn 1978.

25. See Cott 2000; Firmage and Mangrum 1988; Grossberg 1985; Linford 1964; Weisbrod and Sheingorn 1978.

Western world." The justices dismissed the Mormon claim of polygamy as a religious right by comparing polygamy to religious practices that took human life, such as human sacrifice and suttee (widows burning themselves after the deaths of their husbands). The Court concluded: "The State has a perfect right to prohibit polygamy, and all other open offences against the enlightened sentiment of mankind" (48–49, 49, 50).

Lieber went even further than the Supreme Court:

> Monogamy is one of the elementary distinctions—historical and actual—between European and Asiatic humanity. It is one of the frames of our thoughts, and moulds of our feelings; it is a psychological condition of our jural consciousness, of our liberty, of our literature, of our aspirations, of our religious convictions, and of our domestic being and family relation, the foundation of all that is called polity. It is one of the pre-existing conditions of our existence as civilized white men, as much so as our being moral entities is a pre-existing condition of the idea of law, or of the possibility of a revelation. Strike it out, and you destroy our very being; and when we say *our*, we mean our race—a race which has its great and broad destiny, a solemn aim in the great career of civilization, with which no one of us has any right to trifle. (Lieber 1855, 234)

Such arguments represented the overwhelmingly dominant view in America throughout the last half of the 1800s (Cott 2000; Gordon 1995). One of the few dissenting voices was John Stuart Mill, one of the world's foremost advocates of liberty. Although Mill condemned the practice of polygamy, he also felt that Western civilization was strong enough to withstand the test of Mormonism and that, while proselytization and education were in order, the revocation of basic freedoms was not (see Mill 1989a/1859). Most of his American counterparts did not, however, agree.[26]

As I noted earlier, the American crusade against polygamy eventually triumphed over the considerable resistance of the Mormon Church and most

---

26. A fascinating sidelight of the crusade against Mormon polygamy is its intersection with the women's suffrage movement (Cott 2000; Firmage and Mangrum 1988; Gordon 1995; Weisbrod and Sheingorn 1978). Early in the crusade it was suggested that polygamy was so degrading to Mormon women that they themselves would legislate it out of existence if they only had the vote. Realizing that polygamy did in fact have the support of Mormon women, church leaders moved quickly to obtain the vote for women in Utah (becoming in 1870 the second state or territory in the Union—after Wyoming—to do so), hoping both to increase the Mormon vote in Utah and to show the world how enlightened Mormonism truly was. When it became clear, however, that Mormon women voted similarly to Mormon men, the U.S. Congress—the ultimate political power in Utah Territory—rescinded women's franchise.

of its people. However, some individuals with Mormon roots persisted in the practice, and the opposition of the government to polygamy continued, but now in cooperation with the Church itself. In the middle of the 1900s there were raids on polygamists by governmental agencies that rivaled the raids of the late 1800s in their severity and violation of basic civil rights (Bradley 1993). The issue of polygamy again reached the Supreme Court, where its illegality was again upheld, with the majority opinion replicating the arguments of the 1800s, using almost identical developmental language (Cleveland v. United States 1946; also see Bradley 1993; Glendon 1976). And, to this day, polygamists with roots in Mormonism are being prosecuted for their behavior (Janofsky 2001; Wright 2002).

The issue of polygamy remains significant today, however, for reasons that extend beyond the persistence of the practice. Because the Supreme Court decisions in the original Mormon polygamy cases were the first to specify the meaning of the freedom of religion clause of the U.S. Constitution, they have continued to constitute the fundamental judicial interpretation of religious freedom, even though the interpretation of the religious freedom clause has been broadened beyond that prevailing in the 1800s (Firmage and Mangrum 1988; Weisbrod and Sheingorn 1978).

Oneida Group Marriage

American antipathy in the 1800s toward unorthodox marriage practices extended far beyond Mormon polygamy. Particularly repugnant to many Americans was the system of complex or group marriage practiced by the Oneida Community in New York from the late 1840s through the 1870s.

The Oneida movement originated in Vermont in the 1830s under the leadership of John Humphrey Noyes and moved to upstate New York in the 1840s.[27] The community's foundational principles were derived from the Bible and included a belief in the possibility of human perfection, in this world as well as the next. Also important were the beliefs that property must be shared communally and that many of the central activities of life should be organized at the community level.

The principle of communalism in the Oneida Community extended far beyond property and community organization and included family relationships. In the realm of male-female relationships, this meant an abandonment of monogamous marriage and the adoption of complex or group

---

27. This description of the Oneida Community has been distilled from Cott 2000; Foster 1981; Muncy 1973; Robertson 1972; Weisbrod and Sheingorn 1978.

marriage, where, in principle, every woman was to be married to every man, thereby legitimizing heterosexual relations between all consenting adults. In the area of parent-child relations, children were seen as being the collective responsibility of the entire community rather than the exclusive responsibility of individual couples.

Although group marriage was practiced by the Oneida Community for three decades, it was frequently denounced as nothing more than polygamy, free love, or adultery.[28] The community employed several strategies in order to defend itself from these charges. First, community spokesmen articulated the weaknesses of Western social patterns built around private property holding and exclusive sexual relationships.[29] Second, it was pointed out that sexual relationships in the Oneida Community were tightly controlled, because, even though every man was, in principle, married to every woman, the initiation of sexual relationships required community approval (Foster 1981; Muncy 1973). Third, it was further pointed out that reproduction was tightly controlled, in order to improve the quality of offspring (Foster 1981; Muncy 1973). Community approval was, again, required for a couple to bear children, and in the absence of such approval, sexually active couples were required to use contraception.

The Oneida Community never successfully distanced itself from the charges of free love and polygamy. The community had always known criticism, even in its early days, having been run out of Vermont by its opponents. But opposition was reinvigorated when, in its 1878 decision in *Reynolds v. United States,* the U.S. Supreme Court upheld the ban on polygamy and supported the prosecution of polygamists. Shortly thereafter, a substantial campaign emerged to have the New York State legislature ban complex marriage (Cott 2000; Robertson 1972; Weisbrod and Sheingorn 1978).

In response to the threatened legislative action, and at the suggestion of Noyes, the Oneida Community abandoned complex marriage in 1879.[30] The community also, again at Noyes's suggestion, adopted a system of celibacy for those members wanting to be single and monogamy for those wishing to be married. The reasons behind this decision to abandon complex marriage are hard to tease out, but they seem to have included the deteriorating health of Noyes (who moved to Canada shortly after the legislative initiative was introduced), divisions among the community's leaders, and growing independence

---

28. See Cott 2000; Muncy 1973; Robertson 1972; Weisbrod and Sheingorn 1978.

29. See Cott 2000; Foster 1981; Muncy 1973; Weisbrod and Sheingorn 1978.

30. See Cott 2000; Olin 1980; Robertson 1972; Weisbrod and Sheingorn 1978.

among the younger generation (Muncy 1973; Olin 1980; Robertson 1972). It is also likely that the 1878 Supreme Court decision upholding the ban on polygamy was a very important factor, because it sent the clear signal that, in the United States, straying from the bounds of monogamous marriage would not be tolerated. Instead of resisting for additional decades, as the Mormons did, the Oneida Community chose to conform.

Summary

The experiences of Native Americans, immigrants, the Mormons, and the Oneida Community demonstrate that the application of the developmental model and ideology to American family life did not always promote individual freedom, equality, and choice, as one would have expected. Developmental ideology could, in fact, be utilized to restrict the free exercise of conscience in family matters when that freedom led to family forms perceived as threatening American progress and development. In these instances, the fight against the perceived evils of barbarism and backwardness clearly took precedence over the promotion of the principles of freedom, equality, and individual conscience.

This failure to apply the principles of freedom, equality, and consent equally to all groups in America also illustrates the ambiguities involved in the process. There are many different behaviors in which individuals can in theory engage, but the preference of a group (or a government) for one form of behavior over another will almost always limit the choices actually available to people. And, as we have seen, the perception that the Native American, immigrant, Mormon, and Oneida Community family systems were backward and threatened the American way of life limited those groups' choices so drastically as to result in the revocation of the freedom to choose their own way of life.

11

Government Pathways of Influence
outside Northwest Europe

Although the developmental paradigm, reading history sideways, and developmental idealism originated in the West, they have, over the past several centuries, been widely disseminated around the non-Western world by the same travelers, colonial administrators, and missionaries who gathered the cross-sectional data for the histories discussed in the first part of this book. Assisting in this distribution in recent years have been educational institutions, international organizations, development programs, family-planning programs, the women's movement, and the mass media. This dissemination has also been aided by the widespread adoption of Western languages and the phenomenon of growing urbanization. And the diffusion of developmental idealism has occurred at multiple levels—locally, nationally, and internationally (Montgomery and Casterline 1993; Rogers 1973; Rosero-Bixby and Casterline 1993).

It should be noted, however, that developmental idealism did not just passively ride the coattails of political, economic, and religious change but was often an active force facilitating, guiding, and even creating the mechanisms by which it was spread. Examples of this include European exploration and conquest, the forms and policies of colonial governments, and such social forces as Marxism, feminism, the family-planning movement, and evangelical Christianity. It has also played a role in the expansion of educational opportunities, the growth of industry, the improvement of the socioeconomic infrastructure, urbanization, and the establishment and growth of the mass media—all structural changes that have the potential to modify social relations and individual and family aspirations and behavior.

Of course, the enormous differentials in wealth, resources, technology, and military power between the West and the rest of the world reinforced the power of developmental idealism, convincing non-Westerners that the West was at the apex of development and that the rest of the world was underdeveloped and in need of remaking itself in the image of the West. Those differentials were also employed to force the spread of developmental idealism, with the economic and military power of the West directed toward overcoming what was often considerable indigenous resistance.

In this chapter and the next, I consider more fully the dissemination of developmental idealism. This chapter takes up three pathways: European colonization, revolutionary movements and governments, and family-planning programs. The next takes up such factors as educational opportunities, industrialization, urbanization, and the mass media. In both, I consider the influence of developmental idealism on these factors as well as the influence of these factors in the dissemination of developmental idealism. These chapters are not meant to offer an exhaustive discussion, as they explore only certain pathways—and those in only an abbreviated fashion—ignoring many others of equal importance.

European Colonization and Reform Movements

The perceived preeminence of the West was well established in the West before the era of Western exploration and expansion. It was especially strong in the religious and cultural arenas where Christianity was seen as both the one true religion and the height of religious development. The association between Christianity and civilization was, in fact, so strong that civilization became known as "Christian civilization." As the custodians of Christian civilization, the Northwest Europeans considered it their responsibility to spread both Christianity and civilization around the world (Comaroff and Comaroff 1991).[1] In so doing, they were, they believed, both obeying the word of God and helping those less fortunate souls mired in savagery and barbarism (Dussel 1995/1992; LiPuma 2000).

The period of European colonization lasted more than four hundred years, from the early 1500s to the mid-1900s. Virtually all the world's populations experienced European colonization or were threatened by it. They witnessed the power and wealth of Northwest Europe and saw the connection of this power and wealth to the Northwest European family system.[2] The ideology of European superiority was widely propagated, as was the notion

---

1. Colonists often explicitly saw themselves as exporters of modernity (see Comaroff and Comaroff 1991, 1997; Dussel 1995/1992; Moaddel 2005; Mody 2002).

2. See Bernard and Gruzinski 1996/1986; Dozon 1996/1986; Lardinois 1996/1986; Moaddel 2005; Nisbet 1980; Watkins 2000.

that only by adopting Western ways could the non-Western world hope to achieve such a state of development (Blaut 1993). Of course, the experience of colonization was not uniform but depended both on who was doing the colonizing and who was being colonized. In this section, I discuss various colonial reform movements initiated worldwide.

The reform movements initiated in Asia, Africa, and South America by European legislators and colonial administrators paralleled in many respects the efforts of Britain and the United States to deal with indigenous North American populations.[3] The goals of the reformers were many. Particularly pertinent to our purposes here, however, were attempts to modernize (i.e., Westernize) the family systems of the colonized.

The means used by the colonists to achieve the goal of modern family systems varied. In some places, laws were passed regulating who made the decision regarding choice of marriage partner, how marriages could be arranged, who had the authority to perform marriages, at what age marriage could occur, the nature and amount of exchanges at marriage, how many wives a man could have, whether divorce was allowed, and whether widows could remarry.[4] Laws were also passed regulating infanticide, female circumcision, and inheritance.[5] Many colonial systems also adopted elements of Western European legal and judicial philosophy and practice that emphasized the notions of universalism, egalitarianism, and the rights of individuals in contrast to the traditional notions of hierarchy and the authority of the family and community.[6]

Often, these reform movements continued after indigenous people gained control of their own governments.[7] In fact, reform efforts could sometimes be more forcefully and directly pursued after indigenous people gained power because the efforts were no longer directly linked to a colonial or

3. Interestingly, one of the key colonial government reformers in India was Henry Maine, who in the 1800s wrote a very important book about developmental change (Maine 1888/1861; see also Mody 2002).

4. See Bernard and Gruzinski 1996/1986; Bledsoe and Cohen 1993; Buxbaum 1968; Cooper 1997; Dozon 1996/1986; Frank 1989; Gray 1941; Hetherington 2001; Kapadia 1958; Lardinois 1996/1986; LiPuma 2000; Mayhew 1941; Moaddel 1992, 2005; Mody 2002; O'Malley 1941.

5. See Comaroff and Comaroff 1997; Hetherington 2001; Kapadia 1958; Lardinois 1996/1986; Mayhew 1941; O'Malley 1941.

6. See Bernard and Gruzinski 1996/1986; Dozon 1996/1986; Kapadia 1958; Lardinois 1996/1986; Mayhew 1941; Mody 2002; O'Malley 1941; Singh 1976.

7. See Bledsoe and Cohen 1993; Buxbaum 1968; Frank 1989; McNicoll 1994; Mody 2002; Myrdal 1968.

minority white government (Chambers, 2002; Mody 2002). For example, in Indonesia it was only with independence after World War II that reform movements could be initiated at all (Cammack, Young, and Heaton 1996). And in South Africa in the 1990s, certain new reforms not attempted by the previous, white government found a window of opportunity under the new, black government (Chambers, 2002).

It should be noted, however, that reform movements were initiated not just by, or under the influence or guidance of, or in the wake of colonial governments, but also by governments attempting to ward off colonization. The case of Japan is especially noteworthy (see Beillevaire 1996/1986; Goode 1970/1963; Macfarlane 2002). Feeling threatened by Western military and economic might, the Japanese government sent representatives to the West in the latter half of the 1800s in an attempt to understand the forces underpinning that might and, thus, resist it. In the process, those representatives imbibed and brought back with them the principles of developmental idealism, principles after which many reforms were eventually modeled. For example, with the aid of European advisers, a new legal code was introduced in Japan that abolished concubinage, made it easier for individuals rather than families to own property, provided for gender equality in education, and recognized individual rights. Such reforms were thus aimed largely at those aspects of the family system that European reformers had targeted in places colonized by Europeans. They were, however, carefully framed so as not to stray unacceptably far from historical Japanese cultural patterns (Beillevaire 1996/1986; Goode 1970/1963).[8]

Legal reforms were also instituted in Thailand and Turkey. In the early 1900s, Thais began debating new laws designed to change indigenous family forms, bringing them more into line with those in the West. Eventually, in 1935, a new marriage law was passed outlawing polygamy, imposing age restrictions, and requiring that marriages be registered. As Buxbaum suggests: "The substance of the rules in the new family law generally conforms to the international standard as expressed in most legal systems of Western nations" (1968, 98). Also in the early 1900s, revolutionary leaders in Turkey mounted a social revolution to modernize that country (Starr 1989). Laws were passed outlawing polygamy, giving women the right to divorce their husbands, setting minimum ages at which marriage could take place, and giving women the right to own property.

---

8. As will be seen below, the desire to avoid Western domination was an equally important motivation in the transformation of Chinese society that occurred through the 1900s (Cartier 1996/1986; Greenhalgh 1989).

Of course, vowing reform and passing laws are the easy parts. Effecting actual change in behavior is harder. Reform efforts can often have little effect on the general population, either because knowledge of them is restricted to the educated and urban portions of populations or because they are ignored, resisted, or weakly enforced.[9] Reform efforts can also have unintended effects, as in Afghanistan in the early 1900s and Iran in the 1970s, where government reform efforts have not only been strongly resisted but have also contributed to rebellion and regime change (Jayavardene 2002; Moaddel 1992, 2005; Moghadam 2002). Still, some reforms efforts have been successful, those in Central and South America (see below) in particular. What can be said about reform efforts generally is that, even where they have little obvious immediate and direct effect, they plant the seeds of change, which may eventually grow and produce actual changes in norms, values, and family forms.[10]

Among the most powerful and effective forces for change was the combined assault of the Spanish and Portuguese governments and the Catholic Church on indigenous Central and South American social, cultural, and religious forms that were very different from those existing in Western Europe (Bernard and Gruzinski 1996/1986; McCaa 1994a, 2003). The military leaders, colonial administrators, and missionaries moved energetically and forcefully to replace indigenous culture and social organization with Western lifestyles. Especially important to them was the replacement of indigenous religious beliefs and practices with those of Christian Europe. On the family front, the goal was the institution of Christian marriage and family life (Bernard and Gruzinski 1996/1986). The Europeans worked hard—and with force and coercion—to extinguish polygamy, family alliances, the marriages of close relatives, child marriage, and the authority of the family and community in spouse choice.

Given the gulf between the indigenous social, marriage, and family structures and those of Western Europe, the Christianization of society, religion, and marriage was met with strong resistance in many places in South and Central America (Bernard and Gruzinski 1996/1986; Dussel 1995/1992).[11]

---

9. See Beillevaire 1996/1986; Bledsoe and Cohen 1993; Cammack, Young, and Heaton 1996; Cartier 1996/1986; Frank 1989; Gray 1941; Lardinois 1996/1986; McNicoll 1994; O'Malley 1941.

10. See Bledsoe and Cohen 1993; Cammack, Young, and Heaton 1996; Cartier 1996/1986; Kapadia 1958; Lardinois 1996/1986.

11. The superior military power of the European conquerors frequently overpowered indigenous resistance. In addition, the native inhabitants had little resistance to the new diseases from Europe, and the resultant epidemics decimated both the population and the ability of the survivors to resist.

Despite this initial—and sometimes persistent—resistance, within a century of first contact many people in this region were Christian, attending church in Catholic chapels, being married by Catholic priests, speaking European languages, experiencing a more individualistic way of life, and living in family systems that had changed to be more like those of Western Europe (Bernard and Gruzinski 1996/1986; McCaa 1994a, 2003). For various reasons, however, European religion, languages, and family systems were differentially diffused across Central and South America. In addition, European family ideas and practices were frequently modified as they were adopted and often came to coexist alongside family patterns prevalent before the European conquest (Castro Martin 2002).

Revolutionary Movements and Governments

The ideas of developmental idealism have been circulated widely through academic and political networks. Non-Westerners learned of the developmental paradigm and its narrative of world history as they traveled and received educations in the West. The developmental literature also became accessible to non-Westerners through widely disseminated translations of important works.[12] Developmental thought provided the non-Western world with both a narrative of world history and a prescription for social change. Of central importance was the message that change—whether social, political, or economic—was both good and possible, that there was a better life, and that this better life could be attained by breaking the shackles of tradition.

One of the most important of the ideas circulated is the Marxist version of the developmental paradigm.[13] In the model of social change formulated by Marx and Engels, societies progress through various stages of development, eventually reaching the penultimate stage of capitalism, and finally culminating in a socialist utopia. Those societies that have reached the capitalist stage of development are, according to Marx and Engels, ripe for revolution and the subsequent adoption of socialism. The Marxist model was later expanded to suggest that in precapitalist non-Western societies revolution and strong government intervention could rapidly achieve the socialist utopia without passing through capitalism. This model of social and political change has proved to be an enormously powerful motivational force in

12. See Beillevaire 1996/1986; Lie 1996; Macfarlane 2002; Nisbet 1980; O'Malley 1941; Peel 1971; Pillai 1976a; Schwartz 1964; Spence 1999/1990; Wang 1999.

13. See Davis and Harrell 1993; Geiger 1968; Kerblay 1996/1986; Meijer 1971; Nisbet 1980; Sanderson 1990; Spence 1999/1990.

many parts of the world (Giddens 1981; Lie 1996; Nisbet 1980), inspiring movements leading to revolution and the establishment of socialist governments in several countries, most notably China and Russia in the first half of the 1900s.[14]

Particularly important to our concerns here is the fact that the Marxist version of developmental idealism included a strong focus on family structures and relationships.[15] It condemned family forms identified as traditional, linking these family forms with feudalism and a repressive social, political, and economic order. It advocated replacing such family patterns with the socialist version of the modern family, which emphasized gender equality and intergenerational independence. Consequently, dramatic family change has been central to the agendas of many revolutionary socialist movements. This was true in the Soviet Union (Geiger 1968; Kerblay 1996/1986; Northrop 1999), and it was also true in China, a country that I will now discuss in some detail.

The Case of China

China provides a particularly poignant example of the power of developmental idealism when coupled with a revolutionary movement (Davis and Harrell 1993). The Chinese have historically thought of their country as the Middle Kingdom, located at the center of the universe (Spence 1999/1990), and of their culture as representing the sum of wisdom and virtue. And, while they have historically been aware of other peoples and cultures, these were seen as largely irrelevant as sources of knowledge and wisdom. The basic elements of Chinese social life had persisted for centuries, and before the 1800s, there was nothing in the Chinese experience to suggest any need to question the ethnocentric assumption of superiority. The idea that China might look to Northwest Europe as a model for change would have been preposterous.

Much of this changed in the early 1800s as Europe and America gained considerable military and economic control in China (Spence 1999/1990; Wright 1968; Wang 1999). Over the course of the 1800s, China was defeated in numerous battles and Western governments were granted zones of influence in parts of the country. Although China never experienced colonization in the same way that India and Africa did, the influence of Western governments in Chinese affairs was still substantial. Faced first with the possibility

---

14. See Davis and Harrell 1993; Geiger 1968; Meijer 1971; Spence 1999/1990; Wang 1999.

15. See Andors 1983; Davis and Harrell 1993; Geiger 1968; Kerblay 1996/1986; Meijer 1971; Whyte, n.d.

of partitioning among the various Western powers and then with the actuality of military defeat at the hands of the Japanese in 1895, many influential Chinese became convinced of China's military and economic inferiority, a conviction that was reinforced by a comparison of the Chinese standard of living with that in the Western enclaves that had been established in some Chinese cities (Spence 1999/1990).

That conviction led to numerous efforts among China's elite to discover the key to social progress and international security. Many young Chinese traveled and studied abroad in search of the sources—and, thus, the ability to duplicate—Western technological, economic, and military power.[16] As part of this education outreach, much of Western thought was translated into Chinese, including specifically developmental and feminist works, which turned out to be especially influential (Schwartz 1964; Spence 1999/1990; Wang 1999). Most important for our purposes, however, was the fact that the Chinese were taught that Western power was embedded in a social system that differed markedly from the Chinese system. Furthermore, the Chinese were taught that this Western social system was an essential causal force producing Western wealth and power.

The ideas of developmental idealism soon convinced many Chinese intellectuals and political reformers that social and economic development along Western lines was necessary if Chinese culture and society were to survive and prosper. Changes in the family and political system were seen as particularly crucial to the achievement of economic development, technological innovation, and military power. Consequently, such change became the focus of various reform movements. Patriarchal power was attacked, to be replaced with autonomy within the family and democracy in the larger polity. Late marriage and consensual marriage were advocated as replacements for early marriage and arranged marriage. The ancient Chinese practice of minor marriage—the adoption of future daughters-in-law into the future husband's family as infants—was also attacked. In addition, the central Chinese cosmology linking the ancestors, the living, and future generations through the family line was denounced as superstition. The practices of concubinage and foot-binding were also condemned. And education for all, including both men and women, was encouraged as especially necessary to modernization.[17]

16. See Cartier 1996/1986; Gasster 1968; Lang 1968/1946; Schwartz 1964; Spence 1999/1990; Wang 1999; Wright 1968.

17. See Cartier 1996/1986; Gasster 1968; Goode 1970/1963; Lang 1968/1946; Meijer 1971; Spence 1999/1990; Wang 1999; Whyte, n.d.; Wright 1968; Yang 1959.

Knowledge and acceptance of developmental ideas spread during the late 1800s and early 1900s, first only among the educational and political elite, but then more generally among other segments of the population. Developmental ideas eventually percolated through enough of Chinese society to become a driving force for political, economic, and family change through most of the 1900s. These ideas helped spark the Republican Revolution of 1911 and motivated both the nationalist and Communist parties after World War I. With the victory of the Communists over the nationalists and the establishment of the People's Republic of China in 1949, these ideas became an important guide for government policy throughout the second half of the 1900s, affecting virtually every aspect of Chinese society.[18]

Particularly powerful in China have been the first and third propositions of developmental idealism: modern society is good and attainable; and the modern family is a cause as well as an effect of a modern society. Together, these propositions have motivated virtually every major political party and every government in China since 1911 to work toward the transformation of the indigenous Chinese family system into the modern family system of developmental idealism.[19]

Probably the first large-scale effect of this movement to modernize the Chinese family was the abolition of foot-binding, a widely endorsed and practiced element of Chinese society for a thousand years (Lang 1968/1946; Levy 1966). Because small feet had historically been seen as attractive, the feet of many female children were tightly bound from a young age to restrict growth, resulting in small and irregularly shaped feet that greatly limited mobility. In the late 1800s reformers began to denounce the practice of foot-binding (Levy 1966; Wang 1999).[20] With help from Christian missionaries, a mass movement emerged in China to abolish foot-binding, and this goal was endorsed by the leaders of the Republican Revolution of 1911 (Levy 1966). The new government soon issued a series of decrees outlawing foot-binding which "reached into every provincial town, hamlet, and village" (Levy 1966, 89).

18. See Cartier 1996/1986; Goode 1970/1963; Lang 1968/1946; Meijer 1971; Murphy 2001; Spence 1999/1990; Wang 1999; Whyte, n.d.; Wright 1968; Yang 1959.

19. See Cartier 1996/1986; Goode 1970/1963; Lang 1968/1946; Meijer 1971; Spence 1999/1990; Wang 1999; Yang 1959.

20. The reformer Kang Youwei said that "foreigners laugh at us for these things and criticize us for being barbarians. There is nothing which makes us objects of ridicule so much as foot-binding" (Levy 1966, 72). Kang and other reformers argued that foot-binding and other indigenous family practices subjugated women and prevented economic development.

In one rural area south of Beijing, the incidence of foot-binding decreased from 94 percent of the birth cohort of 1890–95 to 6 percent of the birth cohort of 1910–15 (Levy 1966). Of course, the rapidity of the abolishment of foot-binding varied considerably across China, but ultimately the practice was eradicated nationwide. This change became one of the success stories for the proponents of developmental idealism (Levy 1966).

There is also some evidence of additional effects of developmental idealism on family change in China during the first half of the 1900s.[21] Lang (1968/1946) reported that most high school and college students surveyed in the 1930s verbally endorsed reform of the indigenous Chinese family to be more like the modern family of developmental idealism. Several scholars have also suggested actual changes along these same lines in the educated urban elements of Chinese society (Lang 1968/1946; Levy 1949). Lang (1968/1946) reported that by the 1930s Chinese brides had shifted from wearing a red wedding dress indigenous to Chinese society to wearing wedding attire more similar to Western wedding dresses, a change that will be discussed more fully in the next chapter. In addition, a recent retrospective study in one urban center suggests that there may have been significant declines in arranged marriages before the middle of the 1900s (Whyte 1990, 1993).

With the Communist victory in 1949, the drive to modernize intensified, aided by the extension of government power to the local grassroots level (Yang 1959). In the family arena, a new marriage law was passed in 1950 that was essentially an agenda to replace central elements of the indigenous Chinese family system that had been in existence for centuries with the modern family outlined in developmental idealism.[22] This program for family modernization did not initially include efforts to reduce the number of children born, but in the last three decades of the 1900s the government, in its efforts to achieve socioeconomic development, instituted one of the world's most energetic population control and family-planning programs, including a policy to restrict couples to having a maximum of one child.[23]

Of course, historical patterns of family life were deeply ingrained in the Chinese social fabric, and, not surprisingly, the reform efforts of the Communist government met with considerable resistance. Despite this resist-

21. See Cartier 1996/1986; Lang 1968/1946; Levy 1949; Whyte 1990, 1993.

22. See Banister 1987; Cartier 1996/1986; Davis and Harrell 1993; Meijer 1971; Murphy 2001; Whyte 1990; Yang 1959.

23. See Banister 1987; Greenhalgh 1994, 2003a, 2003b; Greenhalgh and Winkler 2001; Lee and Wang 1999; Spence 1999/1990; Wolf 1986.

ance, which was often overcome through coercion, the Communist reform efforts have been successful in many respects, with family and demographic changes being widespread.[24] The power of the family lineages has been broken, reverence for the ancestors has declined, and the party-state has partially replaced parents as the authority in the lives of young people. Arranged marriages have declined dramatically, dowries play a less important role in marriage, and concubinage and minor marriage have largely disappeared. Age at marriage has increased substantially, and fertility has decreased substantially.

Chinese political life has been incredibly volatile over the last half century. One result of that volatility has been that family reforms have not been enforced consistently, although actual trends in marriage and fertility have been related closely to the strength of efforts to enforce the reforms (Greenhalgh 1994; Wolf 1986). Also, in recent years the government has relaxed its hold on family life, a change that has led to decreased age at marriage, among other things.[25]

Family-Planning Movements

Understanding of and commitment to the ideas of developmental idealism have been greatly facilitated in the last half century by the rise of the international population-control and family-planning movement (discussed in chapter 8). This movement was energized—as was the modernization movement in China—by the first and third propositions of developmental idealism: modern society is good and attainable; and the modern family is a cause as well as an effect of modern society. It also received legitimation and power as its advocates successfully linked family planning to the developmental idealism principle of freedom, a principle widely endorsed by respected international organizations (United Nations 2003). At the same time that the family-planning movement was, in large part, the product of developmental idealism, it was also to become one of developmental idealism's most vigorous proponents (Hodgson and Watkins 1997; Johnson 1987; Lapham and Simmons 1987). And it is the role of family-planning programs in propagating the ideas of developmental idealism to which I now turn.

24. See Banister 1987; Davis and Harrell 1993; Greenhalgh 1994, 2001, 2003a; Greenhalgh and Winkler 2001; Meijer 1971; Murphy 2001; Selden 1993; Siu 1993; Unger 1993; Whyte 1988, 1990, 1993; Wolf 1986; Yang 1959.

25. See Davis and Harrell 1993; Greenhalgh 1993; Murphy 2001; Selden 1993; Siu 1993; Whyte 1993.

Family-planning programs were initiated by a group of academics, foundations, Western governments, and international agencies that, together, provided the necessary intellectual justification, organizational and financial resources, and international legitimacy.[26] The international family-planning movement trained policymakers, scholars, government officials, and aid organizations. It created new forms of contraception, and provided to family-planning organizations in many countries contraceptive supplies and training in their distribution and use. It also successfully linked fertility control and small families to aspirations for economic development.

In addition, this international movement provided both incentives and sanctions to motivate the adoption of population and family-planning programs.[27] Some observers have suggested that the West pushed these programs on non-Westerners with missionary zeal and demanded contraception programs and the decline of fertility (Caldwell and Caldwell 1986, 1997, 1998; Donaldson 1990a). International aid for programs designed to foster socio-economic development was sometimes linked directly to the adoption of family-planning programs—either as an incentive for adopting a program or as a sanction for failure to do so.

This international family-planning movement has proved to be exceptionally powerful and effective in accomplishing its goals. Many non-Western governments shifted from a pronatalist to an antinatalist point of view—and in many instances in a remarkably short period of time.[28] In fact, Everett Rogers (1973, 6), an eminent expert on diffusion processes, has commented that "probably no other idea in . . . history has spread so rapidly from nation to nation." By 1969, two-thirds of the population in the so-called developing

26. See Cabrera 1994; Demeny 1988; Donaldson 1990a, 1990b; Finkle 2001; Finkle and McIntosh 1994; Freedman 1987; Greenhalgh 1996; Johnson 1987, 1994; Krannich and Krannich 1980; Mundigo 1996; Ness 1979; Nortman 1987; Notestein 1968; Reed 1978; Salas 1976; Warwick 1982; Watkins and Hodgson 1998.

27. See Barrett and Tsui 1999; Cabrera 1994; Caldwell and Caldwell 1986, 1997, 1998; Cleland, Onuoha, and Timaeus 1994; Donaldson 1990a; Kamuzora 1989; Kasun 1988; Lee et al. 1995; Rogers 1973; Watkins and Hodgson 1998.

28. See Banister 1987; Cabrera 1994; Caldwell 2001; Chamie 1994; Cleland, Onuoha, and Timaeus 1994; Finkle and Crane 1985; Finkle and McIntosh 1994; Freedman 1979; Hull and Hull 1997; Hull, Hull, and Singarimbun 1977; Johnson 1994; Kamuzora 1989; Kaufman 1983; Knodel, Chamratrithirong, and Debavalya 1987; Krannich and Krannich 1980; Mosley and Branic 1989; Mundigo 1996; Ness 1979; Notestein 1983/1964; Raftery, Lewis, and Aghajanian 1995; Thomas and Grindle 1994; Tsui 2001; Warwick 1982; Watkins 2000; Watkins and Hodgson 1998; White 1994.

countries had governments whose policy it was to limit population growth, and that proportion had grown to 93 percent by 1984.[29]

Individual countries have used a wide variety of approaches and methods to foster contraceptive use and lower fertility. Among these approaches have been the provision of family-planning supplies and services, efforts to reduce the number of children wanted, efforts to modernize family structures and relationships, and implicit and explicit incentives and coercion.[30] Not surprisingly, the mix of approaches used has varied greatly across the countries of the world.

A common feature of the program in most countries has been the provision of the necessary means to meet the already existing needs of individual couples to limit the number of children born to them. This individual demand for fewer children can come from many sources. Among the possible sources is the nearly universal decline in mortality, and especially child mortality, in non-Western settings in recent decades (Cleland 2001; Freedman 2001), the effect of which is the same as an increase in fertility since more children live to adulthood. Another source is social and economic change, which can modify personal circumstances and thus bring a desire for fewer children. Yet another is the global reach of the Western mass media, which, implicitly and explicitly, promote Western family forms, including lower fertility.

In order to meet the perceived need for controlled fertility and smaller numbers of children born, the programs have generally created an infrastructure of family-planning clinics and health workers. These organizations have provided contraceptive supplies, information about proper use, and support and follow-up (Freedman 1997; Freedman et al. 1994). Many couples around the world have taken advantage of these services.

In addition to meeting already existing demand, many programs have tried to increase demand for small families and contraception. Three general approaches have been used for this purpose: mass media campaigns meant to educate the general public about the need for controlled fertility; programs

29. See Johnson 1994; and Nortman 1985. See also Casterline 1994; Chamie 1994; Finkle and McIntosh 1994; Hodgson and Watkins 1997; Kaufman 1983; Lapham and Simmons 1987; United Nations 1998, 2003.

30. The countries where coercion has been particularly extensive at times include China, India, and Indonesia, three countries that together account for a substantial fraction of the world's population. See Banister 1987; Caldwell 1993; Caldwell, Reddy, and Caldwell 1988; David 1987; Greenhalgh 1994, 2001, 2003a; Greenhalgh and Winkler 2001; Hodgson and Watkins 1997; Hull and Hull 1997; Kasun 1988; Kaufman 1983; McNicoll 1997; Rogers 1973; Warwick 1986; Wolf 1986.

aimed at specific target audiences (students, military personnel, health-care workers, religious leaders, neighborhood groups, etc.); and the direct dissemination of information and ideas through field-workers.[31] And the messages conveyed have been simple: small families are part of a modern lifestyle; there are advantages of controlled fertility, particularly an improved standard of living; and it is acceptable to use contraception to control fertility.[32] It is likely that, as a minimum, these efforts have been effective in crystallizing or transforming existing demand for reduced childbearing and family planning into the acceptance and use of contraceptive services. They may also have been successful in reducing the number of children desired by couples (Donaldson 1990a; Simmons et al. 1988).

As an aid to reducing family-size ideals and increasing contraceptive use, some in the population-control and family-planning movement endorsed additional elements of the modern family complex of developmental idealism. This was probably due to the fact that in the mid-1900s, when the family-planning programs were first formulated, it was believed that family change had been an essential element of fertility decline in the West (see chapter 4). This made it easy to believe that a transformation of indigenous family systems in non-Western populations would be helpful—if not necessary—to fertility decline in these groups.[33]

This perspective on the importance of family change for fertility decline was endorsed, at least in principle, by numerous governments and international agencies. Even the 1974 Bucharest Population and Development Conference, sharply divided over many issues,[34] adopted a resolution recommending that efforts be made to bring indigenous non-Western family forms

---

31. These field-workers also often provide encouragement and social support for the adoption of contraception and sometimes become active participants in the decision-making process of families (Caldwell, Reddy, and Caldwell 1988; Donaldson 1990a; Simmons et al. 1988).

32. See Abbasi-Shavazi 2000a, 2000b; Berelson 1964; Bongaarts 1997; Cabrera 1994; Caldwell, Reddy, and Caldwell 1988; Critchlow 1999; Donaldson 1990a; Duza and Nag 1993; Finkle and McIntosh 1994; Freedman et al. 1994; Guzmán 1994; Hodgson and Watkins 1997; Hull and Hull 1997; Hull, Hull, and Singarimbun 1977; Johnson 1994; Kaufman 1983; Krannich and Krannich 1980; Kwon 1989; Mehryar et al. 2000; Middleton and Lapham 1987; Robinson and Rachapaetayakom 1993; Rogers 1973; Simmons et al. 1988; Watkins 2000; Watkins and Hodgson 1998; Warwick 1982, 1986.

33. See Davis 1967; Donaldson 1990a; Kwon 1989; McNicoll 1989; Notestein 1950.

34. Delegates disagreed, for example, over the nature of the relation between population programs and socioeconomic development—over whether development caused fertility decline or whether fertility decline caused development—but few disputed that there was a connection (Mauldin et al. 1974).

into closer conformity with modern Western family forms. Although the resolution recognized the importance of the indigenous cultural patterns of countries, it also supported such keystones of developmental idealism as individualism within the family; gender equality, including the full participation of women in society; mature marriage; and consent in marriage. Similar positions were taken by subsequent conferences, both regional and global, and the 1994 Cairo conference went even further by placing some aspects of the modern family higher in its hierarchy of goals than population stabilization itself.[35] This endorsement of the modern family by the family-planning movement would give the modern family additional legitimation, even if the family-planning movement took no further action to actually change family forms other than fertility (McNicoll 1989; Kwon 1989).

There have been many family changes in non-Western settings in recent decades, but they have not been as large and pervasive as previous generations believed were necessary for fertility to decline. Yet fertility has declined in many places. In addition, it has been difficult to identify a close connection between fertility decline and other changes in family forms.[36] Thus, experience outside the West is consistent with Western experience in that the adoption of family planning and the decline of fertility have not been dependent on a wholesale transformation of family forms.

There is widespread consensus that the worldwide family-planning movement has contributed significantly to the decline in fertility outside the West in recent decades.[37] Because developmental idealism was largely respon-

---

35. Among the elements of personal and family life especially endorsed by the Cairo conference were individualism, gender equality, and the empowerment of women (see Finkle and McIntosh 2002; Hodgson and Watkins 1997; Johnson 1994; McNicoll 1997). Nevertheless, the international population-control effort remains focused largely on family-planning programs (see Bongaarts 1997). For more on international support for the proposition that the modern family is good, see generally Abbasi-Shavazi 2000a, 2000b; Banister 1987; Demeny 1985; Kasun 1988; Kaufman 1983; Kwon 1989; Lapham and Mauldin 1985; McDonald 1993; McIntosh and Finkle 1995; McNicoll 1989, 1994; Mehryar et al. 2000; Ndeti and Ndeti 1980; Rogers 1973; Salas 1976; Simmons et al. 1988; United Nations Economic Commission for Africa 1984; Warwick 1986; Watkins and Hodgson 1998.

36. See Cleland 1985; Cleland and Wilson 1987; Freedman 1979; Mason 1997b.

37. See Abbasi-Shavazi 2000b; Abbasi-Shavazi et al. 2002; Banister 1987; Bongaarts 1993, 1997; Bongaarts, Mauldin, and Phillips 1990; Cabrera 1994; Caldwell and Caldwell 1986, 1988; Casterline 1994; Chamie 1994; Donaldson 1990a; Duza and Nag 1993; Freedman 1979; Freedman et al. 1994; Guzmán 1994, 1996; Hirschman 1994; Hirschman and Guest 1990; Hull and Hull 1997; Hull, Hull, and Singarimbun 1977; Knodel, Chamratrithirong, and Debavalya 1987; Kwon 1993; Lapham and Mauldin 1985, 1987; Mehryar et al. 2000; Mundigo 1996; Phillips et al. 1988; Rele

sible for the creation of this family-planning movement, much of the fertility decline can be attributed to it.

Of course, the timing of the introduction of fertility control programs has varied, as have the timing and pace of fertility declines. Also, there are still areas where the use of contraception is limited and fertility levels continue to be high. Although there are undoubtedly many factors contributing to differences in fertility levels and trends across countries, it is very likely that differential acceptance of developmental idealism has played a significant role. Fertility declines have been especially limited in populations that are isolated from the West and Western ideas because of geography, large cultural differences, or strong antipathies.[38] This is apparently true for some parts of Africa and in some Islamic countries where people have been very distrustful of the West and Western ideas and have seen family-planning programs as a foreign-policy conspiracy of Western governments rather than as a route to prosperity and the good life. And, in parts of Asia some people explicitly link their resistance to birth limitation to their belief that family patterns in the West are decadent.

Conclusion

The central conclusion of this chapter is simple: numerous political and government forces have been important factors in the spread of developmental idealism outside the West. Among these forces were European colonization, socialist revolutionary movements and governments, and family-planning movements. Also important, although not discussed in detail in this chapter, were international development efforts, the work of nongovernment organizations, the feminist and other international movements, and Christian missionary efforts.

These political, social, economic, and religious forces were all powered at least to some extent by developmental thinking and ideology. All were also conduits for the spread of developmental idealism. And, because they were

---

and Alam 1993; Robinson and Rachapaetayakom 1993; Tsui 2001; Watkins 2000; Watkins and Hodgson 1998; Warwick 1986. For exceptions, see Aramburú 1994; Pritchett 1994; and Raftery, Lewis, and Aghajanian 1995.

38. See Abbasi-Shavazi 2000b; Abbasi-Shavazi et al. 2002; Caldwell and Caldwell 1998; Chesnais 1992; Cleland 1985; Cleland and Wilson 1987; Knodel and van de Walle 1979; Kokole 1994; Lee et al. 1995; Mazrui 1994; McDonald 1993; Mehryar et al. 2000; Watkins 2000; Watkins and Hodgson 1998.

usually associated with economic, political, and legislative power, the principles of developmental idealism could be legislated and enforced. Such legislation and enforcement were often necessary to achieve change, the foreign nature of many elements of developmental idealism provoking resistance vigorous enough that it could be overcome only with force. The results varied, but most commonly found was a mixture of persistence and change in family forms.

12

Social and Economic Pathways of Influence outside Northwest Europe

I now shift our attention from the direct efforts of governments to spread developmental idealism to the ways in which more general social and economic forces have helped disseminate developmental idealism world-wide. Motivated partially by developmental idealism, and especially by its first proposition (modern society is good and attainable), socioeconomic development—including the expansion of educational opportunities, increases in the market for the mass media, industrialization, and urbaniza-tion—has become the goal of nearly every non-Western nation, greatly affecting the options available to individuals and the constraints binding them, and leading to changes in family life. The resulting new social and eco-nomic institutions have also been infused with developmental idealism, thereby becoming conduits for the very ideas that motivated them.

Social and Economic Change

The Expansion of Educational Opportunities

Education has, in many ways, come to be seen as the primary engine of socioeconomic development. The demand for the knowledge, the technical skills, and the credentials that an education can provide has become enor-mous (Brock-Utne 2000; Dore 1976; Hill and King 1993), often growing beyond the ability of societies to employ all graduates (Meyer et al. 1997). The expansion of educational opportunities is, in fact, one of the most remarkable phenomena of the past century, as very large percentages of the world's children now attend elementary school, and substantial fractions go on to high school and, in some cases, even college.[1] That expansion has

---

1. See Aghajanian and Mehryar 1999; Bledsoe and Cohen 1993; Bledsoe et al. 1999; Caldwell, Reddy, and Caldwell 1988; Chesnais 1992; Cohen 1993; Conway and Borque 1995/1993; Heaton

occurred in all regions of the world, including the poorest, although education levels still vary greatly by country. It has also occurred among females as well as males, although in many places females still lag behind males in terms of attendance (Stromquist 1999; Unesco 1999).

Taiwan provides an example of the enormous increase in school attendance and educational achievement in the 1900s. At the end of the 1800s, very few Taiwanese children attended school at all. But, with the Japanese occupation of the island (1895–1945), rates of elementary school attendance grew, and the rate of expansion of educational opportunities accelerated in the second half of the 1900s. A junior high school education had become compulsory by 1968. And by the end of the 1980s, three-quarters of the high-school-age population were attending school and nearly one-third of the college-age population were attending college (Hermalin, Liu, and Freedman 1994, 68).

Parts of Nepal provide similar examples of increases in educational achievement, although the increases there came later and current levels are lower than in Taiwan. In the Western Chitwan Valley in the south central part of Nepal, the first formal educational institution was created only in 1954. Both the number of schools and the rate of school attendance in the valley increased so dramatically in subsequent years that by the early 1970s the average distance from a neighborhood to a school was less than twenty minutes by foot, and by the mid-1990s elementary school attendance was nearly universal (Axinn and Barber 2001; Beutel and Axinn 2002). Furthermore, although most students were male through the 1950s, the gender disparity decreased so much that by the mid-1990s nearly half of all students were female. Educational aspirations in the valley are currently so high that about nine-tenths of parents feel that attending college is very important for both their daughters and their sons (Beutel and Axinn 2002).

Similar changes have occurred in other parts of Nepal. For example, in a rural community on the edge of the Kathmandu Valley in 1987, the proportions of males and females, respectively, who had ever attended school by age fifteen increased from 8 and 0 percent of the cohort born before 1936 to 73 and 22 percent of the cohort born between 1966 and 1975 (Fricke, Thornton, and Dahal 1990, 298). Even in a remote mountain village in north central Nepal (a four- or five-day walk from a road suitable for motorized traffic), the proportions of males who had ever attended school increased from none of those born before 1955 to 45 percent of those born between 1966 and 1975

and Forste 1998; Hill and King 1993; Hull and Hull 1997; Jejeebhoy 1995; Lapham and Simmons 1987; Rosen 1967; Unesco 1999.

(Fricke et al. 1991, 46).[2] In this particular isolated village there were still almost no females attending school, even among the most recent cohorts.

As the theorists of the 1700s and 1800s recognized, a growth in the number and types of schools and an increase in school attendance can profoundly change relationships with family and community members (see Cleland 2001; Jejeebhoy 1995; Thornton et al. 1994). For example, with increased school attendance, children spend much of the day at school, where they are socialized and supervised by teachers rather than by parents, which creates alternative authority structures. Also created is a generation gap in education level that reduces the prestige of the older, less-educated generation. Skills increase with education level, opening up more remunerative job opportunities. School attendance is also a time-consuming activity that can lead to the postponement of marriage, childbearing, and entrance into the workforce.

Most importantly for our purposes, schools have an ideational influence as they are designed explicitly to provide people new information and ideas. School attendance also equips students with the skills to gain expanded access to new ideas and information across their entire lifetimes. As a result, the educated are more likely to adopt many new ideas, including those of developmental idealism.

The messages of developmental idealism have permeated the educational systems outside of Europe for centuries (Masemann 1999; Samoff 1999; Welch 1999). Centrally important here are the messages that non-Western societies are inferior and undeveloped and that Western societies are superior, highly developed, and prosperous (Brock-Utne 2000). Also important in non-Western school systems are positive images of Western family forms and the link between these family forms and socioeconomic prosperity and well-being.[3]

The linkage of schooling and developmental idealism was so tight in some settings that the motivation for the establishment of schools came, at least partially, from the desire to indoctrinate children in developmental idealism (Conway and Bourque 1995/1993; Comaroff and Comaroff 1997; Brock-Utne 2000). This is particularly true of the many schools established by Christian missionaries who viewed education as an opportunity to impart not only

2. Even more dramatic increases in education levels have been reported by Ahearn (2001) for a village several hours' walk from a road in west central Nepal.

3. See Ahearn 2001; Bledsoe and Cohen 1993; Caldwell 1982; Caldwell, Reddy, and Caldwell 1988; Diamond, Newby, and Varle 1999; Stromquist 1999.

basic skills but Christianity itself, with its particular forms of family life labeled as modern.[4] It is also true that in some settings opportunities for female education were increased at least partially because of the desire to give women the resources and opportunities to achieve equal status with men.[5] In addition, women's education was sometimes justified as a positive force generally, promoting the well-being of the individual, the family, and the nation as a whole.[6]

Of course, education can also be used to maintain and strengthen indigenous cultures. And it can also represent a mix of the old and the new. Quite often, however, and especially in former European colonies such as the countries of Africa, the education process continues to be dominated by Western materials, and the language of instruction often continues to be the colonial European language instead of the indigenous language (Brock-Utne 2000).

Another route that non-Westerners took to education—besides taking advantage of the expanded school systems in their own countries—was pursuing an education in the West, particularly at the college level.[7] As we saw in the previous chapter, beginning in the late 1800s many Chinese students sought an education in the West in order to learn the secrets of Western economic and military power. Similar motivations existed for students from other countries, including Egypt and Japan (Fahmy 1998; Macfarlane 2002; Moaddel 2005). For those unable or unwilling to travel, many works by Western scholars were translated into indigenous languages (Fahmy 1998).

Industrialization and Urbanization

The ambition on the part of a society's leaders to convert their society into a modern one has helped to drive the transformation from a predominantly rural agricultural society into a predominantly urban industrial one, a process that has been dramatic in much of the non-Western world in recent decades. The result has been a transformation in the ways in which people make their livings, deal with their families and communities, and organize their lives.

---

4. See Brock-Utne 2000; Comaroff and Comaroff 1991; Gray 1941; O'Malley 1941; Wang 1999.

5. See Abu-Lughod 1998a; Belarbi 1999; Conway and Bourque 1995/1993; Mar'iyah 2002; Najmabadi 1998; Roose and Swift 2002; Wang 1999.

6. See Ahmed 2002; Hill and King 1993; Mar'iyah 2002; Rorlich 2002; Schultz 1993; Stromquist 1999.

7. See Ahmed 2002; Escobar 1988; Hermalin, Liu, and Freedman 1994; Macfarlane 2002; Moaddel 2005; Myrdal 1968; O'Malley 1941; Rosen 1967; Schwartz 1964; Spence 1999/1990; Wang 1999.

Again, we can see in Taiwan an example of rapid and substantial industrialization and urbanization (Fricke et al. 1994; Hermalin, Liu, and Freedman 1994; Thornton and Fricke 1987). In the early 1900s Taiwan was primarily rural and agricultural, the urban population representing only about one-ninth of the total. This proportion increased slowly at first, reaching approximately one-quarter by midcentury, and then more dramatically, reaching nearly three-quarters by the end of the 1980s. Similarly, the proportion of the labor force in agriculture declined from 56 percent in 1952 to 14 percent in 1988 (Hermalin, Liu, and Freedman 1994). This shift away from agriculture was also associated with a dramatic decline in the number of families organizing and controlling their own means of production in a family farm or business under the authority of a household head, as well as with an increase in the number of people earning their livings as employees in non-family-controlled organizations. This socioeconomic transformation has probably been among the more rapid and substantial in the world, but similar significant transformations have occurred elsewhere.

Such transformations can have substantial implications for individuals and their relationships with family members.[8] The shift from a system where families control and organize the means of production to one where people work outside the home or family network in a bureaucratic organization dramatically reduces the control of the family—and its head—over the means of production and consumption. As generations of scholars have suggested, this can have dramatic implications for household authority patterns, the independence of individuals in the labor force, patterns of interactions with the opposite sex, marriage negotiations, and relationships with peers (Thornton et al. 1994). Migration from rural areas to cities and the process of urbanization can also divide families geographically, lead to new living arrangements, and modify the nature of interactions with peers, neighbors, and the larger community (Thornton et al. 1994).

Such transformations also facilitate the flow of ideas. Whereas the flow of information in rural agricultural societies is controlled primarily through families and communities, in industrial urban societies information flows through both family links and industrial and bureaucratic networks. Specifically, the size and density of cities permit communication flows that are not possible in more rural settings. As a result, individuals are much more likely to come into contact with new ideas—including those about socioeconomic and family development associated with developmental idealism.

8. See Goode 1982/1964; Thornton and Fricke 1987; Thornton et al. 1994; Tilly and Scott 1978.

Mass Media and Travel

The mass media and travel are two more mechanisms by means of which the ideas of developmental idealism have been spread. Modes of communication have changed greatly in recent years, with national and international news and programming now reaching even the most remote parts of the world.[9] With the increase in education levels and the growth of literacy, the market for magazines and newspapers has also increased dramatically. In addition, radios, televisions, and computers bring information into the homes of even the illiterate. Modes of transportation have also changed dramatically in recent years. New networks of roads and airline routes have facilitated the movement of goods, people, and ideas across long distances.

Taiwan, again, offers an example of this rapid and striking change (Hermalin, Liu, and Freedman 1994). Starting from a baseline of great isolation, Taiwan substantially expanded its communication networks over the course of the past century, especially the last few decades. By the late 1980s, 89 percent of all Taiwanese households had a telephone, and 97 percent had color televisions (Hermalin, Liu, and Freedman 1994, 86). Millions of Taiwanese traveled to other countries, including thousands of young people studying abroad, and, in turn, millions of foreigners visited Taiwan. Although Taiwan has had some contact with Westerners since the 1600s, such contact has been especially extensive from the end of World War II to the present. Taiwan has been closely aligned with the United States since 1949, when the Nationalist government of China was defeated by the Communists and forced to retreat from mainland China to Taiwan after 1949. There was for many years a substantial Western military presence in Taiwan, a presence that brought with it Western television programs, movies, and magazines. As is clear to consumers worldwide, Taiwan has long been integrated in the global economy by both buying and selling goods and services.

Although Taiwan may have a higher density of media and transportation networks than many other non-Western societies, the trends in most non-Western countries are moving in the same direction as those in Taiwan. Relatively extensive media exposure could, according to Westoff and Bankole (1997), be found in the 1990s in the countries of sub-Saharan Africa. For example, in Namibia more than four-fifths of married women had access to radio once a week and more than one-quarter had access to television at least once a week (see also Bankole, Rodríguez, and Westoff 1996). Media exposure in

---

9. See Bledsoe and Cohen 1993; Caldwell, Reddy, and Caldwell 1988; de Carvalho and Wong 1996; Lerner 1958; Unesco 1999.

the 1990s was also extensive among married women in South Asia, with one-third listening to the radio weekly and nearly one-half watching television weekly in Pakistan (Westoff and Bankole 1999, 4) In India and Bangladesh nearly one-third of the married women watched television weekly, and about two-fifths listened to the radio weekly (Westoff and Bankole 1999, 13, 19; see also Simmons 1996).

Much of the mass media worldwide is permeated with the ideas of developmental idealism. Although a great deal of indigenous programming (especially news and commentary) does exist, there is also extensive Western programming. And Western programming inevitably brings with it images and messages of Western values and lifestyles. For example, images of socioeconomic prosperity convey the message of the value of socioeconomic development (Faria and Potter 1999; Hornik and McAnany 2001; Kottak 1990). And images of family life convey the message of the value of modern families with autonomy and equality in interpersonal relationships.[10]

Frequently the mass media has been employed for the express purpose of disseminating the ideas of developmental idealism. There is, of course, the obvious but still important example of advertising generating consumer demand (Hornik and McAnany 2001; Kottak 1990; Potter et al. 1998). Equally important from our point of view, however, is the employment of the mass media in family-planning programs. Bledsoe and Cohen (1993) suggest that the mass media may disseminate information about family planning more effectively than do schools. Surveys indicate that significant proportions of respondents report media exposure to family-planning information—for example, three-fifths of married women in Pakistan and nearly half of married women in India and Bangladesh, according to a 1990–91 survey (Westoff and Bankole 1999).[11]

This is not, of course, to suggest that, in the non-Western world, the ideas of developmental idealism have entirely taken over the mass media. Many media programs do continue to endorse the historical values and family forms of the indigenous culture. But much indigenous programming also reflects Western influences.[12] And the result is that, as time passes, in many

---

10. See Ahearn 2001; Faria and Potter 1999; Hornik and McAnany 2001; Kottak 1990; Schak 1975.

11. Widespread exposure has also been reported for Ghana, Tanzania, and Kenya (see Bledsoe and Cohen 1993; Jato et al. 1999; Olaleye and Bankole 1994; Westoff and Rodriguez 1995).

12. See Ahearn 2001; Bledsoe and Cohen 1993; Faria and Potter 1999; Hornik and McAnany 2001; Kottak 1990; Potter et al. 1998.

places the historical indigenous images and messages are increasingly sharing the media stage with Western programming and messages.

The Effects of Social and Economic Change on Family Life

Extensive data collected from many places around the world demonstrate that all the socioeconomic factors discussed above—the expansion of educational opportunities, industrialization, urbanization, and mass media exposure—are empirically related to family attitudes, beliefs, and behavior and that recent changes in these factors can explain a significant amount of the recent change in family life. Furthermore, although causal conclusions are always difficult to draw with nonexperimental data, these correlations likely reflect the influence of these socioeconomic factors on family life. I now turn to a brief discussion of this research, with illustrations primarily drawn from work conducted in Taiwan and Nepal.

Education, Urban Living, and Industrial Employment

Among the relevant socioeconomic factors, I turn first to educational attainment, which has been found to be strongly correlated with all the various aspects of family life. For example, Thornton and Lin (1994) have found that, in Taiwan, educational attainment is strongly related to virtually every family structure and process available for study. As expected, highly educated people in Taiwan tend to be situated on the modern end of the traditional/modern family continuum defined in the second proposition of developmental idealism. Compared to the less educated, they have more say in the choice of their spouse, are more involved in dating, and are more likely to meet their future spouse independent of parents and matchmakers. They endorse higher ages at marriage and are more likely to postpone marriage. And they are more likely to live independently of their parents at marriage and to give less reverence to their ancestors. Higher levels of education are also associated with lower desired and actual fertility and more extensive use of contraception. And all these empirical associations persist even with a substantial set of controls for other socioeconomic influences on family structures and relationships. This is consistent with the interpretation that the empirical relations are the result of education influencing family patterns, with the caveat that uncontrolled factors might still explain the association.

A similar set of empirical associations exists between education and family structures and processes in Nepal. Research indicates that having access to schools and school attendance are significantly related to a range of family attitudes and behaviors, including the use of contraception and whether a person has an arranged marriage.[13] Particularly interesting in the context of the current discussion is the strong association of high levels of education with negative attitudes toward such indigenous practices as child marriage, arranged marriage, polygamy, and mother-in-law obedience. High levels of education are also associated positively with attitudes toward practices—for example, intercaste marriage, divorce, and widow remarriage—that were historically prohibited among many groups in Nepal (Barber 1999). In Nepal, as in Taiwan, these empirical relationships are typically strong and persist in the presence of a substantial array of controls, suggesting that the effects may be causal rather than the result of other factors influencing both education and family life.

These findings can be replicated in numerous additional populations.[14] Educational attainment is also strongly correlated with other dimensions related to developmental idealism in countries outside Northwest Europe (Kahl 1968). It is important to note, however, that the influence of education can vary across both time and space—a fact that is undoubtedly related to variation in cultural circumstances and the role of education in the society (Cleland 2001).

Industrial non-family employment and urban living have also been found to be correlated with various aspects of family life. In Taiwan, for example, compared to those who grow up in agricultural families, young people who grow up in nonagricultural families have more dating experience before marriage, have more say in the choice of their spouse, have higher preferred and actual ages at marriage, and tend to be less reverential of their ancestors. Personal experience with nonfamily employment is associated with similar preferences and behaviors as well as with a lower likelihood of living with parents after marriage. Urban living is also associated with nuclear households. These empirical associations persist in the presence of controls (Thornton and Lin 1994).

Similar correlations exist in Nepal (Axinn and Yabiku 2001; Barber 1999; Ghimire et al. 2002). For example, in Nepal nonfamily employment and urban living are associated with more say in the choice of spouse, a greater likelihood of using contraception, and having a negative attitude toward indigenous marriage practices and a positive attitude toward historically pro-

---

13. See Axinn 1993; Axinn and Yabiku 2001; Barber 1999; Ghimire et al. 2002.

14. See Ainsworth, Beegle, and Nyamete 1996; Cleland 2001; Heaton and Forste 1998; Hill and King 1993; Jejeebhoy 1995; LeVine et al. 1991; Schultz 1993.

hibited marriage practices. As in Taiwan, these correlations persist in the presence of a broad array of controls.

Research has also shown that socioeconomic change can explain a significant part of family change in both Taiwan and Nepal. In Taiwan, for example, change in the socioeconomic factors under consideration here can account for between one-third and one-half of the substantial trend in preferred age at marriage, between one-half and two-thirds of the significant trends in dating and choice of spouse, and virtually all the trends in marriage formation and living arrangements immediately after marriage. However, it can explain only about one-fourth of the trend in the prevalence of Taiwanese living with parents in the years following marriage (Thornton and Lin 1994). Evidence from Nepal also suggests that change in these socioeconomic factors can account for much of the substantial trend in the mate-selection process in that country (Ghimire et al. 2002).

It is important to note that family behaviors and preferences are typically much more strongly correlated with education level than with such socioeconomic predictors as occupation, income, and place of residence. This is especially true in Taiwan, where educational attainment dominates over nonfamily employment and urban living in explaining most dimensions of family life (Thornton and Lin 1994). This also appears to be true in Nepal (Axinn and Yabiku 2001; Barber 1999; Ghimire et al. 2002), but the difference appears to be smaller there than in Taiwan. Furthermore, researchers studying fertility in multiple countries have found that childbearing is more strongly correlated with education level than with occupational status or income.[15]

Just as education level is usually a more powerful predictor of family behaviors and preferences than are occupation and income, change in education level is usually a more powerful predictor of change in family forms than are occupation or income change. For example, in Taiwan, change in education level alone can account for much of the change in family forms explained by the combined effects of several socioeconomic factors (Thornton and Lin 1994). Most strikingly, it can account for virtually all the change in the timing of marriage between the Taiwanese birth cohorts of 1941 and 1966. It can also account for a substantial fraction of change in other

15. See Bledsoe and Cohen 1993; Caldwell and Caldwell 1997; Chesnais 1992; Cleland and Jejeebhoy 1996; Cleland and Wilson 1987; Diamond, Newby, and Varle 1999; Jejeebhoy 1995; Jones 1997; Pritchett 1994; Psacharopoulos and Rosenhouse 1999; Rele and Alam 1993. Also see Inkeles 1969 and Inkeles and Smith 1974 for discussion of the predominant influence of education on a wide range of attitudes and values.

aspects of family life, including that in dating, marital arrangements and introductions, living arrangements, and respect for ancestors. These findings have generally been replicated in Nepal for trends in mate-selection processes (Ghimire et al. 2002). And similar conclusions have been reached in studies of other populations (Cleland and Wilson 1987; Heaton and Forste 1998).[16]

The exceptionally strong role of education—as compared to industry, city life, and occupational status—in predicting a wide range of family ideas and behaviors and in accounting for family change has important theoretical implications. Although industrialization and urbanization can facilitate the communication of ideas and information, that they do so is only a by-product of the economic and social relationships they produce. The education process, by contrast, has been explicitly designed to have the direct effect of spreading information and ideas. In addition, schools are sometimes established, at least in part, for the purpose of disseminating ideas and information to facilitate the adoption of family ideals associated with the modern family of developmental idealism. It is most likely these elements of education that make education level a particularly powerful predictor of family form and change in education level an especially powerful predictor of change in family form. Although additional differences between education and the other socioeconomic factors may also be important, this line of reasoning suggests that changing ideas may be more important than changing socioeconomic structures in explaining changing family ideas and behavior.

There is considerable evidence suggesting that education facilitates access to the mass media[17]—probably because more highly educated people are more likely to be able to afford media access, to have the skills and the knowledge required to access and understand the media, or to be required by their jobs to have access to the media. With more media exposure, highly educated people have more access to new ideas such as those of developmental idealism.

As noted earlier, changes in socioeconomic factors can statistically explain an important part of family change. However, there is also a substantial part of family change that cannot be explained by socioeconomic change (Ghimire et al. 2002; Thornton and Lin 1994). It is possible that the inclusion

16. The substantial role of education in fertility decline has been the subject of several excellent discussions. For example, see Cleland and Jejeebhoy 1996; Cleland and Wilson 1987; Jeffery and Basu 1996; Jejeebhoy 1995.

17. See Bankole, Rodríguez, and Westoff 1996; Jato et al. 1999; Olaleye and Bankole 1994; Westoff 1999; Westoff and Bankole 1997, 1999; Westoff and Rodriguez 1995.

of an even larger set of socioeconomic factors might explain the rest of this family change,[18] but it seems more likely that at least part of the explanation for the unexplained portion of the change lies outside the domain of socio-economic factors. My contention is that the explanations for the remaining family change are likely to lie in the changing content of ideas and values available and accepted in society, with the dissemination of developmental idealism being a particularly important part of the story.

The Mass Media

Another relevant factor found to be strongly correlated with many aspects of family life is exposure to the mass media. The association between media exposure and family patterns remains strong even when several socioeconomic factors are controlled. Several researchers have concluded, for example, that Brazilian television has played a significant role in the modification of gender-role ideology, marriage attitudes, fertility desires and behavior, and attitudes about premarital sex.[19] Kottak (1990) goes so far as to suggest that ideas about family relationships are among the things most susceptible to media influence in Brazil.

Research conducted in Nepal also confirms the importance of the media. Higher levels of media exposure are strongly correlated with an inclination to prefer smaller families, an inclination not to prefer sons over daughters, and more positive attitudes toward contraception (Axinn and Yabiku 2001; Barber and Axinn 2001). Media exposure is also strongly negatively correlated with attitudes toward certain practices permitted by indigenous cultural patterns (e.g., child marriage, arranged marriage, polygamy, and mother-in-law obedience) and strongly positively correlated with attitudes toward certain practices prohibited by indigenous cultural patterns (e.g., intercaste marriage, divorce, and widow remarriage) as well as with whether couples enter into arranged marriages (Ghimire et al. 2002). These estimated effects remain strong even when other socioeconomic factors are controlled.

Change in media exposure alone can explain substantial amounts of family change in Nepal. In fact, one analysis suggests that change in media exposure is among the most important sources of change in marriage

18. It is also possible that a more refined analysis that takes into account measurement error and alternative specifications of the functional form in the statistical analysis might explain more of the trend.

19. See Dunn 2000; Faria and Potter 1999; Hornik and McAnany 2001; Kottak 1990; Potter et al. 1998.

arrangements in recent decades, accounting for about three-fifths of the substantial shift toward young people's involvement in spouse selection. By contrast, only about one-fourth of the change in spouse selection can be explained by other socioeconomic changes (Ghimire et al. 2002).

In other settings, such as Bangladesh, Burkina Faso, Egypt, Ghana, Honduras, India, Indonesia, Kenya, Madagascar, Morocco, Namibia, Nigeria, Pakistan, Peru, the Philippines, Tanzania, and Zambia, media exposure is similarly strongly correlated with fertility and the use of contraception. This correlation holds for both general media exposure and exposure to specific messages about controlled fertility. For example, studies indicate that people with extensive media exposure generally have more knowledge of and more positive attitudes toward family planning, exhibit more actual use of contraception, and show a greater preference for smaller families and later marriage than do those with less media exposure, associations that persist even when other socioeconomic factors are controlled.[20]

Furthermore, qualitative studies conducted in Bangladesh indicate that all but the oldest people are aware of family-planning messages in the media and believe that these messages have made a difference in their relationships and behavior. For example, the mass media is reported to have provided the information and ideas with which to resist preestablished cultural scripts and, instead, pursue the goal of lower fertility by adopting family-planning practices (Simmons 1996). Other qualitative studies indicate similar effects (Freedman 1997; Hornik and McAnany 2001).

Of course, conclusive proof of the effect of media exposure is very difficult to obtain because currently available evidence comes from observational rather than experimental data. Consequently, it is possible that the strong observed correlations could be the product of selectivity and misspecification bias. That is, they could simply reflect the influence of unmeasured factors or the influence of family patterns on media exposure rather than the influence of media exposure on family patterns. Conclusive proof will come only with unambiguously properly specified models or long-term experiments.

Nevertheless, empirical analyses do exist that demonstrate the persistence of the association between media exposure and family patterns in the presence of controls. Some analyses have even been conducted using panel data, permitting an enhanced—although still incomplete—level of confidence in

20. See Bankole, Rodríguez, and Westoff 1996; Bledsoe and Cohen 1993; Dunn 2000; Freedman 1997; Hornik and McAnany 2001; Jato et al. 1999; Kincaid et al. 1999; Olaleye and Bankole 1994; Westoff 1999; Westoff and Bankole 1997, 1999; Westoff and Rodriguez 1995.

their results (Westoff and Bankole 1999; Kincaid et al. 1999; Potter et al. 1998). Thus, the current evidence suggests that media exposure does, in fact, influence family patterns. Furthermore, the problems of selectivity, endogeneity, and misspecification bias exist in all research utilizing observational data and do not appear to be more severe in the current instance than in many others.

In addition, there are theoretical reasons for believing that current studies underestimate rather than overestimate the effects of the mass media (Hornik and McAnany 2001). This underestimation occurs because most studies assume that the effects of the mass media operate only at the individual level as people have direct contact with the media. That is, mass media studies generally estimate the effects of the media by comparing the family behavior and ideas of individuals with various levels of mass media exposure. In order for this comparison to be a true reflection of the influence of the mass media, we must assume that people reporting no direct media experience are in fact not influenced at all by the media. This assumption is thus tantamount to saying that individuals are never influenced indirectly by the media as they communicate with friends, relatives, and neighbors who have direct media exposure. It also assumes that the mass media does not change the general culture, which in turn influences all individuals—both those with and those without direct media exposure. These are all very problematic assumptions whose violation biases downward estimates of the effects of the media.

Summary and Conclusions

In this chapter I have argued that numerous socioeconomic changes, such as industrialization, urbanization, and increases in the mass media and educational opportunities, have been important forces for spreading developmental idealism around the world. These changes have modified the structural relationships among individuals and between individuals and society, but even more crucial for present purposes is the fact that these changes have been important mechanisms for spreading developmental idealism. In addition, these socioeconomic changes are, in part, generated by developmental idealism and its endorsement of modern society, making developmental idealism a force for generating the mechanisms facilitating its spread.

These social and economic changes have had dramatic influence on family behavior and beliefs worldwide, both because they have changed the social structure and because they have facilitated the spread of developmental idealism, with its messages about desirable family forms. It is extremely difficult to evaluate whether these socioeconomic changes have affected family life more because of the structural changes they have brought or because they provide pathways for the spread of new ideas. Nevertheless, it is likely that the ideational pathways are the most important, a conclusion consistent with the fact that increases in the mass media and education (two factors designed to spread ideas and information) are more closely related to family change than are industrialization and urbanization (two factors that are only indirectly related to the spread of ideas and information). Further support for the importance of ideational pathways of family change is provided by the fact that in certain cases change can be plausibly explained only by ideational influences.

Changes in clothing styles serve as one example of a social change that can be plausibly attributed only to the influence of ideational changes. In many parts of the world, clothing styles—including those associated with important family rituals such as weddings—have changed from indigenous to Western forms. Although clothing styles may not be central parts of social and family life, change in them illustrates the power and pervasiveness of the influence of Western ideas. Such change can also have significant symbolic value that influences other aspects of social life, including family processes and relationships.

Take, for example, the shift in wedding attire that has occurred in both Taiwan and mainland China. Chinese brides historically wore red wedding dresses, red being an auspicious color in Chinese society, thought to bring good luck. By the 1930s, however, use of the red wedding dress was declining in some elements of the population. In the cities of mainland China it was being replaced by pink wedding dresses that were patterned largely after the style of wedding gowns in the West (Lang 1968/1946). Interestingly, the white color of Western gowns was not immediately adopted on the mainland because in Chinese culture white was the color historically associated with death.

In more recent decades, the red wedding dress has virtually disappeared in Taiwan. The white wedding gown of Western origins has now become popular in Taiwan, although pink dresses are also common. Also, some brides wear multiple gowns, with the different dresses having varying shades of white and pink. Although the change in the color of wedding dresses from red to white or pink may not seem consequential, the change is important symbolically. What is significant about this change in color is that, while it may have been facilitated by certain structural changes (urbanization, industrialization, etc.), it probably could not have taken place without there having first been an ideational shift in color preferences from the historically auspicious red to either pink or white, which were historically inauspicious colors for wedding gowns.

A similar process of Westernization has occurred in Kenya, where Western gowns "are preferred to the traditional ones, as young women want to signal that they are 'modern' and have mastered the idioms of modernity, style and fashion" (Fuglesang 1992, 142). Some also arrange additional ceremonies, "if they can afford it, wearing the so called 'traditional' . . . gowns to demonstrate that they are also proud of their various (ethnic) heritages and have a firm identity in their culture of origin" (Fuglesang 1992, 142). As in Taiwan and mainland China, this shift in wedding attire was probably, at least in part, a consequence of the spread of developmental idealism.[21]

This brings me to the final conclusion of the chapter. Although I do not claim that developmental idealism offers a complete explanation of change in family forms, the evidence suggests that it is a crucial factor. It certainly must be included in any comprehensive understanding of worldwide family change.

21. Transformation of clothing was apparently an explicit goal of some Western colonizers in Africa (Comaroff and Comaroff 1997). Some saw the dressing of Africans in Western attire as part of the civilizing process. These efforts have met with substantial success.

13

The Power of Developmental Thinking

I begin this closing chapter with the simple assertion that the developmental paradigm and its associated methodology and ideational program have been dominant forces in the world for centuries. They have largely controlled the social sciences, influenced national and international organizations, touched the lives of countless ordinary people, and affected the course of world history. This overwhelming influence has occurred, not just in Europe, but throughout the world.

The magnitude of these propositions and the evidence for their verity raise the immediate question of how such simple ideas could have had such an overwhelming influence. Are they really that powerful? Or did they happen to be located within the minds and cultures of people with the power to impose them on others? In what follows, I suggest that the answer to both questions is yes. In addition, when strong ideas are held by people who are wealthy and powerful, the result can be a rather irresistible force. At the same time, the forces spreading developmental idealism encountered many societies that put up extremely strong resistance, with the result often being conflict, adjustment, and hybridization of cultures.

The ideas of developmental idealism were powerful because the developmental paradigm and reading history sideways provided a model and a method through which to view and understand the world (Fricke 1997a, 1997b; Geertz 1973). This model of a common humanity on the pathway of life, a pathway with uniform and necessary stages, helped make sense out of the enormous differences among contemporaneous societies. It was not that societies were fundamentally different from each other, but that they were ordered at different stages along the ladder of development. The model thus explained both historical and geographic differences and provided useful predictions about future change.

The developmental paradigm and reading history sideways explained not only why societies were different with respect to a particular attribute but also why some social and economic attributes could be observed together in the same societies at the same time. The model, for example, explained why some social and family characteristics were associated with economic and military prowess. For instance, specific social, family, economic, and military attributes were seen as being associated with particular stages of the trajectory of development. In addition, some of these attributes, such as education and knowledge, were seen as causal agents producing certain family structures and processes. And certain family forms were seen as causal influences producing economic and military power.

Additional support for the developmental model came from two other sources. First, it had a long and respected history, extending back to Roman and even Greek antiquity (see chapter 2). Second, its core notion that societies moved through uniform and necessary stages was consistent with the perception that all biological organisms progressed through uniform and necessary stages over their lifetimes. As a result, the developmental model has since the 1700s largely been taken for granted by many scholars and ordinary people in Northwest Europe as one of the commonsense facts of the world—much as it was once taken for granted that the sun went around the earth. The taken-for-granted status of the developmental model has also spread to much of the rest of the world.

The Power of Developmental Models and Methods in Scholarly Work

Because of the power of the developmental paradigm, it should not be surprising that the Northwest European scholars of the 1700s and 1800s read history sideways to construct accounts of human history that covered virtually every dimension of human life, including the economic, political, social, familial, religious, psychological, and cultural. As we have seen in the family arena, this reading of history sideways led to the construction of an account of a great family transition in the Northwest European past that was discovered later to have little resemblance to the actual historical experience of that region. And despite the lack of correspondence with actual historical experience, this account went unchallenged until the middle of the 1900s.

The scholars of the 1700s and 1800s could have abandoned the assumption of necessary and uniform change across societies, eschewed the reading of history sideways, and contented themselves with writing detailed accounts of changes in family life in specific populations—an approach that would have brought them close to the principles of path dependency, contingency, and cultural descent with modification advocated by most scholars of social change today (Durham 1990; Quadagno and Knapp 1992; Sewell 1996). While that approach might have led to an understanding of how societies change, it would not have led to an explanation of the very great diversity that in fact existed. Even today, convincing alternative theories of that diversity remain elusive. It is no wonder, then, that in the 1700s and 1800s, the lack of a plausible account of diversity motivated scholars toward the developmental paradigm, reading history sideways, and the elegant accounts of social change they produced.

The developmental paradigm and reading history sideways came under serious attack in the 1900s, despite their long history, taken-for-granted status, and explanatory power. The numerous critiques that appeared during the 1900s suggest that the developmental paradigm and reading history sideways are fundamentally flawed and should be rejected.[1] These extensive critiques cannot be reviewed at length here, but I will note two main objections. First, the developmental model is teleological. That is, it assumes the existence of some fundamental and irresistible force that not only moves societies through a series of natural, uniform, and unidirectional changes toward some end state, but also does so at varying speeds. And it has been difficult to identify such a force without invoking metaphor, the hand of deity, or a general law of nature. Second, the historical record has not been kind to the assumption of a uniform trajectory of social change or to the accounts of social change derived from reading history sideways.[2]

These theoretical and empirical difficulties have dramatically decreased the influence of the developmental paradigm and reading history sideways in the social sciences. Very few scholars today directly utilize the assumptions of uniform, necessary, and directional change, using instead the ideas of path dependence and contingency. In addition, the perils of using cross-sectional

1. See Baker 1998; Boas 1940; Bock 1956; Giddens 1984; Gillis 1985; Goldenweiser 1937; Goldscheider 1971; Greenhalgh 1993, 1996; Hodgen 1964; Jennings 1975; Kreager 1986; Mandelbaum 1971; Nisbet 1975/1969, 1980; Popper 1964/1957; Szreter 1993; Tilly 1978, 1984; Wallerstein 1991, 1997/1979.

2. Interestingly, as Carneiro (1968) documents using English historical data, developmental histories derived from cross-sectional data can sometimes match those derived from the archival record relatively closely. However, Carneiro's research involved only one family factor and could not, therefore, investigate sequences of family change.

data to make conclusions about social change and to draw causal inferences are now widely understood and appreciated.[3]

Thus, in many ways the history of the developmental paradigm and reading history sideways in the social sciences, including demography and family studies, has followed the standard scientific model. That is, at any point in time observers describe and explain the world using the tools and conceptual apparatus available to them. These approaches, conclusions, and explanations remain in effect until disconfirming evidence and new ways of thinking accumulate and eventually overturn and replace the old models and conclusions.

As I suggested in chapter 6, any pronouncement of the demise of the developmental paradigm and reading history sideways would be premature. The developmental paradigm is more than an irrelevant artifact or a historical curiosity. Its influence can be seen in the continued use of the concept of a uniform trajectory through developmental stages, the continued identification of grand developmental epochs and transitions, the continued reliance on the language of developmental categories, and the continued invocation of the processes of development and modernization. In addition, many social scientists continue to make longitudinal inferences from cross-sectional data despite the existence of large quantities of longitudinal data and numerous warnings about the dangers of reading history sideways.

There are several possible explanations for this. First, it is very difficult and time-consuming to break old habits and ways of thinking. Second, the developmental paradigm and reading history sideways provide elegant and comprehensive accounts of the world and its history. Third, as I will discuss in more detail below, the model of progress and development retains power as an ideational guide to many individuals and groups, including social scientists, thereby providing support to developmental thinking in scholarly work. Fourth, although there is a great deal of longitudinal data available today, there is still a shortage of *reliable* longitudinal data, especially for the more distant past. This leads some social scientists to use whatever information is available.

---

3. The assumption of universal, necessary, and unidirectional change has also been seriously challenged at the individual level. Scholars increasingly view individual change as being influenced by a host of forces, including the biological and the social, and not reducible just to forces emanating from the individual. Thus, individual change is now viewed as more contingent and variable than suggested by the developmental paradigm. See, e.g., Baltes and Nesselroade 1984; Dannefer 1984a, 1984b; Dannefer and Perlmutter 1990; Featherman and Lerner 1985.

Finally, and perhaps most important, alternative paradigms simply do not have the explanatory power of the developmental paradigm and the method of reading history sideways. Although the principles of path dependence, contingency, and cultural descent with modification may provide more reliable accounts of historical processes than do developmental approaches, they are more limited in their ability to provide overarching and general explanations of cross-sectional variance and historical change. Consequently, they form relatively weak alternatives to the more grandiose, although theoretically and empirically flawed, models based on the developmental paradigm.

How are we to minimize the influence of the developmental paradigm and reading history sideways? First, we must have a thorough understanding of developmental models and methods and the ways they have influenced the study of social change. Then we must eliminate developmental models and remove the language of the developmental paradigm from the scientific lexicon and worldview. Next we must place less reliance on the theories formulated in the 1700s and 1800s to explain the family changes that were mistakenly believed to have occurred in Northwest Europe before 1800. This will require the addition of new ideas to explain family change occurring in the world today. Finally, we must identify those secondary reports currently being used to study social change that have been contaminated by the conclusions derived from reading history sideways. Only by making these changes can we completely eliminate the influence of the developmental paradigm and reading history sideways on scholarship today.

The Power of Developmental Models for Ordinary People

The power of the developmental paradigm and reading history sideways in explaining the world has not been limited to scholars. These approaches, along with the conclusions scholars derived from them, provided a powerful framework for ordinary people both to understand and to deal with the world. The approaches and conclusions of scholars were useful for ordinary people because they defined some of the attributes of the good life, specified causal approaches to reaching the good life, and provided statements of fundamental human rights. The positive labels of civilized, modern, enlightened, developed, and progressive were attached to the propositions of developmental idealism. Divergent views were labeled negatively as undeveloped, traditional, backward, barbarous, or savage. The principles of developmental idealism thus provided a structure of goals and motivations to guide individual and community behavior and change. These principles were also seen as inherent in past development and future progress.

With few exceptions, developmental idealism was a force to change social, political, religious, economic, and family systems that had been in existence for centuries. These indigenous social and cultural systems were also powerful in that they had for centuries provided models for understanding and dealing with the world (Fricke 1997a, 1997b; Geertz 1973). As such, these existing ways of believing and doing were deeply embedded within the lives of individuals as well as the social and economic structures of societies. They were also entwined within systems of interest and power, with many stakeholders who wished to maintain the status quo.

Consequently, it is not surprising that the messages of developmental idealism created substantial tension and conflict with indigenous historical social and cultural systems. Indeed, the history of this meeting of developmental idealism with indigenous systems has included substantial "clashes of culture" and both small- and large-scale physical conflict and coercion. In this conflict the power of the people who were supporting developmental idealism was an essential aspect of the spread of the behaviors and values that developmental idealism defined as good.

Such conflicts were substantial even in Northwest Europe, where the ideas of developmental idealism were first formulated and where they would be expected to be more compatible with the existing ideas than in non-European places. In many of these contests the outcome was not determined only by the power of the competing ideas, but also by the relative power of the competing groups.

Furthermore, although I have argued that the propositions of developmental idealism have become more widely endorsed and influential during the past two hundred years, their victory is still far from complete. This can be seen in the continuing inequalities across racial and gender groups in the Western world today. It is also evident in continuing restrictions on sexual expression and childbearing outside of marriage and the rights of homosexual couples to marry and raise children. Moreover, the battle between those wanting to extend the principles of developmental idealism to new family forms and those who want to defend historical family forms is at the center of many of the culture wars currently existing in the United States and elsewhere.

As we saw in chapter 6, developmental idealism has not always been a force for social change in the Western world. Instead it has sometimes been used as a force to prevent or roll back change. The use of developmental idealism to prevent change was evident in the efforts to eliminate Mormon polygamy and Oneida group marriage in the United States. Legal and physical coercion were also essential elements in restricting these innovations, as they were in changing the family forms of Native Americans and immigrants.

As one would expect, the barriers to the spread and adoption of the ideas of developmental idealism have been greater outside of Northwest Europe than inside it. This is due both to the long travel distances and to the barriers of different cultures and social systems. The clash between the principles of developmental idealism and the historical cultures of indigenous societies outside of Northwest Europe was especially apparent when colonial governments attempted to reform the family and social structures of indigenous peoples. In many cases the reform movements of European colonial powers were simply ignored and the European colonists had insufficient resources or will to dictate adoption of their reforms. In other cases the European reforms were met with very effective passive resistance. And in other settings local revolts forced the Europeans to back off from their aggressive programs of reform.

The removal of colonial governments and the establishment of indigenous governments sometimes led to expanded efforts to institute developmental idealism. This occurred because these new governments were imbued with the principles of developmental idealism but did not face the same opposition that a colonial government would have.

At times the elite in non-Western populations voluntarily and aggressively adopted certain Western family, social, and economic approaches as a way of resisting Western military power and the prospects of colonization. They did so because people in non-Western populations recognized their weak economic and military positions relative to those of Western powers and tried to adopt at least some Western ways in order to improve their economic and military power. The consequences of these actions in such places as China were considerable reforms of indigenous family systems so that they became more like the modern family defined by developmental idealism. However, the endorsement of the principles of developmental idealism by political elites in non-Western settings did not often eliminate indigenous resistance to those principles. Many people continued to resist the adoption of developmental idealism, even though it became the official policy of the political elites.

The nature and strength of the resistance to developmental idealism and Western family forms have varied greatly across both space and time. Of particular importance here is the evolution of resistance over the decades and centuries of contact with the forces disseminating developmental idealism.

Resistance movements can accommodate various elements of developmental idealism even as they continue to resist other elements. This accommodation can increase over time as new adjustments are made in the context of assimilation of previous adjustments.

This process has occurred in various places in the Middle East where strong Islamist movements emerged in the late 1900s in opposition to many elements of Western family culture. Such movements have frequently based their resistance to developmental idealism on the historical scriptures and teachings of Islam. However, these recent resistance movements must be evaluated in the context of the previous century of modernist movements to reform indigenous family and political life (Abu-Lughod 1998b; Moaddel 1992, 2005). As a result of the effectiveness of these earlier modernizing movements, the Islamist movements of the present have had to work from a transformed reality. Consequently, these present-day Islamist movements have not argued for the family and social relationships of the distant past but have advocated family and social systems that are hybrids of historical and Western patterns. That is, even as they resist some elements of Western family relationships, they adopt other elements of developmental idealism, without clear recognition of their origins.

Lila Abu-Lughod (1998b) argues that this process is particularly evident in Islamist movements in Egypt. She suggests that feminism, sexual independence, and freedom of women in political circles are sometimes strongly attacked as Western, yet women's employment, female education, companionate marriage, and the nuclear family are only weakly resisted or even openly embraced. Abu-Lughod claims that this acceptance by Islamists of many aspects of Western family systems is the result of long contact with the models of the modern family. Although the rationale often given for espousal of some elements of developmental idealism is that these elements are based on Islamic scripture and tradition, "it is," according to Abu-Lughod, "very hard to deny their sources in the West" (262). In fact, Abu-Lughod concludes that "access to any sort of real 'tradition' has been made impossible by the historical cultural encounter with the West" (261).[4]

Many of these same considerations apply to the Iranian Revolution that overthrew the Shah and his Western-oriented government in the late 1970s.

---

4. Another example of the mixture of Islamic and developmental idealism elements in Egypt is the divorce law reform instituted in 2000 that was justified both by appeals to the modern, enlightened principles of freedom and equality and by appeals to Islamic history and precedents (Duno 2003b; Singerman 2003).

This movement had a very strong Islamist character, emphasizing historical scripture and culture, attacking elements of Western life, and utilizing indigenous elements such as the dress of women to rally support against the Shah (Moaddel 1992; Sullivan 1998). Yet, this revolution cannot be characterized as a general revolt against modernity, but rather as a movement against the repressive features of the Shah's regime and its lack of respect for the role of Islam in Iranian life (Moaddel 1992, 2005). Some of the elements of modern social and family forms were apparently reinterpreted as being Islamic and were incorporated into the revolutionary movement (Sullivan 1998). The revolution was not opposed to modernity; instead, it offered an alternative or hybridized form of modernity (Abbasi-Shavazi et al. 2002; Moaddel 1992; Sullivan 1998).

The modernist tendencies of the Iranian revolutionary regime can be seen in the government's efforts to increase the social and economic well-being of the population through vigorous education, health, and mass media programs involving women as well as men (Abbasi-Shavazi et al. 2002; Hoodfar and Assadpour 2000). In addition, although the new regime initially suspended the official family-planning program of the Shah and emphasized early marriage and pronatalism, these policies were reversed in the late 1980s, and the Iranian government supported an energetic family-planning program.[5] The stated justification for the new family-planning initiative was based upon Muslim heritage rather than on Western ideas (Hoodfar and Assadpour 2000). Interestingly, the past decade in Iran has witnessed substantial increases in age at marriage, women's status, and contraceptive use, while marital fertility and arranged marriage have declined dramatically (Abbasi-Shavazi 2000a, 2000b; Abbasi-Shavazi et al. 2002).

Among the many advantages that developmental idealism has in its confrontations with indigenous cultures is that it is often viewed as an international force, one that transcends political and cultural boundaries and even takes on some of the features of an international religion (Comaroff and Comaroff 1991). Because it links all cultures by positioning them at various points on a single trajectory, it has a universal appeal. In contrast, indigenous cultures are, almost by definition, local entities representing only a modest minority of the world. As such, they have less scope and their resistance to the universal messages of developmental idealism tends to be perceived as petty and backward provincialism.[6]

---

5. See Abbasi-Shavazi et al. 2002; Aghajanian and Mehryar 1999; Hoodfar and Assadpour 2000; Mehryar et al. 2000.

6. I am indebted to Tom Fricke for the ideas expressed in this paragraph.

The general, overarching, and transcendent nature of developmental idealism has made it a primary component of what Meyer et al. (1997) call *world culture,* by which they mean a set of conceptual models, values, and ways of approaching issues that has the power to frame international and national problems and to suggest and impose solutions. Backed as it is by international organizations and strong national states, this world culture has great power and worldwide influence. Most interesting for our purposes, Meyer et al. identify development, freedom, and equality as central principles of this world culture (see also Wallerstein 1991, 1997/1979)—principles that have long been embraced by the United Nations and other international bodies (see, e.g., United Nations 1948, 1962, 1979; Organization of African Unity 1990).

This integration of central aspects of developmental idealism into world culture means that there is a world system to facilitate the spread of developmental idealism. Immanuel Wallerstein has argued that this world system has been in existence for centuries, facilitating the flow of information, goods, and ideas across international boundaries. Most important here is that, with the establishment and spread of international organizations, this world system has in recent decades become increasingly closely integrated, thus further facilitating the spread of developmental idealism.

Of course, the confrontation of developmental idealism with existing family systems involves the lives, agency, and decisions of indigenous people who must make their own decisions about the changes they might make in response to developmental idealism. Any adoption of developmental idealism, thus, involves considerable mixing of indigenous family forms and those of developmental idealism into a hybrid family system that is a combination of elements from the indigenous culture and from developmental idealism.

In such a hybridization process, the historical culture of a population and the ways in which a group encounters developmental idealism are crucial in both the process of change and in the forms of family life that emerge. Because of the great variety of indigenous family systems and the different ways people have come into contact with developmental idealism, it is to be expected that any mixing of indigenous family forms and developmental idealism will produce different results in different societies. And indeed there is today an important diversity of family systems and beliefs across geographical and cultural boundaries.[7] This outcome is consistent with the

---

7. See Billari and Wilson 2001; Bongaarts 2001; Inglehart and Baker 2000; Inglehart, Norris, and Welzel 2003; Kuijsten 1996; Lesthaeghe and Surkyn 2002; Norris and Inglehart 2003; Watkins 1991.

multiple, alternative, or plural modernities that have been discussed by many authors in recent years.[8]

My conclusion about developmental idealism is that it is a powerful force, changing the values, beliefs, and behaviors of people around the world. It is a powerful set of ideas, with an optimistic worldview, a roadmap for achieving success, and considerable consistency with empirical realities about geographical differentials in wealth and power. These features are sufficient to make many people rather enthusiastically embrace many aspects of developmental idealism. However, the appeal of developmental idealism is not universal; many people confronted by it continue to believe in the family and social systems that have sustained them and their ancestors for centuries. To these people, the family systems of Western societies look strange and undesirable, even with the enticements of the paradigm. In these cases developmental idealism is not adopted without force and coercion—which, as we know, are sometimes used to bring conformance to, if not belief in, the principles of developmental idealism. In almost all instances the multitude of forces combine to make developmental idealism an incredibly strong influence on family change for centuries.

Before leaving developmental idealism and its power to influence the lives of people, I emphasize again that developmental idealism is largely a value system indicating basic human rights, the nature of the good life, and the means to achieve the desired ends. My goal has not been to evaluate whether the propositions of developmental idealism are good or bad, helpful or hurtful, true or false, but to show how they have been powerful in changing family life around the world. Furthermore, I emphasize that even though the propositions of developmental idealism have gained much of their legitimacy from the developmental paradigm and reading history sideways and have often been disseminated by repulsive methods, the propositions are, in the end, mostly value statements that can be rejected or accepted independently of their sources and means of dissemination. Such determinations fall outside the parameters of this book.

Researching Developmental Idealism in the 2000s

As I have argued throughout the last part of this book, developmental idealism has been one of the most powerful influences on the lives of ordinary peo-

8. See Kahn 2001; Knauft 2002a; Lee 1994; Taylor 1999.

ple both in Northwest Europe and elsewhere around the world. In fact, the worldwide penetration of the ideas of modernity has led one observer to suggest that the object of anthropology should shift from "premodernity" to "modernity" (Kahn 2001; see also LiPuma 2000). An understanding of the ideas of developmental idealism is clearly necessary to any "anthropology of modernity." But we still know very little about the distribution of developmental thought in the general population, the extent to which beliefs in developmental idealism have changed over time, the precise factors influencing the adoption of such beliefs, and the consequences of beliefs in developmental idealism for family processes and relationships. Our knowledge of these factors and processes is limited because the research community has not focused a systematic research agenda on developmental idealism and its influence on the lives of ordinary people. In order for us to gain this knowledge we need a new program of data collection and analysis devoted to the study of developmental idealism and its role in everyday life. In what follows I outline the four key components of a research program directed to this end.

The first component in this research agenda is the creation of the tools that will allow direct measurement of the extent of belief in the key elements of developmental thinking. More specifically, I propose the creation of tools to measure the extent of belief in each of the four propositions of developmental idealism: modern society is good and attainable; the modern family is good and attainable; the modern family is a cause as well as an effect of a modern society; and individuals have the right to be free and equal, with social relationships being based on consent (see chapter 8). Also important is the creation of tools to measure the extent of belief in the developmental paradigm—the idea that societies go through uniform, necessary, and directional change—and the extent of belief in the method of reading history sideways by discerning one society's past from another society's present (see chapter 2). I also advocate the creation of tools to measure beliefs in a great family transition in Northwest Europe's past (see chapter 3) and in the ranking of countries by their degree of development. The creation of tools to measure the complex ideas of the developmental paradigm and developmental idealism will require extensive effort.[9]

9. In measuring commitment to the proposition that the modern family is good and attainable, it is important to ascertain how individual people define the modern family. This is necessary because the definition of the modern family has varied across time and can vary across individuals and because certain family traits such as divorce and single parenthood are defined by some people as modern and by others as Western (see chapter 8).

The second component of this research agenda is to use the new measurement tools in empirical studies to ascertain the extent to which people accept developmental thinking and incorporate it into their worldviews. Assembling a body of empirical data about developmental beliefs from multiple populations around the world will make it possible to answer such questions as where these beliefs are most widely held, how they are distributed among population subgroups, and how these beliefs are changing.

The third component of this research program is to elucidate the pathways and mechanisms through which beliefs in developmental idealism and the developmental paradigm are disseminated or resisted. As we saw in chapters 8–12, there are many potential pathways for the dissemination of developmental beliefs, which include Northwest European colonization, Christianity, Marxist ideology, education, international travel, the women's movement, family-planning programs, and the mass media. It is important to evaluate which of these have been influential in transmitting beliefs in developmental idealism in particular times and places. This agenda should consider both the content of the messages distributed by these social institutions and the exposure of people to them. It is also important to examine the ways in which developmental idealism has influenced the establishment of many social institutions, such as schools, factories, the mass media, family-planning programs, and feminist initiatives, which have in turn affected family life both by changing constraints and opportunities and by spreading developmental idealism. Equally important is an examination of people's exposure and commitment to forces of resistance to the ideas of developmental idealism.

The fourth component of this research agenda is an investigation of the influence of developmental thinking and beliefs on a wide range of family structures, behaviors, and relationships. This research goal is especially challenging because beliefs in developmental idealism are subjective phenomena and cannot be easily ascertained retrospectively; meeting this goal will require panel designs that begin with a baseline measurement of developmental beliefs followed by additional waves of data collection that measure the relevant family structures and behaviors. Also necessary for this component of the research agenda is an extension of its focus beyond the influence of developmental thought on family structures, behaviors, and relationships. The research must measure and control for factors other than the ideas of developmental idealism. Examples of these other factors include social, economic, and political structures and experiences as well as such ideational forces as belief in the teachings of religion and belief in the ideas and theories of science. This research program must also look at the ways in which structural and ideational factors intersect and mutually reinforce or negate each other as they affect family life. These considerations require special attention to model specification, causal inference, and biases in the estimation of effects, which can be particularly difficult when there are multiple causal influences to be untangled, when the ideational and structural factors involved change over time, and when factors work together as well as independently.

Accomplishment of this ambitious research agenda requires multiple data collection and analysis strategies. Especially relevant are cognitive testing, in-depth interviews, focus groups, ethnographic approaches, and data-gathering through surveys. Archival research and content analysis of published literature would also be useful. A combination of these methods would provide the most insights concerning developmental idealism and its role in changing family life.

Conclusion

I close by observing that the introduction and dominance of the developmental paradigm, reading history sideways, and the conclusions of social science set in motion a worldwide centuries-long experiment concerning the influence of developmental beliefs on family behavior and relationships. This experiment involved the dissemination of developmental idealism and related beliefs through some of the most powerful mechanisms in human history. Unfortunately, from a scientific viewpoint this centuries-long experiment has serious flaws. It was done without control groups, the randomization of treatments, or systematic baseline and follow-up observations. In addition, developmental idealism was not the only explanatory factor allowed to vary. Instead, there were numerous uncontrolled factors—such as wars, scientific and technological change, and change in disease and mortality patterns—the effects of which are potentially confounded with the effects of developmental idealism. Because of these serious shortcomings in the study design, it is difficult to evaluate completely the results of the experiment. Still, the data that do exist suggest strongly that the influence of developmental thought on family life has been substantial worldwide. And there is every reason to believe that that influence continues to be strong today and will remain strong in the future. The study of the influence of developmental thought, both in the past and in the future, must therefore be a high priority.

Postscript: Dealing with the Language of the Developmental Paradigm

One of the most difficult decisions I was faced with while preparing this book centered on language and the values that are embedded in the developmental paradigm. The developmental paradigm is part of a hierarchical view of the world that differentially values the world's various populations, cultures, and societies. It sees some populations as having made more progress than others; that is, it sees some as mature and others as infantile. In fact, it sees some populations as being so developmentally immature as to have no society or culture at all.

The developmental paradigm commands a language that communicates this hierarchical view of the world. In the past, populations that were perceived as being at an early stage of development were referred to as *savage, barbarous, rude, unpolished, uncivilized, traditional, undeveloped,* or *backward.* Populations perceived as being at the pinnacle of development were called *developed, civilized, modern, advanced, enlightened, progressive,* and *polished.*

Embedded within this developmental hierarchy was a hierarchy of social value. Societies perceived as being at the height of development were considered superior and of greater social value, while those seen as being at early stages of development were considered inferior and of lesser value. This reduces to development itself being perceived as being of greater value than traditionality (Williams 1985/1976).

The language used in developmental discourse has evolved dramatically over time. In recent decades, the pejorative nature of such terms as *uncivilized, savage, barbarous, rude, unpolished,* and *backward* has been recognized, and they have largely disappeared from both ordinary and scholarly discourse.[1] Even references to *undeveloped* societies have begun to disappear,

---

1. Interestingly, the 11 September 2001 attacks on the World Trade Center in New York and the Pentagon in Washington, D.C., triggered a brief return to such pejorative language, con-

with the term *undeveloped* being replaced by such terms as *less developed, developing, least developed,* and *newly developed* (most obviously in UN categorization schemes). Interestingly, the term *traditional society* is still frequently used to refer to groups perceived as less developed.

There has been less evolution in the language used to refer to populations perceived as being highly developed. To be sure, developmental discourse seems to have largely abandoned the term *polished* and seems to rely less heavily on the concept of civilization. Yet such terms as *developed, modern, advanced, enlightened,* and *progressive* continue to have wide currency.

Developmental language, by its very nature, implies value distinctions. The use of developmental language perpetuates and legitimates pernicious distinctions among societies, with those (usually Western) labeled *modern* assigned greater value and those (usually non-Western) labeled *traditional* assigned lesser value (Williams 1985/1976). Similar considerations apply to descriptions of social, economic, religious, political, and family systems. For example, categorizing certain family attributes (extended households, arranged marriages, strict parental control, etc.) as *traditional* and others (nuclear households, love marriages, minimal parental control, etc.) as *modern* suggests that the latter are developmentally superior and of greater value and the former developmentally inferior and of lesser value. The use of developmental language is therefore to be eschewed in scientific discourse that aims to be value free.[2]

It might be argued that the traditional/modern continuum can be divorced from the developmental paradigm and used in a value-free way to describe societies and family systems. This approach is problematic because the concepts of modern and traditional are not defined by scientific or theoretical criteria, but by the combination of traits existing among certain groups living in the West—or among groups described in contrast to the West. There is no apparent theoretical construct linking together the dimensions of family life—age at marriage, living arrangements, family size, the arrangement of marriage, parental authority, gender equality, and family solidarity—frequently used to divide family systems into traditional and modern categories. Similarly, there is no apparent theoretical construct to link

---

trasts being made between barbarism and savagery, on the one hand, and civilized society, on the other.

2. The use of developmental language in categorizing societies and economic, political, religious, and family systems also has the potential to damage international goodwill and understanding, because it inherently makes pernicious comparisons in its categorization scheme. This consequence is another reason to eschew the use of developmental language.

together the dimensions of social life frequently used to divide socioeconomic systems along the traditional/modern continuum. Without such theoretical or scientific constructs, the only ideas providing coherence to the traditional/modern continuum are the developmental paradigm and the geographical concentration of particular attributes in Northwest Europe. In the absence of an independent theoretical basis, the continued use of the traditional/modern distinction is without scientific justification and serves only to perpetuate hierarchical notions and to obstruct attempts to attain a true understanding of human social life.

Of course, such an explicit and strong rejection of developmental language does not mean that I have not employed the language myself. In fact, it is obvious that I have used it throughout this book. However, my use of the language was not motivated by any endorsement of the developmental paradigm or the application of the traditional/modern categorization scheme to specific societies or family systems, but by a desire to explain and analyze the developmental models used by others—in the first instance by scholars and in the second instance by people in everyday life.

I used developmental language and categories in the first part of the book, describing the models, methods, and data used by earlier generations of scholars, because the developmental paradigm and its language of hierarchy and differential societal maturity dominated scholarly discourse from the 1600s through the early 1900s. Indeed, I could not have accurately described the work of these scholars without recourse to the developmental concepts and language they used.

I also used developmental language in the second part of the book in order to explain the ways ordinary people have been influenced by various aspects of developmental thinking. Because it was the developmental paradigm, reading history sideways, and the conclusions of several generations of scholars using this model and methods that gave developmental idealism its power, it would have been impossible to describe developmental idealism without the use of developmental language. In fact, the use of the traditional/modern categorization scheme by the general public as well as by scholars dictated its use in the very definition of three of the four propositions of developmental idealism.

It is also important to note that developmental idealism is a conceptual framework and set of propositions that are sometimes included in the understandings of many people outside of academia. The crucial point here is that developmental idealism, with its employment of the traditional/modern distinction, is part of an ideational system available for people in everyday life rather than an analytical system just for scholars. That is, in developmental idealism it is the beliefs and ideas of people in everyday life rather than the categorization system of a researcher that defines a family or social trait as traditional or modern. This is true even though the frameworks of people outside academia today were derived, at least in part, from the scholarly models and conclusions of the past.

A central thesis of this book is that the power of developmental ideology and language is so strong today that many individuals outside academia routinely use the paradigm and its terminology. This is true not only for people in the West but also for people outside the West, even though the application of the concepts of less developed or developing to one's own community and culture implies acceptance of the social and cultural immaturity and inferiority such labels denote. Because developmental models and concepts can be a central part of people's lives, it is essential that these models and concepts be actively studied by the social science community. It is important for scholars to understand the extent to which people around the world accept and use the developmental worldview and the propositions of developmental idealism.

Of course, as scholars study the influence of developmental models, propositions, and motivations on people in everyday life, they themselves will need to employ the same developmental models and propositions. However, this study of developmental models, language, and motivations can be done without scholars themselves categorizing any societies, social forms, or family systems as modern, traditional, developing, or developed. Scholars can avoid using these labels to categorize people even when the people studied identify and categorize themselves as modern, traditional, developed, or developing. Admittedly, this line between studying the distribution and effects of developmental definitions, ideology, and thinking in the world and using developmental models and language to categorize and label people and their social forms is a thin one. Yet it is crucially important.

References

Abbasi-Shavazi, Mohammad J. 2000a. "Effects of Marital Fertility and Nuptiality on Fertility Transition in the Islamic Republic of Iran, 1976–1996." Working paper. Demography and Sociology Program, Australian National University.

———. 2000b. "National Trends and Social Inclusion: Fertility Trends and Differentials in the Islamic Republic of Iran, 1972–1996." Paper presented at the seminar "Family Planning Programmes in the Twenty-first Century," International Union for the Scientific Study of Population, Dhaka, Bangladesh, 16–21 January.

Abbasi-Shavazi, Mohammad J., Amir Mehryar, Gavin Jones, and Peter McDonald. 2002. "Revolution, War, and Modernization: Population Policy and Fertility Change in Iran." *Journal of Population Research* 19 (1): 25–46.

Abma, Joyce C., Anjani Chandra, William D. Mosher, Linda S. Peterson, and Linda J. Piccinino. 1997. "Fertility, Family Planning, and Women's Health: New Data from the 1995 National Survey of Family Growth." In *Vital and Health Statistics* vol. 23, no. 19, pp. 1–114. Washington, D.C.: U.S. Government Printing Office, for U.S. Department of Health and Human Services.

Abray, Jane. 1975. "Feminism in the French Revolution." *American Historical Review* 80 (1): 43–62.

Abu-Lughod, Lila. 1998a. "Feminist Longings and Postcolonial Conditions." In *Remaking Women: Feminism and Modernity in the Middle East*, ed. Lila Abu-Lughod, 3–32. Princeton, N.J.: Princeton University Press.

———. 1998b. "The Marriage of Feminism and Islamism in Egypt: Selective Repudiation as a Dynamic of Postcolonial Cultural Policies." In *Remaking Women: Feminism and Modernity in the Middle East*, ed. Lila Abu-Lughod, 243–69. Princeton, N.J.: Princeton University Press.

Aghajanian, Akbar, and Amir H. Mehryar. 1999. "Fertility Transition in the Islamic Republic of Iran: 1976–1996." *Asia-Pacific Population Journal* 14 (1): 21–42.

Ahearn, Laura M. 2001. *Invitations to Love: Literacy, Love Letters, and Social Change in Nepal.* Ann Arbor: University of Michigan Press.

Ahlburg, Dennis A., and Carol J. DeVita. 1992. "New Realities of the American Family." *Population Bulletin* 47 (2): 1044.

Ahmad, S. 2002. "Feminist Movement for Democratic Rights." In *Muslim Feminism and*

Feminist Movement: South-East Asia, ed. Abida Samiuddin and R. Khanam, 367–84. Delhi: Global.

Ahmed, L. 2002. "Egyptian Reformism and Women's Rights." In *Muslim Feminism and Feminist Movement: Africa*, ed. Abida Samiuddin and R. Khanam, 1:135–51. Delhi: Global.

Ainsworth, Martha, Kathleen Beegle, and Andrew Nyamete. 1996. "The Impact of Women's Schooling on Fertility and Contraceptive Use: A Study of Fourteen Sub-Saharan African Countries." *World Bank Economic Review* 10 (1): 85–122.

Aldous, Joan. 1978. *Family Careers*. New York: Wiley.

Alexander, Jeffrey C. 1995. *Fin de Siècle Social Theory: Relativism, Reduction, and the Problem of Reason*. London: Verso.

Alexander, William. 1995/1779. *The History of Women from the Earliest Antiquity to the Present Time*. 2 vols. Bristol: Thoemmes.

Alison, Archibald. 1840. *The Principles of Population*. Vol. 1. Edinburgh: William Blackwood.

Alwin, Duane F. 1984. "Trends in Parental Socialization Values: Detroit, 1958–1983." *American Journal of Sociology* 90 (2): 359–82.

———. 1986. "Religion and Parental Child-Rearing Orientations: Evidence of a Catholic-Protestant Convergence." *American Journal of Sociology* 92 (2): 412–40.

———. 1987. "Changes in Qualities Valued in Children in the United States." Institute for Social Research, University of Michigan. Typescript.

———. 1988a. "From Obedience to Autonomy: Changes in Traits Desired in Children, 1924–1978." *Public Opinion Quarterly* 52 (1): 33–52.

———. 1988b. "Structural Equation Models in Research on Human Development and Aging." In *Methodological Advances in Aging Research*, ed. T. W. Schaie et al., 71–170. New York: Springer-Verlag.

Amin, Qasim. 1992/1899. *The Liberation of Women*. Translated by Samiha Sidhom Peterson. Cairo: American University in Cairo Press.

Amin, Sajeda, and Nagah H. Al-Bassusi. 2002. "Wage Work to Prepare for Marriage: Labor Force Entry for Young Women in Egypt." Paper presented at the annual meeting of the Population Association of America, Atlanta, 9–11 May.

Amin, Sajeda, and Mead Cain. 1997. "The Rise of Dowry in Bangladesh." In *The Continuing Demographic Transition*, ed. Gavin W. Jones, Robert M. Douglas, Jack C. Caldwell, and Rennie M. D'Souza, 290–306. Oxford: Oxford University Press.

Amin, Samir. 1989. *Eurocentrism*. New York: Monthly Review Press.

Ammons, Linda L. 1999. "What's God Got to Do with It? Church and State Collaboration in the Subordination of Women and Domestic Violence." *Rutgers Law Review* 51:1207–89.

Anderson, Barbara A. 1986. "Regional and Cultural Factors in the Decline of Marital Fertility in Europe." In *The Decline of Fertility in Europe*, ed. Ansley J. Coale and Susan C. Watkins, 293–313. Princeton, N.J.: Princeton University Press.

Anderson, Michael. 1986/1980. *Approaches to the History of the Western Family*. London: Macmillan.

Andors, Phyllis. 1983. *The Unfinished Liberation of Chinese Women, 1949–1980.* Bloomington: Indiana University Press.

Anglim, John. 1978. "On Locke's State of Nature." *Political Studies* 26 (1): 78–90.

Anthony, Susan B. 1897. "The Status of Woman, Past, Present, and Future." *Arena* 17:901–8.

Aramburú, Carlos. 1994. "Is Population Policy Necessary? Latin America and the Andean Countries." In *The New Politics of Population: Conflict and Consensus in Family Planning,* ed. Jason L. Finkle and C. A. McIntosh, 159–78. New York: Population Council.

Ariés, Phillippe. 1962/1960. *Centuries of Childhood.* New York: Vintage.

Ashcraft, Richard. 1968. "Locke's State of Nature: Historical Fact or Moral Fiction?" *American Political Science Review* 62 (3): 898–915.

———. 1969. "John Locke's Library: Portrait of an Intellectual." *Transactions of the Cambridge Bibliographical Society* 5, pt. 1:47–60.

———. 1987. *Locke's Two Treatises on Government.* London: Allen & Unwin.

Astell, Mary. 1970/1730. *Some Reflections upon Marriage.* 4th ed. New York: Source Book.

Audinarayana, N., and S. Krishnamoorthy. 2000. "Contribution of Social and Cultural Factors to the Decline in Consanguinity in South India." *Social Biology* 47 (3–4): 189–200.

Axinn, William G. 1993. "The Effects of Children's Schooling on Fertility Limitation." *Population Studies* 47 (3): 481–93.

Axinn, William G., and Jennifer S. Barber. 2001. "Mass Education and Fertility Transition." *American Sociological Review* 66 (4): 481–505.

Axinn, William G., and Arland Thornton. 2000. "The Transformation in the Meaning of Marriage." In *Ties That Bind: Perspectives on Marriage and Cohabitation,* ed. L. Waite, C. Bachrach, M. Hindin, E. Thomson, and A. Thornton, 147–65. Hawthorne, N.Y.: Aldine de Gruyter.

Axinn, William G., and Scott T. Yabiku. 2001. "Social Change, the Social Organization of Families, and Fertility Limitation." *American Journal of Sociology* 106 (5): 1219–61.

Axtell, James. 1981. *The European and the Indian: Essays in the Ethnohistory of Colonial North America.* New York: Oxford University Press.

Aziz, F. A. 2002. "Survey of Female Circumcision in Ibadan, Nigeria." In *Muslim Feminism and Feminist Movement: Africa,* ed. Abida Samiuddin and R. Khanam, 2:591–96. Delhi: Global.

Bailey, Joanne. 2002. "Favoured or Oppressed? Married Women, Property, and 'Coverture' in England, 1660–1800." *Continuity and Change* 17 (3): 351–72.

Bailey, William B. 1907. "Comments in Edward A. Ross's 'Western Civilization and the Birth-Rate.'" *American Journal of Sociology* 12 (5): 619–21.

Bailyn, Bernard. 1967. *The Ideological Origins of the American Revolution.* Cambridge, Mass.: Belknap.

Baker, Keith M. 1975. *Condorcet: From Natural Philosophy to Social Mathematics.* Chicago: University of Chicago Press.

———. 1990. *Inventing the French Revolution.* Cambridge: Cambridge University Press.

Baker, Lee D. 1998. *From Savage to Negro: Anthropology and the Construction of Race, 1896–1954.* Berkeley and Los Angeles: University of California Press.

Baltes, Paul B., and John R. Nesselroade. 1984. "Paradigm Lost and Paradigm Regained: Critique of Dannefer's Portrayal of Life-Span Development Psychology." *American Sociological Review* 49 (6): 841–47.

Banister, Judith. 1987. *China's Changing Population*. Stanford, Calif.: Stanford University Press.

Bankole, Akinrinola, Germán Rodríguez, and Charles F. Westoff. 1996. "Mass Media Messages and Reproductive Behaviour in Nigeria." *Journal of Biosocial Science* 28 (2): 227–39.

Barber, Jennifer S. 1999. "Communities and Attitudes: The Influence of Nonfamily Institutions and Experiences on Dispositions toward Marriage." Paper presented at the annual meeting of the American Sociological Association, Chicago, 6–10 August.

Barber, Jennifer S., and William G. Axinn. 2001. *New Ideas and Fertility Limitations: The Role of Mass Media*. Institute for Social Research, University of Michigan. Typescript.

Barrett, David B., ed. 1982. *World Christian Encyclopedia: A Comparative Study of Churches and Religions in the Modern World, AD 1900–2000*. Nairobi: Oxford University Press.

Barrett, Deborah, and David J. Frank. 1999. "Population Control for National Development: From World Discourse to National Policies." In *Constructing World Culture: International Nongovernmental Organizations since 1875*, ed. John Boli and George M. Thomas, 198–221. Stanford, Calif.: Stanford University Press.

Barrett, Deborah, and Amy O. Tsui. 1999. "Policy as Symbolic Statement: International Response to National Population Policies." *Social Forces* 78 (1): 213–34.

Bartlett, Elizabeth A., ed. 1988. *Sarah Grimké: Letters on the Equality of the Sexes and Other Essays*. New Haven, Conn.: Yale University Press.

Bartlett, Robert. 1993. *The Making of Europe: Conquest, Colonization, and Cultural Change, 950–1350*. Princeton, N.J.: Princeton University Press.

Batz, William G. 1974. "The Historical Anthropology of John Locke." *Journal of the History of Ideas* 35 (4): 663–70.

Beard, Mary. 1946. *Woman as a Force in History: A Study in Traditions and Realities*. New York: Macmillan.

Becker, Howard, and Harry E. Barnes. 1961. *Social Thought from Love to Science*. New York: Dover.

Beillevaire, Patrick. 1996/1986. "The Family: Instrument and Model of the Japanese Nation." In *A History of the Family*, ed. Andrè Burguière, Christiane Klapisch-Zuber, Martine Segalen, and Françoise Zonabend, 2:242–67. Cambridge, Mass.: Harvard University Press.

Béjin, Andre. 1983. "Social Darwinists and Malthus." In *Malthus Past and Present*, ed. J. Dupâquier, A. Fauve-Chamoux, and E. Grebenik, 299–312. London: Academic Press.

Belarbi, Aicha. 1999. "Islam, Women, and Politics." In *Islam and Equality: Debating the Future of Women's and Minority Rights in the Middle East and North Africa*, 185–205. New York: Lawyers Committee for Human Rights.

Ben-Amos, Ilana K. 2000. "Reciprocal Bonding: Parents and Their Offspring in Early Modern England." *Journal of Family History* 25 (3): 291–312.

Benefo, Kofi D. 1999. "Cultural Perspectives on West African Fertility Change." In *Dynamics of Values in Fertility Change*, ed. Richard Leete, 331–42. Oxford: Oxford University Press.

Berelson, Bernard. 1964. "On Family Planning Communication." *Demography* 1 (1): 94–105.

Berg, Barbara J. 1978. *Remembered Gate: Origins of American Feminism: The Woman and the City, 1800–1860*. New York: Oxford University Press.

Berger, Brigitte, and Peter L. Berger. 1984. *The War over the Family: Capturing the Middle Ground*. Garden City, N.Y.: Anchor.

Berkhofer, Robert F. 1978. *The White Man's Indian: Images of the American Indian from Columbus to the Present*. New York: Knopf.

Berkovitch, Nitza. 1999. "The Emergence and Transformation of the International Women's Movement." In *Constructing World Culture: International Nongovernmental Organizations since 1875*, ed. John Boli and George M. Thomas, 100–126. Stanford, Calif.: Stanford University Press.

Bernard, Carmen, and Serge Gruzinski. 1996/1986. "Children of the Apocalypse: The Family in Meso-America and the Andes." In *A History of the Family*, ed. Andrè Burguière, Christiane Klapisch-Zuber, Martine Segalen, and Françoise Zonabend, 2:161–215. Cambridge, Mass.: Harvard University Press.

Bernard, Jessie. 1982/1972. *The Future of Marriage*. 2d ed. New Haven, Conn.: Yale University Press.

Betts, C. J. 1973. Introduction to *Persian Letters*, by Charles-Louis de Secondat, Baron de Montesquieu, trans. C. J. Betts, 17–23. Harmondsworth: Penguin.

Beutel, Ann M., and William G. Axinn. 2002. "Gender, Social Change, and Educational Attainment." *Economic Development and Cultural Change* 51 (1): 109–34.

Bianchi, Suzanne M., and Daphne Spain. 1986. *American Women in Transition*. New York: Sage.

Billari, Francesco C., and Chris Wilson. 2001. "Convergence towards Diversity? Cohort Dynamics in the Transition to Adulthood in Contemporary Western Europe." Working Paper no. WP 2001–039. Rostock, Germany: Max Planck Institute for Demographic Research.

Biller, Peter. 2001. *The Measure of Multitude: Population in Medieval Thought*. Oxford: Oxford University Press.

Billings, John S. 1893. "The Diminishing Birth-Rate in the United States." *Forum* 15:467–77.

Blaut, James M. 1993. *The Colonizer's Model of the World: Geographical Diffusionism and Eurocentric History*. New York: Guilford.

Bledsoe, Caroline. 1994. "'Children Are Like Young Bamboo Trees': Potentiality and Reproduction in Subsaharan Africa." In *Population, Economic Development, and the Environment*, ed. Kerstin Lindahl-Kiessling and Hans Landberg, 105–38. Oxford: Oxford University Press.

Bledsoe, Caroline H., and Barney Cohen. 1993. *Social Dynamics of Adolescent Fertility in Sub-Saharan Africa*. Washington, D.C.: National Academy Press.

Bledsoe, Caroline H., John B. Casterline, Jennifer A. Johnson-Kuhn, and John G. Haaga, eds. 1999. *Critical Perspectives on Schooling and Fertility in the Developing World*. Washington, D.C.: National Academy Press.

Boas, Franz. 1940. *Race, Language, and Culture*. New York: Macmillan.

Bobbio, Norberto. 1993/1989. *Thomas Hobbes and the Natural Law of Tradition.* Chicago: University of Chicago Press.

Bock, Kenneth E. 1956. *The Acceptance of Histories: Toward a Perspective for Social Science.* Berkeley: University of California Press.

Bogue, Donald J. 1993. "How Demography Was Born." *Demography* 30 (4): 519–22.

Boles, Janet K. 1979. *The Politics of the Equal Rights Amendment: Conflict and the Decision Process.* New York: Longman.

Bolgar, R. R., ed. 1979. *Classical Influences on Western Thought, A.D. 1650–1870.* Cambridge: Cambridge University Press.

Bongaarts, John. 1993. *The Fertility Impact of Family Planning Programs.* New York: Population Council.

———. 1997. "The Role of Family Planning Programmes in Contemporary Fertility Transitions." In *The Continuing Demographic Transition,* ed. Gavin W. Jones, Robert M. Douglas, John C. Caldwell, and Rennie M. D'Souza, 422–43. Oxford: Oxford University Press.

———. 2001. "Household Size and Composition in the Developing World in the 1990s." *Population Studies* 55:263–79.

Bongaarts, John, W. Parker Mauldin, and James F. Phillips. 1990. "The Demographic Impact of Family Planning Programs." *Studies in Family Planning* 21 (6): 299–310.

Bongaarts, John, and Susan C. Watkins. 1996. "Social Interactions and Contemporary Fertility Transitions." *Population and Development Review* 22 (4): 639–82.

Book of Common Prayer, Church of England: The Second Prayer-Book of King Edward VI; Reprinted from a Copy in the British Museum. 1888/1552. London: Griffith, Farran, Okeden & Welsh.

Bosanquet, Helen. 1915/1906. *The Family.* London: Macmillan.

Boserup, Ester. 1971/1970. *Woman's Role in Economic Development.* London: Allen & Unwin.

———. 1990. *Economic and Demographic Relationships in Development: Essays Selected and Introduced by T. Paul Schultz.* Baltimore: Johns Hopkins University Press.

Bowman, Cynthia G. 1996. "A Feminist Proposal to Bring Back Common Law Marriage." *Oregon Law Review* 75:709–80.

Brace, Laura. 2000. "'Not Empire, but Equality': Mary Wollstonecraft, the Marriage State, and the Sexual Contract." *Journal of Political Philosophy* 8 (4): 433–55.

Bradley, Martha S. 1993. *Kidnapped from That Land: The Government Raids on the Polygamists of Short Creek.* Salt Lake City: University of Utah Press.

Brentano, Lujo. 1992/1910. "The Doctrine of Malthus and the Increase of Population during the Last Decades." *Population and Development Review* 18 (1): 147–66.

Brock-Utne, Birgit. 2000. *Whose Education for All?* New York: Falmer.

Brooke, Michael Z. 1970. *Le Play: Engineer and Social Scientist.* London: Longman.

Broude, Gwen J. 1994. *Marriage, Family, and Relationships: A Cross-Cultural Encyclopedia.* Santa Barbara, Calif.: ABC-CLIO.

Brundage, James A. 1987. *Law, Sex, and Christian Society in Medieval Europe.* Chicago: University of Chicago Press.

———. 1993. "Implied Consent to Intercourse." In *Consent and Coercion to Sex and*

Marriage in Ancient Medieval Societies, ed. Angeliki E. Laiou, 245–57. Washington, D.C.: Dumbarton Oaks Research Library and Collection.

Bryson, Gladys. 1945. *Man and Society: The Scottish Inquiry of the Eighteenth Century.* Princeton, N.J.: Princeton University Press.

Bulatao, Rodolfo A. 1979. "Further Evidence of the Transition in the Value of Children." Papers of the East-West Population Institute: Current Studies on the Value of Children, no. 60-B. Honolulu: East-West Population Institute.

———. 1980. "The Transition in the Value of Children and the Fertility Transition." In *Determinants of Fertility Trends: Theories Re-Examined (Proceedings of a Seminar Held in Bad Homburg, F.R. Germany)*, ed. Charlotte Höhn and Rainer MacKensen, 95–122. Liège: Derouaux Ordina Editions.

Bumpass, Larry, and Hsien-Hen Lu. 2000. "Trends in Cohabitation and Implications for Children's Family Contexts in the U.S." *Population Studies* 54 (1): 29–42.

Bumpass, Larry, and James A. Sweet. 1989. "National Estimates of Cohabitation." *Demography* 26 (4): 615–25.

Burch, Thomas K. 1996. "Icons, Straw Men, and Precision: Reflections on Demographic Theories of Fertility Decline." *Sociological Quarterly* 37 (1): 59–81.

Burgess, Ernest W., and Harvey J. Locke. 1953/1945. *The Family.* New York: American Book Co.

Burguière, Andrè. 1987. "The Formation of the Couple." *Journal of Family History* 12 (1–3): 39–53.

Burguière, Andrè, Christiane Klapisch-Zuber, Martine Segalen, and Françoise Zonabend, eds. 1996/1986. *A History of the Family.* 2 vols. Cambridge, Mass.: Harvard University Press.

Burguière, Andrè, and François Lebrun. 1996/1986. "The One Hundred and One Families of Europe." In *A History of the Family*, ed. Andrè Burguière, Christiane Klapisch-Zuber, Martine Segalen, and Françoise Zonabend, 2:11–94. Cambridge, Mass.: Harvard University Press.

Burrow, John W. 1981. *Evolution and Society.* Cambridge: Cambridge University Press.

Butler, Melissa A. 1978. "Early Liberal Roots of Feminism: John Locke and the Attack on Patriarchy." *American Political Science Review* 72 (1): 135–50.

Buxbaum, David C. 1968. *Family Law and Customary Law in Asia: A Contemporary Legal Perspective.* The Hague: Martinus Nijhoff.

Cabrera, Gustavo. 1994. "Demographic Dynamics and Development: The Role of Population Policy in Mexico." In *The New Politics of Population: Conflict and Consensus in Family Planning*, ed. Jason L. Finkle and C. A. McIntosh, 105–20. New York: Population Council.

Cain, Mead. 1977. "The Economic Activities of Children in a Village in Bangladesh." *Population and Development Review* 3 (3): 201–27.

———. 1978. "The Household Life Cycle and Economic Mobility in a Village in Bangladesh." *Population and Development Review* 4 (3): 421–38.

Caldwell, John C. 1982. *Theory of Fertility Decline.* London: Academic.

———. 1993. "The Asian Fertility Revolution: Its Implications for Transition Theories."

In *The Revolution in Asian Fertility: Dimensions, Causes, and Implications*, ed. Richard Leete and Iqbal Alam, 299–316. Oxford: Clarendon.

———. 1999. "The Delayed Western Fertility Decline in English-Speaking Countries." *Population and Development Review* 25 (3): 479–513.

———. 2001. "The Globalization of Fertility Behavior." In *Global Fertility Transition*, ed. John B. Casterline and Rodolfo Bulatao, 93–115. *Population and Development Review*, vol. 27 (suppl.).

Caldwell, John C., and Pat Caldwell. 1986. *Limiting Population Growth and the Ford Foundation Contribution.* London: Frances Pinter.

———. 1988. "Is the Asian Family Planning Program Model Suited to Africa?" *Studies in Family Planning* 19 (1): 19–28.

———. 1997. "What Do We Know about Fertility Transition." In *The Continuing Demographic Transition*, ed. Gavin W. Jones, Robert M. Douglas, John C. Caldwell, and Rennie M. D'Souza, 15–25. Oxford: Oxford University Press.

———. 1998. "Regional Paths to Fertility Transition." Paper presented at the Ford Foundation conference "Global Fertility Transition," Bellagio Center, Bellagio, Italy, 18–22 May.

Caldwell, John C., P. H. Reddy, and Pat Caldwell. 1988. *The Causes of Demographic Change: Experimental Research in South India.* Madison: University of Wisconsin Press.

Calhoun, Arthur W. 1960a/1917. *A Social History of the American Family.* Vol. 1, *Colonial Period.* New York: Barnes & Noble.

———. 1960b/1918. *A Social History of the American Family.* Vol. 2, *From Independence through the Civil War.* New York: Barnes & Noble.

———. 1960c/1919. *A Social History of the American Family.* Vol. 3, *From 1865 to 1919.* New York: Barnes & Noble.

Cammack, Mark, Lawrence A. Young, and Tim Heaton. 1996. "Legislating Social Change in an Islamic Society—Indonesia's Marriage Law." *American Journal of Comparative Law* 44 (1): 45–73.

Caplow, Theodore, Howard M. Bahr, and Bruce A. Chadwick. 1983. *All Faithful People.* Minneapolis: University of Minnesota Press.

Caplow, Theodore, Howard M. Bahr, Bruce A. Chadwick, Reuben Hill, and Margaret H. Williamson. 1982. *Middletown Families.* Minneapolis: University of Minnesota Press.

Carneiro, Robert L. 1968. "Ascertaining, Testing, and Interpreting Sequences of Cultural Development." *Southwestern Journal of Anthropology* 24:354–74.

———. 1973. "Classical Evolution." In *Main Currents in Cultural Anthropology*, ed. Raoul Naroll and Frada Naroll, 57–121. Englewood Cliffs, N.J.: Prentice-Hall.

Carr-Saunders, Alexander M. 1922. *The Population Problem: A Study in Human Evolution.* Oxford: Clarendon.

———. 1936. *World Population: Past Growth and Present Trends.* Oxford: Clarendon.

Cartier, Michael. 1996/1986. "The Long March of the Chinese Family." In *A History of the Family*, ed. André Burguière, Christiane Klapisch-Zuber, Martine Segalen, and Françoise Zonabend, 2:216–41. Cambridge, Mass.: Harvard University Press.

Casterline, John B. 1994. "Fertility Transition in Asia." In *The Onset of Fertility Transition* in *Sub-Saharan Africa*, ed. Thérèsa Locoh and Véronique Hertrick, 69–86. Liège: Derouaux Ordina.

———. 1999. *The Onset and Pace of Fertility Transition: National Patterns in the Second Half of the Twentieth Century*. New York: Population Council.

———, ed. 2001. *Diffusion Processes and Fertility Transition*. Washington, D.C.: National Academy Press.

Casterline, John B., and Rodolfo Bulatao, eds. 2001. *Global Fertility Transition. Population and Development Review*, vol. 27 (suppl.).

Castro Martin, Teresa. 2002. "Consensual Unions in Latin America: Persistence of a Dual Nuptiality System." *Journal of Comparative Family Studies* 33 (1): 35–55.

Chackiel, Juan, and Susana Schkolnik. 1996. "Latin America: Overview of the Fertility Transition, 1950–1990." In *The Fertility Transition in Latin America*, ed. José M. Guzmán, Susheela Singh, Germán Rodriguez, and Edith A. Pantelides, 3–26. Oxford: Clarendon.

Chambers, David. 2002. "Civilizing the Natives: Customary Marriage in Post-Apartheid South Africa." In *Engaging Cultural Differences: The Multicultural Challenge in Liberal Democracies*, ed. Richard Shweder, Martha Minow, and Hazel Rose Markus. New York: Sage.

Chambers-Schiller, Lee V. 1984. *Liberty, a Better Husband? Single Women in America: The Generations of 1780–1840*. New Haven, Conn.: Yale University Press.

Chamie, Joseph. 1994. "Trends, Variations, and Contradictions in National Policies to Influence Fertility." In *The New Politics of Population: Conflict and Consensus in Family Planning*, ed. Jason L. Finkle and C. A. McIntosh, 37–50. New York: Population Council.

Chaytor, Miranda. 1980. "Household and Kinship: Ryton in the Late 16th and Early 17th Centuries." *History Workshop Journal* 10:25–60.

Chesnais, Jean-Claude. 1992. *The Demographic Transition: Stages, Patterns, and Economic Implications*. Oxford: Oxford University Press.

Chester, Robert. 1977. *Divorce in Europe*. Leiden: Martinus Nijoff.

Chiappelli, Fredi, Michael J. B. Allen, and Robert L. Benson, eds. 1976. *First Images of America: The Impact of the New World on the Old*. Berkeley: University of California Press.

Cleland, John. 1985. "Marital Fertility Decline in Developing Countries: Theories and the Evidence." In *Reproductive Change in Developing Countries*, ed. John Cleland and John Hobcraft, 223–52. London: Oxford University Press.

———. 2001. "The Effects of Improved Survival on Fertility: A Reassessment." In *Global Fertility Transition*, ed. John B. Casterline and Rodolfo Bulatao, 60–92. *Population and Development Review*, vol. 27 (suppl.).

Cleland, John, and John Hobcraft, eds. 1985. *Reproductive Change in Developing Countries: Insights from the World Fertility Survey*. London: Oxford University Press.

Cleland, John, and Shireen Jejeebhoy. 1996. "Maternal Schooling and Fertility: Evidence from Censuses and Surveys." In *Girls' Schooling, Women's Autonomy, and Fertility Change in South Asia*, ed. Roger Jeffery and Alaka M. Basu, 72–106. New Delhi: Sage.

Cleland, John, Nelson Onuoha, and Ian Timaeus. 1994. "Fertility Change in Sub-Saharan

Africa: A Review of the Evidence." In *The Onset of Fertility Transition in Sub-Saharan Africa*, ed. Thérèsa Locoh and Véronique Hertrick, 1–20. Liège: Derouaux Ordina Editions.

Cleland, John, and Christopher Wilson. 1987. "Demand Theories of the Fertility Transition: An Iconoclastic View." *Population Studies* 41 (1): 5–30.

Cleveland v. United States. 329 U.S. 14 (1946).

Coale, Ansley J. 1973. "The Demographic Transition." In *International Population Conference, Liège 1973*, 1:53–72. Liège: International Union for the Scientific Study of Population.

Coale, Ansley J., Barbara A. Anderson, and Erna Härm. 1979. *Human Fertility in Russia since the Nineteenth Century*. Princeton, N.J.: Princeton University Press.

Coale, Ansley J., and Edgar M. Hoover. 1958. *The Effects of Economic Development on Population Growth and the Effects of Population Growth on Economic Development*. Princeton, N.J.: Princeton University Press.

———. 1969. "The Effects of Economic Development on Population Growth and the Effects of Population Growth on Economic Development." In *Population in Industrialization*, ed. Michael Drake, 11–29. London: Methuen.

Coale, Ansley J., and Roy Treadway. 1986. "A Summary of the Changing Distribution of Overall Fertility, Marital Fertility, and the Proportion Married in the Provinces of Europe." In *The Decline of Fertility in Europe*, ed. Ansley J. Coale and Susan C. Watkins, 31–181. Princeton, N.J.: Princeton University Press.

Cohen, Barney. 1993. "Fertility Levels, Differentials, and Trends." In *Demographic Change in Sub-Saharan Africa*, ed. Karen A. Foote, Kenneth H. Hill, and Linda G. Martin, 8–67. Washington, D.C.: National Academy Press.

Cohen, Myron L. 1970. "Development Process in the Chinese Domestic Group." In *Family and Kinship in Chinese Society*, ed. Maurice Freedman, 21–36. Stanford, Calif.: Stanford University Press.

———. 1976. *House United, House Divided*. New York: Columbia University Press.

Colden, Cadwallader. 1973/1727. *The History of the Five Indian Nations*. Ithaca, N.Y.: Cornell University Press.

Cole, Thomas R. 1993. *The Journey of Life: A Cultural History of Aging in America*. Cambridge: Cambridge University Press.

Coleman, David. 1988/1986. "Population Regulation: A Long Range View." In *The State of Population Theory*, ed. David Coleman and Roger Schofield, 14–41. Oxford: Blackwell.

Coleman, James S. 1990. *Foundations of Social Theory*. Cambridge, Mass.: Harvard University Press.

Collini, Stefan. 1989. Introduction to *On Liberty and Other Writings*, by J. S. Mill, ed. Stefan Collini, vii–xxvi. New York: Cambridge University Press.

Comaroff, Jean, and John L. Comaroff. 1991. *Of Revelation and Revolution: Christianity, Colonialism, and Consciousness in South Africa*. Chicago: University of Chicago Press.

———. 1997. *Of Revelation and Revolution: The Dialectics of Modernity on a South African Frontier*. Chicago: University of Chicago Press.

Comte, Auguste. 1858/1830–42. *The Positive Philosophy of Auguste Comte*. Translated by Harriett Martineau. New York: Calvin Blanchard.

Condorcet, Marquis de. N.d./1795. *Outlines of an Historical View of the Progress of the Human Mind.* Ann Arbor, Mich.: Edwards Bros.

Conklin, Paul K. 1974. *Self-Evident Truths.* Bloomington: Indiana University Press.

Conway, Jill K., and Susan C. Bourque, eds. 1995/1993. *The Politics of Women's Education: Perspectives from Asia, Africa, and Latin America.* Ann Arbor: University of Michigan Press.

Coontz, Stephanie. 1991/1988. *The Social Origins of Private Life: A History of American Families, 1600–1900.* New York: Verso.

Cooper, Barbara M. 1997. *Marriage in Maradi: Gender and Culture in a Hausa Society in Niger, 1900–1989.* Portsmouth, N.H.: Heinemann.

Cott, Nancy F. 1994. "Early Twentieth-Century Feminism in Political Context: A Comparative Look at Germany and the United States." In *Suffrage and Beyond,* ed. Caroline Daley and Melanie Nolan, 234–51. New York: New York University Press.

———. 2000. *Public Vows: A History of Marriage and the Nation.* Cambridge, Mass.: Harvard University Press.

Cranston, Maurice. 1957. *John Locke.* New York: Macmillan.

———. 1983. *Jean-Jacques: The Early Life and Work of Jean-Jacques Rousseau, 1712–1754.* London: Penguin.

———. 1984. Introduction to *A Discourse on Inequality,* by Jean-Jacques Rousseau, ed. Maurice Cranston, 9–53. Harmondsworth: Penguin.

———. 1991. *The Noble Savage: Jean-Jacques Rousseau, 1754–1762.* London: Penguin.

Critchlow, Donald T. 1999. *Intended Consequences: Birth Control, Abortion, and the Federal Government in Modern America.* New York: Oxford University Press.

Crook, Stephen, Jan Pakulski, and Malcolm Waters. 1992. *Postmodernization: Change in Advanced Society.* Newbury Park, Calif.: Sage.

Cuno, Kenneth M. 2003a. "Ambiguous Modernization: The Transition to Monogamy in the Khedival House of Egypt." In *Family History in the Middle East,* ed. Barbara Doumani, 247–70. Albany: State University of New York Press.

———. 2003b. "Divorce and the Fate of the Family in Modern Egypt." Paper presented at the conference "Institutions, Ideologies, and Agency: Changing Family Life in the Arab Middle East and Diaspora," University of North Carolina at Chapel Hill, 11–12 April.

Czap, Peter, Jr. 1983. "A Large Family, the Peasant's Greatest Wealth: Serf Households in Mishino, Russia, 1814–1858." In Family Forms in Historic Europe, ed. Richard Wall, 105–53. Cambridge: Cambridge University Press.

Dahl, Gudrun, and Annika Rabo, eds. 1992. *Kam-Ap or Take-Off: Local Notions of Development.* Stockholm: Stockholm Studies in Social Anthropology.

Dannefer, Dale. 1984a. "Adult Development and Social Theory." *American Sociological Review* 49 (1): 100–116.

———. 1984b. "The Role of the Social in Life-Span Developmental Psychology, Past and Future: Rejoinder to Baltes and Nesselroade." *American Sociological Review* 49 (6): 847–50.

Dannefer, Dale, and Marion Perlmutter. 1990. "Development as a Multidimensional Process: Individual and Social Constituents." *Human Development* 33:108–37.

David, Henry P. 1987. "Incentives and Disincentives in Family Planning Programs." In *Organizing for Effective Family Planning Programs*, ed. Robert Lapham and George B. Simmons, 521–42. Washington, D.C.: National Academy Press.

Davies, Kathleen M. 1981. "Continuity and Change in Literary Advice on Marriage." In *Marriage and Society: Studies in the Social History of Marriage*, ed. R. B. Outhwaite, 58–80. London: Europa.

Davis, Deborah, and Stevan Harrell, eds. 1993. *Chinese Families in the Post-Mao Era*. Berkeley and Los Angeles: University of California Press.

Davis, Kingsley. 1948. *Human Society*. New York: Macmillan.

———. 1951. *The Population of India and Pakistan*. Princeton, N.J.: Princeton University Press.

———. 1967. "Population Policy: Will Current Programs Succeed?" *Science* 158 (3802): 730–39.

———. 1984. "Wives and Work: The Sex Role Revolution and Its Consequences." *Population and Development Review* 10 (3): 397–417.

———. 1985. "The Meaning and Significance of Marriage in Contemporary Society." In *Contemporary Marriage*, ed. Kingsley Davis, 1–21. New York: Sage.

———. 1997/1937. "Reproductive Institutions and the Pressure for Population." *Population and Development Review* 23 (3): 611–24.

d'Avray, David L. 1985. "The Gospel of the Marriage Feast of Cana and Marriage Preaching in France." In *The Bible in the Medieval World: Essays in Memory of Beryl Smalley*, ed. Katherine Walsh and Diana Wood, 207–24. Oxford: Blackwell.

d'Avray, David L., and M. Tausche. 1981. "Marriage Sermons in *ad status* Collections of the Central Middle Ages." In *Archives d'histoire doctrinale et littéraire du moyen âge*, ed. Étienne Gilson, Gabriel Théry, M.-T. d'Alverny, and M.-D. Chenu, 71–119. Year 1980, vol. 47. Paris: J. Vrin.

de Carvalho, José A. M., and Laura R. Wong. 1996. "The Fertility Transition in Brazil: Causes and Consequences." In *The Fertility Transition in Latin America*, ed. José M. Guzmán, Susheela Singh, Germán Rodríguez, and Edith A. Pantelides, 373–96. Oxford: Clarendon.

de Jongh, Eddy. 1997/1971. "Realism and Seeming Realism in Seventeenth-Century Dutch Painting." In *Looking at Seventeenth-Century Dutch Art: Realism Reconsidered*, ed. Wayne Franity, 21–56. Cambridge: Cambridge University Press.

Debeer, Esmond S. 1969. "Locke and English Liberalism: The *Second Treatise of Government* in Its Contemporary Setting." In *John Locke: Problems and Perspectives*, ed. John W. Yolton, 34–44. London: Cambridge University Press.

Degler, Carl N. 1980. *At Odds*. New York: Oxford University Press.

Demeny, Paul. 1968. "Early Fertility Decline in Austria-Hungary: A Lesson in Demographic Transition." *Daedalus* 97 (2): 502–22.

———. 1985. "The World Demographic Situation." Center for Policy Studies Working Paper no. 121. New York: Population Council.

———. 1988. "Social Science and Population Policy." *Population and Development Review* 14 (3): 451–80.

Demos, John. 1970. *A Little Commonwealth: Family Life in Plymouth Colony.* London: Oxford University Press.

Diamond, Ian, Margaret Newby, and Sarah Varle. 1999. "Female Education and Fertility: Examining the Links." In *Critical Perspectives on Schooling and Fertility in the Developing World*, ed. Carolyn H. Bledsoe, John B. Casterline, Jennifer A. Johnson-Kuhn, and John G. Haaga, 23–48. Washington, D.C.: National Academy Press.

Diamond, Jared M. 1997. *Guns, Germs, and Steel: The Fates of Human Societies.* New York: Norton.

Dike, Samuel W. 1885. "Important Review of the Divorce Question for Pulpit Treatment." *Homiletic Review* 10:388–92.

Dippie, Brian W. 1982. *The Vanishing American: White Attitudes and U.S. Indian Policy.* Middletown, Conn.: Wesleyan University Press.

Dixon, Ruth. 1978. "Late Marriage and Non-Marriage as Demographic Responses: Are They Similar?" *Population Studies* 32 (3): 449–66.

Donahue, C. J., Jr. 1976. "The Policy of Alexander the Third's Consent Theory of Marriage." In *Proceedings of the Fourth International Congress of Medieval Canon Law*, ed. Stephan Kuttner, 5:251–81. Vatican City: Biblioteca Apostolica Vaticana.

———. 1983. "The Canon Law on the Formation of Marriage and Social Practice in the Later Middle Ages." *Journal of Family History* 8 (2): 144–58.

Donaldson, Peter J. 1990a. *Nature against Us: The United States and the World Population Crisis, 1965–1980.* Chapel Hill: University of North Carolina Press.

———. 1990b. "On the Origins of the United States Government's International Population Policy." *Population Studies* 44 (3): 385–99.

Dore, Ronald. 1976. *The Diploma Disease: Education, Qualification, and Development.* London: Allen & Unwin.

Dozon, Jean-Pierre. 1996/1986. "Africa: The Family at the Crossroads." In *A History of the Family*, ed. André Burguière, Christiane Klapisch-Zuber, Martine Segalen, and Françoise Zonabend, 2:301–38. Cambridge, Mass.: Harvard University Press.

DuBois, Ellen C. 1994. "Woman Suffrage around the World: Three Phases of Suffragist Internationalism." In *Suffrage and Beyond*, ed. Caroline Daley and Melanie Nolan, 252–76. New York: New York University Press.

Dunn, Janet S. 2000. "Television and Declining Fertility in Northeastern Brazil." Institute for Social Research, University of Michigan. Typescript.

Dunn, John. 1969. *The Political Thought of John Locke.* London: Cambridge University Press.

Durch, Jane S. 1980. *Nuptiality Patterns in Developing Countries: Implications for Fertility.* Washington, D.C.: Population Reference Bureau.

Durham, William H. 1990. "Advances in Evolutionary Culture Theory." *Annual Review of Anthropology* 19:187–210.

Durkheim, Emile. 1978/1892. "The Conjugal Family." In *Emile Durkheim on Institutional Analysis*, ed. Mark Traugott, 229–39. Chicago: University of Chicago Press.

———. 1984/1893. *The Division of Labor in Society.* New York: Free Press.

Dussel, Enrique. 1995/1992. *The Invention of the Americas.* New York: Continuum.

Duvall, Evelyn M., and Reuben L. Hill. 1948. *Report of the Committee on the Dynamics of Family Interaction.* Washington, D.C.: National Conference on Family Life.

Duza, M. Badrud, and Moni Nag. 1993. "High Contraceptive Prevalence in Matlab, Bangladesh: Underlying Processes and Implications." In *The Revolution in Asian Fertility,* ed. Richard Leete and Iqbal Alam, 67–82. Oxford: Clarendon.

Easterlin, Richard A., and Eileen M. Crimmins. 1985. *The Fertility Revolution: A Supply-Demand Analysis.* Chicago: University of Chicago Press.

Ekirch, Arthur A., Jr. 1951. *The Idea of Progress in America, 1815–1860.* New York: Peter Smith.

Elder, Glen H., Jr. 1977. "Family History and the Life Course." *Journal of Family History* 2 (4): 279–304.

———. 1978. "Family History and the Life Course." In *Transitions: The Family and the Life Course in Historical Perspective,* ed. Tamara K. Hareven, 17–64. New York: Academic.

Elliott, John H. 1972/1970. *The Old World and the New, 1492–1650.* Cambridge: Cambridge University Press.

Ellwood, Charles A. 1910. *Sociology and Modern Social Problems.* New York: American.

Emerick, Charles F. 1909. "College Women and Race Suicide." *Political Science Quarterly* 24 (2): 269–83.

Engelmann, George J. 1903. "Education Not the Cause of Race Decline." *Popular Science Monthly* 63:172–84.

Engels, Friedrich. 1971/1884. *The Origin of the Family, Private Property, and the State.* New York: International.

England, Paula. 2000. "Marriage, the Costs of Children, and Gender Inequality." In *Ties That Bind: Perspectives on Marriage and Cohabitation,* ed. L. Waite, C. Bachrach, M. Hindin, E. Thomson, and A. Thornton, 320–42. Hawthorne, N.Y.: Aldine de Gruyter.

Erikson, Eric H. 1963/1950. *Childhood and Society.* 2d rev. and enlarged ed. New York: Norton.

Escobar, Arturo. 1988. "Power and Visibility: Development and the Invention and Management of the Third World." *Cultural Anthropology* 3 (4): 428–43.

Eversley, David E. C. 1959. *Social Theories of Fertility and the Malthusian Debate.* London: Oxford University Press.

Ewen, Elizabeth. 1985. *Immigrant Women in the Land of Dollars: Life and Culture on the Lower East Side, 1890–1925.* New York: Monthly Review Press.

Fabian, Johannes. 1983. *Time and the Other: How Anthropology Makes Its Object.* New York: Columbia University Press.

Fahmy, Khaled. 1998. "Women, Medicine, and Power in Nineteenth-Century Egypt." In *Remaking Women: Feminism and Modernity in the Middle East,* ed. Lila Abu-Lughod, 35–72. Princeton, N.J.: Princeton University Press.

Faria, Vilmar E., and Joseph E. Potter. 1999. "Television, Telenovelas, and Fertility Change in North-East Brazil." In *Dynamics of Values in Fertility Change,* ed. Richard Leete, 252–72. New York: Oxford University Press.

Farmer, Paul. 1954. *The Social Theory of Frederic Le Play.* Ithaca, N.Y.: Cornell University Press.

Featherman, David L., and Richard M. Lerner. 1985. "Ontogenesis and Sociogenesis:

Problematics for Theory and Research about Development and Socialization across the Lifespan." *American Sociological Review* 50 (5): 659–76.

Fenton, William N., and Elizabeth L. Moore. 1974. Introduction to *Customs of the American Indians Compared with the Customs of Primitive Times*, by Joseph F. Lafitau, ed. and trans. W. N. Fenton and E. L. Moore, xxix–cxix. Toronto: Champlain Society.

Ferguson, Adam. 1980/1767. *An Essay on the History of Civil Society*. New Brunswick, N.J.: Transaction.

Ferrero, Guglielmo. 1994/1922. "An Historian's View of Population." *Population and Development Review* 20 (4): 893–387.

Filmer, Robert S. 1949/1680. *Patriarcha*. Oxford: Blackwell.

Finkle, Jason L. 2001. "Politics of Population Policies." In *International Encyclopedia of the Social and Behavioral Sciences*, ed. Neil J. Smelser and Paul B. Baltes, 11793–98. Amsterdam: Elsevier.

Finkle, Jason L., and Barbara B. Crane. 1985. "Ideology and Politics at Mexico City: The United States at the 1984 International Conference on Population." *Population and Development Review* 11 (1): 1–28.

Finkle, Jason L., and C. Allison McIntosh. 1994. "The New Politics of Population: Conflict and Consensus in Family Planning." *Population and Development Review* 20 (suppl.): 3–34.

———. 2002. "United Nations Population Conferences: Shaping the Policy Agenda for the Twenty-First Century." *Studies in Family Planning* 33 (1): 11–23.

Firmage, Edwin B., and Richard C. Mangrum. 1988. *Zion in the Courts: A Legal History of the Church of Jesus Christ of Latter-Day Saints, 1830–1900*. Urbana: University of Illinois Press.

Flandrin, Jean-Louis. 1980. "Repression and Change in the Sexual Life of Young People in Medieval and Early Modern Times." In *Family and Sexuality in French History*, ed. Robert Wheaton and Tamara K. Hareven, 27–48. Philadelphia: University of Pennsylvania Press.

Fletcher, Ronald. 1969. "Frederic Le Play." In *The Founding Fathers of Social Science*, ed. Timothy Raison, 51–58. London: Penguin.

———. 1973/1962. *The Family and Marriage in Britain*. London: Penguin.

Flew, Antony, ed. 1986/1970. *Thomas Malthus: An Essay on the Principle of Population*. New York: Penguin.

Flexner, Eleanor. 1975. *Century of Struggle: The Woman's Rights Movement in the United States*. Cambridge, Mass.: Harvard University Press.

Fliegelman, Jay. 1982. *Prodigals and Pilgrims*. Cambridge: Cambridge University Press.

Foner, Eric. 1970. *Free Soil, Free Labor, Free Men: The Ideology of the Republican Party before the Civil War*. New York: Oxford University Press.

Fortes, Meyer. 1958. "Introduction: Cambridge Papers in Social Anthropology." In *The Developmental Cycle in Domestic Groups*, ed. Jack Goody, 1–14. Cambridge: Cambridge University Press.

Foster, Lawrence. 1981. *Religion and Sexuality: Three American Communal Experiments of the Nineteenth Century*. New York: Oxford University Press.

————. 2001. "Introduction: The Roots of an Extraordinary Community." In *Free Love in Utopia: John Humphrey Noyes and the Origin of the Oneida Community*, ed. George W. Noyes, ix–xlvii. Urbana: University of Illinois Press.

Fox-Genovese, Elizabeth. 1987. "Women and the Enlightenment." In *Becoming Visible: Women in European History* (2d ed.), ed. Renate Bridenthal, Claudia Koonz, and Susan Stuard, 251–77. Boston: Houghton Mifflin.

Foyster, Elizabeth. 2001. "Parenting Was for Life, Not Just for Childhood: The Roles of Parents in the Married Lives of Their Children in Early Modern England." *History* 86:313–27.

France, Peter. 1992. *Politeness and Its Discontents.* Cambridge: Cambridge University Press.

Frank, Odile. 1989. "Family Welfare Policies in Sub-Saharan Africa: Views from Africa." Paper presented at a seminar organized by the IUSSP Committee on Policy and Population in Kenshasa, Zaire, International Union for the Scientific Study of Population, Liège, 27 February–2 March.

Franklin, Benjamin. 1961/1751. "Observations concerning the Increase of Mankind." In *The Papers of Benjamin Franklin*, ed. Leonard W. Labaree and Whitfield J. Bell Jr., 225–34. New Haven, Conn.: Yale University Press.

Freed, Doris J., and Henry H. Foster. 1980. "Divorce in the Fifty States: An Overview as of August 1, 1980." *Family Law Reporter* 6 (42): 4043–66.

Freedman, Joseph S. 2002. "Philosophical Writings on the Family in Sixteenth- and Seventeenth-Century Europe." *Journal of Family History* 27 (3): 292–342.

Freedman, Ronald, ed. 1964. *Population: The Vital Revolution.* New York: Anchor.

————. 1979. "Theories of Fertility Decline: A Reappraisal." *Social Forces* 58 (1): 1–17.

————. 1984. "The William and Flora Hewlett Foundation Program in Support of U.S. Population Studies Centers: An Evaluation." Institute for Social Research, University of Michigan. Typescript.

————. 1987. "The Contribution of Social Science Research to Population Policy and Family Planning Program Effectiveness." *Studies in Family Planning* 18 (2): 57–82.

————. 1997. "Do Family Planning Programs Affect Fertility Preferences? A Literature Review." *Studies in Family Planning* 28 (1): 1–13.

————. 2001. "Fertility in the Next Fifty Years." Paper presented at the annual meeting of the Population Association of America, Washington, D.C., 29–31 March.

Freedman, Ronald, Ming-Cheng Chang, Te-Hsiung Sun, and Maxine Weinstein. 1994. "The Fertility Transition in Taiwan." In *Social Change and the Family in Taiwan*, ed. A. Thornton and H. S. Lin, 264–304. Chicago: University of Chicago Press.

Freeze, ChaeRan Y. 2002. *Jewish Marriage and Divorce in Imperial Russia.* Hanover, N.H.: University Press of New England.

Fricke, Thomas. 1986. *Himalayan Households: Tamang and Domestic Processes.* Studies in Cultural Anthropology no. 11. Ann Arbor, Mich.: UMI.

————. 1997a. "Culture Theory and Population Process: Toward a Thicker Demography." In *Anthropological Demography: Toward a New Synthesis*, ed. David I. Kertzer and Thomas Fricke, 248–77. Chicago: University of Chicago Press.

————. 1997b. "Marriage Change as Moral Change: Culture, Virtue, and Demographic

Transition." In *The Continuing Demographic Transition*, ed. Gavin W. Jones, Robert M. Douglas, Jack C. Caldwell, and Rennie M. D'Souza, 183–212. Oxford: Oxford University Press.

Fricke, Thomas, Dilli R. Dahal, Arland Thornton, William G. Axinn, and Krishna P. Rimal. 1991. "Tamang Family Research Project: Summary Report on Ethnographic and Survey Research Conducted in the Budhanilkantha Area, Kathmandu Valley, and Tipling Gaon Panchayat in the Upper Ankhu Khola Valley, March 1987–January 1988." In *Report to Center for Nepal and Asian Studies*, 1–111. Kirtipir, Nepal: Tribhuvan University.

Fricke, Thomas, Paul K. C. Liu, Arland Thornton, D. Freedman, and Li-Shou Yang. 1994. "The Changing Organization of Individual Activities." In *Social Change and the Family in Taiwan*, ed. A. Thornton and H. S. Lin, 116–47. Chicago: University of Chicago Press.

Fricke, Thomas, Arland Thornton, and Dilli R. Dahal. 1990. "Family Organization and the Wage Labor Transition in a Tamang Community of Nepal." *Human Ecology* 18 (3): 283–313.

————. 1998. "Netting in Nepal: Social Change, the Life Course, and Brideservice in Sangila." *Human Ecology* 26 (2): 213–37.

Friedl, Erika. 2003. "Tribal Enterprises and Marriage Issues in Twentieth-Century Iran." In *Family History in the Middle East*, ed. Barbara Doumani, 151–70. Albany: State University of New York Press.

Fuglesang, Minou. 1992. "No Longer Ghosts: Women's Notions of 'Development' and 'Modernity' in Lamu Town, Kenya." In *Kam-Ap or Take-Off: Local Notions of Development*, ed. Gudrun Dahl and Annika Rabo, 123–56. Stockholm: Stockholm Studies in Social Anthropology.

Fuller, Margaret. 1941/1845. "Woman in the Nineteenth Century." In *The Writings of Margaret Fuller*, ed. Mason Wade, 109–218. New York: Viking.

Gallin, Bernard. 1966. *Hsin Hsing, Taiwan: A Chinese Village in Change*. Berkeley: University of California Press.

Gaskin, John C. A., ed. 1996. Introduction to *Leviathan*, by Thomas Hobbes, xi–xliii. Oxford: Oxford University Press.

Gasster, Michael. 1968. "Reform and Revolution in China's Political Modernization." In *China in Revolution: The First Phase, 1900–1913*, ed. Mary C. Wright, 67–96. New Haven, Conn.: Yale University Press.

Gatrell, Peter. 1982. "Historians and Peasants: Studies of Medieval English Society in a Russian Context." *Past and Present*, no. 96:22–50.

Geertz, Clifford. 1973. *The Interpretation of Cultures*. New York: Basic.

Geiger, H. Kent. 1968. *The Family in Soviet Russia*. Cambridge, Mass.: Harvard University Press.

George, Henry. 1938/1880. *Progress and Poverty*. New York: Robert Schalkenbach Foundation.

Ghimire, Dirgha J., William G. Axinn, Scott G. Yabiku, and Arland Thornton. 2002. "Social Change, Premarital Non-Family Experience, and Spouse Choice in an Arranged Marriage Society." Institute for Social Research, University of Michigan. Typescript.

Giddens, Anthony. 1981. *A Contemporary Critique of Historical Materialism: Power, Property, and the State.* London: Macmillan.

———. 1984. *The Constitution of Society: Outline of the Theory of Structuration.* Cambridge: Polity.

———. 1991. *Modernity and Self-Identity.* Stanford, Calif.: Stanford University Press.

Gies, Frances, and Joseph Gies. 1987. *Marriage and the Family in the Middle Ages.* New York: Harper & Row.

Gillis, John R. 1985. *For Better, for Worse: British Marriages, 1600 to the Present.* New York: Oxford University Press.

Glendon, Mary A. 1976. "Marriage and the State: The Withering Away of Marriage." *Virginia Law Review* 62 (4): 663–720.

———. 1977. *State, Law, and Family: Family Law in Transition in the United States and Western Europe.* Amsterdam: North-Holland.

Glenn, Norval D. 1997. *Closed Hearts, Closed Minds: The Textbook Story of Marriage: A Report to the Nation from the Council on Families.* New York: Institute for American Values.

Glenn, Susan A. 1990. *Daughters of the Shtetl: Life and Labor in the Immigrant Generation.* Ithaca, N.Y.: Cornell University Press.

Godelier, Maurice. 1983. "Malthus and Ethnography." In *Malthus Past and Present*, ed. J. Dupâquier, A. Fauve-Chamoux, and E. Grebenik, 125–50. London: Academic.

Godwin, William. 1926/1793. *An Enquiry concerning Political Justice and Its Influence on General Virtue and Happiness.* New York: Knopf.

———. 1964/1820. *Of Population.* London: Longman, Hurst, Rees, Orme & Brown.

Goldenweiser, Alexander. 1937. *Anthropology: An Introduction to Primitive Culture.* New York: F. S. Crofts.

Goldin, Claudia. 1990. *Understanding the Gender Gap: An Economic History of American Women.* New York: Oxford University Press.

Goldscheider, Calvin. 1971. *Population, Modernization, and Social Structure.* Boston: Little, Brown.

———. 2002. *Cultures in Conflict: The Arab-Israeli Conflict.* Westport, Conn.: Greenwood.

Goldscheider, Frances K., and Calvin Goldscheider. 1993. *Leaving Home before Marriage: Ethnicity, Familism, and Generational Relationships.* Madison: University of Wisconsin Press.

Goldscheider, Frances K., and Linda J. Waite. 1991. *New Families, No Families? The Transformation of the American Home.* Berkeley and Los Angeles: University of California Press.

Goode, William J. 1970/1963. *World Revolution and Family Patterns.* New York: Free Press.

———. 1982/1964. *The Family.* 2d ed. Englewood Cliffs, N.J.: Prentice-Hall.

Goodman, Dena. 1994. *The Republic of Letters: A Cultural History of the French Enlightenment.* Ithaca, N.Y.: Cornell University Press.

Goody, Jack. 1983. *The Development of the Family and Marriage in Europe.* Cambridge: Cambridge University Press.

———. 1990. *The Oriental, the Ancient, and the Primitive: Systems of Marriage and the Family in the Pre-Industrial Societies of Eurasia.* Cambridge: Cambridge University Press.

Gordon, Daniel. 1994. *Citizens without Sovereignty.* Princeton, N.J.: Princeton University Press.

Gordon, Sarah B. 1995. "'The Twin Relic of Barbarism': A Legal History of Anti-Polygamy in Nineteenth-Century America." Ph.D. diss., Princeton University.

Gottlieb, Beatrice. 1980. "The Meaning of Clandestine Marriage." In *Family and Sexuality in French History,* ed. Robert Wheaton and Tamara K. Hareven, 49–83. Philadelphia: University of Pennsylvania Press.

Gough, E. Kathleen. 1959. "The Nayars and the Definition of Marriage." *Journal of the Royal Anthropological Institute* 89:23–34.

Gourevitch, Victor. 1988–89. "Rousseau's Pure State of Nature." *Interpretation* 16:23–59.

———. 1997. Introduction to *The Social Contract and Other Later Political Writings,* by Jean-Jacques Rousseau, ed. Victor Gourevitch, ix–xxxi. New York: Cambridge University Press.

Granqvist, Hilma. 1968. "Edward Westermark." In *The International Encyclopedia of the Social Sciences,* ed. David L. Sills, 16:529–31. New York: Macmillan/Free Press.

Grant, Ruth W., and Nathan Tarcov. 1996. Introduction to *Some Thoughts concerning Education and Of the Conduct of the Understanding,* by John Locke, ed. Ruth W. Grant and Nathan Tarcov, vii–xix. Indianapolis: Hackett.

Gray, H. 1941. "The Progress of Women." In *Modern India and the West: A Study of the Interaction of Their Civilizations,* ed. L. S. S. O'Malley, 445–83. London: Oxford University Press.

Greenhalgh, Susan. 1982. "Income Units: The Ethnographic Alternative to Standardization." *Population and Development Review* 8 (suppl.): 70–91.

———. 1985. "Sexual Satisfaction in East Asia." *Population and Development Review* 11 (2): 265–314.

———. 1989. "Chinese Family Policy: Negative Lessons for Sub-Saharan Africa." Paper presented at a seminar organized by the IUSSP Committee on Policy and Population in Kenshasa, Zaire, International Union for the Scientific Study of Population, Liège, 27 February–2 March.

———. 1990. "Toward a Political Economy of Fertility: Anthropological Contributions." *Population and Development Review* 16 (1): 85–106.

———. 1993. "The Peasantization of the One-Child Policy in Shaanxi." In *Chinese Families in the Post-Mao Era,* ed. Deborah Davis and Stevan Harrell, 219–50. Berkeley and Los Angeles: University of California Press.

———. 1994. "Controlling Births and Bodies in Village China." *American Ethnologist* 21 (1): 3–30.

———. 1996. "The Social Construction of Population Science: An Intellectual, Institutional, and Political History of Twentieth-Century Demography." *Comparative Studies in Society and History* 38 (1): 26–66.

———. 2001. "Fresh Winds in Beijing: Chinese Feminists Speak Out on the One-Child Policy and Women's Lives." *Signs: Journal of Women in Culture and Society* 26 (3): 847–86.

———. 2003a. "Planned Births, Unplanned Persons: 'Population' in the Making of Chinese Modernity." *American Ethnologist* 30 (2): 196–215.

———. 2003b. "Science, Modernity, and the Making of China's One-Child Policy." *Population and Development Review* 29 (2): 163–96.

Greenhalgh, Susan, and Edwin A. Winkler. 2001. *Chinese State Birth Planning in the 1990s and Beyond.* Washington, D.C.: U.S. Government Printing Office, for Resource Information Center, Immigration and Naturalization Service.

Grimké, Sarah. 1988/1838. *Letters on the Equality of the Sexes and Other Essays.* Edited by Elizabeth Ann Bartlett. New Haven, Conn.: Yale University Press.

Grossberg, Michael. 1985. *Governing the Hearth: Law and the Family in Nineteenth Century America.* Chapel Hill: University of North Carolina Press.

Groves, Ernest R., and William F. Ogburn. 1928. *American Marriage and Family Relationships.* New York: Henry Holt.

Gruber, Jacob. 1973. "Forerunners." In *Main Currents in Cultural Anthropology*, ed. Raoul Naroll and Frada Naroll, 25–56. Englewood Cliffs, N.J.: Prentice-Hall.

Guengant, Jean-Pierre. 1996. "Demographic Transition in the Caribbean: An Attempt at Interpretation." In *The Fertility Transition in Latin America*, ed. José M. Guzmán, Susheela Singh, Germán Rodriguez, and Edith A. Pantelides, 74–94. Oxford: Clarendon.

Gutmann, Myron P., Sara M. Pullum-Piñón, and Thomas W. Pullum. 2002. "Three Eras of Young Adult Home Leaving in Twentieth-Century America." *Journal of Social History* 35 (3): 533–76.

Guzmán, José M. 1994. "The Onset of Fertility Decline in Latin America." In *The Onset of Fertility Transition in Sub-Saharan Africa*, ed. Thérèsa Locoh and Véronique Hertrick, 43–67. Liège: Derouaux Ordina.

———. 1996. "Introduction: Social Change and Fertility Decline in Latin American." In *The Fertility Transition in Latin America*, ed. José M. Guzmán, Susheela Singh, Germán Rodriguez, and Edith A. Pantelides, xxii–xxxi. Oxford: Clarendon.

Guzmán, José M., Susheela Singh, Germán Rodriguez, and Edith A. Pantelides, eds. 1996. *The Fertility Transition in Latin American.* Oxford: Clarendon.

Haag, Pamela. 1999. *Consent: Sexual Rights and the Transformation of American Liberalism.* Ithaca, N.Y.: Cornell University Press.

Hajnal, John. 1965. "European Marriage Patterns in Perspective." In *Population in History*, ed. D. V. Glass and D. E. C. Eversley, 101–43. Chicago: Aldine.

———. 1982. "Two Kinds of Preindustrial Household Formation System." *Population and Development Review* 8 (3): 449–94.

Hall, Peter D. 1977. "Family Structure and Economic Organization: Massachusetts Merchants, 1700–1850." In *Family and Kin in Urban Communities*, ed. Tamara K. Hareven, 38–61. New York: New View Points.

Halpern, Joel M. 1972. "Town and Countryside in Serbia in the Nineteenth Century: Social and Household Structure as Reflected in the Census of 1863." In *Household and Family in Past Time*, ed. Peter Laslett and Richard Wall, 401–27. London: Cambridge University Press.

Hanawalt, Barbara A. 1986. *The Ties That Bound: Peasant Families in Medieval England.* New York: Oxford University Press.

———. 1993. *Growing Up in Medieval London: The Experience of Childhood in History.* New York: Oxford University Press.

Hannerz, Ulf. 1987. "The World in Creolization." *Africa* 57 (4): 546–59.

Hardy, Carmon. 1992. *Solemn Covenant.* Urbana: University of Illinois Press.

Hareven, Tamara K., ed. 1977. *Family and Kin in Urban Communities, 1700–1930.* New York: New View Points.

———. 1987. "Family History at the Crossroads." *Journal of Family History* 12 (1–3): ix–xxiii.

———. 1991. "The History of the Family and the Complexity of Social Change." *American Historical Review* 96 (1): 95–124.

Harkavy, Oscar. 1995. *Curbing Population Growth: An Insider's Perspective on the Population Movement.* New York: Plenum.

Harrell, Stevan. 1997. *Human Families.* Boulder, Colo.: Westview Press.

Harris, Marvin. 1968. *The Rise of Anthropological Theory.* New York: Thomas Y. Crowell.

Hart, Harold H. 1972. *Marriage: For and Against.* New York: Hart.

Harvey, Paul H., and Mark D. Pagel. 1991. *The Comparative Method in Evolutionary Biology.* Oxford: Oxford University Press.

Harwood-Lejeune, Audrey. 2001. "Rising Age at Marriage and Fertility in Southern and Eastern Africa." *European Journal of Population* 17 (3): 261–80.

Haskell, Ann S. 1973. "The Paston Women on Marriage in Fifteenth-Century England." *Viator: Medieval and Renaissance Studies* 4:459–71.

Hauser, Philip M. 1964. "The Population of the World: Recent Trends and Prospects." In *Population: The Vital Revolution*, ed. Ronald Freedman, 15–29. New York: Anchor.

Heaton, Tim B., and Renata Forste. 1998. "Education as Policy: The Impact of Education on Marriage, Contraception, and Fertility in Colombia, Peru, and Bolivia." *Social Biology* 45 (3–4): 194–213.

Hegel, George W. F. 1878/1837. *Lectures on the Philosophy of History.* London: George Bell & Sons.

Henrich, Joe, and Robert Boyd. 1998. "The Evolution of Conformist Transmission and the Emergence of between-Group Differences." *Evolution and Human Behavior* 19 (4): 215–41.

Herlihy, David. 1985. *Medieval Households.* Cambridge, Mass.: Harvard University Press.

Hermalin, Albert, Paul K. C. Liu, and Deborah Freedman. 1994. "The Social and Economic Transformation of Taiwan." In *Social Change and the Family in Taiwan*, ed. Arland Thornton and Hui-Sheng Lin, 49–87. Chicago: University of Chicago Press.

Herodotus. 1942/n.d. *The Persian Wars.* Translated by George Rawlinson. New York: Modern Library.

Hetherington, Penelope. 2001. "Generational Changes in Marriage Patterns in the Central Province of Kenya, 1930–1990." *Journal of Asian and African Studies* 36 (2): 157–80.

Hicks, Neville. 1978. *This Sin and Scandal: Australia's Population Debate, 1891–1911.* Canberra: Australian National University Press.

Higgs, Henri. 1890. "Frederic Le Play." *Quarterly Journal of Economics* 4 (4): 408–33.

Hill, M. Anne, and Elizabeth M. King. 1993. "Women's Education in Developing Countries: An Overview." In *Women's Education in Developing Countries: Barriers, Benefits, and Policies*, ed. Elizabeth M. King and M. Anne Hill, 1–50. Baltimore: Johns Hopkins University Press.

Hirschman, Charles. 1994. "Why Fertility Changes." *Annual Review of Sociology* 20:203–33.

Hirschman, Charles, and Philip Guest. 1990. "Data and Perspectives: The Emerging Demographic Transitions in Southeast Asia." *Population and Development Review* 16 (1): 121–52.

Hirschman, Charles, and Nguyen H. Minh. 2002. "Tradition and Change in Vietnamese Family Structure in the Red River Delta." *Journal of Marriage and the Family* 64 (4): 1063–79.

Ho, Mae-Wan, ed. 1988. *Evolutionary Processes and Metaphors.* Chichester: Wiley.

Hobbes, Thomas. 1991/1642. *Man and Citizen.* Edited by Bernard Gert. Indianapolis: Hackett.

———. 1996/1651. *Leviathan.* Edited by J. C. A. Gaskin. Oxford: Oxford University Press.

Hodgen, Margaret T. 1964. *Early Anthropology in the Sixteenth and Seventeenth Centuries.* Philadelphia: University of Pennsylvania Press.

Hodgson, Dennis. 1983. "Demography as Social Science and Policy Science." *Population and Development Review* 9 (1): 1–34.

———. 1988. "Orthodoxy and Revisionism in American Demography." *Population and Development Review* 14 (4): 541–69.

Hodgson, Dennis, and Susan C. Watkins. 1997. "Feminists and Neo-Malthusians: Past and Present Alliances." *Population and Development Review* 23 (3): 469–524.

Hole, Judith, and Ellen Levine. 1971. *Rebirth of Feminism.* New York: Quadrangle/New York Times Book Co.

———. 1984. "The First Feminists." In *Women: A Feminist Perspective* (3d ed.), ed. Jo Freeman, 543–56. Palo Alto, Calif.: Mayfield.

Home, Henry K. 1813/1774. *Sketches of the History of Man in Two Volumes.* Edinburgh: Printed for W. Creech, Edinburgh, and for W. Strahan and T. Cadell, London.

Hoodfar, Homa. 2002. "The Feminist Movement in Egypt." In *Muslim Feminism and Feminist Movement: Africa*, ed. Abida Samiuddin and R. Khanam, 1:129–34. Delhi: Global.

Hoodfar, Homa, and Samad Assadpour. 2000. "The Politics of Population Policy in the Islamic Republic of Iran." *Studies in Family Planning* 31 (1): 19–34.

Hornik, Robert, and Emile McAnany. 2001. "Mass Media and Fertility Change." In *Diffusion Processes and Fertility Transition*, ed. John B. Casterline, 208–39. Washington, D.C.: National Academy Press.

Howard, George E. 1904. *A History of Matrimonial Institutions.* Chicago: University of Chicago Press.

Howell, Nancy. 1986. "Feedback and Buffers in Relation to Scarcity and Abundance: Studies of Hunter-Gatherer Populations." In *The State of Population Theory*, ed. David Coleman and Roger Schofield, 156–87. New York: Blackwell.

Huddleston, Lee E. 1967. *Origins of the American Indians; European Concepts, 1492–1729*. Austin: University of Texas Press, for Institute of Latin American Studies.

Hufton, Olwen. 1995. *The Prospect before Her: A History of Women in Western Europe*. Vol. 1, *1500–1800*. London: Harper Collins.

Hull, Terence H., and Valerie J. Hull. 1997. "Politics, Culture, and Fertility: Transitions in Indonesia." In *The Continuing Demographic Transition*, ed. Gavin W. Jones, Robert M. Douglas, John C. Caldwell, and Rennie M. D'Souza, 383–421. Oxford: Oxford University Press.

Hull, Terence H., Valerie J. Hull, and Masri Singarimbun. 1977. "Indonesia's Family Planning Story: Success and Challenge." *Population Reference Bureau* 32 (6): 3–53.

Hume, David. 1825/1742. *Essays and Treatises*. Edinburgh: James Walker.

Hunt, Lynn. 1994. "Psychoanalysis, Feminism, and the French Revolution." In *Main Trends in Cultural History*, ed. Willem Melching and Wyger Velema, 164–81. Amsterdam: Rodopi.

Hunter, James D. 1991. *Culture Wars: The Struggle to Define America*. New York: Basic.

Ihara, Toni, and Ralph Warner. 1978. *The Living Together Kit*. Berkeley, Calif.: Nolo.

Inglehart, Ronald, and Wayne E. Baker. 2000. "Modernization, Cultural Change, and the Persistence of Traditional Values." *American Sociological Review* 65 (1): 19–51.

Inglehart, Ronald, Pippa Norris, and Christian Welzel. 2003. "Gender Equality and Democracy." In *Human Values and Social Change: Findings from the Values Survey*, ed. Ronald Inglehart, 91–115. Leiden: Brill.

Ingram, Martin. 1981. "Spousal Litigation in the English Ecclesiastical Courts, c. 1350–1640." In *Marriage and Society: Studies in the Social History of Marriage*, ed. R. B. Outhwaite, 35–57. London: Europa.

———. 1985. "The Reform of Popular Culture? Sex and Marriage in Early Modern England." In *Popular Culture in Seventeenth-Century England*, ed. Barry Reay, 129–65. London: Croom Helm.

Inkeles, Alex. 1969. "Making Men Modern: On the Causes and Consequences of Individual Change in Six Developing Countries." *American Journal of Sociology* 75 (2): 208–25.

Inkeles, Alex, and David H. Smith. 1974. *Becoming Modern: Individual Change in Six Developing Countries*. Cambridge, Mass.: Harvard University Press.

Jacobson, Paul H. 1959. *American Marriage and Divorce*. New York: Rinehart.

Janofsky, Michael. 2001. "Utahan Is Sentenced to 5 Years in Prison in Polygamy Case." *New York Times*, 25 August, A9.

Jato, Miriam N., Calista Simbalakia, Joan M. Tarasevich, David N. Awasum, Clement N. B. Kihinga, and Edith Ngirwamungu. 1999. "The Impact of Multimedia Family Planning Promotion on the Contraceptive Behavior of Women in Tanzania." *International Family Planning Perspectives* 25 (2): 60–67.

Jayavardene, Kumari. 2002. "Women's Emancipation in Afghanistan." In *Muslim Feminism and Feminist Movement: Central Asia*, ed. Abida Samiuddin and R. Khanam, 1:3–5. Delhi: Global.

Jeaffreson, John C. 1872. *Brides and Bridals*. London: Hurst & Blackett.

Jeffery, Roger, and Alaka M. Basu. 1996. "Schooling as Contraception?" In *Girls' Schooling, Women's Autonomy, and Fertility Change in South Asia*, ed. Roger Jeffery and Alaka M. Basu, 15–47. New Delhi: Sage.

Jejeebhoy, Shireen J. 1995. *Women's Education, Autonomy, and Reproductive Behaviour: Experience from Developing Countries*. Oxford: Clarendon.

Jennings, Francis. 1975. *The Invasion of America: Indians, Colonialism, and the Cant of Conquest*. Chapel Hill: University of North Carolina Press.

Johnson and Graham's Lessee v. William McIntosh. 21 U.S. (8 Wheaton) 543 (1823).

Johnson, Stanley P. 1987. *World Population and the United Nations: Challenge and Response*. Cambridge: Cambridge University Press.

———. 1994. *World Population—Turning the Tide: Three Decades of Progress*. London: Graham & Trotman/Martinus Nijhoff.

Jones, Gavin W. 1981. "Malay Marriage and Divorce in Peninsular Malaysia: Three Decades of Change." *Population and Development Review* 7 (2): 255–78.

———. 1997. "The Decline of University Marriage in East and South-East Asia." In *The Continuing Demographic Transition*, ed. Gavin W. Jones, Robert M. Douglas, John C. Caldwell, and Rennie M. D'Souza, 51–79. Oxford: Oxford University Press.

Jones, Gavin W., Robert M. Douglas, John C. Caldwell, and Rennie M. D'Souza, eds. 1997. *The Continuing Demographic Transition*. Oxford: Oxford University Press.

Jones, Rev. Richard. 1859. *Literary Remains of the Late Rev. Richard Jones*. Edited by Rev. W. Whewell. London: John Murray.

Kahl, Joseph A. 1968. *The Measurement of Modernism*. Austin: University of Texas Press.

Kahn, Joel S. 2001. "Anthropology and Modernity." *Current Anthropology* 42 (5): 51–80.

Kamuzora, C. L. 1989. "The Evolution of Policy on Fertility in Tanzania: Drawing on and Influence of International Experience." Paper presented at a seminar organized by the IUSSP Committee on Policy and Population in Kenshasa, Zaire, International Union for the Scientific Study of Population, Liège, 27 February–2 March.

Kandiyoti, Deniz. 1998. "Some Awkward Questions on Women and Modernity in Turkey." In *Remaking Women: Feminism and Modernity in the Middle East*, ed. Lila Abu-Lughod, 270–88. Princeton, N.J.: Princeton University Press.

Kapadia, Karin M. 1958. *Marriage and Family in India*. Oxford: Oxford University Press.

Kasun, Jacqueline. 1988. *The War against Population: The Economics and Ideology of World Population Control*. San Francisco: Ignatius.

Kaufman, Joan. 1983. *A Billion and Counting: Family Planning Campaigns and Policies in the People's Republic of China*. San Francisco: San Francisco Press.

Keely, Charles B. 1994. "Limits to Papal Power: Vatican Inaction after *Humanae Vitae*." In *The New Politics of Population: Conflict and Consensus in Family Planning*, ed. Jason L. Finkle and C. A. McIntosh, 220–40. New York: Population Council.

Kellner, Hans D. 1972. *Frederic Le Play and the Development of Modern Sociology*. Rochester, N.Y.: University of Rochester.

Kelly, Henry A. 1973. "Clandestine Marriage and Chaucer's 'Troilus.'" *Viator: Medieval and Renaissance Studies* 4:435–57.

Kent, James. 1873. *Commentaries on American Law*. 12th ed. Vol. 2. Edited by O. W. Holmes Jr. Boston: Little, Brown.

Kerblay, Basile. 1996/1986. "Socialist Families." In *A History of the Family*, ed. Andrè Burguière, Christiane Klapisch-Zuber, Martine Segalen, and Françoise Zonabend, 2:442–75. Cambridge, Mass.: Harvard University Press.

Kertzer, David I. 1989. "The Joint Family Household Revisited: Demographic Constraints and Household Complexity in the European Past." *Journal of Family History* 14 (1): 1–15.

———. 1991. "Household History and Sociological Theory." *Annual Review of Sociology* 17:155–79.

Kertzer, David I., and Marzio Barbagli, eds. 2001. *The History of the European Family: Family Life in Early Modern Times*. Vol. 1. New Haven, Conn.: Yale University Press.

Khater, Akram F. 2003. "'Queen of the House'? Making Immigrant Lebanese Families in the Mahjar." In *Family History in the Middle East*, ed. Barbara Doumani, 271–99. Albany: State University of New York Press.

Kincaid, D. Larry, Maria E. Figueroa, Douglas Storey, and Carol Underwood. 1999. "Ideation and Fertility Control: The Relationship Observed in Five Countries." Paper presented at the annual meeting of the Population Association of America, New York, 25–27 March.

Kirk, Dudley. 1944. "Population Changes and the Postwar World." *American Sociological Review* 9 (1): 28–35.

Klassen, Albert D., Colin J. Williams, and Eugene E. Levitt. 1989. *Sex and Morality in the U.S.* Middletown, Conn.: Wesleyan University Press.

Kloeze, Jan W. te, and Kees de Hoog. 1999. "Between Freedom and Commitment: The Postmodern Family Discovered: A Sociological Study of Typologies of Family and Leisure Domains in the Netherlands." *Society and Leisure* 22 (1): 171–86.

Kluge, Arnold G. N.d. "Testing the Comparative and Lineage Methods for Inferring Adaptation." Museum of Zoology, University of Michigan. Typescript.

Knauft, Bruce M., ed. 2002a. *Critically Modern: Alternatives, Alterities, Anthropologies*. Bloomington: Indiana University Press.

———. 2002b. "Critically Modern: An Introduction." In *Critically Modern: Alternatives, Alterities, Anthropologies*, ed. Bruce M. Knauft, 1–54. Bloomington: Indiana University Press.

———. 2002c. "Trials of the Oxymodern: Public Practice at Nomad Station." In *Critically Modern: Alternatives, Alterities, Anthropologies*, ed. Bruce M. Knauft, 105–43. Bloomington: Indiana University Press.

Knibbs, George H. 1928. *The Shadow of the World's Future*. London: Ernest Benn.

Knodel, John. 1978. "European Populations in the Past: Family-Level Relations." In *The Effects of Infant and Child Mortality on Fertility*, ed. Samuel H. Preston, 21–45. New York: Academic.

Knodel, John, Aphichat Chamratrithirong, and Nibhon Debavalya. 1987. *Thailand's Reproductive Revolution*. Madison: University of Wisconsin Press.

Knodel, John, and Gavin W. Jones. 1996. "Post-Cairo Population Policy: Does Promoting Girls' Schooling Miss the Mark?" *Population and Development Review* 22 (4): 683–702.

Knodel, John, and Etienne van de Walle. 1979. "Lessons from the Past: Policy Implications of Historical Fertility Studies." *Population and Development Review* 5 (2): 217–45.

Kobrin, Frances E. 1976. "The Fall of Household Size and the Rise of the Primary Individual in the United States." *Demography* 13 (1): 127–38.

Koegel, Otto E. 1922. *Common Law Marriage and Its Development in the United States.* Washington, D.C.: John Byrne.

Koehler, Lyle. 1980. *A Search for Power: The "Weaker Sex" in Seventeenth-Century New England.* Urbana: University of Illinois Press.

Kokole, Omari H. 1994. "The Politics of Fertility in Africa." In *The New Politics of Population: Conflict and Consensus in Family Planning,* ed. Jason L. Finkle and C. A. McIntosh, 73–88. New York: Population Council.

Kottak, Conrad P. 1990. *Prime-Time Society.* Belmont, Calif.: Wadsworth.

Kraditor, Aileen S. 1965. *The Ideas of the Woman Suffrage Movement.* New York: Columbia University Press.

Krannich, Ronald L., and Caryl R. Krannich. 1980. *Politics of Family Planning Policy: Thailand—a Case of Successful Implementation.* Berkeley: Center for South and Southeast Asia Studies, University of California.

Kreager, Philip. 1986. "Demographic Regimes as Cultural Systems." In *The State of Population Theory,* ed. David Coleman and Roger Schofield, 131–55. New York: Blackwell.

Kuijsten, Anton C. 1996. "Changing Family Patterns in Europe: A Case of Divergence?" *European Journal of Population* 12 (2): 115–43.

Kulick, Don. 1992. "'Coming Up' in Gapun: Conceptions of Development and Their Effect on Language in a Papua New Guinean Village." In *Kam-Ap or Take-Off: Local Notions of Development,* ed. Gudrun Dahl and Annika Rabo, 10–34. Stockholm: Stockholm Studies in Social Anthropology.

Kussmaul, A. 1981. *Servants in Husbandry in Early-Modern England.* Cambridge: Cambridge University Press.

Kwon, Tai-Hwan. 1989. "Sociocultural Context of Fertility Control Policy in Korea." Paper presented at a seminar organized by the IUSSP Committee on Policy and Population in Kenshasa, Zaire, International Union for the Scientific Study of Population, Liège, 27 February–2 March.

———. 1993. "Exploring Socio-Cultural Explanations of Fertility Transition in South Korea." In *The Revolution in Asian Fertility,* ed. Richard Leete and Iqbal Alam, 41–53. Oxford: Clarendon.

Lafitau, Joseph F. 1974/1724. *Customs of the American Indians Compared with the Customs of Primitive Times.* Edited and translated by W. N. Fenton and E. L. Moore. Toronto: Champlain Society.

Lang, Olga. 1968/1946. *Chinese Family and Society.* New York: Anchor.

Lapham, Robert J., and W. Parker Mauldin. 1985. "Contraceptive Prevalence: The Influence of Organized Family Planning Programs." *Studies in Family Planning* 16 (3): 117–37.

———. 1987. "The Effects of Family Planning on Fertility: Research Findings." In

Organizing for Effective Family Planning Programs, ed. Robert J. Lapham and George B. Simmons, 647–80. Washington, D.C.: National Academy Press.

Lapham, Robert J., and George B. Simmons, eds. 1987. *Organizing for Effective Family Planning Programs*. Washington, D.C.: National Academy Press.

Lardinois, Roland. 1996/1986. "India: The Family, the State, and Women." In *A History of the Family*, ed. Andrè Burguière, Christiane Klapisch-Zuber, Martine Segalen, and Françoise Zonabend, 2:268–300. Cambridge, Mass.: Harvard University Press.

Larson, Gustive O. 1971. *The "Americanization" of Utah for Statehood*. San Marino, Calif.: Huntington Library.

Laslett, Peter. 1965. "John Locke and His Books." In *The Library of John Locke*, ed. John Harrison and Peter Laslett, 1–61. Oxford: Oxford University Press.

———. 1978/1977. *Family Life and Illicit Love in Earlier Generations*. Cambridge: Cambridge University Press.

———. 1984/1965. *The World We Have Lost: England before the Industrial Age*. 3d ed. New York: Scribner's.

———. 1988/1960. Introduction to *Two Treatises of Government: A Critical Edition with an Introduction and Apparatus Criticus by Peter Laslett*. Cambridge: Cambridge University Press.

Laslett, Peter, and Richard Wall, eds. 1974/1972. *Household and Family in Past Time*. London: Cambridge University Press.

The Late Corporation of the Church of Jesus Christ of Latter-Day Saints v. United States. 136 U.S. 1 (1890).

Latham, Michael E. 2000. *Modernization as Ideology*. Chapel Hill: University of North Carolina Press.

Laumann, Edward O., John H. Gagnon, Robert T. Michael, and Stuart Michaels. 1994. *The Social Organization of Sexuality: Sexual Practices in the United States*. Chicago: University of Chicago Press.

Le Play, Frédéric. 1879. Les Ouvriers européens. Vol. 1. Tours: Alfred Mame et Fils, Libraires-Editeurs.

———. 1937/1879. "Les Ouvriers européens." In *Family and Society*, ed. Carle C. Zimmerman and Merle E. Framptons, trans. Samuel Dupertuis, 361–595. New York: D. Van Nostrand.

———. 1982a/1881. "La Constitution essentielle de l'humanité (Tours: Mame, 1881)." In *Frédéric Le Play on Family, Work, and Social Change*, ed. and trans. Catherine Bodard Silver, 48–78. Chicago: University of Chicago Press.

———. 1982b/1862. "Instruction sur la méthode d'observation." In *Frédéric Le Play on Family, Work, and Social Change*, ed. and trans. Catherine Bodard Silver, 179–83. Chicago: University of Chicago Press.

———. 1982c/1855. "Les Ouvriers européens." In *Frédéric Le Play on Family, Work, and Social Change*, ed. and trans. Catherine Bodard Silver, 151–62, 239–47, 263–87. Chicago: University of Chicago Press.

———. 1982d/1879. "Les Ouvriers européens." In *Frédéric Le Play on Family, Work, and*

Social Change, ed. and trans. Catherine Bodard Silver, 184–205. Chicago: University of Chicago Press.

———. 1982e/1872. "La Réforme sociale." In *Frédéric Le Play on Family, Work, and Social Change*, ed. and trans. Catherine Bodard Silver, 259–62. Chicago: University of Chicago Press.

Leclercq, Jean. 1982. "The Development of a Topic in Medieval Studies in the Eighties: An Interdisciplinary Perspective on Love and Marriage." In *Literary and Historical Perspectives on the Middle Ages*, ed. Patricia W. Cummins, Patrick W. Conner, and Charles W. Cornell, 20–37. Morgantown: West Virginia University Press.

Leder, Lawrence H. 1968. *Liberty and Authority: Early American Political Ideology, 1689–1763*. Chicago: Quadrangle.

Lee, James Z., and Cameron D. Campbell. 1997. *Fate and Fortune in Rural China: Social Organization and Population Behavior in Liaoning, 1774–1873*. Cambridge: Cambridge University Press.

Lee, James Z., and Feng Wang. 1999. *One Quarter of Humanity: Malthusian Mythology and Chinese Realities, 1700–2000*. Cambridge, Mass.: Harvard University Press.

Lee, James Z., Feng Wang, and Emiko Ochiai. 2000. "Domestic Group Organization and Demographic Behavior in Eurasia, 1750–1900: A Reassessment of Metageography." Humanities and Social Sciences, California Institute of Technology. Typescript.

Lee, Kelley, Gill Walt, Louisiana Lush, and John Cleland. 1995. *Population Policies and Programmes: Determinants and Consequences in Eight Developing Countries*. London: London School of Hygiene and Tropical Medicine and United Nations Population Fund.

Lee, Raymond L. M. 1994. "Modernization, Postmodernism, and the Third World." *Journal of the International Sociological Association* 42 (2): 1–66.

Lehmann, William C. 1979/1960. *John Millar of Glasgow, 1735–1801*. New York: Arno.

Lenski, Gerhard. 1976. "History and Social Change." *American Journal of Sociology* 82 (3): 548–64.

Lerner, Daniel. 1958. *The Passing of Traditional Society: Modernizing the Middle East*. Glencoe, Ill.: Free Press.

Lesthaeghe, Ron. 1980. "On the Social Control of Human Reproduction." *Population and Development Review* 6 (4): 527–48.

———. 1983. "A Century of Demographic and Cultural Change in Western Europe: An Exploration of Underlying Dimensions." *Population and Development Review* 9 (3): 411–35.

Lesthaeghe, Ron, and K. Neels. 2002. "From the First to the Second Demographic Transition: An Interpretation of the Spatial Continuity of Demographic Innovation in France, Belgium, and Switzerland." Interface Demography, Vrije Universiteit Brussel, Brussels. Typescript.

Lesthaeghe, Ron, and Johan Surkyn. 2002. "New Forms of Household Formation in Central and Eastern Europe: Are They Related to Newly Emerging Value Orientations?" Working Paper no. 2002–2. Interface Demography, Vrije Universiteit Brussel.

Lesthaeghe, Ron, and Chris Wilson. 1986. "Modes of Production, Secularization, and the Pace of Fertility Decline in Western Europe, 1870–1930." In *The Decline of Fertility in Europe*, ed. Ansley J. Coale and Susan C. Watkins, 261–92. Princeton, N.J.: Princeton University Press.

Levine, David. 2001. *At the Dawn of Modernity: Biology, Culture, and the Material Life in Europe after the Year 1000.* Berkeley: University of California Press.

LeVine, Robert A., Sarah E. LeVine, Amy Richman, F. M. T. Uribe, Clara S. Correa, and Patrice M. Miller. 1991. "Women's Schooling and Child Care in the Demographic Transition: A Mexican Case Study." *Population and Development Review* 17 (3): 459–96.

Levy, Darline G., Harriet B. Applewhite, and Mary D. Johnson, eds. 1979. *Women in Revolutionary Paris, 1789–1795.* Urbana: University of Illinois Press.

Levy, Howard S. 1966. *Chinese Footbinding: The History of a Curious Erotic Custom.* New York: Walton Rawls.

Levy, Marion J., Jr. 1949. *The Family Revolution in Modern China.* Cambridge, Mass.: Harvard University Press.

Liao, Tim F. 2001. "Were Past Chinese Families Complex? Household Structures during the Tang Dynasty, 618–907 AD." *Continuity and Change* 16 (3): 331–55.

Lie, John. 1996. *Sociology of Contemporary Japan.* London: Sage.

Lieber, Francis. 1855. "The Mormons: Shall Utah Be Admitted into the Union?" *Putnam's Monthly* 5:225–36.

———. 1876/1838. *Manual of Political Ethics.* 2d rev. ed. Philadelphia: J. B. Lippencott.

Linford, Orma. 1964. "The Mormons and the Law: The Polygamy Cases." *Utah Law Review* 9 (1): 308–70.

LiPuma, Edward. 2000. *Encompassing Others: The Magic of Modernity in Melanesia.* Ann Arbor: University of Michigan Press.

Locke, John. 1988/1690. *Two Treatises of Government: A Critical Edition with an Introduction and Apparatus Criticus by Peter Laslett.* Cambridge: Cambridge University Press.

———. 1996/1693. *Some Thoughts concerning Education.* In *Some Thoughts concerning Education; and Of the Conduct of the Understanding,* by John Locke, ed. Ruth W. Grant and Nathan Tarcov, 1–162. Indianapolis: Hackett.

Locoh, Thérèsa. 1988. "Evolution of the Family in Africa." In *The State of African Demography,* ed. Etienne van de Walle, Patrick O. Ohadike, and Mpembele D. Sala-Diakanda, 47–65. Liège: International Union for the Scientific Study of Population.

Loomis, Charles P. 1934. "The Growth of the Farm Family in Relation to Its Activities." *North Carolina Agricultural Experiment Station Bulletin* 198:297–331.

Löwith, Karl. 1949. *Meaning in History.* Chicago: University of Chicago Press.

Lubbock, Sir J. 1889/1870. *The Origin of Civilization and the Primitive Condition of Man.* New York: D. Appleton.

Lynd, Robert S., and Helen M. Lynd. 1929. *Middletown: A Study in Contemporary American Culture.* New York: Harcourt, Brace.

Lystra, Karen. 1989. *Searching the Heart: Women, Men, and Romantic Love in Nineteenth-Century America.* New York: Oxford University Press.

Macaulay, Catharine. 1974/1790. *Letters on Education.* New York: Garland.

MacDonald, Michael. 1981. *Mystical Bedlam*. Cambridge: Cambridge University Press.

Macfarlane, Alan. 1970. *The Family Life of Ralph Jasselin, a Seventeenth-Century Clergyman: An Essay in Historical Anthropology*. Cambridge: Cambridge University Press.

———. 1979a/1978. *The Origins of English Individualism: The Family, Property, and Social Transition*. Cambridge: Cambridge University Press.

———. 1979b. Review of *The Family, Sex, and Marriage in England, 1500–1800*, by Lawrence Stone. *History and Theory* 18 (1): 103–26.

———. 1986. *Marriage and Love in England: Modes of Reproduction, 1300–1840*. Oxford: Blackwell.

———. 1987. *The Culture of Capitalism*. Oxford: Blackwell.

———. 2000. *The Riddle of the Modern World*. New York: St. Martin's.

———. 2002. *The Making of the Modern World: Visions from the West and East*. London: Palgrave.

Macpherson, C. B. 1962. *The Political Theory of Possessive Individualism*. London: Oxford University Press.

Madan, T. N. 2000. "The Hindu Family and Development." In *The Indian Family: Change and Persistence*, ed. Parimal K. Roy, 257–80. New Delhi: Gyan.

Maine, Henry S. 1888/1861. *Ancient Law*. New York: Henry Holt.

Malcolmson, Robert. 1980. "A Set of Ungovernable People." In *An Ungovernable People*, ed. John Brewer and John Styles, 85–127. London: Hutchinson.

Malthus, Thomas R. 1986a/1798. *An Essay on the Principle of Population*. In *Thomas Malthus: An Essay on the Principle of Population and a Summary View of the Principle of Population*, ed. Antony Flew, 67–217. New York: Penguin.

———. 1986b/1803. *An Essay on the Principle of Population*. Vols. 2–3 in *The Works of Thomas Robert Malthus*, ed. Edward A. Wrigley and David Souden. London: William Pickering. This 1803 *Essay* (republished in 1826) is a thoroughly revised and vastly expanded version of the 1798 *Essay*.

———. 1986c/1830. "A Summary View of the Principle of Population." In *Thomas Malthus: An Essay on the Principle of Population*, ed. Antony Flew, 219–72. New York: Penguin.

Mandelbaum, Maurice. 1971. *History, Man, and Reason: A Study in Nineteenth-Century Thought*. Baltimore: Johns Hopkins University Press.

Manuel, Frank E. 1962. *The Prophets of Paris*. Cambridge, Mass.: Harvard University Press.

Mar'iyah, C. 2002. "The Feminist Movement for Equal Rights." In *Muslim Feminism and Feminist Movement: South-East Asia*, ed. Abida Samiuddin and R. Khanam, 177–214. Delhi: Global.

Marx, Karl, and Friedrich Engels. 1965/1848. *Manifesto of the Communist Party*. Beijing: Foreign Languages.

Masemann, Vandra L. 1999. "Culture and Education." In *Comparative Education: The Dialectic of the Global and the Local*, ed. Robert F. Arnove and Carlos Alberto Torres, 115–33. Lanham, Md.: Rowman & Littlefield.

Mason, Karen O. 1997a. "Explaining Fertility Transitions." *Demography* 34 (4): 443–54.

———. 1997b. "Gender and Demographic Change: *What Do We Know?*" In *The Continuing*

Demographic Transition, ed. Gavin W. Jones, Robert M. Douglas, John C. Caldwell, and Rennie M. D'Souza, 158–82. Oxford: Oxford University Press.

Mattessich, Paul, and Reuben Hill. 1987. "Life Cycle and Family Development." In *Handbook of Marriage and the Family*, ed. Marvin B. Sussman and Suzanne K. Steinmetz, 437–69. New York: Plenum.

Matthiessen, Paul C., and James C. McCann. 1978. "The Role of Mortality in the European Fertility Transition: Aggregate-Level Relations." In *The Effects of Infant and Child Mortality on Fertility*, ed. Samuel H. Preston, 47–68. New York: Academic.

Mauldin, W. Parker, Nazli Chouchri, Frank W. Notestein, and Michael Teitelbaum. 1974. "A Report on Bucharest." *Studies in Family Planning* 5 (12): 357–95.

May, Henry F. 1976. *The Enlightenment in America*. New York: Oxford University Press.

Mayhew, A. I. 1941. "The Christian Ethic and India." In *Modern India and the West: A Study of the Interaction of Their Civilizations*, ed. L. S. S. O'Malley, 305–37. London: Oxford University Press.

Maynes, Mary J., and Ann Waltner. 2001. "Women's Life-Cycle Transitions in a World-Historical Perspective: Comparing Marriage in China and Europe." *Journal of Women's History* 12 (4): 11–21.

Mazrui, Ali A. 1994. "Islamic Doctrine and the Politics of Induced Fertility Change: An African Perspective." In *The New Politics of Population: Conflict and Consensus in Family Planning*, ed. Jason L. Finkle and C. A. McIntosh, 121–34. New York: Population Council.

McCaa, Robert. 1994a. "Child Marriage and Complex Families among the Nahuas of Ancient Mexico." *Latin American Population History Bulletin* 26 (fall): 2–11.

———. 1994b. "Marriageways in Mexico and Spain, 1500–1900." *Continuity and Change* 9 (1): 11–43.

———. 2003. "The Nahua *calli* of Ancient Mexico: Household, Family, and Gender." *Continuity and Change* 18 (1): 23–48.

McClintock, Anne. 1995. *Imperial Leather: Race, Gender, and Sexuality in the Colonial Conquest*. New York: Routledge.

McDonald, Peter. 1985. "Social Organization and Nuptiality in Developing Societies." In *Reproductive Change in Developing Countries*, ed. John Cleland and John Hobcraft, 87–114. London: Oxford University Press.

———. 1993. "Fertility Transition Hypotheses." In *The Revolution in Asian Fertility: Dimensions, Causes, and Implications*, ed. Richard Leete and Iqbal Alam, 3–14. Oxford: Clarendon.

McIntosh, C. Alison, and Jason L. Finkle. 1995. "The Cairo Conference on Population and Development: A New Paradigm?" *Population and Development Review* 21 (2): 223–60.

McLennan, John F. 1886/1865. *Studies in Ancient History*. London: Macmillan.

McLoughlin, William G. 1986. *Cherokee Renascence in the New Republic*. Princeton, N.J.: Princeton University Press.

McNickle, D'Arcy. 1973. *Native American Tribalism: Indian Survivals and Renewals*. New York: Oxford University Press, for Institute of Race Relations.

McNicoll, Geoffrey. 1989. "Family and Welfare Policies in Sub-Saharan Africa: Drawing on International Experience." Paper presented at a seminar organized by the IUSSP Committee on Policy and Population in Kenshasa, Zaire, International Union for the Scientific Study of Population, Liège, 27 February–2 March.

———. 1994. "Institutional Analysis of Fertility." In *Population, Economic Development, and the Environment,* ed. Kerstin Lindahl-Kiessling and Hans Landberg, 199–230. Oxford: Oxford University Press.

———. 1997. "The Governance of Fertility Transition: Reflections on the Asian Experience." In *The Continuing Demographic Transition,* ed. Gavin W. Jones, Robert M. Douglas, John C. Caldwell, and Rennie M. D'Souza, 365–82. Oxford: Oxford University Press.

McSheffrey, Shannon. 1998. "'I Will Never Have None Ayenst My Faders Will': Consent and the Making of Marriage in the Late Medieval Diocese of London." In *Women, Marriage, and Family in Medieval Christendom,* ed. Constance M. Rousseau and Joel T. Rosenthal, 153–74. Kalamazoo: Medieval Institute Publications, Western Michigan University.

Meek, Ronald L. 1976. *Social Science and the Ignoble Savage.* Cambridge: Cambridge University Press.

Mehryar, Amir H., Joel Montague, Farzaneh Roudi, and Farzaneth Tajdini. 2000. "Iranian Family Planning Program at the Threshold of the t Twenty-first Century." Paper presented at the seminar "Family Planning Programmes in the Twenty-first Century," International Union for the Scientific Study of Population, Dhaka, Bangladesh, 16–21 January.

Mehryar, Amir H., M. Tabibian, and R. Ghoulipour. N.d. *Correlates and Determinants of Fertility Decline in Iran, 1986–1996: A District Level Analysis.* Tehran: Institute for Research on Planning and Development.

Meijer, Marimus J. 1971. *Marriage Law and Policy in the Chinese People's Republic.* Hong Kong: Hong Kong University Press.

Mennell, Stephen. 1996. "Asia and Europe: Comparing Civilizing Processes." In *The Course of Human History: Economic Growth, Social Process, and Civilization,* ed. Johan Goudsblom, Eric Jones, and Stephen Mennell, 117–34. Armonk, N.Y.: M. E. Sharpe.

Meyer, John W., John Boli, George M. Thomas, and Francisco O. Ramirez. 1997. "World Society and the Nation-State." *American Journal of Sociology* 103 (1): 144–81.

Michael, Robert T., John H. Gagnon, Edward O. Laumann, and Gina Kolata. 1994. *Sex in America: A Definitive Survey.* Boston: Little, Brown.

Middleton, John, and Robert J. Lapham. 1987. "Demand Generation." In *Organizing for Effective Family Planning Programs,* ed. Robert Lapham and George B. Simmons, 295–323. Washington, D.C.: National Academy Press.

Mill, J. S. 1989a/1859. "On Liberty." In *On Liberty and Other Writings,* by J. S. Mill, ed. Stefan Collini, 1–116. New York: Cambridge University Press.

———. 1989b/1859–69. *On Liberty and Other Writings,* ed. Stefan Collini. New York: Cambridge University Press.

———. 1989c/1869. "The Subjection of Women." In *On Liberty and Other Writings,* by J. S. Mill, ed. Stefan Collini, 117–218. New York: Cambridge University Press.

Millar, John. 1979/1779. *The Origin of the Distinction of Ranks.* Edited by William C. Lehmann. New York: Arno.

Mitterauer, Michael, and Reinhard Sieder. 1982/1977. *The European Family: Patriarchy to Partnership from the Middle Ages to the Present.* Chicago: University of Chicago Press.

Moaddel, Mansoor. 1992. *Class, Politics, and Ideology in the Iranian Revolution.* New York: Columbia University Press.

———. 2005. *Islamic Modernism, Nationalism, and Fundamentalism: Episode and Discourse.* Chicago: University of Chicago Press.

Moaddel, Mansoor, and Taqhi Azadarmaki. 2003. "The Worldviews of Islamic Publics: The Cases of Egypt, Iran, and Jordan." In *Human Values and Social Change: Findings from the Values Survey,* ed. Ronald Inglehart, 69–89. Leiden: Brill.

Modell, John. 1989. *Into One's Own: From Youth to Adulthood in the United States, 1920–1975.* Berkeley and Los Angeles: University of California Press.

Modell, John, Frank Furstenberg, and Theodore Hershberg. 1976. "Social Change and Transitions to Adulthood in Historical Perspective." *Journal of Family History* 1 (1): 7–32.

Modell, John, and Tamara K. Hareven. 1973. "Urbanization and the Malleable Household: An Examination of Boarding and Lodging in American Families." *Journal of Marriage and the Family* 35 (3): 467–79.

Mody, Perveez. 2002. "Love and the Law: Love-Marriage in Delhi." *Modern Asian Studies* 36 (1): 223–56.

Moghadam, Valentine. 2002. "Gender Politics in Iran and Afghanistan." In *Muslim Feminism and Feminist Movement: Central Asia,* ed. Abida Samiuddin and R. Khanam, 1:45–78. Delhi: Global.

Montaigne, Michel de. 1946/1580. *Essays.* New York: Heritage.

Montesquieu, Charles-Louis de Secondat, Baron de. 1973/1721. *Persian Letters.* Translated by C. J. Betts. Harmondsworth: Penguin.

———. 1997/1748. *The Spirit of the Laws.* Translated and edited by Anne M. Cohler, Basia C. Miller, and Harold S. Stone. Cambridge: Cambridge University Press.

Montgomery, Mark R., and John B. Casterline. 1993. "The Diffusion of Fertility Control in Taiwan: Evidence from Pooled Cross-Section Time-Series Models." *Population Studies* 47 (3): 457–79.

More, Sir Thomas. 1997/1516. *Utopia.* Edited by Paul Negri. Mineola, N.Y.: Dover.

Morgan, Edmund S. 1966/1944. *The Puritan Family: Religion and Domestic Relations in Seventeenth-Century New England.* New York: Harper & Row.

Morgan, Lewis H. 1985/1877. *Ancient Society.* Tucson: University of Arizona Press.

Morgan, S. Phillip. 1996. "Characteristic Features of Modern American Fertility." In *Fertility in the United States,* ed. John B. Casterline, Ronald Lee, and Karen A. Foote, 19–63. *Population and Development Review,* vol. 22 (suppl.).

Mosley, M. H., and Gladys Branic. 1989. "Population Policy in Sub-Saharan Africa: Agenda of International Agencies." Paper presented at a seminar organized by the IUSSP Committee on Policy and Population in Kenshasa, Zaire, International Union for the Scientific Study of Population, Liège, 27 February–2 March.

Mount, Ferdinand. 1982. *The Subversive Family: An Alternative History of Love and Marriage.* London: Jonathan Cape.

Muncy, Raymond L. 1973. *Sex and Marriage in Utopian Communities: Nineteenth Century America.* Bloomington: Indiana University Press.

Mundigo, Axel I. 1996. "The Role of Family Planning Programmes in the Fertility Transition of Latin America." In *The Fertility Transition in Latin America,* ed. José M. Guzmán, Susheela Singh, Germán Rodriguez, and Edith A. Pantelides, 192–210. Oxford: Clarendon.

Murphy, Eugene T. 2001. "Changes in Family and Marriage in a Yangzi Delta Farming Community, 1930–1990." *Ethnology* 40 (3): 213–35.

Murray, Jacqueline. 1998. "Individualism and Consensual Marriage: Some Evidence from Medieval England." In *Women, Marriage, and Family in Medieval Christendom,* ed. Constance M. Rousseau and Joel T. Rosenthal, 121–51. Kalamazoo: Medieval Institute Publications, Western Michigan University.

Myrdal, Gunnar. 1968. *Asian Drama: An Inquiry into the Poverty of Nations.* Vol. 2. New York: Twentieth Century Fund.

Myres, John L. 1916. *The Influence of Anthropology on the Course of Political Science.* Berkeley: University of California Press.

Najmabadi, Afsaneh. 1998. "Crafting an Educated Housewife in Iran." In *Remaking Women: Feminism and Modernity in the Middle East,* ed. Lila Abu-Lughod, 91–125. Princeton, N.J.: Princeton University Press.

Ndeti, Kivuto, and Cecilia Ndeti. 1980. *Cultural Values and Population Policy in Kenya.* Nairobi: Kenya Literature Bureau.

Nearing, Nellie S. 1914. "Education and Fecundity." *Publications of the American Statistical Association* 14 (106): 156–74.

Ness, Gayl D. 1979. "Organizational Issues in International Population Assistance." In *World Population and Development,* ed. P. M. Hauser, 615–49. Syracuse, N.Y.: Syracuse University.

Nevitt, H. Rodney, Jr. 2001. "Vermeer on the Question of Love." In *The Cambridge Companion to Vermeer,* ed. Wayne E. Franits, 89–110. Cambridge: Cambridge University Press.

"The New England Family." 1882. *New Englander* 41 (165): 137–59.

Newman, Stephen L. 1992. "Locke's Two Treatises and Contemporary Thought: Freedom, Community, and the Liberal Tradition." In *John Locke's Two Treatises of Government: New Interpretations,* ed. Edward J. Harpham, 173–208. Lawrence: University Press of Kansas.

Nicholas, David. 1985. *The Domestic Life of a Medieval City: Women, Children, and the Family in Fourteenth-Century Ghent.* Lincoln: University of Nebraska Press.

Nicholson, Linda J. 1986. *Gender and History: The Limits of Social Theory in the Age of the Family.* New York: Columbia University Press.

Nisbet, Robert A. 1975/1969. *Social Change and History.* New York: Oxford University Press.

———. 1980. *History of the Idea of Progress.* New York: Basic.

Nock, Steven L. 1998. *Marriage in Men's Lives.* New York: Oxford University Press.

———. 2000. "The Divorce of Marriage and Parenthood." *Journal of Family Therapy* 22:245–63.

Noonan, John T., Jr. 1967. "Marital Affection in the Canonists." In *Collectanea Stephan Kuttner,* vol. 2 (vol. 12 of *Studia Gratiana: post octava Decreti saeculari: Collectanea historiae iuris canonici,* ed. Giuseppe Forchielli and Alphonso M. Stickler), pp. 479–509. Bologna: Institutum Gratianum.

———. 1973. "Power to Choose." *Viator: Medieval and Renaissance Studies* 4:419–34.

Norris, Pippa, and Ronald Inglehart. 2003. "Islamic Culture and Democracy: Testing the 'Clash of Civilizations' Thesis." In *Human Values and Social Change: Findings from the Values Survey,* ed. Ronald Inglehart, 5–33. Leiden: Brill.

Northrop, Douglas Taylor. 1999. "Uzbek Women and the Veil: Gender and Power in Stalinist Central Asia." Ph.D. diss., Stanford University.

Nortman, Dorothy L. 1985. *Population and Family Planning Programs: A Compendium of Data through 1983.* 12th ed. New York: Population Council.

———. 1987. "Family Planning Resources: Focus on Funds." In *Organizing for Effective Family Planning Programs,* ed. Robert Lapham and George B. Simmons, 111–41. Washington, D.C.: National Academy Press.

Norton, Mary B. 1980. *Liberty's Daughters and the Revolutionary Experience of American Women, 1750–1800.* Boston: Little, Brown.

Notestein, Frank W. 1945. "Population—the Long View." In *Food for the World,* ed. Theodore W. Schultz, 37–57. Chicago: University of Chicago Press.

———. 1950. "The Reduction of Human Fertility as an Aid to Programs of Economic Development in Densely Settled Agrarian Regions." In *Modernization Programs in Relation to Human Resources and Population Problems,* 89–100. New York: Milbank Memorial Fund.

———. 1968. "The Population Council and the Demographic Crisis of the Less Developed World." *Demography* 5 (2): 553–61.

———. 1982. "Demography in the United States: A Partial Account of the Development of the Field." *Population and Development Review* 8 (4): 651–88.

———. 1983/1964. "Population Growth and Economic Development." *Population and Development Review* 9 (2): 345–60.

O'Donnell, William J., and David A. Jones. 1982. *The Law of Marriage and Marital Alternatives.* Lexington, Mass.: Lexington.

Offen, Karen. 2000. *European Feminism, 1700–1950.* Stanford, Calif.: Stanford University Press.

O'Hara, Diana. 1991. "'Ruled by My Friends': Aspects of Marriage in the Diocese of Canterbury, c. 1540–1570." *Continuity and Change* 6 (1): 9–41.

———. 2000. *Courtship and Constraint: Rethinking the Making of Marriage in Tudor England.* Manchester: Manchester University Press.

Okin, Susan M. 1982. "Women and the Making of the Sentimental Family." *Philosophy and Public Affairs* 11 (1): 65–88.

Olaleye, David O., and Akinrinola Bankole. 1994. "The Impact of Mass Media Family Planning Promotion on Contraceptive Behavior of Women in Ghana." *Population Research and Policy Review* 13:161–77.

Olin, Spencer C., Jr. 1980. "The Oneida Community and the Instability of Charismatic Authority." *Journal of American History* 67 (2): 285–300.

Olsen, Glenn W. 2001. "Marriage in Barbarian Kingdom and Christian Court: Fifth through Eleventh Centuries." In *Christian Marriage: A Historical Study*, ed. Glenn W. Olsen, 146–212. New York: Crossroad.

O'Malley, L. S. S., ed. 1941. *Modern India and the West: A Study of the Interaction of Their Civilizations*. London: Oxford University Press.

O'Rand, Angela M., and Margaret L. Krecker. 1990. "Concepts of the Life Cycle: Their History, Meanings, and Uses in the Social Sciences." *Annual Review of Sociology* 16:241–62.

Organization of African Unity. 1990. *African Charter on the Rights and Welfare of the Child*. Addis Ababa, Ethiopia: Organization of African Unity.

Outhwaite, R. Brian. 1995. *Clandestine Marriage in England, 1500–1850*. Rio Grande, Ohio: Hambledon.

Ozment, Steven. 1983. *When Fathers Ruled: Family Life in Reformation Europe*. Cambridge, Mass.: Harvard University Press.

———. 2001. *Ancestors: The Loving Family in Old Europe*. Cambridge, Mass.: Harvard University Press.

Pagden, Anthony. 1982. *The Fall of Natural Man: The American Indian and the Origins of Comparative Ethnology*. Cambridge: Cambridge University Press.

Pagnini, D. L., and Robert R. Rindfuss. 1993. "The Divorce of Marriage and Childbearing: Changing Attitudes and Behavior in the United States." *Population and Development Review* 19 (2): 331–47.

Paine, Thomas. 1879/1776. *Common Sense*. In *The Political Works of Thomas Paine*, 7–51. Chicago: Belfords, Clark.

———. 1984/1791–92. *Rights of Man*. With an introduction by Eric Foner. New York: Penguin.

Paley, William. 1793. *The Principles of Moral and Political Philosophy*. 9th ed. London: Faulder.

Pearce, Roy H. 1967/1953. *Savagism and Civilization*. Baltimore: Johns Hopkins University Press.

Peel, John D. Y. 1971. *Herbert Spencer: The Evolution of a Sociologist*. New York: Basic.

Pembroke, S. G. 1979. "The Early Human Family: Some Views, 1770–1870." In *Classical Influences on Western Thought, A.D. 1650–1870*, ed. R. R. Bolgar, 275–91. Cambridge: Cambridge University Press.

Perkin, Joan. 1989. *Women and Marriage in Nineteenth-Century England*. London: Routledge.

Phillips, James F., Ruth Simmons, Michael A. Koenig, and J. Chakraborty. 1988. "Determinants of Reproductive Change in a Traditional Society: Evidence from Matlab, Bangladesh." *Studies in Family Planning* 19 (6): 313–34.

Phillips, Roderick. 1988. *Putting Asunder: A History of Divorce in Western Society.* Cambridge: Cambridge University Press.

Pierre, Teresa O. 2001. "Marriage, Body, and Sacrament in the Age of Hugh of St. Victor." In *Christian Marriage: A Historical Study,* ed. Glenn W. Olsen, 213–68. New York: Crossroad.

Pigg, Stacy L. 1992. "Inventing Social Categories through Place: Social Representations and Development in Nepal." *Comparative Studies in Society and History* 34 (3): 491–513.

Pillai, S. Devadas. 1976a. "The Sociology of Ghurye." In *Aspects of Changing India: Studies in Honour of Professor G. S. Ghurye,* ed. S. D. Pillai, 27–40. Bombay: Popular Prakashan.

———. 1976b. "Western Perspectives on India: Some Views and Counter-Views." In *Aspects of Changing India: Studies in Honour of Professor G. S. Ghurye,* ed. S. D. Pillai, 1–26. Bombay: Popular Prakashan.

Pinchbeck, Ivy. 1969. *Women Workers and the Industrial Revolution, 1750–1850.* London: Virago.

Piotrow, Phyllis T. 1973. *World Population Crisis: The United States Response.* New York: Praeger.

Plane, Ann M. 2000. *Colonial Intimacies: Indian Marriage in Early New England.* Ithaca, N.Y.: Cornell University Press.

Poll, Richard D. 1957. "The Mormon Question Enters National Politics, 1850–1856." *Utah Historical Quarterly* 25 (2): 117–31.

Pollock, Frederick, and Frederick W. Maitland. 1968. *The History of English Law before the Time of Edward I.* Cambridge: Cambridge University Press.

Pollock, Linda A. 1985/1983. *Forgotten Children: Parent-Child Relations from 1500 to 1900.* Cambridge: Cambridge University Press.

Popenoe, David. 1988. *Disturbing the Nest.* New York: Aldine de Gruyter.

Popper, Karl R. 1964/1957. *The Poverty of Historicism.* New York: Harper & Row.

Porter, H. C. 1979. *The Inconstant Savage: England and the North American Indian, 1500–1660.* Dallas: Duckworth.

Potter, Joseph E., R. M. Assuncão, Suzana M. Cavenaghi, and Andre J. Caetano. 1998. "The Spread of Television and Fertility Decline in Brazil: A Spatial-Temporal Analysis, 1970–1991." Paper presented at the annual meeting of the Population Association of America, Chicago, 2–4 April.

Preston, Samuel H., ed. 1978. *The Effects of Infant and Child Mortality on Fertility.* New York: Academic.

Preston, Samuel H., and John McDonald. 1979. "The Incidence of Divorce within Cohorts of American Marriages Contracted since the Civil War." *Demography* 16 (1): 1–25.

Price, Richard. 1776. *Observations on the Nature of Civil Liberty, and the Principles of Government, from Dr. Price's Much Esteemed and Popular Essay, Published Anno 1776: With the Declaration of Principles, and Regulations of the Friends of Liberty, United for Promoting Constitutional Learning.* London: Printed by the Order of the Society and Sold by Joyce and Toone, Eaton, Lee, Ballard, Riebau.

Prinz, Christopher. 1995. *Cohabiting, Married, or Single.* Aldershot: Avebury.

Pritchett, Lant H. 1994. "Desired Fertility and the Impact of Population Policies." *Population and Development Review* 20 (1): 1–55.

Prucha, Francis P., ed. 1973. *Americanizing the American Indians*. Cambridge, Mass.: Harvard University Press.

———. 1984. *The Great Father*. Lincoln: University of Nebraska Press.

Psacharopoulos, George, and Sandra Rosenhouse. 1999. "Population Growth, Education, and Employment in Latin America, with an Illustration from Bolivia." In *Population Growth and Demographic Structure*, 155–72. New York: United Nations, Department of Economic and Social Affairs, Population Division.

Quadagno, Jill, and Stan J. Knapp. 1992. "Have Historical Sociologists Forsaken Theory?" *Sociological Methods and Research* 20 (4): 481–507.

Quinn, D. Michael. 1985. "LDS Church Authority and New Plural Marriages, 1890–1904." *Dialogue: A Journal of Mormon Thought* 18 (1): 9–105.

———. 1998. "Plural Marriage and Mormon Fundamentalism." *Dialogue: A Journal of Mormon Thought* 31 (2): 1–68.

Raftery, Adrian E., Steven M. Lewis, and Akbar Aghajanian. 1995. "Demand or Ideation? Evidence from the Iranian Marital Fertility Decline." *Demography* 32 (2): 159–82.

Raymo, James M. 1998. "Later Marriages or Fewer? Changes in the Marital Behavior of Japanese Women." *Journal of Marriage and the Family* 60 (4): 1023–34.

Raymo, James M., and Yu Xie. 2000. "Temporal and Regional Variation in the Strength of Educational Homogamy." *American Sociological Review* 65 (5): 773–81.

Razi, Zvi. 1993. "The Myth of the Immutable English Family." *Past and Present*, no. 140:3–44.

Reed, James. 1978. *Private Vice to Public Virtue: The Birth Control Movement and American Society since 1830*. New York: Basic.

Reiss, Ira L. 1967. *The Social Context of Premarital Sexual Permissiveness*. New York: Holt, Rinehart & Winston.

Rele, J. R., and Iqbal Alam. 1993. "Fertility Transition in Asia: The Statistical Evidence." In *The Revolution in Asian Fertility: Dimensions, Causes, and Implications*, ed. Richard Leete and Iqbal Alam, 15–37. Oxford: Clarendon.

Rendall, Jane. 1985. *The Origins of Modern Feminism: Women in Britain, France, and the United States, 1780–1860*. London: Macmillan.

———. 1994. "Citizenship, Culture, and Civilization: The Languages of British Suffragists, 1866–1874." In *Suffrage and Beyond*, ed. Caroline Daley and Melanie Nolan, 127–50. New York: New York University Press.

Reynolds v. United States. 98 U.S. 145 (1878).

Rheinstein, Max. 1972. *Marriage Stability, Divorce, and the Law*. Chicago: University of Chicago Press.

Riley, Glenda. 1991. *Divorce: An American Tradition*. New York: Oxford University Press.

Rives, J. B. 1999. *Tacitus: Germania*. Oxford: Clarendon.

Roberts-Jones, Philippe, and Françoise Roberts-Jones. 1997. *Pieter Bruegel*. Paris: Harry N. Adams.

Robertson, Constance N. 1972. *Oneida Community: The Breakup, 1876–1881*. Syracuse, N.Y.: Syracuse University Press.

Robertson, Robert. 1992. *Globalization: Social Theory and Global Culture.* London: Sage.

Robertson, William. 1780/1777. *The History of America by William Robertson.* Dublin: Printed for Messrs. Price, Whitestone, W. Watson, Corcoran, R. Cross and 41 Others in Dublin.

———. 1860/1762. *The History of the Reign of the Emperor Charles V with a View of the Progress of Society in Europe.* 1st American ed., from 10th London ed. New York: Hopkins & Seymour.

Robinson, Warren C., and Jawalaksana Rachapaetayakom. 1993. "The Role of Government Planning in Thailand's Fertility Decline." In *The Revolution in Asian Fertility*, ed. Richard Leete and Iqbal Alam, 54–66. Oxford: Clarendon.

Rockefeller, John D. 1977/1952. "On the Origins of the Population Council." *Population and Development Review* 3 (4): 493–502.

Rogers, Everett M. 1973. *Communication Strategies for Family Planning.* New York: Free Press.

Roof, Wade C., and William McKinney. 1987. *American Mainline Religion.* New Brunswick, N.J.: Rutgers University Press.

Roose, H., and M. Swift. 2002. "Malaysian Feminism and Feminist Movement." In *Muslim Feminism and Feminist Movement: South-East Asia*, ed. Abida Samiuddin and R. Khanam, 11–40. Delhi: Global.

Rorlich, A. A. 2002. "Muslim Feminism and Nationalism: Crimea, Middle Volga, and Caucasus." In *Muslim Feminism and Feminist Movement: Central Asia*, ed. Abida Samiuddin and R. Khanam, 1:245–67. Delhi: Global.

Rosen, George. 1967. *Democracy and Economic Change in India.* Berkeley: University of California Press.

Rosero-Bixby, Luis, and John B. Casterline. 1993. "Modelling Diffusion Effects in Fertility Transition." *Population Studies* 47 (1): 147–67.

Ross, Edward A. 1907. "Western Civilization and the Birth-Rate." *American Journal of Sociology* 12 (5): 607–32.

———. 1927. *Standing Room Only.* New York: Century.

Rotenstreich, Nathan. 1971. "The Idea of Historical Progress and Its Assumptions." *History and Theory* 10 (2): 197–221.

Rothman, Ellen K. 1984. *Hands and Hearts: A History of Courtship in America.* New York: Basic.

Rousseau, Jean-Jacques. 1984/1755. *A Discourse on Inequality.* Edited by Maurice Cranston. Harmondsworth: Penguin.

———. 1997/1762. *The Social Contract and Other Later Political Writings.* Edited by Victor Gourevitch. New York: Cambridge University Press.

Rubinow, I. M. 1907. "Comments in Edward A. Ross's 'Western Civilization and the Birth-Rate.'" *American Journal of Sociology* 12 (5): 627–31.

Ruggles, Steven. 1987. *Prolonged Connections: The Rise of the Extended Family in Nineteenth-Century England and America.* Madison: University of Wisconsin Press.

———. 1994. "The Transformation of American Family Structure." *American Historical Review* 99 (1): 103–28.

————. 1996. "The Effects of Demographic Change on Multigenerational Family Structure: United States Whites, 1880–1980." In *Les Systèmes démographiques du passé*, ed. A. Bideau, A. Perrenoud, K.-A. Lynch, and G. Brunet, 22–40. Lyon: Centre Jacques Cartier.

————. 2001. "Living Arrangements and Well-Being of Older Persons in the Past." In *Living Arrangements of Older Persons: Critical Issues and Policy Responses* (Population Bulletin of the United Nations), ed. Alberto Palloni, 111–61. New York: United Nations.

Salas, Rafael M. 1976. *People: An International Choice: The Multilateral Approach to Population*. Oxford: Pergamon.

Samoff, Joel. 1999. "Institutionalizing International Influence." In *Comparative Education: The Dialectic of the Global and the Local*, ed. Robert F. Arnove and Carlos Alberto Torres, 51–89. Lanham, Md.: Rowman & Littlefield.

Sandberg, John F. 2002. "Child Mortality, Family Building, and Social Learning in a Nepalese Mountain Community." Ph.D. diss., University of Michigan.

Sanderson, Stephen K. 1990. *Social Evolutionism: A Critical History*. Oxford: Blackwell.

Sarsby, Jacqueline. 1983. *Romantic Love and Society*. New York: Penguin.

Schak, David C. 1975. *Dating and Mate-Selection in Modern Taiwan*. Taipei: Chinese Association for Folklore.

Schneider, Carl E. 1985. "Moral Discourse and the Transformation of American Family Law." *Michigan Law Review* 83 (8): 1803–79.

Schochet, Gordon J. 1975. *Patriarchalism in Political Thought*. New York: Basic.

Schultz, T. Paul. 1993. "Returns to Women's Education." In *Women's Education in Developing Countries: Barriers, Benefits, and Policies*, ed. Elizabeth M. King and M. A. Hill, 51–99. Baltimore: Johns Hopkins University Press.

Schwartz, Benjamin. 1964. *In Search of Wealth and Power: Yen Fu and the West*. Cambridge, Mass.: Belknap.

Scott, Jacqueline. 1998. "Changing Attitudes to Sexual Morality: A Cross-National Comparison." *Sociology* 32 (4): 815–45.

Sears, Elizabeth. 1986. *The Ages of Man: Medieval Interpretations of the Life Cycle*. Princeton, N.J.: Princeton University Press.

Seccombe, Wally. 1992. *A Millennium of Family Change: Feudalism to Capitalism in Northwestern Europe*. London: Verso.

Segalen, Martin. 1986. *Historical Anthropology of the Family*. Cambridge: Cambridge University Press.

Selden, Mark. 1993. "Family Strategies and Structures in Rural North China." In *Chinese Families in the Post-Mao Era*, ed. Deborah Davis and Stevan Harrell, 139–64. Berkeley and Los Angeles: University of California Press.

Senior, Nassau. 1831. *Two Lectures on Population*. London: John Murray.

Seward, Rudy R. 1978. *The American Family*. Beverly Hills, Calif.: Sage.

Sewell, William H., Jr. 1996. "Three Temporalities: Toward an Eventful Sociology." In *The Historic Turn in the Human Sciences*, ed. Terrence J. McDonald, 245–80. Ann Arbor: University of Michigan Press.

Shah, A. M. 1974. *The Household Dimension of the Family in India: A Field Study in a Gujarat Village and a Review of Other Studies.* Berkeley: University of California Press.

Shahar, Shulamith. 1983. *The Fourth Estate: A History of Women in the Middle Ages.* London: Methuen.

Shakry, Omnia. 1998. "Schooled Mothers and Structured Play: Child Rearing in Turn-of-the-Century Egypt." In *Remaking Women: Feminism and Modernity in the Middle East,* ed. Lila Abu-Lughod, 126–70. Princeton, N.J.: Princeton University Press.

Shammas, Carole. 1995. "Anglo-American Household Government in Comparative Perspective." *William and Mary Quarterly* 52 (1): 104–44.

Shanin, Teodor. 1972. *The Awkward Class.* Glasgow: Oxford University Press.

Shanley, Mary L. 1979. "Marriage Contract and Social Contract in Seventeenth Century English Political Thought." *Western Political Quarterly* 32 (1): 79–91.

Sharpless, John. 1996. "World Population Growth, Family Planning, and American Foreign Policy." In *The Politics of Abortion and Birth Control in Historical Perspective,* ed. Donald T. Critchlow, 72–102. University Park: Pennsylvania State University Press.

Sheehan, Bernard W. 1980. *Savagism and Civility: Indians and Englishmen in Colonial Virginia.* Cambridge: Cambridge University Press.

Sheehan, Michael M. 1971. "The Formation and Stability of Marriage in Fourteenth-Century England: Evidence of an Ely Register." *Medieval Studies* 33:228–63.

———. 1978. "Choice of Marriage Partner in the Middle Ages: Development and Mode of Application and a Theory of Marriage." *Studies in Medieval and Renaissance History,* n.s., 1:1–33.

———. 1991a. "The Bishop of Rome to a Barbarian King on the Rituals of Marriage." In *Iure Veritas: Studies in Canon Law in Memory of Shafer Williams,* ed. Steven B. Bowman and Blanche E. Cody, 187–99. Cincinnati: University of Cincinnati College of Law.

———. 1991b. "Maritalis Affectio Revisited." In *The Old Daunce: Love, Friendship, Sex, and Marriage in the Medieval World,* ed. Robert R. Edwards and Stephen Spector, 32–43. Albany: State University of New York Press.

Shorter, Edward. 1977/1975. *The Making of the Modern Family.* New York: Basic.

Simmons, Ruth. 1996. "Women's Lives in Transition: A Qualitative Analysis of the Fertility Decline in Bangladesh." *Studies in Family Planning* 27 (5): 251–68.

Simmons, Ruth, Laila Baqee, Michael A. Koenig, and James F. Phillips. 1988. "Beyond Supply: The Importance of Female Family Planning Workers in Rural Bangladesh." *Studies in Family Planning* 19 (1): 29–38.

Singerman, Diane. 2003. "Contemporary Reform of Personal Status Law in Egypt." Paper presented at the conference "Institutions, Ideologies, and Agency: Changing Family Life in the Arab Middle East and Diaspora," University of North Carolina at Chapel Hill, 11–12 April.

Singh, Yogendra. 1976. "Legal System, Legitimation, and Social Change." In *Changing India: Essays in Honour of Professor G. S. Ghurye,* ed. S. D. Pillai, 381–409. Bombay: Popular Prakashan.

Siu, Helen F. 1993. "Reconstituting Dowry and Brideprice in South China." In *Chinese*

Families in the Post-Mao Era, ed. Deborah Davis and Stevan Harrell, 165–88. Berkeley and Los Angeles: University of California Press.

Sklar, June L. 1974. "The Role of Marriage Behavior in the Demographic Transition: The Case of Eastern Europe around 1900." *Population Studies* 28 (2): 231–47.

Sluijter, Eric J. 2000. *Seductress of Sight: Studies in Dutch Art of the Golden Age*. Zwolle: Waanders.

Smith, Adam. 1937/1776. *The Wealth of Nations*. Vol. 1. London: J. M. Dent; New York: E. P. Dutton.

———. 1976/1759. *The Theory of Moral Sentiments*. Edited by D. D. Raphael and A. L. Macfie. Oxford: Clarendon.

———. 1978/1762–63. *Lectures on Jurisprudence*. Oxford: Oxford University Press.

Smith, Anthony D. 1973. *The Concept of Social Change*. London: Routledge & Kegan Paul.

Smith, Daniel B. 1977. "Autonomy and Affection: Parents and Children in Eighteenth-Century Chesapeake Families." *Psychohistory Review* 6:32–51.

Smith, Daniel S. 1978. "Parental Power and Marriage Patterns: An Analysis of Historical Trends in Hingham, Massachusetts." In *The American Family in Social-Historical Perspective*, 2d ed., ed. Michael Gordon, 87–100. New York: St. Martin's.

———. 1981. "Historical Change in the Household Structure of the Elderly in Economically Developed Countries." In *Aging: Stability and Change in the Family*, ed. Robert W. Fogel, Elaine Hatfield, Sara B. Kiesler, and Ethel Shanas, 91–114. New York: Academic.

———. 1993. "The Curious History of Theorizing about the History of the Western Nuclear Family." *Social Science History* 17 (3): 325–53.

———. 1994. "The Periodization of American Family History." Department of History, University of Illinois at Chicago. Typescript.

Smith, David P. 1980. "Age at First Marriage." In *World Fertility Survey Comparative Studies*, vol. 7. Voorburg, Netherlands: International Statistical Institute.

Smith, George D. 1994. "Nanvoo Roots of Mormon Polygamy: A Preliminary Demographic Report." *Dialogue: A Journal of Mormon Thought* 27 (1): 1–72.

Smith, Peter C. 1980. "Asian Marriage Patterns in Transition." *Journal of Family History* 5 (1): 58–97.

Smith, Richard M. 1979. "Some Reflections on the Evidence for the Origins of the 'European Marriage Pattern' in England." In *The Sociology of the Family: New Directions for Britain*, ed. Chris Harris, Michael Anderson, Robert Chester, D. H. J. Morgan, and Diana Leonard, 74–112. Chester: Bemrose.

———. 1981. "Fertility, Economy, and Household Formation in England over Three Centuries." *Population and Development Review* 7 (4): 595–622.

———. 1986. "Marriage Processes in the English Past: Some Continuities." In *The World We Have Gained: Histories of Population and Social Structure*, ed. Lloyd Bonfield, Richard M. Smith, and Keith Wrightson, 43–99. Oxford: Blackwell.

———. 1992. "Geographical Diversity in the Resort to Marriage in Late Medieval Europe: Work, Reputation, and Unmarried Females in the Household Formation Systems of

Northern and Southern Europe." In *Woman Is a Worth Wight: Women in English Society c. 1200–1500*, ed. P. J. P. Goldberg, 16–59. Wolfeboro Falls, N.H.: Alan Sutton.

———. 1999. "Relative Prices, Forms of Agrarian Labour, and Female Marriage Patterns in England, 1350–1800." In *Marriage and Rural Economy: Western Europe since 1400*, ed. Isabelle Devos and Liam Kennedy, 19–48. Belgium: Brepols.

Smith, Tom W. 1990. "Liberal and Conservative Trends in the United States since World War II." *Public Opinion Quarterly* 54 (4): 479–507.

Smits, Jeroen, Wout Ultee, and Jan Lammers. 1998. "Educational Homogamy in 65 Countries: An Explanation of Differences in Openness Using Country-Level Explanatory Variables." *American Sociological Review* 63 (2): 264–85.

———. 2000. "More or Less Educational Homogamy? A Test of Different Versions of Modernization Theory Using Cross-Temporal Evidence for 60 Countries." *American Sociological Review* 65 (5): 781–89.

Snell, Keith D. M. 2002. "English Rural Societies and Geographical Marital Endogamy, 1700–1837." *Economic History Review* 55 (2): 262–98.

Soloway, Richard A. 1969. *Prelates and People: Ecclesiastical Social Thought in England, 1783–1852.* Toronto: University of Toronto Press.

Sorkin, Alan L. 1978. *The Urban American Indian.* Lexington, Mass.: Lexington.

Spain, Daphne, and Suzanne M. Bianchi. 1996. *Balancing Act: Motherhood, Marriage, and Employment among American Women.* New York: Sage.

Spanier, Graham B., and Paul C. Glick. 1980. "The Life Cycle of American Families: An Expanded Analysis." *Journal of Family History* 5 (1): 98–112.

Spence, Jonathan D. 1999/1990. *The Search for Modern China.* 2d ed. New York: Norton.

Spencer, Herbert. 1851. *Social Statics; or, The Conditions Essential to Human Happiness Specified, and the First of Them Developed.* London: J. Chapman.

Spengler, Joseph J. 1972. *Population Economics.* Durham, N.C.: Duke University Press.

———. 1991/1932. "The Birth Rate—Potential Dynamite." *Population and Development Review* 17 (1): 157–69.

Spitulnik, Debra A. 2002. "Accessing 'Local' Modernities: Reflections on the Place of Linguistic Evidence in Ethnography." In *Critically Modern: Alternatives, Alterities, Anthropologies*, ed. Bruce M. Knauft, 194–219. Bloomington: Indiana University Press.

Srinivas, M. N. 1956. "A Note on Sanskritization and Westernization." *Far Eastern Quarterly* 15 (4): 481–96.

Stanton, Elizabeth C. 1900. "Progress of the American Woman." *North American Review* 171 (529): 904–8.

Stanton, Glenn T. 1997. *Why Marriage Matters.* Colorado Springs, Colo.: Piñon.

Starr, June. 1989. "The Role of Turkish Secular Law in Changing the Lives of Rural Muslim Women, 1950–1970." *Law and Society Review* 23 (3): 497–523.

Stimson, Frederic J. 1886–92. *American Statute Law: An Analytical and Compared Digest.* 2 vols. Boston: Charles C. Soule.

Stocking, George W., Jr. 1968. *Race, Culture, and Evolution.* New York: Free Press.

———. 1987. *Victorian Anthropology.* New York: Free Press.

Stoertz, Fiona H. 2001. "Young Women in France and England, 1050–1300." *Journal of Women's History* 12 (4): 22–46.

Stolnitz, George J. 1964. "The Demographic Transition: From High to Low Birth Rates and Death Rates." In *Population: The Vital Revolution*, ed. Ronald Freedman, 30–46. New York: Anchor.

Stone, Lawrence. 1977. *The Family, Sex, and Marriage in England, 1500–1800*. New York: Harper & Row.

———. 1982. "Family History in the 1980's, Past Achievements, and Future Trends." In *The New History: The 1980's and Beyond*, ed. Theodore K. Rabb and Robert I. Rotberg, 51–87. Princeton, N.J.: Princeton University Press.

Stromquist, Nelly P. 1999. "Women's Education in the Twenty-first Century: Balance and Prospects." In *Comparative Education: The Dialectic of the Global and the Local*, ed. Robert F. Arnove and Carlos Alberto Torres, 179–205. Lanham, Md.: Rowman & Littlefield.

Sullivan, Zohreh. 1998. "Eluding the Feminist, Overthrowing the Modern? Transformation." In *Remaking Women: Feminism and Modernity in the Middle East*, ed. Lila Abu-Lughod, 215–42. Princeton, N.J.: Princeton University Press.

Sumner, William G. 1934/1880. *Essays of William Graham Sumner*. Edited by Albert G. Keller and Marucie R. Davie. Vol. 2. New Haven, Conn.: Yale University Press.

Sumner, William G., and Albert G. Keller. 1927. *The Science of Society*. Vol. 1. New Haven, Conn.: Yale University Press.

———. 1929. *The Science of Society*. Vol. 3. New Haven, Conn.: Yale University Press.

Swindlehurst, Albert. 1916. "Some Phases of the Law of Marriage." *Harvard Law Review* 30:124–40.

Symonds, Richard, and Michael Carder. 1973. *The United Nations and the Population Question*. New York: McGraw-Hill.

Szreter, Simon. 1993. "The Idea of Demographic Transition and the Study of Fertility Change." *Population and Development Review* 19 (4): 659–702.

———. 1996. *Fertility, Class, and Gender in Britain, 1860–1940*. Cambridge: Cambridge University Press.

Tadmor, Naomi. 2001. *Family and Friends in Eighteenth-Century England: Household, Kinship, and Patronage*. Cambridge: Cambridge University Press.

Tarcov, Nathan. 1984. *Locke's Education for Liberty*. Chicago: University of Chicago Press.

Tarrow, Sidney G. 1998. *Power in Movement: Social Movements and Contentious Politics*. 2d ed. Cambridge: Cambridge University Press.

Taylor, Charles. 1999. "Two Theories of Modernity." *Public Culture* 11 (1): 153–74.

Teggart, Frederick J. 1925. *Theory of History*. New Haven, Conn.: Yale University Press.

Teitelbaum, Michael S., and Jay M. Winter. 1985. *The Fear of Population Decline*. Orlando, Fla.: Academic.

Thomas, John W., and Merilee S. Grindle. 1994. "Political Leadership and Policy Characteristics in Population Policy Reform." In *The New Politics of Population: Conflict and Consensus in Family Planning*, ed. Jason L. Finkle and C. A. McIntosh, 51–70. New York: Population Council.

Thomas, William I., and Florian Znaniecki. 1974/1918. *The Polish Peasant in Europe and America*. New York: Octagon.

Thompson, Warren S. 1929. "Population." *American Journal of Sociology* 34 (6): 959–75.

———. 1930a. *Danger Spots in World Population*. New York: Knopf.

———. 1930b. *Population Problems*. New York: McGraw-Hill.

———. 1952. "Type of Knowledge Needed for an Adequate Approach to Problems of (High) Fertility in Agrarian Societies." In *Approaches to Problems of High Fertility in Agrarian Societies: Papers Presented at the 1951 Annual Conference of the Milbank Memorial Fund*, 139–52. New York: Milbank Memorial Fund.

Thompson, William, and Anna Wheeler. 1994/1825. *Appeal of One Half the Human Race, Women, against the Pretensions of the Other Half, Men, to Retain Them in Political, and Thence in Civil and Domestic, Slavery*. Bristol: Thoemmes.

Thornton, Arland. 1984. "Transformations of American Society and Family Life." In *Broken Families: Hearings before the Subcommittee on Family and Human Services, United States Senate, Part 2*, 14–27. Washington, D.C.: U.S. Government Printing Office.

———. 1985. "Reciprocal Influences of Family and Religion in a Changing World." *Journal of Marriage and the Family* 47 (2): 381–94.

———. 1989. "Changing Attitudes toward Family Issues in the United States." *Journal of Marriage and the Family* 51 (4): 873–93.

———. 2001. "The Developmental Paradigm, Reading History Sideways, and Family Change." *Demography* 38 (4): 449–65.

Thornton, Arland, William G. Axinn, Tom Fricke, and Duane F. Alwin. 2001. "Value and Beliefs in the Lives of Children and Families." In *The Well-Being of Children and Families*, ed. Arland Thornton, 215–43. Ann Arbor: University of Michigan Press.

Thornton, Arland, and Deborah Freedman. 1982. "Changing Attitudes toward Marriage and Single Life." *Family Planning Perspectives* 14 (6): 297–303.

———. 1983. "The Changing American Family." *Population Bulletin* 38 (4): 85–90.

Thornton, Arland, and Thomas Fricke. 1987. "Social Change and the Family: Comparative Perspectives from the West, China, and South Asia." *Sociological Forum* 2 (4): 746–72.

Thornton, Arland, Thomas Fricke, Li-Shou Yang, and Jui-Shan Chang. 1994. "Theoretical Mechanisms of Family Change." In *Social Change and the Family in Taiwan*, ed. Arland Thornton and Hui-Sheng Lin, 88–115. Chicago: University of Chicago Press.

Thornton, Arland, and Hui-Sheng Lin, eds. 1994. *Social Change and the Family in Taiwan*. Chicago: University of Chicago Press.

Thornton, Arland, and Linda Young-DeMarco. 2001. "Four Decades of Trends in Attitudes toward Family Issues in the United States: The 1960s through the 1990s." *Journal of Marriage and the Family* 63 (4): 1009–37.

Thwing, Charles Franklin, and Carrie F. B. Thwing. 1887. *The Family: An Historical and Social Study*. Boston: Lee & Shepard.

Tilly, Charles, ed. 1978. *Historical Studies of Changing Fertility*. Princeton, N.J.: Princeton University Press.

———. 1984. *Big Structures, Large Processes, Huge Comparisons*. New York: Sage.

———. 1986. Review of *The Decline of Fertility in Europe*, ed. Ansley J. Coale and Susan Cotts Watkins. *Population and Development Review* 12 (2): 323–28.

Tilly, Louise A., and Joan W. Scott. 1978. *Women, Work, and Family*. New York: Hold, Rinehart, & Winston.

Tocqueville, Alexis de. 1955/1835. *Democracy in America*. Vol. 2. New York: Vintage.

Todd, Emmanuel. 1985. *The Explanation of Ideology: Family Structures and Social Systems*. Oxford: Blackwell.

Tomaselli, Sylvana. 1985. "The Enlightenment Debate on Women." *History Workshop Journal* 20: 101–24.

Traer, John F. 1980. *Marriage and the Family in Eighteenth-Century France*. Ithaca, N.Y.: Cornell University Press.

Trost, Jan. 1981. "Cohabitation in the Nordic Countries." *Alternative Lifestyles* 4 (4): 401–27.

Tsui, Amy O. 2001. "Population Policies, Family Planning Programs, and Fertility: The Record." In *Global Fertility Transition*, ed. John B. Casterline and Rodolfo Bulatao, 184–204. *Population and Development Review*, vol. 27 (suppl.).

Turgot, Anne-Robert-Jacques. 1895/1750. *The Life and Writings of Turgot*. Edited by W. Walker Stephens. London: Longmans, Green.

Tylor, Edward B. 1871. *Primitive Culture*. Vol. 1. London: John Murray.

Ulrich, Laurel T. 1982. *Good Wives: Image and Reality in the Lives of Women in Northern New England, 1650–1750*. New York: Knopf.

Unesco. 1999. *Statistical Yearbook*. Paris: Unesco/Bernan.

Unger, Jonathan. 1993. "Urban Families in the Eighties: An Analysis of Chinese Surveys." In *Chinese Families in the Post-Mao Era*, ed. Deborah Davis and Stevan Harrell, 25–49. Berkeley and Los Angeles: University of California Press.

Ungern-Sternberg, Roderich von. 1931. *The Causes of the Decline in Birth-Rate within the European Sphere of Civilization*. Monograph Series 4. Cold Spring Harbor, N.Y.: Eugenics Research Association.

United Nations. 1948. *Universal Declaration of Human Rights*. General Assembly Resolution 217 A (III). New York: United Nations.

———. 1953. *The Determinants and Consequences of Population Trends*. Population Studies, no. 17. New York: Department of Social Affairs, Population Division, United Nations.

———. 1962. *Convention on Consent to Marriage, Minimum Age for Marriage, and Registration of Marriages*. General Assembly Resolution 1763 A (XVII). Geneva: Office of the United Nations High Commissioner for Human Rights.

———. 1979. *Convention on the Elimination of All Forms of Discrimination against Women*. Vol. 00. General Assembly Resolution 34/180. Geneva: Office of the United Nations High Commissioner for Human Rights.

———. 1998. *National Population Policies*. New York: Department of Economic and Social Affairs, Population Division, United Nations.

———. 2003. *Fertility, Contraception, and Population Policies*. New York: United Nations.

United Nations Economic Commission for Africa. 1984. *Kilimanjaro Programme of Action for African Population and Self-Reliant Development.* Arusha: United Republic of Tanzania.

van de Kaa, Dirk J. 1987. "Europe's Second Demographic Transition." *Population Bulletin* 42 (1): 1–59.

———. 1994. "The Second Demographic Transition Revisited: Theories and Expectations." In *Population and Family in the Low Countries, 1993: Late Fertility and Other Current Issues*, ed. Gijs Beets, Hans van den Brekel, Robert Cliquet, Gilbert Dooghe, and Jenny de Jong Gierveld, 81–126. Lisse, Netherlands: Swets & Zeitlinger.

———. 1996. "Anchored Narratives: The Story and Findings of Half a Century of Research into the Determinants of Fertility." *Population Studies* 50 (3): 389–432.

———. 2001. "Postmodern Fertility Preferences: From Changing Value Orientation to New Behaviour." In *Global Fertility Transition*, ed. John B. Casterline and Rodolfo Bulatao, 290–331. *Population and Development Review*, vol. 27 (suppl.).

———. In press. "Demographic Revolutions or Transitions? A Forward." In *Childbearing Prospects in Low-Fertility Countries: A Cohort Analysis*, by Thomas Frejka and Jean-Paul Sardon. Dordrecht, Netherlands: Kluwer Academic Press.

van de Walle, Etienne. 1978. "Alone in Europe: The French Fertility Decline until 1850." In *Historical Studies of Changing Fertility*, ed. Charles Tilly, 257–334. Princeton, N.J.: Princeton University Press.

———. 1993. "Recent Trends in Marriage Ages." In *Demographic Change in Sub-Saharan Africa*, ed. Karen A. Foote, Kenneth H. Hill, and Linda G. Martin, 117–52. Washington, D.C.: National Academy Press.

van de Walle, Francine. 1986. "Infant Mortality and the European Demographic Transition." In *The Decline of Fertility in Europe*, ed. Ansley J. Coale and Susan C. Watkins, 201–33. Princeton, N.J.: Princeton University Press.

Van Wagoner, Richard S. 1986. *Mormon Polygamy: A History.* Salt Lake City, Utah: Signature.

Vance, Rupert B. 1952a. "The Demographic Gap: Dilemmas of Modernization Programs." In *Approaches to Problems of High Fertility in Agrarian Societies: Papers Presented at the 1951 Annual Conference of the Milbank Memorial Fund*, 9–17. New York: Milbank Memorial Fund.

———. 1952b. "Is Theory for Demographers?" *Social Forces* 31 (1): 9–13.

Varenne, Hervé. 1996/1986. "Love and Liberty: The Contemporary American Family." In *A History of the Family*, ed. Andrè Burguière, Christiane Klapisch-Zuber, Martine Segalen, and Françoise Zonabend, 2:416–41. Cambridge, Mass.: Harvard University Press.

Vaughan, Alden T. 1995/1965. *New England Frontier: Puritans and Indians, 1620–1675.* 3d ed. Norman: University of Oklahoma Press.

Ventura, S. J., C. A. Bachrach, L. Hill, K. Kaye, P. Holcomb, and E. Koff. 1995. "The Demography of Out-of-Wedlock Childbearing." In *Report to Congress on Out-of-Wedlock Childbearing* (DHHS Publication no. [PHS] 95–1257), 1–133. Washington, D.C.: U.S. Government Printing Office, for Department of Health and Human Services.

Vergara, Lisa. 2001. "Perspectives on Women in the Art of Vermeer." In *The Cambridge Companion to Vermeer*, ed. Wayne E. Franits, 54–72. Cambridge: Cambridge University Press.

Veroff, Joseph, Elizabeth A. M. Douvan, and Richard A. Kulka. 1981. *The Inner American: A Self-Portrait from 1957 to 1976*. New York: Basic.

Waite, Linda. 1995. "Does Marriage Matter?" *Demography* 32 (4): 483–507.

Waite, Linda, Christine Bachrach, Michelle Hinden, Elizabeth Thomson, and Arland Thornton, eds. 2000. *Ties That Bind: Perspectives on Marriage and Cohabitation*. Hawthorne, N.Y.: Aldine de Gruyter.

Waite, Linda, and M. Gallagher. 2000. *The Case for Marriage*. Cambridge, Mass.: Harvard University Press.

Wall, Richard. 1983. Introduction to *Family Forms in Historic Europe*, ed. Richard Wall, Jean Robin, and Peter Laslett, 1–64. Cambridge: Cambridge University Press.

———. 1995. "Elderly Persons and Members of Their Households in England and Wales from Preindustrial Times to the Present." In *Aging in the Past: Demography, Society, and Old Age*, ed. David I. Kertzer and Peter Laslett, 81–105. Berkeley and Los Angeles: University of California Press.

Wallerstein, Immanuel. 1974. *The Modern World-System: Capitalist Agriculture and the Origins of the European World-Economy in the Sixteenth Century*. New York: Academic.

———. 1991. *Unthinking Social Science: The Limits of Nineteenth-Century Paradigms*. Cambridge: Polity.

———. 1997/1979. *The Capitalist World-Economy: Essays by Immanuel Wallerstein*. Cambridge: Cambridge University Press.

Wang, Zheng. 1999. *Women in the Chinese Enlightenment: Oral and Textual Histories*. Berkeley and Los Angeles: University of California Press.

Warwick, Donald P. 1982. *Bitter Pills: Population Policies and Their Implementation in Eight Developing Countries*. Cambridge: Cambridge University Press.

———. 1986. "The Indonesian Family Planning Program: Government Influence and Client Choice." *Population and Development Review* 12 (3): 453–90.

———. 1994. "The Politics of Research on Fertility Control." In *The New Politics of Population: Conflict and Consensus in Family Planning*, ed. Jason L. Finkle and C. A. McIntosh, 179–93. New York: Population Council.

Washburn, Wilcomb E. 1971. *Red Man's Land/White Man's Law*. New York: Scribner's.

Watkins, Susan C. 1986a. "Conclusions." In *The Decline of Fertility in Europe*, ed. Ansley J. Coale and Susan C. Watkins, 420–49. Princeton, N.J.: Princeton University Press.

———. 1986b. "Regional Patterns of Nuptiality in Western Europe, 1870–1960." In *The Decline of Fertility in Europe*, ed. Ansley J. Coale and Susan C. Watkins, 314–36. Princeton, N.J.: Princeton University Press.

———. 1991. *From Provinces into Nations: Demographic Integration in Western Europe, 1870–1960*. Princeton, N.J.: Princeton University Press.

———. 1993. "If All We Knew about Women Was What We Read in *Demography*, What Would We Know?" *Demography* 30 (4): 551–78.

———. 2000. "Local and Foreign Models of Reproduction in Nyanza Province, Kenya." *Population and Development Review* 26 (4): 725–59.

Watkins, Susan C., and Dennis Hodgson. 1998. "From Mercantilists to Neo-Malthusians: The International Population Movement and the Transformation of Population Ideology in Kenya." Paper presented at the workshop "Social Processes Underlying Fertility Change in Developing Countries," Committee on Population, National Academy of Sciences, Washington, D.C., 29–30 January.

Weber, Max. 1958a/1904–5. *The Protestant Ethic and the Spirit of Capitalism.* Translated by Talcott Parsons. New York: Scribner's.

———. 1958b/1916–17. *The Religion of India: The Sociology of Hinduism and Buddhism.* Translated and edited by Hans H. Gerth and Don Martindale. Glencoe, Ill.: Free Press.

———. 1968a/1922. *Economy and Society: An Outline of Interpretive Sociology.* Edited by Guenther Roth and Claus Wittich. Translated by Ephraim Fischoff et al. New York: Bedminster.

———. 1968b/1916. *The Religion of China: Confucianism and Taoism.* Translated and edited by Hans H. Gerth. Glencoe, Ill.: Free Press.

Weisbrod, Carol, and Pamela Sheingorn. 1978. "*Reynolds v. United States*: Nineteenth-Century Forms of Marriage and the Status of Women." *Connecticut Law Review* 10 (4): 828–58.

Weitzman, Lenore J. 1981. *The Marriage Contract: Spouses, Lovers, and the Law.* New York: Free Press.

Welch, Anthony. 1999. "The Triumph of Technocracy or the Collapse of Certainty: Modernity, Postmodernity, and Postcolonialism in Comparative Education." In *Comparative Education: The Dialectic of the Global and the Local,* ed. Robert F. Arnove and Carlos Alberto Torres, 25–49. Lanham, Md.: Rowman & Littlefield.

Westermarck, Edward A. 1894/1891. 2d ed. *The History of Human Marriage.* London: Macmillan.

———. 1922. *The History of Human Marriage.* 5th ed. New York: Allerton.

———. 1929/1927. *Memories of My Life.* New York: Macaulay.

———. 1970/1936. *The Future of Marriage in Western Civilisation.* Freeport, N.Y.: Books for Libraries.

———. 1971/1908. *The Origin and Development of the Moral Ideas.* London: Macmillan.

Westoff, Charles F. 1999. "Mass Communications and Fertility." In *Dynamics of Values in Fertility Change,* ed. Richard Leete, 237–51. Oxford: Oxford University Press.

Westoff, Charles F., and Akinrinola Bankole. 1997. "Mass Media and Reproductive Behavior in Africa." Demographic and Health Surveys Analytical Report no. 2. Calverton, Md.: Macro International.

———. 1999. "Mass Media and Reproductive Behavior in Pakistan, India, and Bangladesh." Demographic and Health Surveys Analytical Report no. 10. Calverton, Md.: Macro International.

Westoff, Charles F., and Germán Rodríguez. 1995. "The Mass Media and Family Planning in Kenya." *International Family Planning Perspectives* 21 (1): 26–31, 36.

Weyrauch, Walter O. 1965. "Informal Marriage and Common Law Marriage." In *Sexual Behavior and the Law*, ed. Robert Slovenko, 297–340. Springfield, Ill.: Charles C. Thomas.

White, Tyrene. 1994. "Two Kinds of Production: The Evolution of China's Family Planning Policy in the 1980s." In *The New Politics of Population: Conflict and Consensus in Family Planning*, ed. Jason L. Finkle and C. A. McIntosh, 137–58. New York: Population Council.

Whitelock, Dorothy. 1952. *The Beginnings of English Society.* Baltimore: Penguin.

"Why Is Single Life Becoming More General?" 1868. *The Nation* 6 (140): 190–91.

Whyte, Martin K. 1988. "Death in the People's Republic of China." In *Death Ritual in Late Imperial and Modern China*, ed. James Watson and Evelyn Rawski, 289–316. Berkeley and Los Angeles: University of California Press.

———. 1990. "Changes in Mate Choice in Chengdu." In *Chinese Society on the Eve of Tiananmen*, ed. Deborah Davis and Ezra Vogel, 181–213. Cambridge, Mass.: Harvard University Press.

———. 1993. "Wedding Behavior and Family Strategies in Chengdu." In *Chinese Families in the Post-Mao Era*, ed. Deborah Davis and Stevan Harrell, 189–216. Berkeley and Los Angeles: University of California Press.

———. N.d. "China's Revolutions and Parent-Child Relations." Department of Sociology, Harvard University. Typescript.

Willcox, Walter F. 1891. "The Divorce Problem: A Study in Statistics." In *Studies in History, Economics, and Public Law* (vol. 1, no. 1), 9–74. New York: University Faculty of Political Science of Columbia University.

———. 1907. "Comments in Edward A. Ross's Western Civilization and the Birth-Rate." *American Journal of Sociology* 12 (5): 631–32.

Williams, George C. 1966. *Adaptation and Natural Selection: A Critique of Some Current Evolutionary Thought.* Princeton, N.J.: Princeton University Press.

Williams, Raymond. 1985/1976. *Key Words: A Vocabulary of Culture and Society.* Rev. ed. New York: Oxford University Press.

Wills, Gary. 1978. *Inventing America: Jefferson's Declaration of Independence.* Garden City, N.Y.: Doubleday.

Wilmoth, John R., and Patrick Ball. 1992. "The Population Debate in American Popular Magazines." *Population and Development Review* 18 (4): 631–68.

Wilson, Chris, and Tim Dyson. 1992. "Family Systems and Cultural Change: Perspectives from Past and Present." In *Family Systems and Cultural Change*, ed. Elza Berquo and Peter Xenos, 31–45. Oxford: Clarendon Press.

Wilson, James Q. 2002. *The Marriage Problem.* New York: Harper Collins.

Winchester, Simon. 2001. *The Map That Changed the World: William Smith and the Birth of Modern Geology.* New York: Harper Collins.

Witte, John, Jr. 1997. *From Sacrament to Contract: Marriage, Religion, and Law in the Western Tradition.* Louisville: Westminister/John Knox.

Wolf, Arthur P. 1986. "The Preeminent Role of Government Intervention in China's Family Revolution." *Population and Development Review* 12 (1): 101–16.

Wollstonecraft, Mary. 1975/1792. *A Vindication of the Rights of Women.* Edited by Carol H. Poston. New York: Norton.

Wood, Gordon S. 1969. *The Creation of the American Republic, 1776–1789.* Chapel Hill: University of North Carolina Press.

Woods, Robert I. 1987. "Approaches to the Fertility Transition in Victorian England." *Population Studies* 41 (2): 283–311.

Wright, Caroll D. 1899. *Outline of Practical Sociology.* New York: Longmans, Green.

Wright, Lawrence. 2002. "Lives of the Saints." *New Yorker,* 21 January, 40–57.

Wright, Mary C. 1968. "Introduction: The Rising Tide of Change." In *China in Revolution: The First Phase, 1900–1913,* ed. Mary C. Wright, 1–63. New Haven, Conn.: Yale University Press.

Wrightson, Keith. 1982. *English Society, 1580–1680.* London: Hutchinson.

Wrigley, Edward A., and Roger S. Schofield. 1981. *The Population History of England, 1541–1871: A Reconstruction.* Cambridge, Mass.: Harvard University Press.

Wrigley, Edward A., and David Souden. 1986. Introduction to *The Works of Thomas Robert Malthus,* ed. Edward A. Wrigley and David Souden, 1:7–39. London: William Pickering.

Yanagisako, Sylvia J. 1979. "Family and Household: The Analysis of Domestic Groups." *Annual Review of Anthropology* 8:161–205.

Yang, C. K. 1959. *The Chinese Family in the Communist Revolution.* Cambridge, Mass.: Technology.

Zafiri, Fatima. 2002. "Islamic Feminism and the Soviet Legacy of Modernisation." In *Muslim Feminism and Feminist Movement: Central Asia,* ed. Abida Samiuddin and R. Khanam, 1:81–114. Delhi: Global.

Zagarri, Rosemarie. 1998. "The Rights of Man and Woman in Post-Revolutionary America." *William and Mary Quarterly* 55 (2): 203–30.

Index